PHYSICAL FLUID DYNAMICS

THE MODERN UNIVERSITY PHYSICS SERIES

This series is intended for readers whose main interest is in physics, or who need the methods of physics in the study of science and technology. Some of the books will provide a sound treatment of topics essential in any physics training, while other, more advanced, volumes will be suitable as preliminary reading for research in the field covered. New titles will be added from time to time.

Clark: *A First Course in Quantum Mechanics*
Littlefield and Thorley: *Atomic and Nuclear Physics* (3rd Edn.)
Lothian: *Optics and Its Uses*
Lovell, Avery and Vernon: *Physical Properties of Materials*
Tritton: *Physical Fluid Dynamics*
Wolbarst: *Symmetry and Quantum Systems*

Physical Fluid Dynamics

D. J. TRITTON

School of Physics
University of Newcastle-upon-Tyne

VNR VAN NOSTRAND REINHOLD COMPANY

New York - Cincinnati - Toronto - London - Melbourne

© D. J. Tritton, 1977

First published 1977, two printings
Reprinted 1979, 1980

**Published by Van Nostrand Reinhold Company Ltd.,
Molly Millars Lane, Wokingham, Berkshire, England**

*Published in 1977 by Van Nostrand Reinhold Company
A Division of Litton Educational Publishing, Inc.,
135 West 50th Street, New York, N.Y. 10020 U.S.A.*

*Van Nostrand Reinhold Limited
1410 Birchmount Road, Scarborough, Ontario, M1P 2E7,
Canada*

*Van Nostrand Reinhold Australia Pt. Limited
17 Queen Street, Mitcham, Victoria 3132, Australia*

Library of Congress Cataloguing in Publication Data
Tritton, D. J.
 Physical fluid dynamics.
 (The Modern university physics series)
 Bibliography: p. 346
 Includes index.
 1. Fluid dynamics. 1. Title.
QC151.T74   532   76–41890
ISBN 0 442 30131 6
     0 442 30132 4 pbk.

Typeset in Great Britain by Preface Ltd., Salisbury
Printed and bound in Great Britain by
Henry Ling Ltd., at the Dorset Press, Dorchester, Dorset

Preface

To classify a book as 'experimental' rather than 'theoretical' or as 'pure' rather than 'applied' is liable to imply unreal distinctions. Nevertheless, some classification is necessary to tell the potential reader whether the book is for him. In this spirit, this book may be said to treat fluid dynamics as a branch of physics, rather than as a branch of applied mathematics or of engineering. I have often heard expressions of the need for such a book, and certainly I have felt it in my own teaching.

I have written it primarily for students of physics and of physics-based applied science, although I hope others may find it useful. The book differs from existing 'fundamental' books in placing much greater emphasis on what we know through laboratory experiments and their physical interpretation and less on the mathematical formalism. It differs from existing 'applied' books in that the choice of topics has been made for the insight they give into the behaviour of fluids in motion rather than for their practical importance. There are differences also from many existing books on fluid dynamics in the branches treated, reflecting to some extent shifts of interest in recent years. In particular, geophysical and astrophysical applications have prompted important fundamental developments in topics such as convection, stratified flow, and the dynamics of rotating fluids. These developments have hitherto been reflected in the contents of textbooks only to a limited extent.

Much of the book is based on lectures I have given to final year physics students at Newcastle-upon-Tyne University, though I have substantially expanded parts of the material. I have also been influenced by teaching fluid dynamics both at a more elementary level and to postgraduate students of geophysics and planetary physics. I have tried to learn which approaches to various topics students find most informative, and I hope this experience has led to improvements in what I have written.

I have had the final year physics students particularly in mind when deciding what background knowledge to assume of the reader. The mathematical methods used should all be familiar to such students (although substantial parts of the book would be intelligible to a reader at an earlier mathematical stage). Also, it is not really paradoxical that a book aimed at physics students should contain less explanation of basic physics (such as related thermodynamics) than some other fluid dynamics texts; knowledge of this can reasonably be assumed.

Nevertheless, I hope that the book will be of value to a variety of other types of reader and I have tried to extend its usefulness wherever this has been possible without distorting the primary aim. Workers in widely various types of applied science need an understanding of the phenomena of fluid motion. I have in mind particularly, but not solely, geo- and planetary physicists (meteorologists and oceanographers as well as students of planetary interiors), of whose needs I probably have the most immediate appreciation. Where fluid dynamical topics are taught as part of a geophysics course, I believe that this should be a suitable text-book. I believe also that postgraduate students and other research workers, faced with a project involving fluid dynamics, should find this book of value. It is not uncommon for otherwise interesting geophysical papers to be marred by the employment of fluid dynamical concepts in a way that shows serious misunder-standing of their significance. But these misunderstandings are not surprising in the absence of convenient sources of information. Such readers should not imagine that there are easy short-cuts to an understanding of the phenomena of fluid motion, but I trust that this book may make the long route a little less arduous.

The choice of topics in a book of this sort must be controversial. The size of the subject necessitates many arbitrary omissions. The reader wishing to discover just what is included and what is omitted may find it useful to refer not only to the contents list but also to Section 1.2. The major limitation is the restriction to incompressible flow. This will, I know, make the book inadequate for some courses. Compressible flow is, however, such a large topic that it really requires a book of its own; just a chapter would perhaps do it more of an injustice than total omission. Even within the limitation to incompressible flow, I am much aware of omissions that some readers will regret. What I hope I have achieved is a text giving students sufficient knowledge of the basic concepts of fluid dynamics and sufficient insight into the consequences of these concepts that they will be able to use other (probably more advanced) sources to obtain information that is omitted here.

The systematic development of the subject occupies Chapters 5 to 22. After the introduction in Chapter 1, Chapters 2 to 4 treat three particular topics in a descriptive (though hopefully not too superficial) way. These topics have been placed ahead of the systematic treatment for two reasons. Primarily they are intended to give the reader some understanding of the type of phenomena with which one is concerned; it is a long haul through the basic concepts of Chapters 5 to 8 if one does not know what it is all for. Additionally, I hope that Chapters 2 to 4 may make the book more accessible to students at an earlier stage of their studies.

Chapter 23 considers experimental methods; it is convenient to discuss these all together rather than alongside the experimental results. Chapter 24 illustrates applications of fluid dynamics — geophysical, biophysical, technological, and so forth. Its nature is explained more fully in Section 24.1. In a sense, this chapter is included for 'entertainment', but some knowledge of its range of applications should add to the reader's appreciation of the way in which fluid dynamics has developed.

Much of the illustrative material throughout the book has been drawn from research papers. It is a feature of fluid dynamics — probably more than of most branches of physics — that the details of rather simply specified topics are complex and still imperfectly understood. (Others must have shared my experience of having difficulty in convincing a postgraduate student that the topic proposed for him had not been fully elucidated long ago.) It is thus often appropriate to use even for introductory purposes (e.g. Chapters 2 to 4) topics that are still the subject of research. This feature of the subject also makes it easier for a book to serve both as an undergraduate text and as a source of information for research workers.

The figure captions often contain details that students will wish to ignore; these are intended for the more advanced reader who wants to know the particular conditions to which the data refer. However, I hope that these details may sometimes convey to students something of the 'flavour' of experimental fluid dynamics.

The book is more fully referenced than most undergraduate texts. Some of the references indicate sources of material – of illustrations or of ideas. (Sometimes I have thought a reference for a specific point appropriate, because the simplification justifiable for the newcomer to the subject may lead the more experienced reader to ask, 'Just what does he mean by that?') Other references have been included for the reader who is using the book as an information source and wishes to follow up a topic in detail. No attempt at completeness has been made; that would involve far too many references. I have tried to give an appropriate point of entry into the literature of a topic, more often a recent review or significant paper than the pioneering research work. In general, the role of a reference should be apparent from the context. In addition to specific references, there is a bibliography of related books (and films).

Writing the book has been a task of some years. Consequently, some parts are more up-to-date than others in the choice of illustrative material and references. I have tried to modify the parts written earlier in the light of any significant new developments. But there comes a point when one has to say 'that is the final version'; otherwise the process never converges!

The primary purpose of the book being pedagogical, I have compiled a selection of problems for the student to work, although the emphasis on experimentally based information means that not all topics lend themselves readily to problem working. Some of the problems involve bringing together ideas from different chapters, so they are all collected together at the end of the book. The problems are very variable in difficulty and are intended more for selection by the teacher than for use by the student on his own. A few of the problems amount to little more than the substitution of numbers into equations; the quantities have been chosen to be physically realistic and it is hoped that the student will attempt to visualize the situation rather than just make the substitution mechanically. At the opposite end of the spectrum, a few of the problems will be solvable only by students with knowledge of mathematical methods not used in the text. Some of the problems are based on examination questions set to physics students at the University of Newcastle-upon-Tyne; I am grateful to the University for permission to include these.

Many people have been most helpful with information and comments – too many for me to list them individually; my gratitude is nonetheless sincere. I must name my colleagues who have given particular help. Discussions with Drs. P. A. Davies, A. Ibbetson, and C. W. Titman have frequently helped me to clarify my ideas. The material in the appendix to Chapter 14 was developed in collaboration with Dr. D. C. Tozer.

Section 6.2 required specific assistance. Professor S. C. R. Dennis provided numerical details of the velocity field. He kindly recomputed these more accurately and in a more suitable form than in Ref. [95]; these computations were carried out in the Data Handling Division at CERN, Geneva. The subsequent computations leading to Figs. 6.3–6.5 were made in the Computing Laboratory of Newcastle-upon-Tyne University by Mrs. S. Hofmann, for whose interest and skill I am most grateful.

Acknowledgements to bodies who have given permission for the reproduction of copyright material are listed separately. I am grateful also to the authors who have agreed to my using their material and particularly to those who have provided original prints of their photographs or additional information. Again a blanket 'thank you' must suffice. In many cases, I have presented material in a slightly different form from its original publication and have therefore not needed to seek permission; my debt to the authors is, of course, no less. The originators of all photographs and sets of data are indicated by the references.

I am, of course, particularly indebted to my typists, Mrs. M. Bennison and Miss M. Hopkinson, and I am equally indebted, for their skilful draughting of many of the diagrams, to Mrs. D. Hewett and Mrs. E. R. Thompson. I am grateful also for the services of the University Library (and its inter-library loans service) and of the Photography Department (who made excellent copies of photographs of which the originals were unobtainable) at the University of Newcastle-upon-Tyne.

Finally my thanks go to former and present staff of Van Nostrand Reinhold Co. Ltd., particularly Mr. D. J. Carpenter, Mrs. T. Mozley, Miss L. J. Ward and Mr. D. Winsor, for their encouragement and cooperation.

In conclusion, let me say that I should much welcome any comments on the book that readers may care to send.

Acknowledgements

I am grateful to the following bodies for permission to reproduce figures of which they hold the copyright:

American Institute of Aeronautics and Astronautics (Fig. 22.2)
American Institute of Physics (Figs. 4.9 and 15.10)
American Meteorological Society (Fig. 24.1)
American Society of Mechanical Engineers (Fig. 16.1)
Annual Reviews Inc. (Figs. 16.3 and 16.7)
Artemis Press (Fig. 24.3)
Barth J. A. Verlag (Fig. 19.9)
Boeing Scientific Research Laboratories (Fig. 16.8)
Cambridge University Press (Figs. 14.7, 14.11, 15.9, 16.14, 17.4, 19.2, 22.13, 22.20 and 22.21)
Central Electricity Generating Board (Figs. 24.9 and 24.10)
Company of Biologists Ltd. (Fig. 24.18)
Gordon and Breach Ltd. (Figs. 16.4 and 16.6)
Her Majesty's Stationery Office, by permission of the Controller (Fig. 20.1)
Her Majesty's Stationery Office, by permission of the Controller, courtesy Hydraulics Research Station, Wallingford (Figs. 24.5 and 24.6)
Indian Association for the Cultivation of Science (Fig. 4.15)
Macmillan Journals Ltd. (Fig. 24.2)
Microfilms International Marketing Corp. Inc. (Figs. 4.5, 4.8 and 4.11)
National Aeronautics and Space Administration (Fig. 14.5)
Physical Society of Japan (Figs. 3.4, 11.10, 19.7 and 19.8)
Royal Meteorological Society (Figs. 15.15 and 15.17)
Royal Society (Figs. 18.4 and 18.5)
Scientific American (Fig. 24.22)
Springer-Verlag (Figs. 2.10(a) and (b), 3.7 and 14.6)
Tellus (Fig. 16.9)
University of Chicago Press (Fig. 24.4)
VDI Verlag (Figs. 4.16, 14.1 and 14.4)
Vieweg und Sohn (Fig. 4.6)

Those silent waters weave for him
A fluctuant mutable world and dim,
Where wavering masses bulge and gape
Mysterious, and shape to shape
Dies momently through whorl and hollow,
And form and line and solid follow
Solid and line and form to dream
Fantastic down the eternal stream;
An obscure world, a shifting world,
Bulbous, or pulled to thin, or curled,
Or serpentine, or driving arrows,
Or serene slidings, or March narrows.

From "The Fish" by Rupert Brooke.

Contents

1
Introduction

1.1 Preamble

We know from everyday observation that liquids and gases in motion behave in very
varied and often complicated ways. When one observes them in the controlled
conditions of a laboratory, one finds that the variety and complexity of flow
patterns arise even if the arrangement is quite simple. Fluid dynamics is the study
of these phenomena. Its aims are to know what will happen in a given arrangement
and to understand why.

One believes that the basic physical laws governing the behaviour of fluids in
motion are the usual well-known laws of mechanics — essentially conservation of
mass and Newton's laws of motion, together with, for some problems, the laws of
thermodynamics. The complexities arise in the consequences of these laws. The
way in which observed flow patterns do derive from the governing laws is often by
no means apparent. A large theoretical and conceptual structure, built, on the one
hand, on the basic laws and, on the other hand, on experimental observation, is
needed to make the connection.

In most investigations in fluid mechanics, the physical properties of the fluid, its
density, viscosity, compressibility, etc., are supposed known. The study of such
properties and the explanation in terms of molecular structure of their values for
different fluids do, of course, constitute another important branch of physics.
However, the overlap between the two is, in most cases, slight. This is essentially
because most flows can be described and understood entirely in macroscopic terms
without reference to the molecular structure of the fluid.

Thus, for the most part, fluid dynamical problems are concerned with the
behaviour, subject to known laws, of a fluid of specified properties in a specified
configuration. One might for example want to know what happens when oil flows
through a pipe as the result of a pressure difference between its ends; or when a
column of hot air rises above a heat source; or when a solid sphere is moved
through a tank of water — the whole of which might be placed on a rotating table.
Ideally one would like to be able to solve such problems through an appropriate
mathematical formulation of the governing laws; the role of experiment would then
be to check that solutions so obtained do correspond to reality. In fact the mathematical difficulties are such that a formal theory often has to be supplemented or
replaced by experimental observations and measurements. Even in cases where a
fairly full mathematical description of a flow has been obtained, this has often been
possible only after experiments have indicated the type of theory needed. The
subject involves an interplay between theory and experiment. The proportion each
contributes to our understanding of flow behaviour varies greatly from topic to

topic. This book is biassed towards some of those topics where experimental work
has been particularly important.

On the other hand, the book is primarily concerned with 'pure' fluid mechanics
rather than with applications. It attempts to develop an understanding of the
phenomena of fluid flow by considering simple configurations – simple, that is, in
their imposed conditions – rather than more complicated ones that might be of
importance in particular applications. This is not to deny the influence of applications on the development of the subject. Fluid dynamics has numerous and
important applications to engineering, to geo- and astrophysics, and to biophysics;
if this is not evident a glance forward to Chapter 24 will make the point. The
topics chosen for investigation, even in fundamental studies, owe much to the
applications currently considered significant. For example, it is doubtful whether
the intriguing phenomena that arise when the whole body of the fluid is rotating
would have received much attention but for the importance of such effects in
atmospheric and oceanic motions.

1.2 Scope of book

Fluid dynamics has many facets. It is necessary in any book to make some
restrictions to the range of topics considered. The principal restrictions in this book
are the following six.

(i) The laws of classical mechanics apply throughout. Since other restrictions will
limit the flows considered to low speeds, the exclusion of relativistic effects is not
significant. The exclusion of quantum mechanical effects just means that we are not
dealing with liquid helium.

(ii) The length scale of the flow is always taken to be large compared with the
molecular mean-free-path, so that the fluid can be treated as a continuum. More
precise meaning will be given to this statement in Section 5.2. It excludes the flow
of gases at very low pressures (rarified gases) from our considerations.

(iii) We consider only incompressible flow; that is flow in which the pressure
variations do not produce any significant density variations. In isothermal flows
this means that the density is a constant; in other flows that it is a function of the
temperature alone.

There are two ways in which fulfilment of this condition can come about. The
fluid may have such a small compressibility (such a large bulk modulus) that, even
if large pressure variations are present, they produce only slight density variations.
Or the pressure variations may be sufficiently small that, even if the compressibility
is not so small, the density variations are small. Liquid flows can usually be treated
as incompressible for the former reason. More surprisingly, gas flows can often be
similarly treated for the latter reason – whenever, as we shall see in Section 5.8, the
flow speed is everywhere low compared with the speed of sound. Thus, although
this restriction excludes the many interesting phenomena of the high speed flow of
gases (compressible flow), it still retains a wide range of important situations in the
dynamics of gases as well as of liquids.

(iv) We consider only Newtonian fluids. This is a statement about the physical
properties that affect the stresses developed within a fluid as a result of its motion
and thus enter the dynamics of a flow. To see what is meant by a Newtonian fluid
we consider a simple configuration, Fig. 1.1; the relationship of this to a general

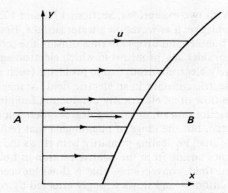

Figure 1.1 Schematic diagram of viscous stress generated by simple velocity variation, $u(y)$. Short arrows represent forces acting in plane of AB, drawn on side of fluid on which force acts.

flow configuration, and thus a more rigorous definition of a Newtonian fluid, will be considered in Section 5.6. In Fig. 1.1, all the fluid is moving in the same direction but with a speed that varies in a perpendicular direction; i.e. the only non-zero component of the velocity is the x-component, u, and this is a function, $u(y)$, of the co-ordinate y. Across any arbitrary plane, perpendicular to y, within the fluid, a stress will act. As drawn in Fig. 1.1, the faster fluid above the plane AB will drag the fluid below forward, and the slower fluid below will drag the fluid above back. Equal and opposite forces will thus act on the fluid above and below as shown (although the arrows are drawn on the sides of the fluid *on* which they act, the lines of action of both forces are actually in the dividing plane AB). The generation of this internal stress is known as viscous action. In a Newtonian fluid the stress is directly proportional to the velocity gradient; if τ is the force per unit area,

$$\tau = \mu \frac{\partial u}{\partial y} \tag{1.1}$$

μ is the coefficient of viscosity of the fluid, often called just the viscosity. Another way of stating the definition of a Newtonian fluid is to say that it is a fluid of constant viscosity. Constant here means that it does not depend on the velocity field; the viscosity of a Newtonian fluid may (and usually does) vary with temperature or it may (but usually does not) vary with pressure.

All gases and liquids with small molecules interacting in a simple way are observed to be very closely Newtonian. Non-Newtonian behaviour can arise in liquids with long molecules (polymers), in solutions of polymers, in liquids where the molecules tend to gather in more organized structures than usual, and in suspensions and emulsions (the former name being used when solid material is dispersed through a liquid and the latter when drops of one liquid are dispersed through another). Thus all the common fluids one is likely to use in the laboratory are Newtonian, as are many of the fluids occurring in important applications. However, by restricting ourselves to Newtonian fluids, we are excluding various fluids of importance in biophysics (e.g., blood flowing through small capillaries), industrial applications (e.g., many paints), and chemical engineering.

(v) We shall not (with two exceptions, Sections 17.2 and 17.4) consider flows with free surfaces. Topics such as waves on a water surface, flow in open channels, and the dynamics of bubbles and drops are thus outside the scope of the book.

(vi) We shall not consider any problems in which electromagnetic effects are important, either purely electrohydrodynamic problems (such as the behaviour of a liquid of variable dielectric constant in an electric field) or magnetohydrodynamic problems (such as the flow of an electrically conducting fluid in a magnetic field).

All the above restrictions mean, in varying degrees, that important and interesting topics are being omitted. But the range of phenomena that remains within our scope is wide and varied. We shall be dealing primarily with flows induced by imposed pressure gradients, flows arising from the relative motion of boundaries or of one boundary and ambient fluid, convection – that is flows induced by or associated with temperature variations – and flows strongly affected by rotation of the whole system or by density stratification. This may not at first sight seem a very broad spectrum of topics, but each has many facets. A major reason for this is the frequent occurrence of instabilities, leading to the breakdown of one type of flow into another. The next three chapters will illustrate the variety and complexity of the phenomena that occur, and illustrate in particular that the complexity can arise even for very simple imposed conditions. We may also remark here that the examples of applications of fluid dynamics in Chapter 24, drawn from widely assorted branches of applied science, have all been chosen as cases that can be understood, at least in part, within the limitations of this book.

Throughout most of this book, except where specific experimental arrangements are concerned, we shall talk about fluids, without making any distinction between liquids and gases. This is because the range of situations within the above limitations is just the range in which liquids and gases exhibit the same phenomena (provided the comparison is made in the correct quantitative way – see Chapter 7); circumstances in which any one of the limitations, except (vi), did not apply would normally refer specifically either to a liquid or to a gas. Points (iii) and (iv) are particularly important. The facts that in many flows gases behave as if they were incompressible and that the same law of viscous behaviour applies to gases and many liquids are central to the development of a common dynamical description for the two phases.

1.3 Notation and definitions

A list of symbols used in this book is given on pages 324–328. This is intended as an aid when a symbol reappears in the text sometime after it has been first introduced.

Here we may just note the symbols for the basic fluid dynamical quantities appearing throughout the book. Fluid velocity is denoted by $\mathbf{u}$ (with Cartesian components (u, v, w) in directions (x, y, z)), the pressure by p, the temperature by T, fluid density by ρ, the viscosity (already introduced in Section 1.2) by μ, the kinematic viscosity (μ/ρ) by ν, and time by t.

Many of the dynamical and physical quantities appearing in fluid dynamics are standard quantities with accepted definitions familiar to a physicist. It has not been thought necessary to define such quantities in the text, but their dimensions are quoted in the list of symbols when this provides a useful reminder of the definition.

It is conventional to use a double letter symbol for most non-dimensional quantities (e.g., Re for Reynolds number, Ra for Rayleigh number). Such symbols will be printed non-italicized to distinguish them from products of two quantities.

Two terms that will be used frequently require definition. Both refer to particular classes of flow that are often considered because of their relative simplicity.

Firstly, a steady flow is one which does not change with time. An observer looking at such a flow at two different instants will see exactly the same flow pattern, although the fluid at each position in this pattern will be different at the two instants. Mathematically (using the Eulerian system to be introduced in Section 5.3), steady flow may be expressed

$$\partial/\partial t = 0 \tag{1.2}$$

where the derivative operates on any parameter associated with the flow. Steady flow can occur only if all the imposed conditions are constant in time. This means that a flow is steady only in the appropriate frame of reference (flow past a fixed obstacle may be steady, but the same situation seen as the obstacle moving through the fluid is not steady, even though the two cases are dynamically equivalent — see Section 3.1). However, one would normally choose that frame for study of the flow. A flow that is changing with time is, of course, called unsteady. An intrinsically unsteady flow is one that is not steady in any frame of reference. Such a flow must occur if there is no frame in which the imposed conditions remain fixed. We shall be seeing that intrinsically unsteady flow also sometimes arises spontaneously even when the imposed conditions are steady.

Secondly, a two-dimensional flow is one in which the motion is confined to parallel planes (the velocity component in the perpendicular direction is zero everywhere) and the flow pattern in every such plane is the same. Formally,

$$w = 0, \quad \partial/\partial z = 0 \tag{1.3}$$

Such a motion may occur in an effectively two-dimensional geometry with the ends in the third direction so distant that they have negligible effect on the flow in the region of interest.

The significance of these concepts will become clearer through specific examples in the following chapters.

2
Pipe and Channel Flow

2.1 Introduction

In this and the next two chapters, we take three geometrically simple flow configurations and have a look at the principal flow phenomena. These will provide a more specific introduction than the last chapter to the character of fluid dynamics. We consider these examples now, before starting on the formal development of the subject in Chapter 5; we can then approach the setting up of the equations of motion with an idea of the types of phenomena that one hopes to understand through these equations. Although these chapters are primarily phenomenological, the present chapter will also be used to introduce some simple theoretical ideas.

The first topic is viscous incompressible flow through pipes and channels. Consider a long straight pipe or tube of uniform circular cross-section. One end of this is supplied by a reservoir of fluid maintained at a constant pressure, higher than the constant pressure at the other end. A simple arrangement for doing this in principle, using a liquid as the working fluid, is shown in Fig. 2.1; practical arrangements for investigating the phenomena to be described require some refinement of this arrangement. Fluid is pushed through the pipe from the high pressure end to the low. We suppose that the gravitational force on the fluid is irrelevant, either because the pipe is horizontal or because this force is small compared with the forces associated with the pressure differences. Although there are other experiments that one can do with pipes, this configuration is usually known as pipe flow.

Channel flow is the two-dimensional counterpart of pipe flow. Flow is supposed

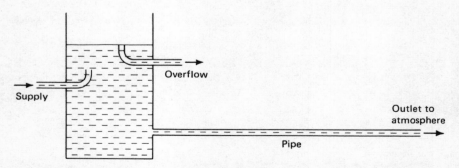

Figure 2.1   Simple pipe flow experimental arrangement. The pipe length is reduced in scale.

to occur between two parallel planes close together. The pressure difference is maintained between two opposite sides of the gap. The other two sides must be walled but are supposed to be so far away from the working region that they have no effect there. This is obviously a more difficult arrangement to set up experiment-ally, and the description of observations will be given in the context of pipe flow. However, a simple piece of theory can be developed about one possible flow pattern, and it is convenient to consider this first for channel flow.

2.2 Laminar flow theory: channel

Figure 2.2 shows the notation for this theory. The channel width is taken as $2a$ and its length as l; we are supposing that l is much larger compared with a than one can show in the diagram. Pressures p_1 and p_2 $(p_1 > p_2)$ are maintained at the ends of the channel. Co-ordinates are chosen as shown with the zero of y on the mid-plane of the channel.

It is observed (see Section 5.7) that the fluid immediately next to the walls remains at rest — a fact known as the no-slip condition. The speed, u, with which the fluid moves in the x-direction must thus be a function of y — zero at $y = \pm a$, non-zero elsewhere. This distribution $u(y)$ is known as the velocity profile.

The remoteness of the other walls, in the z-direction, is taken to imply that the flow is two-dimensional (see Section 1.3). We can thus consider all processes to be occurring in the plane of Fig. 2.2.

For the present theory we also suppose that the velocity profile is the same at all distances down the channel; that is at all x. Since the density ρ is taken to be constant as discussed in Section 1.2(iii), this is obviously one way of satisfying the requirement that the flow should conserve mass. The same velocity profile trans-ports the same amount of mass per unit time past every station.

The pressure varies with x, obviously, but is constant across the pipe at each x. We shall see below that a pressure gradient in a given direction generates a force in that direction; there is nothing to balance such a force in the y- or z-direction.

We consider now the forces acting on a small element of fluid of sides δx and δy as shown in Fig. 2.2 and side δz in the third direction. There are two processes giving rise to such forces — the action of viscosity as described in Section 1.2(iv), and the pressure.

The expression for the viscous force illustrates an important general point that, although the viscous stress depends on the first spatial derivative of the velocity, the viscous force on a fluid element depends on the second derivative. The net force

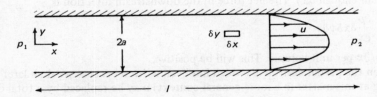

Figure 2.2 Definition diagram for channel flow. Width of channel is shown exaggerated with respect to length.

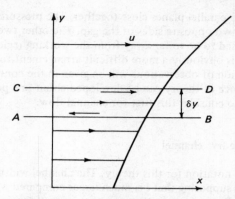

Figure 2.3   Extension of Fig. 1.1 to show viscous stresses acting on fluid element.

on the element is the small difference of the viscous stresses on either side of it. Figure 2.3 extends Fig. 1.1 to show this. Per unit area perpendicular to the y-direction, forces $\mu(\partial u/\partial y)_{y+\delta y}$ and $-\mu(\partial u/\partial y)_y$ act in the x-direction on the region between planes AB and CD. The net force on our element is

$$\left[\mu\left(\frac{\partial u}{\partial y}\right)_{y+\delta y} - \mu\left(\frac{\partial u}{\partial y}\right)_y\right]\delta x\delta z = \frac{\partial}{\partial y}\left(\mu\frac{\partial u}{\partial y}\right)\delta y\delta x\delta z$$

(when δy is small enough)

$$= \mu\frac{\partial^2 u}{\partial y^2}\delta x\delta y\delta z \qquad \text{(when } \mu \text{ is constant)}$$

$$(2.1)$$

The viscous force per unit volume is $\mu\partial^2 u/\partial y^2$. In the present case, for which u is independent of x and z, this may be written $\mu d^2 u/dy^2$. From the general shape of the velocity profile in Fig. 2.2, or from the physical expectation that viscous action will oppose the flow, we anticipate that d^2u/dy^2 will be negative.

The pressure decreases as one goes downstream; there will be slightly different pressure forces acting on the two ends of the element. Since pressure is force per unit area, that at the upstream end acting in the downstream direction on the element is $p_x\delta y\delta z$ (p_x denoting the value of p at x) and that at the downstream end acting in the upstream direction is

$$p_{x+\delta x}\delta y\delta z = \left(p_x + \frac{\partial p}{\partial x}\delta x\right)\delta y\delta z \qquad (2.2)$$

(for small enough δx). The net force in the downstream direction is

$$-\frac{\partial p}{\partial x}\delta x\delta y\delta z \qquad (2.3)$$

or $-\partial p/\partial x$ per unit volume. This will be positive.

Again the partial derivative (which has been written because we shall later be looking at this matter in a more general context) may be replaced by a total derivative, because p varies only with x. Further, the assumption of an unchanging velocity profile makes the dynamical processes the same at all stations downstream; the pressure force per unit volume — i.e. the pressure gradient — must be independent of x. Hence,

$$-\frac{\partial p}{\partial x} = -\frac{\mathrm{d}p}{\mathrm{d}x} = \frac{p_1 - p_2}{l} = G, \text{say} \qquad (2.4)$$

The momentum of the element $\delta x \delta y \delta z$ is not changing; each fluid particle travels downstream at a constant distance from the centre of the channel and so with a constant speed. Hence, the total force acting must be zero,

$$\mu \frac{\partial^2 u}{\partial y^2} \delta x \delta y \delta z - \frac{\partial p}{\partial x} \delta x \delta y \delta z = 0 \qquad (2.5)$$

that is

$$\mu \frac{\mathrm{d}^2 u}{\mathrm{d}y^2} = -G \qquad (2.6)$$

With the boundary conditions

$$u = 0 \quad \text{at} \quad y = \pm a \qquad (2.7)$$

this integrates to give

$$u = \frac{G}{2\mu}(a^2 - y^2) \qquad (2.8)$$

We have ascertained that the velocity profile is a parabola.

The mass of fluid passing through the channel per unit time and per unit length in the z-direction is

$$\int_{-a}^{a} \rho u \mathrm{d}y = 2G\rho a^3 / 3\mu \qquad (2.9)$$

2.3 Laminar flow theory: pipe

The corresponding flow in a pipe is usually known as Poiseuille flow (or sometimes, in the interests of historical accuracy, Hagen–Poiseuille flow). This case is marginally more complicated because of the cylindrical geometry. Figure 2.4 shows a cross-section of the pipe; the flow direction (the x-axis) is normal to the page. The velocity profile now represents the speed as a function of radius, $u(r)$, and we again

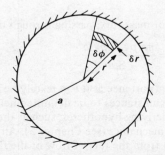

Figure 2.4 Definition sketch for pipe flow.

consider the case when this is independent of x. We consider an element of fluid as shaded in Fig. 2.4 and having length δx in the flow direction. The viscous forces on the two faces of this now differ slightly not only because the velocity gradients differ but also because the two faces have different areas. The force on one face is

$$\mu(\partial u/\partial r)r\delta\phi\delta x \tag{2.10}$$

and, by an argument parallel to that in Section 2.2, the net viscous force on the element is

$$\mu\frac{\partial}{\partial r}\left(r\frac{\partial u}{\partial r}\right)\delta r\delta x\delta\phi \tag{2.11}$$

The pressure force on one end of the element is

$$pr\delta\phi\delta r \tag{2.12}$$

and the net pressure force

$$-(\partial p/\partial x)r\delta x\delta\phi\delta r \tag{2.13}$$

Arguing in the same way as for channel flow we get

$$\mu\frac{d}{dr}\left(r\frac{du}{dr}\right) = -Gr \tag{2.14}$$

Integration gives

$$u = -\frac{Gr^2}{4\mu} + A\ln r + B \tag{2.15}$$

A must be zero for the velocity not to become infinite on the axis and B can be evaluated from the fact that

$$u = 0 \quad \text{at} \quad r = a \tag{2.16}$$

giving

$$u = \frac{G}{4\mu}(a^2 - r^2) \tag{2.17}$$

The velocity profile is a paraboloid with a maximum speed

$$u_{\max} = \frac{Ga^2}{4\mu} \tag{2.18}$$

The mass per unit time, or mass flux, passing through the pipe is

$$\int_0^a \rho 2\pi r u\, dr = \frac{\pi\rho Ga^4}{8\mu} = \frac{\pi\rho(p_1 - p_2)a^4}{8\mu l} \tag{2.19}$$

This is a quantity of some importance as it can readily be measured. Agreement with observation (under circumstances to be delimited below) provides an important check of the validity of underlying hypotheses, such as the no-slip condition and the applicability of continuum mechanics (see Chapter 5). Alternatively, an unknown viscosity can be determined from the rate of flow of the fluid through a tube under a known pressure gradient. This is the principle of one important type of viscometer.

An average speed can be defined as the mass flux divided by the density and cross-sectional area

$$u_{av} = \frac{Ga^2}{8\mu} \qquad (2.20)$$

2.4 The Reynolds number

We have determined above one theoretically possible flow behaviour. It is not the only possibility. Sometimes the actual flow behaviour corresponds to the theory, sometimes not. In order to specify the circumstances in which the different types of flow occur, we need to introduce the concept of the Reynolds number.

There are several types of variable associated with the pipe flow configuration: the dimensions of the pipe, the rate of flow, the physical properties of the fluid. For present purposes, we will suppose that the situation is fully specified if we know:

d (= $2a$), the pipe diameter
u_{av}, the average flow speed
ρ, the fluid density
μ, the viscosity

Two omissions from this list require some comment. The pipe length is not included on the supposition that, provided the pipe is long enough, the type of flow is determined before the downstream end can have any influence. The pressure gradient is not included because it cannot be varied independently of the above parameters. To produce the same average flow-speed of the same fluid through the same pipe will require the same imposed pressure gradient — whether or not the Poiseuille flow relationship applies. Hence, the pressure gradient need not be included in the specification of the situation. It is arguable that one should include the pressure gradient and omit the average speed, since the former is the controlled variable in most experiments. In Section 19.3 we shall see that there is one case in which this would certainly be the better procedure. However, this has not been conventional practice, and to adopt it would make for confusion. We notice that u_{av} relates directly to the total rate of flow through the pipe and must be the same at every station along the length — unlike u_{max} and other speeds one might define that depend on the detailed velocity profile.

We are now concerned with the question: what type of flow occurs for given values of d, u_{av}, ρ, and μ? But these four parameters are dimensional quantities, whereas the concept of a 'type of flow' does not have dimensions associated with it. Just as it is meaningless to write down an equation, $A = B$, with A and B of different dimensions, so it is meaningless to associate a type of flow with certain values of any dimensional quantity. For example, one would not expect a particular type of flow to occur over the same range of u_{av} for pipes of different diameter or for different fluids. The values of u_{av} specifying the range must be expressible (in principle, whether or not in practice) in terms of the things that determine it. There must be some (known or unknown) expression for it, and this expression must bring in other dimensional quantities in order to be dimensionally satisfactory. Thus we look for the factors that determine the type of flow in terms of dimensionless, not dimensional, parameters. Such dimensionless parameters must be provided as combinations of the specifying dimensional parameters. (We have arrived by a plausibility argument at a conclusion that we shall be examining more systematically in Chapter 7.)

There is one dimensional combination of the four parameters for the present configuration

$$\text{Re} = \frac{\rho u_{av} d}{\mu} \tag{2.21}$$

This is known as the Reynolds number of pipe flow.

It is one example of the general definition of the Reynolds number as

$$\text{Re} = \frac{\rho UL}{\mu} = \frac{UL}{\nu} \tag{2.22}$$

where U and L are velocity and length scales; that is typical measures of how fast the fluid is moving and the size of the system. As the book proceeds, we shall be seeing the relevance of forms of Reynolds number to a variety of situations.

Hence, it is appropriate to discuss the different types of flow in a pipe in terms of different ranges of Reynolds number.

2.5 The entry length

When the Reynolds number is less than about 30, the Poiseuille flow theory always provides an accurate description of the flow. In fact Equation (2.21) was first established empirically by Hagen and Poiseuille and the theory was given later by Stokes — a somewhat surprising historical fact if one knows how easy it is to fail to verify the theory as a result of having the Reynolds number too high!

At higher Reynolds numbers, the Poiseuille flow theory applies only after some distance down the pipe. The fluid is unlikely to enter the pipe with the appropriate parabolic velocity profile. Consequently, there is an entry length in which the flow is tending towards the parabolic profile. At low Reynolds number, this is so short that it can be ignored. But it is found both experimentally and theoretically that, as the Reynolds number is increased, this is no longer true. The details of the entry length depend, of course, on the actual velocity profile at entry, which in turn depends on the detailed geometry of the reservoir and its connection to the pipe. However, an important case is that in which the fluid enters with a uniform speed over the whole cross-section. Because of the no-slip condition, the fluid next to the wall must immediately be slowed down. This retardation spreads inward, whilst fluid at the centre must move faster, so that the average speed remains the same and mass is conserved. One thus gets a sequence of velocity profiles as shown in Fig. 2.5. Ultimately, the parabolic profile is approached and from there onwards the Poiseuille flow theory applies.

We can use this case to illustrate the dependence of the extent of the entry length on the Reynolds number. Defining X as the distance downstream from the entry at which u_{max} is within 5 per cent of its Poiseuille value [233]

$$\frac{X}{d} \approx \frac{\text{Re}}{30} \tag{2.23}$$

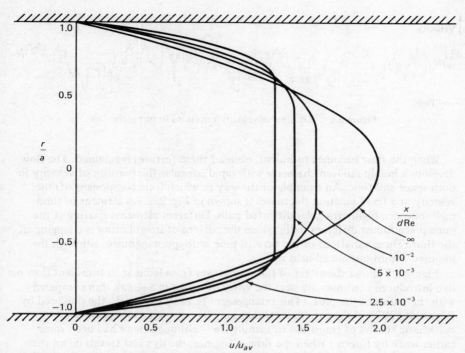

Figure 2.5 Laminar velocity profiles in pipe entry length. Based on average of various experimental and theoretical profiles, as collected together in Ref. [233].

This means, for example, that for flow at a Reynolds number of 10^4 (chosen as a high value at which this type of flow can occur) in a pipe of diameter 3 cm the entry length is 10 m long. Evidently there will be many practical situations in which the Poiseuille flow pattern is never reached. Even if it is reached, it will often not occupy a sufficiently large fraction of the length for equation (2.19) to be a good approximation to the relationship between pressure drop and mass flux.

Incidentally, the length at the other end over which the presence of the outlet has an effect is always relatively small.

2.6 Transition to turbulent flow

The above is an important, but perhaps rather uninteresting limitation to the occurrence of Poiseuille flow. As the Reynolds number is increased further, there is a much more dramatic change in the flow. It undergoes transition to the type of motion known as turbulent, the flows considered so far being called laminar.

In laminar pipe flow the speed at a fixed position is always the same. Each element of fluid travels smoothly along a simple well-defined path. (In Poiseuille flow, this is a straight line at a constant distance from the axis; in the entry length it is a smooth curve.) Each element starting at the same place (at different times) follows the same path.

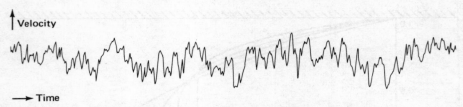

↑ Velocity

—→ Time

Figure 2.6   Example of velocity variations in turbulent flow.

When the flow becomes turbulent, none of these features is retained. The flow develops a highly random character with rapid irregular fluctuations of velocity in both space and time. An example of the way in which (one component of) the velocity at a fixed position fluctuates is shown in Fig. 2.6. An element of fluid now follows a highly irregular distorted path. Different elements starting at the same place follow different paths, since the pattern of irregularities is changing all the time. These variations of the flow in time arise spontaneously, although the imposed conditions are all held steady.

Figure 2.7 shows the effect of the changeover from laminar to turbulent flow on dye introduced continuously near the entry of a pipe in a streak thin compared with the radius of the pipe. (This arrangement is, in its essentials, the one used by Reynolds [207] in the experiments that may be regarded as the genesis of systematic studies of transition to turbulence — although there had been some earlier work by Hagen.) When the flow is laminar, the dye just travels down the pipe in a straight or almost straight line as shown in the upper picture. As the flow rate is increased, thus increasing the Reynolds number, the pattern changes as shown in the lower picture. The dye streak initially travels down the pipe in the same way as before, but, after some distance, it wavers and then suddenly the dye appears diffused over the whole cross-section of the pipe. The motion has become turbulent and the rapid fluctuations have mixed the dye up with the undyed fluid.

The distance fluid travels downstream before becoming turbulent varies with time, and, at any instant, there can be a laminar region downstream of a turbulent region. This comes about in the following way. The turbulence is generated initially

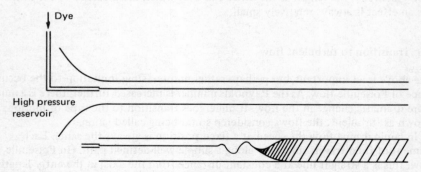

↓ Dye

High pressure
reservoir

Figure 2.7   Dye streaks in laminar and turbulent pipe flow. (Pipe length compressed relative to other dimensions.)

Figure 2.8 Growth and transport of turbulent plug. Shaded regions are turbulent, unshaded laminar. The mean fluid speed is approximately midway between the speeds of the front and rear of the plug.

over a small region. This region is actually localized radially (close to the wall) and azimuthally as well as axially. However, it quickly spreads over a cross-section of the pipe, and there is then a short length of turbulent flow with laminar regions both upstream and downstream of it. This short length is known as a turbulent plug. (We postpone till Section 19.3 further consideration of the origin of turbulent plugs.) The turbulence then spreads — the laminar fluid next to each end of the turbulent plug is brought into turbulent motion — and the plug gets longer. The fluid is, of course, meanwhile travelling down the pipe. Hence, the development of a plug is as shown in Fig. 2.8. The shapes of the interfaces are indicated roughly, based on photographs such as those in Fig. 2.9. As the plug grows the interfaces soon occupy a very short length of the pipe compared with the plug itself, and so the laminar and turbulent regions are well demarcated.

After a while another plug is born in a similar way. By this time the previous plug has moved off downstream so there is again laminar fluid downstream of the new plug. The plugs sometimes originate randomly in time, sometimes periodically; the circumstances in which the two cases occur will be discussed further in Section 19.3. When the front interface of one plug meets the rear interface of another, as a result of their growth, the two simply merge to give a single longer plug.

Figure 2.9 Photo sequence showing passage of turbulent plug past fixed observation point, similar to those in Refs. [167; 169]. Flow is downwards; time increases from left to right. Plug enters field of view at top of first frame (which also shows end of earlier plug at bottom) and leaves it at bottom of seventh frame. Flow visualization by addition of small amount of birefringent material — refractive index for polarized light affected by shear (Refs. [32, 166]).

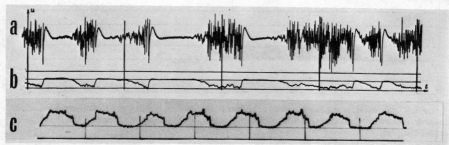

Figure 2.10 Oscillograms of velocity fluctuations at the centre of a pipe. Traces (a) and (b) (from Ref. [211]) show random plug production for Re = 2550, l/d = 322; trace (a) was given by a.c. amplification of the signal and shows the velocity fluctuations in the plugs; trace (b) was given by d.c. amplification of the same signal and shows principally the local mean velocity change between laminar and turbulent flow. Trace (c) (from Ref. [194]) is the counterpart of trace (b) for periodic plug production for Re ≈ 5000, l/d = 290. Note: velocity increases upwards in traces (a) and (b) but decreases upwards in trace (c).

As a result of these processes, a sensor at a fixed point in the pipe observes alternately laminar and turbulent motion. Figure 2.10 shows oscillograms of velocity fluctuations arising in this way, for random and for periodic plug production. The abrupt changes between laminar and turbulent motion illustrate again the sharpness of the interfaces.

The fraction of the time that the motion is turbulent — known as the intermittency factor — increases with distance downstream as a result of the growth of the plugs. Far enough downstream, in a long enough pipe, the laminar regions have all been absorbed and the flow is fully turbulent.

From the considerations earlier in this section, one would expect that there should be a critical value of the Reynolds number, below which the flow is wholly laminar, above which transition to turbulence occurs. In fact, the situation is more complicated than that. The transition process is extremely sensitive to the detailed geometry of the entry from the reservoir and to the level of small disturbances in the incoming fluid. As a result, transition has been observed to start at values of the Reynolds number ranging from 2×10^3 to 10^5. (This will be discussed further in Section 19.3.) The implication of this variation is not that the reasoning establishing the role of the Reynolds number was erroneous, but that dimensional parameters other than the four listed ($d, u_{av}, \rho,$ and μ) are relevant to transition.

2.7 Relationship between flow rate and pressure gradient

The pressure difference needed to produce a given flow rate through a pipe is larger when the flow is turbulent than when it is laminar. This is shown in Fig. 2.11. Since the abscissa is the Reynolds number, it is appropriate that the ordinate should be a non-dimensional form of the average pressure gradient $(p_1 - p_2)/l$, chosen† here as $(p_1 - p_2)d^3\rho/\mu^2 l$. The dotted lines in Fig. 2.11 show this parameter

---

† A more conventional choice would be $(p_1 - p_2)d/\rho u_{av}^2 l$ (the above parameter divided by (Re)^2). However, because it does not contain u_{av}, our choice is more convenient for certain considerations in Section 19.3. It also shows the behaviour in a particular pipe more directly.

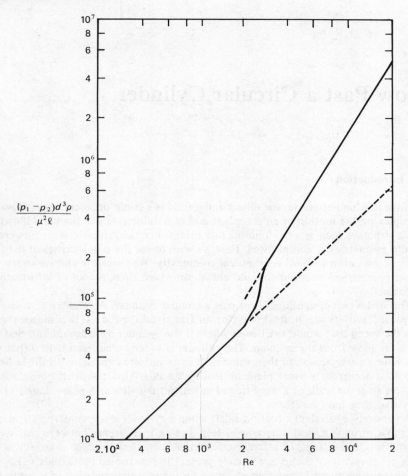

Figure 2.11 Variation of non-dimensional average pressure gradient with Reynolds number for pipe flow. Dotted lines: wholly laminar flow and wholly turbulent flow. Full line: example of actual case. Based on information in Refs. [38, 211].

plotted (logarithmically) against Reynolds number for Poiseuille flow and for wholly turbulent flow. The continuous line shows the behaviour for an actual case. At low Reynolds number it follows the Poiseuille flow line; as transition starts it rises above this, and, ultimately, when transition is complete in a short fraction of the total length, approaches the turbulent flow line. (The case chosen shows transition at a relatively low Reynolds number. With higher Reynolds number transition in a pipe of practicable length, there is likely to be some departure from the Poiseuille law before transition because of the importance of the entry length.)

3
Flow Past a Circular Cylinder

3.1 Introduction

Relative motion between some object and a fluid is a common occurrence. Obvious examples are the motion of an aeroplane and of a submarine and the wind blowing past a structure such as a tall building or a bridge. Practical situations are however usually geometrically complicated. Here we wish to see the complexities of the flow that can arise even without geometrical complexity. We therefore choose a very simple geometrical arrangement, and one about which there is a lot of information available.

This is the two-dimensional flow past a circular cylinder. A cylinder of diameter d is placed with its axis normal to a flow of free stream speed u_0; that means that u_0 is the speed that would exist everywhere if the cylinder were absent and that still exists far away from the cylinder. The cylinder is so long compared with d that its ends have no effect; we can then think of it as an infinite cylinder with the same behaviour occurring in every plane normal to the axis. Also, the other boundaries to the flow (e.g. the walls of a wind-tunnel in which the cylinder is placed) are so far away that they have no effect.

An entirely equivalent situation exists when a cylinder is drawn perpendicularly to its axis through a fluid otherwise at rest. The only difference between the two situations is in the frame of reference from which the flow is being observed. (Aspects of relativity theory are already present in Newtonian mechanics.) The velocity at each point in one frame is given by the vectorial addition of u_0 onto the velocity at the geometrically similar point in the other frame (Fig. 3.1). This transformation does not change the accelerations involved or the velocity gradients giving rise to viscous forces; it thus has no effect on the dynamics of the situation.

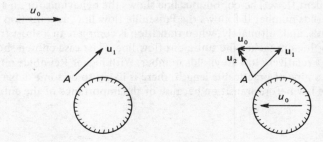

Figure 3.1   Velocity vectors $\mathbf{u}_1$ and $\mathbf{u}_2$ at point A in two frames of reference.

(These remarks apply only when u_0 is constant; if it is changing then one does have to distinguish between the cylinder accelerating and the fluid accelerating.)

It is, however, convenient to use a particular frame of reference for describing the flow. Except where otherwise stated, the following description will use the frame of reference in which the cylinder is at rest.

3.2 The Reynolds number

One can have various values of d and u_0 and of the density, ρ, and viscosity, μ, of the fluid. For reasons like those applying to pipe flow (Section 2.4) the important parameter is the Reynolds number

$$\text{Re} = \frac{\rho u_0 d}{\mu} \tag{3.1}$$

This is the only dimensionless combination and one expects (and finds) that the flow pattern will be the same when Re is the same. We thus consider the sequence of changes that occurs to the flow pattern as Re is changed. We are concerned with a very wide range of Re. In practice this means that both u_0 and d have to be varied to make observations of the full range. For example, $\text{Re} = 10^{-1}$ corresponds in air to a diameter of 10 μm with a speed of 0.15 m s^{-1} (or in glycerine to a diameter of 10 mm with a speed of 10 mm s^{-1}); $\text{Re} = 10^6$ corresponds in air to a diameter of 0.3 m with a speed of 50 m s^{-1}. Thus experiments have been done with cylinders ranging from fine fibres to ones that can be used only in the largest wind tunnels.

3.3 Flow patterns

The following description of the flow patterns is based almost entirely on experimental observations. Only for the lowest Reynolds numbers can the flow as a whole be determined analytically (Section 9.5), although there are theoretical treatments of aspects of the flow at other Reynolds numbers. Some of the flow patterns have also been studied computationally.

Figure 3.2 shows the flow when $\text{Re} \ll 1$. The lines indicate the paths of elements of fluid. The flow shows no unexpected properties, but two points are worth noting for comparison with higher values of the Reynolds number. Firstly, the flow is symmetrical upstream and downstream; the right-hand half of Fig. 3.2 is the mirror image of the left-hand half. Secondly, the presence of the cylinder has an effect over large distances; even many diameters to one side the velocity is appreciably different from u_0.

As Re is increased the upstream—downstream symmetry disappears. The particle paths are displaced by the cylinder for a larger distance behind it than in front of it. When Re exceeds about 4, this leads to the feature shown in the computed flow pattern of Fig. 3.3. Fluid that comes round the cylinder close to it moves away from it before reaching the rear point of symmetry. As a result, two 'attached eddies' exist behind the cylinder; the fluid in these circulates continuously, not moving off downstream. These eddies get bigger with increasing Re; Fig. 3.4 shows a photograph of the flow at $\text{Re} \approx 40$ just before the next flow development takes place. (For further computed flow patterns in this regime see Section 6.2.)

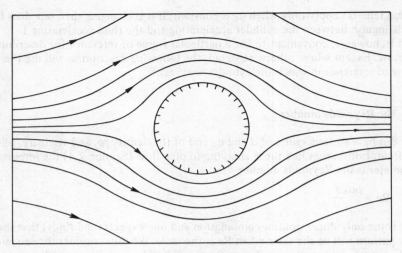

Figure 3.2   Low Reynolds number flow past a circular cylinder.

The tendency for the most striking flow features to occur downstream of the cylinder becomes even more marked as one goes to higher Reynolds numbers. This region is called the wake of the cylinder. The reason why there should be a distinctive velocity distribution in the wake will be considered in Section 3.4, and in Section 17.6 we shall be seeing that this distribution is one of a kind prone to instability. In consequence, for Re > 40, the flow becomes unsteady. As with transition to turbulence in a pipe (Section 2.6), this unsteadiness arises

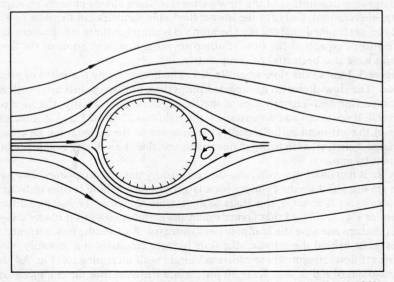

Figure 3.3   Flow past a circular cylinder at Re = 10 (computed: Ref. [95]).

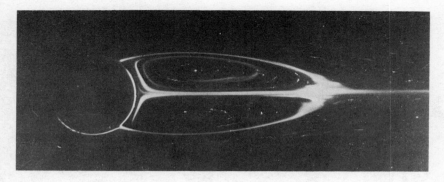

Figure 3.4   Attached eddies on circular cylinder at Re = 41, exhibited by coating cylinder with dye (condensed milk). From Ref. [245].

spontaneously even though all the imposed conditions are being held steady.

Figure 3.5 shows a sequence of patterns in a cylinder wake, produced by dye emitted through a small hole at the rear of the cylinder. The instability develops to give the flow pattern, known as a Kármán vortex street, shown schematically in Fig. 3.6. Concentrated regions of rapidly rotating fluid — more precisely regions of locally high vorticity (a term to be defined in Section 6.4) — form two rows on either side of the wake. All the vortices on one side rotate in the same sense, those on opposite sides in opposite senses. Longitudinally, the vortices on one side are mid-way between those on the other.

The whole pattern of vortices travels downstream, but with a speed rather smaller than u_0. This means that for the other frame of reference, a cylinder pulled through stationary fluid, the vortices slowly follow the cylinder. Figure 3.7 shows a photograph taken with this arrangement. A moderately long exposure shows the motion of individual particles in the fluid. Because the vortices are moving only slowly relative to the camera, the circular motion associated with them is shown well.

Although, at Reynolds numbers a little above 40, the vortex street develops from an amplifying wake instability [62, 296] (Fig. 3.5), increasing Reynolds number leads to an interaction with the flow in the immediate vicinity of the cylinder [60, 274]. When Re is greater than about 100, the attached eddies are periodically shed from the cylinder to form the vortices of the street. Whilst the eddy on one side is being shed that on the other side is re-forming. Figure 3.8 shows a close-up view of the region immediately behind the cylinder, with the same dye system as in Fig. 3.5, during this process.

Figure 3.9 shows a side-view of a vortex street, again shown by dye released at the cylinder. Sometimes the vortices are straight and closely parallel to the cylinder (indicating that the shedding occurs in phase all along the cylinder); sometimes they are straight but inclined to the cylinder, as in the top part of Fig. 3.9 (indicating a linear variation in the phase of shedding); and sometimes they are curved, as in the bottom part of Fig. 3.9 (indicating a more complicated phase variation). The exact behaviour is very sensitive to disturbances and so it is difficult to predict just what will occur at any given Reynolds number. One can, however, say that the lower the Reynolds number the greater is the likelihood of straight, parallel vortices.

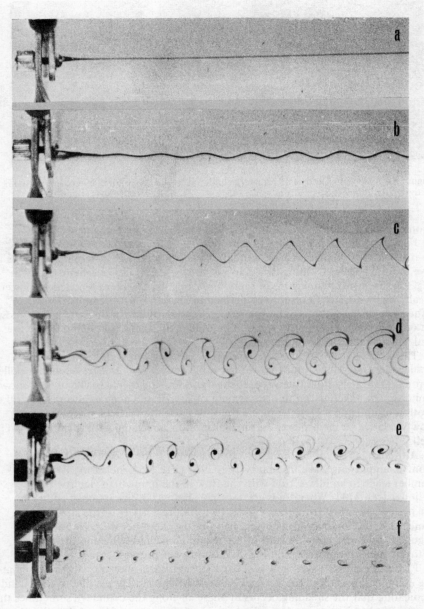

Figure 3.5 Cylinder wakes exhibited by dye introduced through hole in cylinder. (Cylinder is obscured by bracket but can be seen obliquely, particularly in (a) and (f).) (a) Re ≈ 30; (b) Re ≈ 40; (c) Re = 47; (d) Re = 55; (e) Re = 67; (f) Re = 100.

Figure 3.6   Relative positions of vortices in Kármán vortex street.

It should be emphasized that, in Figs. 3.5, 3.8, and 3.9, the introduction of dye was continuous. The gathering into discrete regions is entirely a function of the flow.

Figure 3.10 shows a sequence of oscillograms at two points fixed relative to a cylinder in a wind-tunnel as the main flow velocity is increased. In Fig. 3.10(a) and (b) it can be seen that the passage of the vortex street past the point of observation produces an almost sinusoidal variation. The frequency, n, of this is usually specified in terms of the non-dimensional parameter

$$St = nd/u_0 \tag{3.2}$$

known as the Strouhal number. St is a function of Re (although a sufficiently slowly varying one that it may be said that St is typically 0.2).

With increasing Re the strong regularity of the velocity variation is lost (Fig. 3.10). An important transition occurs at a Reynolds number a little below 200. Below this, the vortex street continues to all distances downstream. Above, it breaks down and produces ultimately a turbulent wake, although, as we shall be seeing below, the intermediate stages take different forms over different Reynolds number ranges. Figure 3.11 is a photograph of a turbulent wake. The name turbulent implies the existence of highly irregular rapid velocity fluctuations, in the same way as in Section 2.6. The turbulence is confined to the long narrow wake region

Figure 3.7   Vortex street exhibited by motion of particles floating on water surface, through which cylinder has been drawn; Re = 200. From Ref. [266].

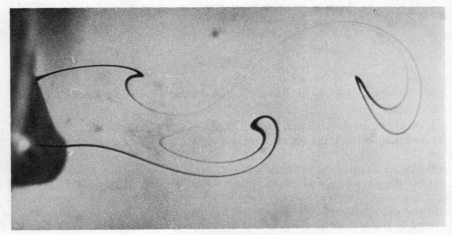

Figure 3.8   Motion immediately behind cylinder; Re = 110.

downstream of the cylinder. The character of a turbulent wake will be discussed in more detail in Section 22.4.

Despite the transition to turbulence, markedly periodic vortex shedding remains a characteristic of the flow up to the highest Reynolds numbers ($\sim 10^7$) at which observations have been made. When this is not immediately apparent from oscillograms like Fig. 3.10, Fourier analysis reveals the presence of a dominant

Figure 3.9   Side-view of vortex street behind cylinder; Re = 150. From Ref. [61].

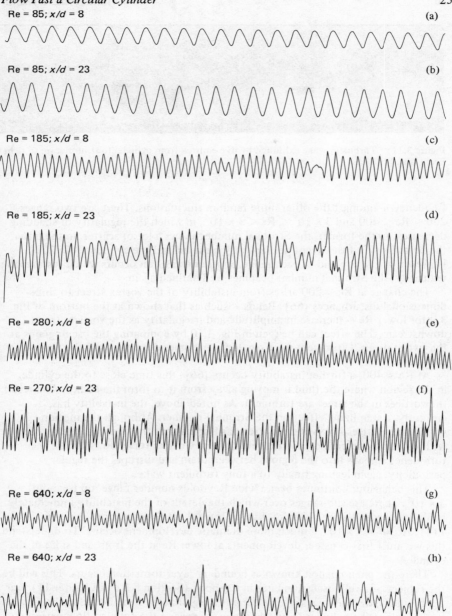

Figure 3.10 Oscillograms of velocity fluctuations in cylinder wake. Traces are in pairs at same Re, but different distances, *x*, downstream from cylinder. For both positions, probe was slightly off-centre to be influenced mainly by vortices on one side of street. (Notes: relative velocity amplitudes are arbitrary; time scale is expanded by factor of about 3 in traces (g) and (h).)

Figure 3.11 Turbulent wake exhibited by dye emitted from cylinder (out of picture to right). From Ref. [118].

frequency n amongst the other more random fluctuations. There are two ranges, $200 < \text{Re} < 400$ and $3 \times 10^5 < \text{Re} < 3 \times 10^6$, in which the regularity of shedding decreases: in the former, the Strouhal number shows a lot of scatter; in the latter, the periodicity is lost except perhaps very close behind the cylinder [62, 209]. However, at the top end of each range, another transition occurs which restores the regularity; the Strouhal number becomes well defined again.

The change at $\text{Re} \approx 200$ arises from instability of the vortex street to three-dimensional disturbances [66]. Bends – such as that shown at the bottom of Fig. 3.9 for lower Re – increase in amplitude and irregularity as the vortices travel downstream. The effect can be seen in Fig. 3.10 by comparing the oscillograms at the two stations. Ultimately the irregularity becomes dominant and the wake is turbulent.

At $\text{Re} \approx 400$, a further instability occurs [66], this time close to the cylinder in the region where the fluid is moving away from it to form the eddies. As a result the vortices in the street are turbulent. As noted above, the instability has, curiously, a stabilizing effect on the Strouhal number. Although the motion within the vortices involves rapid irregular fluctuations the vortex shedding occurs with quite precise periodicity. However, as the vortices travel downstream the turbulence spreads into the regions between them and disrupts the regular periodicity, again leading finally to a fully turbulent wake.

This behaviour continues over a wide Reynolds number range, up to about 3×10^5. There are sub-ranges over which the details of the instability immediately behind the cylinder are different, but we leave these complications aside [66, 113, 114]. At $\text{Re} \approx 3 \times 10^5$, a much more dramatic development occurs. To understand this we must first consider developments at lower Re at the front and sides of the cylinder.

There the phenomenon known as boundary layer formation occurs. This will be the subject of a full discussion later in the book (Section 8.3 and Chapter 11). For the moment, we may just say that there is a region, called the boundary layer, next to the wall of the cylinder in which all the changes to the detailed flow pattern occur. Outside this the flow pattern is independent of the Reynolds number. For these statements to mean anything, the boundary layer must be thin compared with the diameter of the cylinder; this is the case when Re is greater than about 100. (Boundary layer formation does not start by a sudden transition of the sort we have been considering previously; it is an asymptotic condition approached at high enough Re. The figure of 100 is just an order of magnitude.)

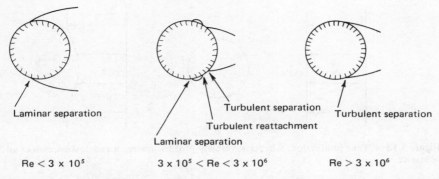

Laminar separation

Turbulent separation

Turbulent reattachment

Laminar separation

Turbulent separation

$Re < 3 \times 10^5$ $3 \times 10^5 < Re < 3 \times 10^6$ $Re > 3 \times 10^6$

Figure 3.12 Separation positions for various Reynolds number ranges (Refs. [209, 248]).

The change in the flow at $Re \approx 3 \times 10^5$ results from developments in the boundary layer. Below this Reynolds number the motion there is laminar. Above it undergoes transition to turbulence. At first, this transition takes a rather complicated form [209, 248]: laminar fluid close to the wall moves away from it as if it were entering the attached eddies; transition then occurs very quickly and the turbulent flow reattaches to the wall only a small distance downstream from the laminar separation. (See Section 11.4 for more precise consideration of these processes.) There are also complications due to the facts that the transition can occur asymmetrically between the two sides of the cylinder [58] and non-uniformly along its length [131].

At higher values of the Reynolds number, above about 3×10^6, transition occurs in the boundary layer itself, thus eliminating the laminar separation and turbulent reattachment. The transition process is now similar to that described for pipe flow.

Whether or not it has previously undergone laminar separation and turbulent reattachment, the turbulent boundary layer itself separates; the fluid in it moves away from the wall of the cylinder and into the wake some distance before the rear line of symmetry. This occurs, however, much further round the cylinder than when the boundary layer remains laminar (Fig. 3.12). As a result the wake is narrower for $Re > 3 \times 10^5$ than for $Re < 3 \times 10^5$. When $Re > 3 \times 10^5$, the fluid entering the wake is already turbulent and so the transition process immediately behind the cylinder is eliminated.

3.4 Drag

An important quantity associated with the relative motion between a body and a fluid is the force produced on the body. One has to apply a force in order to move a body at constant speed through a stationary fluid. Correspondingly an obstacle placed in a moving fluid would be carried away with the flow if no force were applied to hold it in place. The force in the flow direction exerted by the fluid on an obstacle is known as the drag. There is an equal and opposite force exerted by the obstacle on the fluid.

At high Reynolds numbers, this can be thought of as the physical mechanism of wake formation. Because of the force between it and the obstacle, momentum is

Figure 3.13   Wake production: schematic velocity profiles upstream and downstream of an obstacle.

removed from the fluid. The rate of momentum transport downstream must be smaller behind the obstacle than in front of it. There must thus be a reduction in the velocity in the wake region (Fig. 3.13). (At low Reynolds numbers, when the velocity and pressure are modified to large distances on either side of the obstacle, the situation is more complex.)

For the circular cylinder, the important quantity is the drag per unit length; we denote this by D. To show the variation with Reynolds number we need a non-dimensional representation; this is provided by the quantity known as the drag coefficient, defined to be

$$C_D = \frac{D}{\frac{1}{2}\rho u_0^2 d} \tag{3.3}$$

(The factor ½ has, of course, no role in the non-dimensionalization, but is conventionally included because $\frac{1}{2}\rho u_0^2$ has a certain physical significance – see Section 10.7.)

Figure 3.14 shows the variation of the drag coefficient with Reynolds number. The use of the non-dimensional parameters enables all conditions to be covered by a single curve. The curve is based primarily on experimental measurements, too numerous to show individual points. At the low Reynolds number end, the experiments can be matched to theory.

The corresponding plot between Reynolds number and drag coefficient can also be given for a sphere, although with less precision because of the experimental problem of supporting the sphere. The curve, although different in detail, shows all the same principal features as the one for the cylinder.

A few features of the curves merit comment – some of these being points to which we shall return in later chapters.

At low Reynolds numbers,

$$C_D \propto \frac{1}{\text{Re}} \tag{3.4}$$

(This is actually an accurate representation for the sphere, an approximate one for the cylinder – Sections 9.4 and 9.5.) For a given body in a given fluid (fixed d, ρ, and μ) this corresponds to

$$D \propto u_0 \tag{3.5}$$

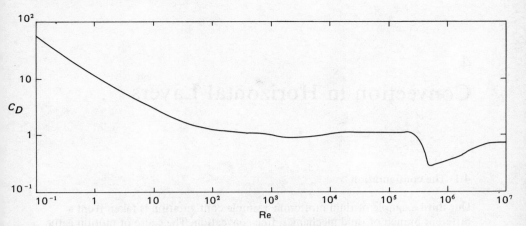

Figure 3.14   Variation of drag coefficient with Reynolds number for circular cylinder. Curve is experimental, based on data in Refs. [94, 105, 209, 250, 274, 292].

Direct proportionality of the drag to the speed is a characteristic behaviour at low speeds.

Over a wide range of Reynolds number (10^2 to 3×10^5) the drag coefficient varies little. For a given body in a given fluid, constant C_D corresponds to

$$D \propto u_0^2 \tag{3.6}$$

Proportionality of the drag to the square of the speed is often a characteristic behaviour at high speeds.

However, there is a dramatic departure from this behaviour at $\text{Re} \approx 3 \times 10^5$. The drag coefficient drops by a factor of over 3. This drop occurs sufficiently rapidly that there is actually a range over which an increase in speed produces a decrease in drag. We have seen that this Reynolds number corresponds to the onset of turbulence in the boundary layer. The consequent delayed separation of the boundary layer results in a narrower wake. Since this in turn corresponds to less momentum extraction from the flow, one might expect the lower drag. The result is nonetheless a somewhat paradoxical one since transition to turbulence usually produces an increased drag. In fact, on the cylinder and sphere, the force exerted directly by the boundary layer does increase on transition. But this is more than counteracted by another effect — changes in the pressure distribution over the surface (see Section 11.5).

4
Convection in Horizontal Layers

4.1 The configuration

Our third example of fluid motion in a simple configuration is taken from a different branch of fluid mechanics, free convection. The cause of motion is the action of a gravitational field on the density variations associated with temperature variations — essentially the well-known fact that hot fluid rises. A systematic discussion of free convection will be given in Chapter 14. Here we discuss the phenomena to be observed in one particular arrangement [72, 145].

A layer of fluid (Fig. 4.1) occupies the space between two horizontal plates, a vertical distance d apart. Each plate is maintained at a steady uniform temperature, the lower one hotter than the upper one ($T_2 > T_1$). The walls limiting the extent of the layer in the horizontal direction are supposed to be so far apart that they have little influence on the motion in most of the layer.

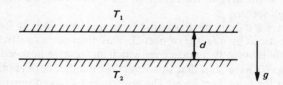

Figure 4.1   Definition sketch for Bénard convection.

This is known as the Bénard configuration. Historically, the name is inaccurate; Bénard's pioneering observations, although for long believed to relate to this configuration, were actually mostly of another phenomenon (Section 17.4) that gives rise to similar effects. However, the name is so well established that its use in this way causes no confusion.

Bénard convection has been extensively investigated both experimentally and theoretically. The theoretical work has provided, for example, the most accurate information about when flow occurs (Section 4.2). On the other hand, most of our knowledge about the detailed flow patterns (the sequence of events to be summarized in Section 4.3) comes from experiment. Such experiments have been carried out with a variety of fluids, as will be illustrated by the figures in this chapter. Considerable ingenuity has been needed to overcome the practical difficulties of approximating well to the theoretical configuration whilst having a way of observing the flow patterns.

4.2 Onset of motion

The Bénard configuration differs from the situations we have been considering hitherto in that one cannot immediately say whether flow will occur. Fluid at rest in a layer of the sort shown in Fig. 4.1 is in equilibrium. However, heavy cold fluid is situated above light hot fluid; if the former moves downwards and the latter upwards, there is a release of potential energy which can provide kinetic energy for the motion. There is thus a possibility that the equilibrium will be unstable. Flow thus arises not because of the absence of equilibrium (i.e. the absence of any solution of the governing equations with the fluid at rest) but because the equilibrium is unstable.

The distinction may be clarified by contrasting the Bénard situation with the flow in a similar fluid layer between vertical plates (to be considered more fully in Section 14.7). In this the fluid next to the hot wall rises and that next to the cold wall falls (Fig. 4.2) because no balance between the gravitational and pressure forces exists with the fluid at rest.

In that case, motion always occurs. In Bénard convection, it occurs only when certain criteria are fulfilled. An obvious first criterion is that the temperature should decrease upwards,

$$T_2 > T_1 \qquad (4.1)$$

so that heavier fluid overlies lighter.† But this is not the only criterion. The instability is opposed by the frictional action of viscosity. It is also opposed by the action of thermal conductivity, which tends to remove the temperature difference between the hot rising regions and the cold falling regions. Motion occurs only when the destabilizing action of the temperature difference is strong enough to overcome these.

This depends on a quantity known as the Rayleigh number, which plays a role for the present problem similar to that played by the Reynolds number in the previous problems. The Rayleigh number is

$$Ra = \frac{g\alpha(T_2 - T_1)d^3}{\nu\kappa} \qquad (4.2)$$

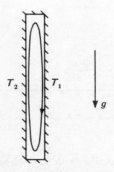

Figure 4.2   Convection in a vertical slot.

†This assumes that the coefficient of expansion is positive. In the few cases where it is negative, such as water below 4°C, the criterion (4.1) is of course reversed.

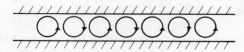

Figure 4.3   Schematic representation of Bénard convection at a Rayleigh number a little above critical.

where d is the depth of the layer, $(T_2 - T_1)$ is the temperature difference across it, g is the acceleration due to gravity, and α, ν, and κ are properties of the fluid, respectively its coefficient of expansion, kinematic viscosity, and thermal diffusivity.† The role of the Rayleigh number will be discussed in Section 14.2 and 18.2; however we may notice here that the factors that drive the motion — the combination of the temperature difference, the consequent expansion, and gravity — appear in the numerator and the factors mentioned above as opposing it appear in the denominator.

Instability occurs when the Rayleigh number exceeds a critical value of about 1700 (see Section 18.2). Below this the fluid remains at rest. Above it comes into motion. The fluid establishes hot rising regions and cold falling regions with horizontal motion at top and bottom to maintain continuity, as shown schematically in Fig. 4.3. The rising fluid loses its heat by thermal conduction when it gets near to the cold top wall and can thus move downwards again. Similarly, the cold downgoing fluid is warmed in the vicinity of the hot bottom wall and can rise again. When the flow is established as a steady pattern, the continuous release of potential energy is balanced by viscous dissipation of mechanical energy. The potential energy is provided by the heating at the bottom and the cooling at the top. From a thermodynamic point of view the system is thus a heat engine (cf. Section 14.4).

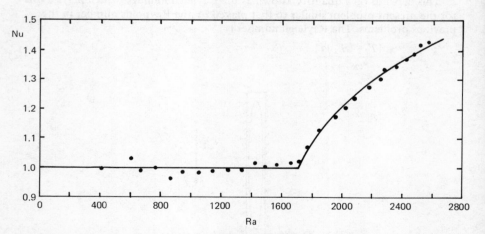

Figure 4.4   Variation of Nusselt number with Rayleigh number for Bénard convection, showing increase of heat transfer with onset of motion. Data obtained by C. W. Titman.

†Thermal diffusivity is defined as $\kappa = k/\rho C_p$ (k = thermal conductivity; ρ = density; C_p = specific heat at constant pressure).

The onset of motion as the Rayleigh number is increased is most readily detected by its effect on the heat transfer. When the fluid is at rest, this is due to conduction (radiative heat transfer is frequently negligible, though it sometimes has to be subtracted out, particularly in experiments with gases); hence, if H is the rate of heat transfer per unit area

$$H = \frac{k(T_2 - T_1)}{d} \tag{4.3}$$

When the fluid comes into motion it carries heat with it and the heat transfer increases above that given by conduction alone. Figure 4.4 shows the observed variation of the quantity

$$\text{Nu} = \frac{Hd}{k(T_2 - T_1)} \tag{4.4}$$

with Rayleigh number. (Nu is known as the Nusselt number — see Sections 13.4 and 14.7.) Nu remains equal to 1 below the critical Rayleigh number, but increases above 1 with the onset of motion.

4.3 Flow regimes

The detailed structure of the convection and, in particular, the planform of the rising and falling regions is a matter of some complexity. For values of the Rayleigh number not too much in excess of the critical value, the convection always occurs in a fairly regular pattern, as was implied by Fig. 4.3. (The individual elements in such a pattern are known as convection cells — or Bénard cells — and the flow as a whole is described as cellular.) The geometry of this pattern can, however, take a variety of forms, as can be seen in Figs. 4.5 to 4.7. The matter is complicated by the fact that the variation of fluid properties (particularly viscosity) with temperature influences the pattern. When this variation is negligible the convection first occurs in long 'rolls' of rising and falling fluid (as in Figs. 4.5 and 4.6). Because these rolls are long, the whole pattern is sensitive to the shape of the vertical walls (e.g., Fig. 4.6).

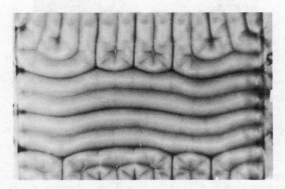

Figure 4.5   Bénard convection at Ra = 3 x 10³, Pr = 367; aluminium powder flow visualization (see Section 23.4). From Ref. [236].

Figure 4.6   Bénard convection at Rayleigh number slightly above critical, Pr ≈ 800;
aluminium powder flow visualization (Section 23.4). From Ref. [143].

As the Rayleigh number is increased, a sequence of changes in the mode of convection occurs. The values of the Rayleigh number corresponding to these changes
depend on a further parameter, the Prandtl number

$$Pr = \nu/\kappa \qquad (4.5)$$

This is a property of the particular fluid. Even when this is allowed for, there are
considerable variations in the quantitative observations, associated with sensitivity
to disturbances and hysteresis (transitions occurring at different Rayleigh number
when this is increasing and when it is decreasing). Hence, no quantitative details will
be provided in the following account,† although values of the Rayleigh and Prandtl

Figure 4.7   Bénard convection at Ra = 2.6 × 10⁴, Pr = 100; aluminium powder flow visualization (Section 23.4). From Ref. [210].

† The account is synthesized from observations in a variety of fluids, and seems to be the most
consistent description that can be given at the present time. However, this means that not all
parts of the account necessarily apply at every Prandtl number. Also, almost certainly, future
work will reveal additional significant stages of development.

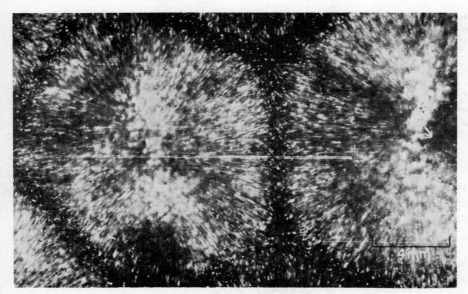

Figure 4.8   Detailed view of cell in Bénard convection, Ra = 1.76 × 10⁴ ; aluminium powder flow visualization (Section 23.4). From Ref. [159].

numbers in the figure captions give some indications. In general, corresponding developments tend to occur at a lower value of the Rayleigh number when the Prandtl number is lower. As an extreme example, in mercury, with Pr = 0.025, it is difficult to observe any form of convection other than turbulent.

The first development is a change in the planform of cellular convection from the rolls shown in Figs. 4.5 and 4.6 to a three-dimensional pattern such as that in Fig. 4.7. The flow remains steady. Quite a variety of three-dimensional patterns has been observed; again, probably, temperature variation of viscosity has influenced some of these. Figure 4.8 shows a close-up of one convection cell in a three-dimensional array. The fluid rises in isolated regions at the centre of polygons like that shown and falls in a continuous network formed by the peripheries of the polygons. The horizontal flow close to the top produces the streaks seen in the photograph.

Further developments involve the motion becoming unsteady. Figure 4.9 shows observations of the temperature variations. At each Rayleigh number, one trace shows the variation with time at a fixed position, the other the variation with position observed by traversing a probe through the fluid. At low Rayleigh numbers, the temperature at a fixed position is effectively constant, whilst the traverse produces a roughly periodic variation associated with the passage of the probe through the cells. At higher Rayleigh numbers unsteadiness is apparent. At first, the time variations are a perturbation of the previous pattern, but with increasing Ra, they become increasingly dominant.

Other experiments have elucidated some of the processes involved. The first unsteadiness is in the form of periodic pulsations within the cellular flow. There is some dispute as to the detailed form of the pulsations [150, 294] – perhaps there is more

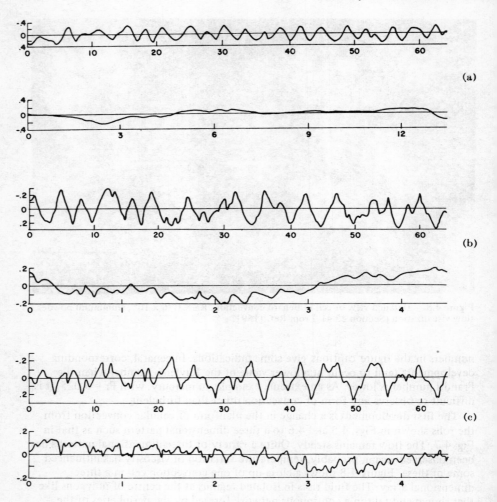

(a)

(b)

(c)

than one mode of oscillation – but their occurrence is well illustrated by Fig. 4.10. This picture was obtained by having the fluid illuminated along only one line and moving the camera so that the image of this line moved across the film. The result is essentially a space–time representation of the flow, and the 'ribbed' pattern indicates the occurrence of periodic fluctuations.

Further increase in Rayleigh number results in the periodic variations giving way to much less regular ones. Convection cells can still be observed (Fig. 4.11), although with greater variability in size and shape. The flow within the cells, however, is turbulent. At Rayleigh numbers well above critical, only fluid passing quite close to the lower boundary is significantly heated. The resulting hot rising regions are thus narrow and so, owing to a similar effect at the upper boundary, are the cold falling regions (Fig. 4.12). Much of the fluid circulates approximately isothermally. This is an example of what, later in the book, we shall come to know

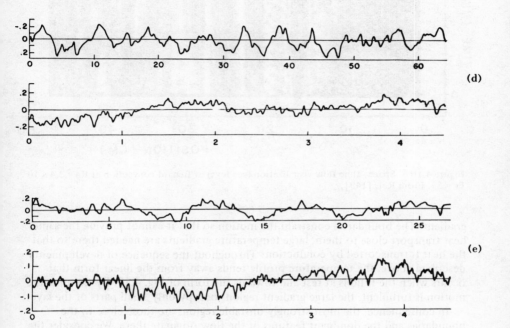

Figure 4.9 Temperature variations in Bénard convection observed by moving and stationary probes. (a) Ra = 5.0 x 10³, (b) 1.21 x 10⁴, (c) 3.03 x 10⁴, (d) 5.61 x 10⁴, (e) 1.55 x 10⁶; Pr = 0.72 (air) throughout. Abscissa scales represent x/d and time (minutes) for the two cases; ordinate scales represent the difference between the instantaneous temperature and the mean temperature divided by $(T_2 - T_1)$. From Ref. [293].

as boundary layer development. The generation of the turbulence within the convection cells occurs in the narrow hot and cold regions. Because of the turbulence the cellular structure is no longer readily apparent from observations of the temperature field (Fig. 4.9c).

At still higher Rayleigh number the cellular structure disappears altogether. One is now in the regime described as turbulent convection. To understand the processes occurring in this regime, it is helpful to look at the mean temperature distribution across the layer. (Averaging is either over time or over horizontal planes. The nature and role of mean quantities in turbulent flows will be discussed in Section 20.3.) This takes the form shown schematically in Fig. 4.13, with large temperature gradients close to the boundaries and a nearly isothermal region in the interior, for the following reason. In the interior the fluid motion transports a large amount of heat across the layer (i.e. Nu ≫ 1), a process requiring negligible vertical temperature

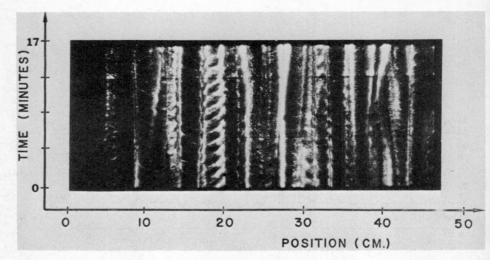

Figure 4.10   Space–time flow visualization (see text) of Bénard convection at Ra = 3.4 x 10⁵, Pᵣ = 57. From Ref. [149].

gradient. The boundaries constrain the motion so that it cannot provide the same heat transport close to them; large temperature gradients are needed there so that the heat is transported by conduction. Throughout the sequence of developments described above, the temperature profile tends away from the linear form that occurs when the fluid is at rest and towards the form of Fig. 4.13. By the time the motion is turbulent, the large gradient regions occupy only small parts of the layer.

In consequence, the most strongly unstable regions are those close to the boundaries and the dominant features of the flow originate there. We consider the hot bottom wall; similar processes occur close to the cold top wall, with the roles of hot and cold fluid reversed. There are intermittent eruptions of hot fluid away from

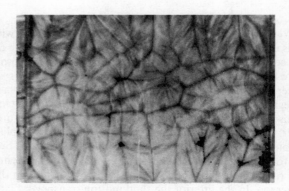

Figure 4.11   Counterpart of Fig. 4.5 at Ra = 1.3 x 10⁵, Pr = 311. From Ref. [236].

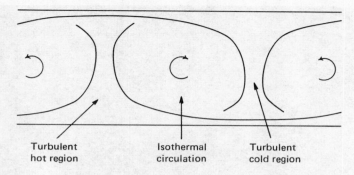

Figure 4.12   Principal features of cellular convection in boundary layer regime.

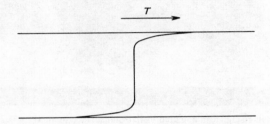

Figure 4.13   General form of mean temperature distribution for Bénard convection at high Rayleigh number.

Figure 4.14   Thermals rising from a heated horizontal surface in water (Pr ≈ 6); dye produced *uniformly* at surface by pH technique (see Section 23.4). From Ref. [237].

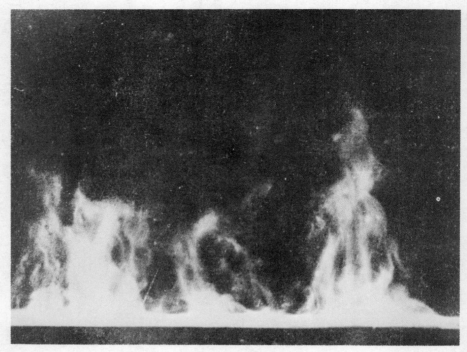

Figure 4.15   Thermals rising from a heated horizontal surface in air (Pr = 0.7); flow visualization using recondensed water vapour evaporated at moist surface. From Ref. [206].

the bottom boundary. Colder fluid moves close to the wall to replace the fluid in an eruption. This is gradually warmed by conduction from the wall until there is a thick enough layer of hot fluid for another eruption to be initiated. The process then repeats itself.

Each eruption gives rise to one or more columns of hot fluid rising through the interior region. These features are sometimes called thermals, sometimes plumes. Over a range of Rayleigh number, the thermals penetrate right across the layer, generating transient stable blobs of fluid close to the opposite boundary [77].

Ultimately, however, at the highest Rayleigh numbers, there is such vigorous mixing associated with the turbulent motion that the thermals lose their identity before reaching the opposite boundary. The processes at each boundary now occur independently of those at the other. They can be investigated by studying the motion above a single heated plate at the bottom of a large expanse of fluid (Figs. 4.14–4.16), corresponding in a sense to infinite Rayleigh number.

Two different types of motion have been observed, the relationship between them being unclear. Both involve the above process of the generation of thermals. However, in some cases, illustrated by Fig. 4.14, the eruptions occur with marked periodicity and the hot rising regions are in the same places each time. In the more usual case, illustrated by Fig. 4.15, the eruptions are not simultaneous over different parts of the plate. At any instant they are randomly distributed in position (Fig. 4.16 shows the random character of the instantaneous temperature field); at a fixed

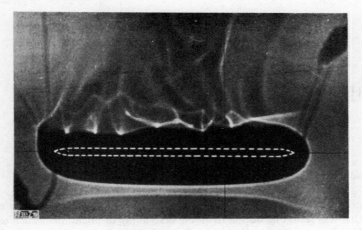

Figure 4.16 Shadowgraph (see Section 23.4) of convection around a heated horizontal plate. Dotted line shows position of shadow of plate in the absence of thermal effects. From Ref. [220].

position they occur randomly in time. Only in the latter case can the motion really be called fully turbulent. However, almost certainly, both types of flow involve vigorous disorganized small-scale motion as well as the rather coherent large-scale motion of the thermals. The former occurs both within the thermals and in the slowly downward drifting cold fluid between the thermals [270].

5
Equations of Motion

5.1 Introduction

We turn now to the formulation of the basic equations — the starting point of the theories that will lead, one hopes, to an understanding of phenomena such as those described in Chapters 2 to 4. These equations are formulations appropriate to a fluid in motion of the usual laws of mechanics — conservation of mass and Newton's laws of motion. In some situations other physical processes may be present, thermodynamic processes for instance, and equations for these are similarly formulated.

5.2 Fluid particles and continuum mechanics

Before we can proceed with this formulation we need certain preliminary ideas, the most important being the concept of a fluid particle.

The equations concern physical and mechanical quantities, such as velocity, density, pressure, temperature, which will be supposed to vary continuously from point to point throughout the fluid. How do we define these quantities at a point? To do so we have to make what is known as the assumption of the applicability of continuum mechanics or the continuum hypothesis. We suppose that we can associate with any volume of fluid, no matter how small, those macroscopic properties that we associate with the fluid in bulk. We can then say that at each point there is a particle of fluid and that a large volume of fluid consists of a continuous aggregate of such particles, each having a certain velocity, temperature, etc.

Now we know that this assumption is not correct if we go right down to molecular scales. We have to consider why it is nonetheless plausible to formulate the equations on the basis of the continuum hypothesis. It is simplest to think of a gas, although the considerations for a liquid are very similar.

The various macroscopic properties are defined by averaging over a large number of molecules. Consider velocity for example. The molecules of a gas have high†️ speeds associated with their Brownian motion, but these do not result in a bulk transfer of gas from one place to another. The flow velocity is thus defined as the average velocity of many molecules. Similarly, the temperature is defined by the average energy of the Brownian motion. The density is defined by the mass of the average number of molecules to be found in a given volume. Other macroscopic

† High in the sense that, for the flows at speeds low compared with the speed of sound that are considered in this book, the r.m.s. Brownian speed is much larger than the flow speed.

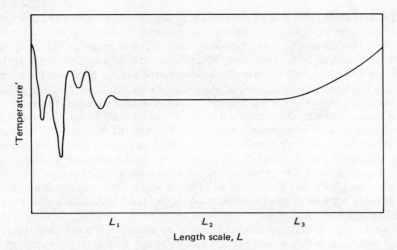

Figure 5.1   Schematic variation of average energy of molecules with length scale. See text.

properties, such as pressure and viscosity, likewise result from the average action of many molecules.

None of these averaging processes is meaningful unless the averaging is carried out over a large number of molecules. A fluid particle must thus be large enough to contain many molecules. It must still be effectively at a point with respect to the flow as a whole. Thus the continuum hypothesis can be valid only if there is a length scale, L_2, which we can think of as the size of a fluid particle, such that

$$L_1 \ll L_2 \ll L_3 \tag{5.1}$$

where the meanings of L_1 and L_3 are illustrated by Fig. 5.1. This figure uses the example of temperature, rather than the natural first choice of velocity, because it is easier to discuss a scalar. It shows schematically the average Brownian energy of the molecules in a volume L^3 plotted against the length scale L (on a logarithmic scale). The centre of the volume may be supposed fixed as its size is varied. When the volume is so small that it contains only a few molecules, there are large random fluctuations; the change produced by increasing the volume depends on the particular speeds of the new molecules then included. As the volume becomes large enough to contain many molecules, the fluctuations become negligibly small. A temperature can then meaningfully be defined. L_1 is proportional to, but an order of magnitude or so larger than, the average distance from a molecule to its nearest neighbour. At the other extreme, the volume may become so large that it extends into regions where the temperature is significantly different. This will result in an increase or decrease in the average. L_3 is a typical length scale associated with the flow; that is a typical distance over which the macroscopic properties vary appreciably.

The applicability of the continuum hypothesis depends on there being a significant plateau between L_1 and L_3 as shown. One may regard L_2 as being an infinitesimal distance so far as macroscopic effects are concerned, and formulate the equations (as differential equations implicitly involving the limit of small separations) ignoring the behaviour on still smaller length scales.

The same fluid particle does not consist of just the same molecules at all times. The interchange of molecules between fluid particles is taken into account in the macroscopic equations by assigning to the fluid diffusive properties such as viscosity and thermal conductivity. For example (again considering a gas for simplicity) the physical process by which the velocity distribution of Fig. 1.1 generates the stress shown is the Brownian movement of molecules across AB; those crossing in, say, the $+y$-direction have on average less x-momentum and so tend to reduce the momentum of the fluid above AB. The same fluid particle may be identified at different times — once the continuum hypothesis is accepted — through the macroscopic formulation. This specifies (in principle) a trajectory for every particle and thus provides meaning to the statement that the fluid at one point at one time is the same as that at another point at another time. For example, for a fluid macroscopically at rest, it is obviously sensible to say that the same fluid particle is always in the same place — even though, because of the Brownian motion, the same molecules will not always be at that place.

However, for the continuum hypothesis to be plausible, it is evidently necessary for the molecules within a fluid particle to be strongly interacting with one another. If each molecule acted just as if the others were not there, there would be little point in identifying the aggregate as a particle. Thus, if λ is the molecular mean free path, continuum mechanics can be applied only if

$$\lambda \ll L_2 \tag{5.2}$$

so that each molecule undergoes many collisions whilst traversing a distance that can still be regarded as infinitesimal. Since λ can be large compared with L_1 as defined above, this is an additional requirement to (5.1).

Once the continuum hypothesis has been introduced, we can formulate the equations of motion on a continuum basis, and the molecular structure of the fluid need not be mentioned any more. Hence, although the concepts developed above underlie the whole formulation, we shall not have much occasion to refer back to them. Velocity, henceforth, will be either a mathematical quantity or something (hopefully equivalent) that one measures experimentally. So will all the other parameters. Their definitions as averages over molecules provide answers to the implicit, but rarely explicit, questions: 'What is the real physical meaning of this mathematical quantity?' 'What quantity does one ideally wish to measure?'

The continuum hypothesis is only a hypothesis. The above discussion suggests that it is plausible, but nothing more. The real justification for it comes subsequently — through the experimental verification of predictions of the equations developed on the basis of the hypothesis.

5.3 Eulerian and Lagrangian co-ordinates

In setting up the equations governing the dynamics of a fluid particle, we evidently need to decide whether we should use co-ordinates fixed in space or co-ordinates that move with the particle. These two procedures are known respectively as the Eulerian and Lagrangian specifications. The equations are much more readily formulated using the former because the Lagrangian specification does not immediately indicate the instantaneous velocity field on which depend the stresses acting between fluid particles. Throughout this book we use only the Eulerian specification; i.e.

we write the velocity

$$\mathbf{u} = \mathbf{u}(\mathbf{r}, t) \tag{5.3}$$

where $\mathbf{r}$ is the position in an inertial frame of reference and t is time. Values of $\mathbf{u}$ at the same $\mathbf{r}$ but different t do not, of course, correspond to the same fluid particle.

It is not always easy to relate Lagrangian aspects, such as the trajectories of fluid particles, to an Eulerian specification. In the context of this book, this is particularly relevant to the interpretation of flow visualization experiments in which dye marks certain fluid particles. The relationship of the observed patterns to the corresponding Eulerian velocity field may not be simple.

5.4 Continuity equation

We are now ready to start on the actual formulation of the equations. We consider first the representation of mass conservation, often called continuity.

Consider an arbitrary volume V fixed relative to Eulerian co-ordinates and entirely within the fluid (Fig. 5.2). Fluid moves into or out of this volume at points over its surface. If $d\mathbf{S}$ is an element of the surface (the magnitude of $d\mathbf{S}$ being the area of the element and its direction the outward normal) and $\mathbf{u}$ is the velocity at the position of this element, it is the component of $\mathbf{u}$ parallel to $d\mathbf{S}$ that transfers fluid out of V. Thus, the outward mass flux (mass flow per unit time) through the element is $\rho\mathbf{u}\cdot d\mathbf{S}$, where ρ is the fluid density. Hence,

$$\text{Rate of loss of mass from } V = \int_S \rho\mathbf{u}\cdot d\mathbf{S} \tag{5.4}$$

(This is, of course, negative if the mass in V is increasing.) We have also

$$\text{Total mass in volume } V = \int_V \rho\, dV \tag{5.5}$$

Hence

$$\frac{d}{dt} \int_V \rho\, dV = \int_V \frac{\partial \rho}{\partial t}\, dV = -\int_S \rho\mathbf{u}\cdot d\mathbf{S} \tag{5.6}$$

We are interested in the mass balance at a point, rather than that over an arbitrary finite volume. Hence, we allow V to shrink to an infinitesimal volume; the integration in $\int(\partial\rho/\partial t)dV$ is redundant and we have

$$\frac{\partial \rho}{\partial t} = -\lim_{V \to 0} \left[\int \rho\mathbf{u}\cdot d\mathbf{S}/V \right] \tag{5.7}$$

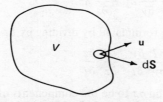

Figure 5.2   Definition sketch for derivation of continuity equation.

That is

$$\frac{\partial \rho}{\partial t} = -\text{div } \rho \mathbf{u} \tag{5.8}$$

by definition of the operator div. This gives the general expression representing mass conservation for a fluid in which both $\mathbf{u}$ and ρ are functions of position,

$$\frac{\partial \rho}{\partial t} + \nabla \cdot (\rho \mathbf{u}) = 0 \tag{5.9}$$

This is known as the continuity equation.

For the important special case when ρ is constant — see Section 1.2 (iii) and Section 5.8 — the continuity equation reduces to the very simple form

$$\nabla \cdot \mathbf{u} = 0 \tag{5.10}$$

The velocity field is a solenoidal vector. We notice that this does not assume steady flow. The time-variation does not appear explicitly in the continuity equation of a constant density fluid even when the flow is unsteady.

5.5 The substantive derivative

The next equation to be derived is the representation of Newton's second law of motion; i.e. the rate of change of momentum of a fluid particle is equal to the net force acting on it. We need first of all an expression for the rate of change of momentum of a fluid particle. It would not be correct to equate the rate of change of momentum at a fixed point to the force, because different particles are there at different times. Even in steady flow, for example, a fluid particle can change its momentum by travelling to a place where the velocity is different; this acceleration requires a force to produce it.

This is one example of a general problem. On occasion, one needs to know the rate of change of other quantities whilst following a fluid particle. In problems where thermal effects are important, for example, various physical processes may heat or cool the fluid. These determine the rate of change of the temperature of a fluid particle, not the rate of change at a fixed point.

In this section, therefore, we examine the general question of rates of change following the fluid. It is easier in the first place to consider a scalar quantity, and we denote this by T, thinking of the example of temperature.

Quite generally, the small change δT produced by a small change δt in time and small changes $\delta x, \delta y, \delta z$ in Cartesian position co-ordinates is

$$\delta T = \frac{\partial T}{\partial t} \delta t + \frac{\partial T}{\partial x} \delta x + \frac{\partial T}{\partial y} \delta y + \frac{\partial T}{\partial z} \delta z \tag{5.11}$$

and a rate of change can be formulated by dividing by δt

$$\frac{\delta T}{\delta t} = \frac{\partial T}{\partial t} + \frac{\partial T}{\partial x} \frac{\delta x}{\delta t} + \frac{\partial T}{\partial y} \frac{\delta y}{\delta t} + \frac{\partial T}{\partial z} \frac{\delta z}{\delta t} \tag{5.12}$$

If now we choose $\delta x, \delta y$, and δz to be the components of the small distance moved by a fluid particle in time δt, then (in the limit $\delta t \to 0$) this is the rate of change of

T of that particle. Also $\delta x/\delta t$, $\delta y/\delta t$ and $\delta z/\delta t$ are then (in the same limit) the three components of the velocity of the particle (u, v, and w). We thus have

$$\frac{DT}{Dt} = \frac{\partial T}{\partial t} + u\frac{\partial T}{\partial x} + v\frac{\partial T}{\partial y} + w\frac{\partial T}{\partial z} \tag{5.13}$$

In general D/Dt denotes the rate of change (of whatever quantity it operates on) following the fluid. This operator is known as the substantive derivative.

We can re-write equation (5.13) as

$$\frac{DT}{Dt} = \frac{\partial T}{\partial t} + \mathbf{u} \cdot \nabla T \tag{5.14}$$

and the operator in general as

$$\frac{D}{Dt} = \frac{\partial}{\partial t} + \mathbf{u} \cdot \nabla \tag{5.15}$$

(exhibiting the physically obvious fact that it does not depend on the particular co-ordinates used).

We see that the relationship combines the two ways in which the temperature of a fluid particle can change. It can change because the whole temperature field is changing — a process present even if the particle is at rest. And it can change by moving to a position where the temperature is different — a process present even if the temperature field as a whole is steady. As one would expect, this latter process depends on the magnitude of the spatial variations of the temperature and on the velocity, determining how quickly the fluid moves through the spatial variations.

Nothing in the above analysis restricts it to scalar quantities, and we can similarly write that the rate of change of a vector quantity $\mathbf{B}$ following a fluid particle is

$$\frac{D\mathbf{B}}{Dt} = \frac{\partial \mathbf{B}}{\partial t} + u\frac{\partial \mathbf{B}}{\partial x} + v\frac{\partial \mathbf{B}}{\partial y} + w\frac{\partial \mathbf{B}}{\partial z} = \frac{\partial \mathbf{B}}{\partial t} + \mathbf{u} \cdot \nabla \mathbf{B} \tag{5.16}$$

Whereas $\mathbf{u} \cdot \nabla T$ is the scalar product of vectors $\mathbf{u}$ and ∇T, $\mathbf{u} \cdot \nabla \mathbf{B}$ cannot be similarly split up. It is meaningful only as a whole. ($\mathbf{u} \cdot \nabla$) operating on a vector must be thought of as a new operator (defined through its Cartesian expansion).

The particular case, $\mathbf{B} = \mathbf{u}$, gives the rate of change of velocity following a fluid particle,

$$\frac{D\mathbf{u}}{Dt} = \frac{\partial \mathbf{u}}{\partial t} + \mathbf{u} \cdot \nabla \mathbf{u} \tag{5.17}$$

$\mathbf{u}$ now enters in two ways, both as the quantity that changes as the fluid moves and as the quantity that governs how fast the change occurs. Mathematically, however, it is just the same quantity in both its roles.

Returning finally to the information that we require for the dynamical equation, we have that the rate of change of momentum per unit volume following the fluid is

$$\rho\frac{D\mathbf{u}}{Dt} = \rho\frac{\partial \mathbf{u}}{\partial t} + \rho\mathbf{u} \cdot \nabla \mathbf{u} \tag{5.18}$$

Why, the reader may ask, is it $\rho D\mathbf{u}/Dt$ and not $D(\rho\mathbf{u})/Dt$? (The distinction is important in the general case when both **u** and ρ are variables.) The only reason why a particular bit of fluid is changing its momentum is that it is changing its velocity. If it is simultaneously changing its density, this is not because it is gaining or losing mass, but because it is changing the volume it occupies. This change is therefore irrelevant to the momentum change. Expressing the distinction verbally instead of algebraically, we may say that '(the rate of change of momentum) per unit volume' is different from 'the rate of change of (momentum per unit volume)', and the former is the relevant quantity.

5.6 The Navier–Stokes equation

From above, the left-hand side of the dynamical equation, representing Newton's second law of motion, is $\rho\,\mathrm{D}u/\mathrm{D}t$. The right-hand side is the sum of the forces (per unit volume) acting on the fluid particle. We now consider the nature of these forces in order to complete the equation.

Some forces are imposed on the fluid externally, and are part of the specification of the particular problem. One may need, for example, to specify the gravity field in which the flow is occurring. On the other hand, the forces due to the pressure and to viscous action – of which simple examples have been given in Section 2.2 – are related to the velocity field. They are thus intrinsic parts of the equations of motion and have to be considered here. Both the pressure and viscous action generate stresses acting across any arbitrary surface within the fluid; the force on a fluid particle is the net effect of the stresses over its surface.

The generalization of the pressure force from the simple case considered in Section 2.2 is straightforward. We saw there that the net force per unit volume in the x-direction as a result of a pressure change in that direction is $-\partial p/\partial x$. For a general pressure field, similar effects act in all directions and the total force per unit volume is $-\mathrm{grad}\,p$. This term always appears in the dynamical equation; when a fluid is brought into motion, the pressure field is changed from that existing when it is at rest (the hydrostatic pressure). We can regard this for the moment as an experimental result. We shall be seeing that it is necessary to have the pressure as a variable in order that the number of variables matches the number of equations.

The general form of the viscous force is not so readily inferred from any simple example. The mathematical formulation is outlined as an appendix to this chapter. Here we shall look at some of the physical concepts underlying viscous action, and then quote the expression for the viscous term in the dynamical equation that is given by rigorous formulation of these concepts. (Some further discussion of the physical action of viscosity will be given in the context of the particular example of jet flow in Section 11.9.)

Viscous stresses oppose relative movements between neighbouring fluid particles. Equivalently, they oppose the deformation of fluid particles. The difference between these statements lies only in the way of verbalizing the rigorous mathematical concepts, as is illustrated by Fig. 5.3. The change in shape of the initially rectangular region is produced by the ends of one diagonal moving apart and the ends of the other moving together. As the whole configuration is shrunk to an infinitesimal one, it may be said either that the particle shown is deforming or that particles on either side of AB are in relative motion. The rate of deformation depends on the velocity gradients in the fluid. The consequence of this behaviour

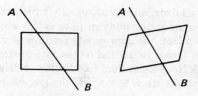

Figure 5.3 Deformation of rectangular element and relative motion of fluid on either side of arbitrary line through the element.

is the generation of a stress (equal and opposite forces on the two sides) across a surface such as *AB*; this stress depends on the properties of the fluid as well as on the rate of deformation.

The stress can have any orientation relative to the surface across which it acts. The special case, considered in Sections 1.2(iv) and 2.2, in which the stress is in the plane of the surface is often thought of as the 'standard' case. We therefore look for a moment at a simple situation in which viscous stresses normal to the surface govern the behaviour. This is the falling column produced for example when a viscous liquid is poured from a container (Fig. 5.4). In the absence of side-walls transverse viscous stresses cannot be generated as they are in channel flow. The reason the fluid at, say, *P* does not fall with an acceleration of *g* is the viscous interaction with the more slowly falling fluid at *Q*.

In the general case, the stress is a quantity with a magnitude and two directions – the direction in which it acts and the normal to the surface – associated with it. It is thus a second-order tensor. (The stresses acting across surfaces of different orientations through the same point are not, of course, independent of one another.) The rate of deformation is also expressed by a second-order tensor – the rate-of-strain tensor. From the considerations above we expect this to involve the velocity

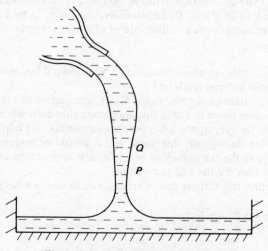

Figure 5.4 Pouring of viscous liquid.

gradients. However, not all distributions of velocity variation lead to deformation; a counter-example is the rotation of a body of fluid as if it were rigid (see Section 6.4). The rate-of-strain tensor selects the appropriate features of the velocity field.

One expects the stress tensor to depend on the rate-of-strain tensor and on the properties of the fluid. A Newtonian fluid (see Section 1.2(iv)) can now be defined rigorously as one in which the stress tensor and the rate-of-strain tensor are linearly related.

The remaining ideas contained in the derivation of the viscous term of the dynamical equation are simply symmetry considerations. For example, a mirror-image flow pattern must generate a mirror-image stress distribution. And the analysis of a flow configuration using different co-ordinates must give the same result.

In Cartesian co-ordinates, the x-component of the viscous force per unit volume (see appendix to this chapter) is

$$\frac{\partial}{\partial x}\left[2\mu\frac{\partial u}{\partial x} + \lambda\,\nabla\cdot\mathbf{u}\right] + \frac{\partial}{\partial y}\left[\mu\left(\frac{\partial u}{\partial y} + \frac{\partial v}{\partial x}\right)\right] + \frac{\partial}{\partial z}\left[\mu\left(\frac{\partial w}{\partial x} + \frac{\partial u}{\partial z}\right)\right] \quad (5.19)$$

Similar expressions for the y- and z-components are given by appropriate permutations.

μ is the coefficient of viscosity, defined through the special case considered in Section 1.2(iv). λ is a second viscosity coefficient. One would expect there to be a second such coefficient, independent of the first, by analogy with the fact that there are two independent elastic moduli. This is a valid analogy. However, it has often been the practice to introduce a relationship between μ and λ ($\lambda = -2\mu/3$). This is done at the cost of redefining the pressure so that it is not the thermodynamic pressure, and the second independent parameter then appears in the relationship between the two pressures [23, 208]. λ is difficult to measure experimentally and is not known for the variety of fluids for which there are values of μ. Hence, the statement that a fluid is Newtonian usually means that μ is observed to be independent of the rate of strain and that λ is assumed to be so too.

However, for a fluid of constant density, the continuity equation (5.10) causes the term involving λ to drop out. If, additionally, μ is taken to be a constant, expression (5.19) reduces (with a further use of (5.10)) to simply

$$\mu\nabla^2 u \quad (5.20)$$

The y- and z-components are correspondingly $\mu\nabla^2 v$ and $\mu\nabla^2 w$, and the vectorial viscous force per unit volume is $\mu\nabla^2\mathbf{u}$.†

Because (5.20) is so much simpler than (5.19), one prefers to use the former whenever possible; one tends to make this approximation even when the density and/or the viscosity do vary appreciably (see also appendix to Chapter 14). That will be the procedure throughout this book. But it should be remembered that situations may arise in the laboratory or in a practical application which are properly described only by the full expression.

Collecting together the various contributions mentioned, we have

$$\rho\frac{D\mathbf{u}}{Dt} = -\nabla p + \mu\nabla^2\mathbf{u} + \mathbf{F} \quad (5.21)$$

† The meaning of ∇^2 operating on a vector is defined through its Cartesian expansion.

This is known as the Navier–Stokes equation. It is the basic dynamical equation expressing Newton's second law of motion for a fluid of constant density.

The term **F** represents the contribution of those forces (such as gravity) mentioned at the beginning of this section that have to be included in the specification of the problem. This is often known as the body force term, because such forces act on the volume of a fluid particle, not over its surface in the way the stresses between fluid particles act. The reaction to a body force is remote from the fluid particle concerned — usually outside the fluid region, although occasionally on distant fluid particles.

We shall often be considering problems in which **F** = 0, the cause of motion being either imposed pressure differences or relative movement of boundaries. No body forces are applied. It might be objected that, although one can well imagine all other sources of body force being eliminated, almost every flow will take place in a gravity field. It can be shown that gravitational body forces act significantly only on density differences. If the density is uniform, the gravitational force is balanced by a vertical pressure gradient which is present whether or not the fluid is moving and which does not interact with any flow. This hydrostatic balance can be subtracted out of the dynamical equation and the problem reduced to one without body forces. This assumes, of course, that the fluid region is supported at the bottom; flow under gravity down a vertical pipe provides an obvious example where this is not so and where the above remarks do not apply. We will consider the justification for subtracting out the hydrostatic balance more mathematically in Section 13.2.

The Navier–Stokes equation may be re-written

$$\frac{\partial \mathbf{u}}{\partial t} + \mathbf{u} \cdot \nabla \mathbf{u} = -\frac{1}{\rho} \nabla p + \nu \nabla^2 \mathbf{u} + \frac{1}{\rho} \mathbf{F} \qquad (5.22)$$

$\nu = \mu/\rho$ and is a property of the fluid called the kinematic viscosity.

We notice that the equation is a non-linear partial differential equation in **u**. The non-linearity arises from the dual role of the velocity in determining the acceleration of a fluid particle, as mentioned in Section 5.5. This non-linearity is responsible for much of the mathematical difficulty of fluid dynamics, and is the principal reason why our knowledge of the behaviour of fluids in motion is obtained in many cases from observation (both of laboratory experiments and of natural phenomena) rather than from theoretical prediction. The physical counterpart of the mathematical difficulty is the variety and complexity of fluid dynamical phenomena; without the non-linearity the range of these would be much more limited.

The continuity equation (5.10) and the Navier–Stokes equation (5.21) constitute a pair of simultaneous partial differential equations. Both represent physical laws which will always apply to every fluid particle. Together they provide one scalar equation and one vector equation — effectively four simultaneous equations — for one scalar variable (the pressure) and one vector variable (the velocity) — effectively four unknown quantities. The number of unknowns is thus correctly matched to the number of equations. We see that the pressure must necessarily be an intrinsic variable in fluid dynamical problems for there to be enough variables to satisfy the basic laws of mechanics.

For many particular problems it is convenient to use the equations referred to a co-ordinate system rather than the vectorial forms. Most often one uses Cartesian co-ordinates, but sometimes a curvilinear system is suggested by the geometry.

Listed below are the forms taken by the continuity equation (5.10) and the three components of the Navier–Stokes equation (5.21) in Cartesian, cylindrical polar, and spherical polar co-ordinates:

(i) Cartesian co-ordinates:

$$\frac{\partial u}{\partial x} + \frac{\partial v}{\partial y} + \frac{\partial w}{\partial z} = 0 \tag{5.23}$$

$$\rho \left[\frac{\partial u}{\partial t} + u \frac{\partial u}{\partial x} + v \frac{\partial u}{\partial y} + w \frac{\partial u}{\partial z} \right] = -\frac{\partial p}{\partial x} + \mu \left[\frac{\partial^2 u}{\partial x^2} + \frac{\partial^2 u}{\partial y^2} + \frac{\partial^2 u}{\partial z^2} \right] + F_x \tag{5.24}$$

together with similar equations for v and w.

(ii) Cylindrical polar co-ordinates (r = distance from axis, ϕ = azimuthal angle about axis, z = distance along axis):

$$\frac{\partial u_r}{\partial r} + \frac{u_r}{r} + \frac{1}{r} \frac{\partial u_\phi}{\partial \phi} + \frac{\partial u_z}{\partial z} = 0 \tag{5.25}$$

$$\rho \left[\frac{\partial u_r}{\partial t} + u_r \frac{\partial u_r}{\partial r} + \frac{u_\phi}{r} \frac{\partial u_r}{\partial \phi} + u_z \frac{\partial u_r}{\partial z} - \frac{u_\phi^2}{r} \right] = -\frac{\partial p}{\partial r}$$

$$+ \mu \left[\frac{\partial^2 u_r}{\partial r^2} + \frac{1}{r} \frac{\partial u_r}{\partial r} - \frac{u_r}{r^2} + \frac{1}{r^2} \frac{\partial^2 u_r}{\partial \phi^2} + \frac{\partial^2 u_r}{\partial z^2} - \frac{2}{r^2} \frac{\partial u_\phi}{\partial \phi} \right] + F_r \tag{5.26}$$

$$\rho \left[\frac{\partial u_\phi}{\partial t} + u_r \frac{\partial u_\phi}{\partial r} + \frac{u_r u_\phi}{r} + \frac{u_\phi}{r} \frac{\partial u_\phi}{\partial \phi} + u_z \frac{\partial u_\phi}{\partial z} \right] = -\frac{1}{r} \frac{\partial p}{\partial \phi}$$

$$+ \mu \left[\frac{\partial^2 u_\phi}{\partial r^2} + \frac{1}{r} \frac{\partial u_\phi}{\partial r} - \frac{u_\phi}{r^2} + \frac{1}{r^2} \frac{\partial^2 u_\phi}{\partial \phi^2} + \frac{\partial^2 u_\phi}{\partial z^2} + \frac{2}{r^2} \frac{\partial u_r}{\partial \phi} \right] + F_\phi \tag{5.27}$$

$$\rho \left[\frac{\partial u_z}{\partial t} + u_r \frac{\partial u_z}{\partial r} + \frac{u_\phi}{r} \frac{\partial u_z}{\partial \phi} + u_z \frac{\partial u_z}{\partial z} \right] = -\frac{\partial p}{\partial z}$$

$$+ \mu \left[\frac{\partial^2 u_z}{\partial r^2} + \frac{1}{r} \frac{\partial u_z}{\partial r} + \frac{1}{r^2} \frac{\partial^2 u_z}{\partial \phi^2} + \frac{\partial^2 u_z}{\partial z^2} \right] + F_z \tag{5.28}$$

(iii) Spherical polar co-ordinates (r = distance from origin, θ = angular displacement from reference direction, ϕ = azimuthal angle about line $\theta = 0$):

$$\frac{\partial u_r}{\partial r} + \frac{2u_r}{r} + \frac{1}{r} \frac{\partial u_\theta}{\partial \theta} + \frac{u_\theta \cot \theta}{r} + \frac{1}{r \sin \theta} \frac{\partial u_\phi}{\partial \phi} = 0 \tag{5.29}$$

$$\rho \left[\frac{\partial u_r}{\partial t} + u_r \frac{\partial u_r}{\partial r} + \frac{u_\theta}{r} \frac{\partial u_r}{\partial \theta} + \frac{u_\phi}{r \sin \theta} \frac{\partial u_r}{\partial \phi} - \frac{u_\theta^2}{r} - \frac{u_\phi^2}{r} \right]$$

$$= -\frac{\partial p}{\partial r} + \mu \left[\frac{\partial^2 u_r}{\partial r^2} + \frac{2}{r} \frac{\partial u_r}{\partial r} - \frac{2u_r}{r^2} + \frac{1}{r^2} \frac{\partial^2 u_r}{\partial \theta^2} + \frac{\cot \theta}{r^2} \frac{\partial u_r}{\partial \theta} \right.$$

$$\left. + \frac{1}{r^2 \sin^2 \theta} \frac{\partial^2 u_r}{\partial \phi^2} - \frac{2}{r^2} \frac{\partial u_\theta}{\partial \theta} - \frac{2u_\theta \cot \theta}{r^2} - \frac{2}{r^2 \sin \theta} \frac{\partial u_\phi}{\partial \phi} \right] + F_r \tag{5.30}$$

$$\rho \left[\frac{\partial u_\theta}{\partial t} + u_r \frac{\partial u_\theta}{\partial r} + \frac{u_r u_\theta}{r} + \frac{u_\theta}{r} \frac{\partial u_\theta}{\partial \theta} + \frac{u_\phi}{r \sin \theta} \frac{\partial u_\theta}{\partial \phi} - \frac{u_\phi^2 \cot \theta}{r} \right]$$

$$= -\frac{1}{r} \frac{\partial p}{\partial \theta} + \mu \left[\frac{\partial^2 u_\theta}{\partial r^2} + \frac{2}{r} \frac{\partial u_\theta}{\partial r} - \frac{u_\theta}{r^2 \sin^2 \theta} + \frac{1}{r^2} \frac{\partial^2 u_\theta}{\partial \theta^2} \right.$$

$$\left. + \frac{\cot \theta}{r^2} \frac{\partial u_\theta}{\partial \theta} + \frac{1}{r^2 \sin^2 \theta} \frac{\partial^2 u_\theta}{\partial \phi^2} + \frac{2}{r^2} \frac{\partial u_r}{\partial \theta} - \frac{2 \cot \theta}{r^2 \sin \theta} \frac{\partial u_\phi}{\partial \phi} \right] + F_\theta \qquad (5.31)$$

$$\rho \left[\frac{\partial u_\phi}{\partial t} + u_r \frac{\partial u_\phi}{\partial r} + \frac{u_r u_\phi}{r} + \frac{u_\theta}{r} \frac{\partial u_\phi}{\partial \theta} + \frac{u_\theta u_\phi \cot \theta}{r} + \frac{u_\phi}{r \sin \theta} \frac{\partial u_\phi}{\partial \phi} \right]$$

$$= -\frac{1}{r \sin \theta} \frac{\partial p}{\partial \phi} + \mu \left[\frac{\partial^2 u_\phi}{\partial r^2} + \frac{2}{r} \frac{\partial u_\phi}{\partial r} - \frac{u_\phi}{r^2 \sin^2 \theta} + \frac{1}{r^2} \frac{\partial^2 u_\phi}{\partial \theta^2} + \frac{\cot \theta}{r^2} \frac{\partial u_\phi}{\partial \theta} \right.$$

$$\left. + \frac{1}{r^2 \sin^2 \theta} \frac{\partial^2 u_\phi}{\partial \phi^2} + \frac{2}{r^2 \sin \theta} \frac{\partial u_r}{\partial \phi} + \frac{2 \cot \theta}{r^2 \sin \theta} \frac{\partial u_\theta}{\partial \phi} \right] + F_\phi \qquad (5.32)$$

(One sometimes requires also the individual stress components in polar co-ordinates. These will be introduced as required. For a more systematic treatment the reader is referred to Refs. [12 and 21].)

5.7 Boundary conditions

Since the governing equations of fluid motion are differential equations, the specification of any problem must include the boundary conditions. We would expect this on physical grounds; the motion throughout a fluid region is evidently influenced by the presence and motion of walls or other boundaries. We examine now the form taken by the conditions on the velocity field applying at boundaries.

There are obviously various types of boundary, giving rise to different possible conditions. However, the only case that we need consider in any detail for the purposes of this book is the most common type of boundary to a fluid region — the rigid impermeable wall.

One condition applying at such a wall is obviously provided by the requirement that no fluid should pass through the wall. If the wall is moving with velocity $\mathbf{U}$ and the velocity of a fluid particle right next to the wall is $\mathbf{u}$, then this means that the normal components of these two velocities must be the same;

$$\mathbf{u} \cdot \hat{\mathbf{n}} = \mathbf{U} \cdot \hat{\mathbf{n}} \qquad (5.33)$$

where $\hat{\mathbf{n}}$ is the unit normal to the surface (Fig. 5.5). One often chooses a frame of reference in which the boundaries are at rest, giving $\mathbf{U} = 0$; this boundary condition then becomes

$$\mathbf{u} \cdot \hat{\mathbf{n}} = 0 \qquad (5.34)$$

or in Cartesian co-ordinates with x and z in the local tangential plane to the wall and y normal to it

$$v = 0 \qquad (5.35)$$

Another condition is provided by the no-slip condition, already mentioned in Section 2.2, that there should be no relative tangential velocity between a rigid wall

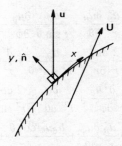

Figure 5.5   Velocity vectors of solid and of fluid particle immediately next to its surface. (Note: **U** and **u** are shown different for definition purposes, although the text subsequently shows them to be the same.)

and the fluid immediately next to it. Formally,

$$\mathbf{u} \times \hat{\mathbf{n}} = \mathbf{U} \times \hat{\mathbf{n}} \tag{5.36}$$

and, when $\mathbf{U} = 0$,

$$\mathbf{u} \times \hat{\mathbf{n}} = 0 \tag{5.37}$$

or

$$u = w = 0 \tag{5.38}$$

It is apparent that some such condition must pertain. For example, without it, there would be no boundary condition on u (equations (2.7) and (2.16)) for pipe or channel flow and the solutions (equations (2.8) and (2.17)) could not be obtained; viscous action would place no limit on the amount of fluid per unit time that could pass through a pipe under a given pressure gradient. However, it is not so apparent that the condition should take this exact form. The notion underlying the no-slip condition is that the interaction between a fluid particle and a wall is similar to that between neighbouring fluid particles. Within a fluid there cannot be any finite discontinuity of velocity. This would involve an infinite velocity gradient and so produce an infinite viscous stress that would destroy the discontinuity in an infinitesimal time. If, therefore, the wall acts like further fluid, the action of viscosity prevents a discontinuity in velocity between the wall and fluid; the no-slip condition must apply. However, this concept that the wall acts like further fluid is itself an assumption and the justification for the no-slip condition lies ultimately in experimental observation. This experimental justification takes two forms. The first is direct observation; dye or smoke introduced very close to a wall does stay at rest relative to the wall. The second is an *a posteriori* justification; the no-slip condition is assumed and the solutions of the equations found in simple cases; agreement between theory and experiment then justifies the original assumption. The no-slip condition is found to be violated only when the molecular mean-free path becomes comparable with the distances involved; then the continuum equations are ceasing to be applicable anyway.

Conditions (5.33) and (5.36) in combination do, of course, give

$$\mathbf{u} = \mathbf{U} \tag{5.39}$$

or, in Cartesian co-ordinates on a wall at rest,

$$u = v = w = 0. \tag{5.40}$$

The total boundary condition is simply that there is no relative motion between a wall and the fluid next to it. It is, however, important to note (and it will be of significance subsequently — Section 8.3) that the physical origins of the two parts of the condition are quite different. The no-slip condition depends essentially on the action of viscosity, whilst the impermeability condition does not.

This is a convenient point to mention the forces exerted by a moving fluid on a rigid boundary, a matter of obvious practical importance. This again uses the notion that the fluid acts on a wall in the same way as it acts on further fluid. However, no assumption is involved here; the stresses must be continuous or a fluid particle at a wall would experience infinite acceleration. Thus we may use the expressions in Section 5.6 for stresses in the interior of the fluid. We use Cartesian co-ordinates as above with the wall at $y = 0$. Then the viscous stresses in the x-, y- and z- directions can be extracted from expression (5.19) and are given in the first place as

$$\mu\left(\frac{\partial u}{\partial y} + \frac{\partial v}{\partial x}\right)_{y=0}; \quad 2\mu\left(\frac{\partial v}{\partial y}\right)_{y=0}; \quad \mu\left(\frac{\partial w}{\partial y} + \frac{\partial v}{\partial z}\right)_{y=0} \tag{5.41}$$

Since, from the continuity equation,

$$\frac{\partial v}{\partial y} = -\frac{\partial u}{\partial x} - \frac{\partial w}{\partial z} \tag{5.42}$$

and since, also,

$$u = v = w = 0 \quad \text{at} \quad y = 0 \quad \text{for all } x \text{ and } z \tag{5.43}$$

these reduce to

$$\mu\left(\frac{\partial u}{\partial y}\right)_{y=0}; \quad 0; \quad \mu\left(\frac{\partial w}{\partial y}\right)_{y=0} \tag{5.44}$$

The first and third quantities are the tangential forces per unit area on the wall. There is no normal viscous force, but there is a pressure force of p per unit area in the $-y$-direction.

There are other important types of boundary besides the rigid impermeable wall. The free surface of a liquid is an obvious example. And a rigid wall with suction or injection of fluid through it has important practical applications, such as some aircraft wings where the flow is controlled by suction of the air. However, we do not need to formulate the corresponding boundary conditions for the purposes of this book.

One other case does need mention — when the boundary condition is applied at infinity. Often any boundaries are far from the region of interest, as in the examples of an aeroplane well above the ground or a small model placed in a wind-tunnel. The motion far from such an obstacle is the same as in the absence of the obstacle, and one has a boundary condition of the form

$$\mathbf{u} \rightarrow \mathbf{u_0} \quad \text{as} \quad \mathbf{r} \rightarrow \infty \tag{5.45}$$

5.8 Condition for incompressibility

We have seen that both the continuity equation and the dynamical equation simplify greatly if one can treat the density, ρ, as a constant. Fortunately, there are many situations in which it is a good approximation to do so. Brief consideration has been given to this matter in Section 1.2(iii) and we now examine more fully the conditions in which one may make this approximation.

The status of the equation

$$\rho = \text{const.} \tag{5.46}$$

is that of an equation of state. That is to say, in circumstances where it is not a good approximation, one needs instead an equation of state giving the density as a function of pressure and temperature.

Correspondingly, when one does take the density as being constant, one is saying that the density variations produced by the pressure and temperature variations are sufficiently small to be unimportant. In this section we shall be principally concerned with the effect of pressure variations, as we have already seen that such variations are intrinsic to any flow. We shall derive a criterion for these to have a negligible effect. Non-fulfilment of this criterion is the most familiar reason for departures from equation (5.46); consequently this equation is called the incompressibility condition, although the name is not a complete summary of the requirements for it to be applicable.

Temperature variations are also in principle intrinsic to any flow. (They may also be introduced specifically — see Chapters 13 and 14 — but we leave to Section 13.2 and the appendix to Chapter 14 the corresponding considerations for that case.) Firstly, the expansions and contractions as the fluid moves through the pressure field involve temperature changes. The effect of these will, however, be covered by the following discussion of the pressure effect; nowhere will it be assumed that the changes are isothermal. Secondly, viscous action involves the dissipation of mechanical energy (see Section 11.9), which reappears as heat; we will consider this briefly at the end of this section.

Liquids are known to change their density very little even for large pressure changes. One would expect to be able to treat these as incompressible. It is less apparent that there are important circumstances in which gases can be so treated — although the result is perhaps not wholly unexpected if one recalls that the fractional change in the atmospheric pressure (and so the fractional change in the air density) is small even when strong winds are blowing. The following derivation of the criterion is thus of importance primarily for gases, although it is in fact quite general.

We can write the density

$$\rho = \rho_0 + \Delta\rho \tag{5.47}$$

where ρ_0 is a reference density — for example, the density at some arbitrarily chosen point — and $\Delta\rho$ is the local departure from this. If

$$\Delta\rho/\rho_0 \ll 1 \tag{5.48}$$

then, for example, the term $\rho\,Du/Dt$ in the dynamical equation can be approximated by $\rho_0\,Du/Dt$. A similar comment applies to the other places where ρ appears in the continuity and dynamical equations. Thus the equations with ρ const. may be used when relationship (5.48) is satisfied.

Since the density changes under consideration result from pressure variations, in order to estimate the typical size of $\Delta\rho$ we need to know the typical size ΔP of these pressure variations. We get this information from the requirement that the pressure force must be balanced by other terms in the Navier–Stokes equation and thus will be of the same order of magnitude as at least one other term. (If the flow is produced by imposed pressure differences, then at the start of the motion the fluid will accelerate until terms involving the velocity become comparable with the pressure force. If the flow is produced by imposed velocity differences, then the flow will generate pressure differences of an appropriate size.) We confine attention to steady flow without body forces, and so, either

$$\nabla p \sim \rho \mathbf{u} \cdot \nabla \mathbf{u} \tag{5.49}$$

or

$$\nabla p \sim \mu \nabla^2 \mathbf{u} \tag{5.50}$$

or both (with the symbol $\sim$ meaning 'is of the same order of magnitude as'). We shall pursue the consequences of (5.49). We shall see in Chapter 8 that the only circumstances when (5.50) applies whilst (5.49) does not are when the Reynolds number is low, and the following analysis does not then apply.

Provided that the x-axis is chosen in a direction in which significant variations occur, (5.49) can be written

$$\frac{\partial p}{\partial x} \sim \rho u \frac{\partial u}{\partial x} = \frac{1}{2} \rho \frac{\partial u^2}{\partial x} \tag{5.51}$$

This indicates that

$$\Delta P/L \sim \rho \Delta(U^2)/L \tag{5.52}$$

where ΔP and $\Delta(U^2)$ are typical differences in p and u^2 between points a distance L apart. This means that, if one arbitrarily chose many such pairs of points, the average difference in p would be of the general size ΔP. Since ΔP and $\Delta(U^2)$ are defined only as order of magnitude quantities they do not require more precise definition than that.

If L is the general length scale of the flow, ΔP and $\Delta(U^2)$ are the orders of magnitude of the variations of p and u^2 within the fluid; and are related by

$$\Delta P \sim \rho \Delta(U^2) \tag{5.53}$$

We do not need to maintain the distinction between a typical difference in the (square of the) velocity and a typical value of the (square of the) velocity itself; i.e. we can write

$$\Delta U \sim U; \quad \Delta(U^2) \sim U^2 \tag{5.54}$$

where U is a velocity-scale. The reason for this is that one always can (and normally will) choose a frame of reference in which some points of the flow — for example those at a boundary — are at rest. (It would be perverse to analyse the dynamics of a low-speed aeroplane from the frame of reference of a high-speed aeroplane.) On the other hand, it is necessary to maintain the distinction between the pressure difference scale and the pressure itself. Since the pressure appears only in the form ∇p in the governing equations, the absolute pressure can be increased indefinitely without directly† altering the dynamics; only pressure differences are relevant

Thus we have

$$\Delta P \sim \rho U^2 \tag{5.55}$$

which indicates the typical pressure variation in a flow of typical speed U. We now use this to determine the typical density variation. This depends on the fluid and in particular on its compressibility, β;

$$\Delta \rho / \rho \sim \beta \Delta P \tag{5.56}$$

(For order of magnitude considerations it does not matter whether β is the isothermal compressibility, the adiabatic compressibility or what.) The final result is given in a convenient form if we now introduce the speed of sound, a, in the fluid;

$$a^2 = \left(\frac{\partial p}{\partial \rho}\right)_S \sim \frac{1}{\rho \beta} \tag{5.57}$$

(S = entropy). a is introduced here simply as a property of the fluid under consideration, a measure of its compressibility.

Combining the various relationships, we have

$$\frac{\Delta \rho}{\rho} \sim \frac{\Delta P}{\rho a^2} \sim \frac{U^2}{a^2} \tag{5.58}$$

Thus criterion (5.48) is fulfilled if

$$(\text{Ma})^2 = U^2 / a^2 \ll 1 \tag{5.59}$$

Flows at speeds low compared with the speed of sound in the fluid thus behave as if the fluid were incompressible.

The ratio U/a is known as the Mach number of the flow, and incompressible flows thus occur at low Mach number. The fact that $(\text{Ma})^2$ is involved in relationship (5.59) means that Ma does not have to be very small; when Ma is less than about 0.2, density variations are only a few per cent, bringing the accuracy of the incompressibility assumption to within the sort of accuracy attainable in many fluid dynamical investigations.

Many important gas flows do occur at low Mach number. For example, the speed of sound in air under atmospheric conditions is around 300 m s^{-1}. Evidently, one will often be concerned with speeds low compared with this.

The fact that liquids are much less compressible than gases is contained in this analysis by the fact they have much higher sound speeds, thus giving lower Mach numbers at the same U.

One general comment about the nature of the above argument may be made. The way in which ρ enters the governing equations is important in deciding that relationship (5.48) is a justification for treating ρ as a constant. Pressure provides an immediate counter-example in the present context. The fractional pressure change

†It can do so indirectly by changing fluid properties.

may also be small; in fact, for a gas,

$$\Delta P/p \sim \Delta \rho/\rho \tag{5.60}$$

This does not mean that the pressure can be treated as a constant. As we have already noted, the pressure appears only in ∇p and the absolute pressure can be altered at will without changing the equations; comparison with it is thus irrelevant.

It was remarked that the above analysis does not apply at low Reynolds number. Then one has to use (5.50) instead of (5.49). The corresponding analysis then gives the criterion for incompressibility as

$$(\text{Ma})^2 \ll \text{Re} \tag{5.61}$$

where Re is the Reynolds number – a somewhat academic result, rarely relevant to real situations. (But see Section 24.4.)

A similar treatment of viscous dissipation shows that it also frequently has negligible effect. (It is, for example, not noticeably warmer swimming at the bottom of a waterfall than at the top.) The details will not be given here; the corresponding matter in the topic of free convection is discussed in the appendix to Chapter 14. As in that case, the criterion for the resulting density changes to be negligible can be expressed in a form not involving the viscosity coefficient and related to the criterion for incompressibility. This effect can be ignored wherever (5.59) is fulfilled. Hence, this provides an adequate criterion for the use of the incompressible flow equations.

Appendix: Derivation of viscous term of dynamical equation

This appendix presents the main points of the mathematical formulation of the ideas described physically in Section 5.6. For a more complete treatment, see, for example Refs. [12 and 23]. We first examine the form of the rate-of-strain tensor and then determine the consequences of a linear relationship between this and the stress tensor.

Consider two material points separated by a distance δl, having components δx_i.

$$(\delta l)^2 = \delta x_i \delta x_i \tag{5.62}$$

with the summation convention for repeated suffixes applying.

$$\frac{D(\delta l)^2}{Dt} = 2\delta x_i \frac{D(\delta x_i)}{Dt} = 2\delta x_i \delta u_i$$

$$= 2\delta x_i \delta x_j \frac{\partial u_i}{\partial x_j} = \delta x_i \delta x_j \left(\frac{\partial u_i}{\partial x_j} + \frac{\partial u_j}{\partial x_i} \right) \tag{5.63}$$

It is thus the symmetrical combinations of the velocity gradients that give rise to distortions opposed by viscous action. (A motion in which

$$\frac{\partial u_i}{\partial x_j} = -\frac{\partial u_j}{\partial x_i} \tag{5.64}$$

for all i and j does not involve any relative movement between two neighbouring points for any δx_i.) Moreover, these symmetrical combinations represent fractional rates of change of the separation for various orientations; for example if

$\delta x_2 = \delta x_3 = 0$,

$$\frac{1}{\delta l} \frac{D(\delta l)}{Dt} = \frac{\partial u_1}{\partial x_1} \tag{5.65}$$

They are thus rates of strain of the fluid. The rate-of-strain tensor e_{ij} is formulated as the symmetrical part of the velocity gradient tensor,

$$\zeta_{ij} = \frac{\partial u_i}{\partial x_j} \qquad e_{ij} = \frac{1}{2}(\zeta_{ij} + \zeta_{ji}) \tag{5.66}$$

[Parenthetically, the antisymmetric part

$$\eta_{ij} = \frac{1}{2}(\zeta_{ij} - \zeta_{ji}) \tag{5.67}$$

corresponds to the vorticity — see Section 6.4;

$$\eta_{ij} = -\frac{1}{2}\epsilon_{ijk}\omega_k] \tag{5.68}$$

The viscous stress tensor is given by defining τ_{ij} as the force per unit area acting in the i-direction across a surface normal to the j-direction. For a Newtonian fluid this is linearly related to e_{ij}:

$$\tau_{ij} = \Lambda_{ijkl}e_{kl} \tag{5.69}$$

The physical processes must be independent of the orientation and handedness of the axes. Λ_{ijkl} must thus be an isotropic tensor and the most general form it can take is [133]

$$\Lambda_{ijkl} = \lambda\delta_{ij}\delta_{kl} + \xi\delta_{ik}\delta_{jl} + \chi\delta_{il}\delta_{jk} \tag{5.70}$$

This gives

$$\tau_{ij} = \lambda\delta_{ij}e_{kk} + (\xi + \chi)e_{ij} \tag{5.71}$$

(since $e_{ij} = e_{ji}$). There are thus two arbitrary constants involved; these are physical properties of the particular fluid. From the particular case $e_{12} = \frac{1}{2}\partial u/\partial y$ and all other e_{ij} equal to zero, we can identify that

$$\xi + \chi = 2\mu \tag{5.72}$$

where μ is the coefficient of viscosity introduced in Section 1.2. Also,

$$e_{kk} = \frac{\partial u_k}{\partial x_k} = \text{div } \mathbf{u} \tag{5.73}$$

and so

$$\tau_{ij} = \mu\left(\frac{\partial u_i}{\partial x_j} + \frac{\partial u_j}{\partial x_i}\right) + \lambda\delta_{ij} \text{ div } \mathbf{u} \tag{5.74}$$

The net viscous force on a fluid particle is given as before (Section 2.2) by the differences in the stresses acting across opposite faces. The force per unit volume is thus $\partial\tau_{ij}/\partial x_j$. Writing this in expanded form gives expression (5.19).

6
Further Basic Ideas

6.1 Streamlines, streamtubes, particle paths and streaklines

A streamline is defined as a continuous line within the fluid of which the tangent at any point is in the direction of the velocity at that point. Its relationship to the velocity field is thus analogous to the relationship of a line of force to an electric field. Patterns of streamlines are useful (particularly in two-dimensional flow) in providing a pictorial representation of a flow.

The streamlines for a known velocity field (u, v, w) are given as solutions of the pair of differential equations

$$\frac{dx}{u} = \frac{dy}{v} = \frac{dz}{w} \tag{6.1}$$

Two streamlines cannot intersect except at a position of zero velocity; otherwise one would have the meaningless situation of a velocity with two directions.

A streamtube is a tubular region within the fluid bounded by streamlines. Because streamlines cannot intersect, the same streamlines pass through a streamtube at all stations along its length.

Consider two stations along a streamtube of cross-sectional areas S_1 and S_2 as in Fig. 6.1. We suppose that the cross-sections are small enough that there is negligible variation of physical quantities over them and we can say that the densities and speeds at the two stations are ρ_1 and q_1 and ρ_2 and q_2 ($q = |\mathbf{u}|$; we can use the scalar quantity, as the direction is by definition along the streamtube). The rate at which mass is entering the volume between the two stations is $\rho_1 q_1 S_1$; the rate at which it is leaving is $\rho_2 q_2 S_2$. If the flow is either steady or incompressible (or, but not necessarily, both) the mass in this region is not changing, and so

$$\rho_1 q_1 S_1 = \rho_2 q_2 S_2 \tag{6.2}$$

If the flow is incompressible, $\rho_1 = \rho_2$ and

$$q_2/q_1 = S_1/S_2 \tag{6.3}$$

or, for a general station along the steamtube,

$$q \propto 1/S \tag{6.4}$$

The speed is inversely proportional to the cross-sectional area. Hence where the streamlines are close together the speed is high; where they are far apart it is low. Convergence of streamlines indicates acceleration, divergence deceleration. These facts are useful in the interpretation of streamline patterns. It is important to note that we have derived them only for incompressible flow. Result (6.4) is, of course,

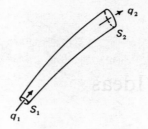

Figure 6.1   Section of a streamtube.

directly related to the continuity equation, div **u** = 0, just as the parallel interpretation that the electric field is large where there is a high density of lines of force applies only when there are no space charges and so div **E** = 0.

One cannot directly observe a streamline by flow visualization. One can synthesize a streamline pattern from pictures, such as Fig. 3.7, showing the change in position of many particles during a short time interval.

In the most common types of flow visualization, dye (or smoke) is introduced at a point. One then sees either a particle path or a streakline: the former if the dye is introduced instantaneously and observed continuously or photographed with a long exposure; the latter if the dye is introduced continuously and observed or photographed instantaneously.

A particle path is effectively defined by its name. It is the trajectory of an individual element of fluid.

A streakline is the locus of all fluid elements that have previously passed through a particular fixed point.

In steady flow, streamlines, particle paths, and streaklines are all identical. A particle is instantaneously moving along a streamline; if that streamline is unchanged at a slightly later time, the particle will continue to move along it, and so it traverses the streamline. Similarly, particles starting from the same point at different times will all follow the same path, and so a streakline will consist of that path.

In unsteady flow, streamlines, particle paths, and streaklines are all different; the remarks in the last paragraph no longer apply. It is then that the interpretation of patterns obtained by flow visualization calls for care; it may not be easy to infer instantaneous flow patterns from the observations.

Thus, in Chapter 3, the steady flow patterns at low Reynolds number are quite fully specified by the illustrations. Although the lines in Figs. 3.2 and 3.3 were there defined as particle paths, we can now say that these figures show streamline patterns. Further, Fig. 3.4, which is in principle a sort of streakline pattern, can be used to illustrate one of these flows. When the flow becomes unsteady, any individual illustration tells a more partial story. For example, the streakline patterns in Fig. 3.5 and the streamline pattern deducible from Fig. 3.7 complement one another.

The relationships between the streamlines, particle paths, and streaklines in an unsteady flow — and the fact that they can look quite different from one another — are best seen through an example. Section 6.2 will consider one case in some detail, and we will take up the introduction of the basic ideas of fluid dynamics again in Section 6.3.

6.2 Computations for flow past a circular cylinder

In this section we look at some computed flow patterns that illustrate the relationship between streamlines, particle paths and streaklines. They concern a flow that is steady in one frame of reference. However, we consider it also in another frame so that the flow is then unsteady. (The computations thus also illustrate the relationship between patterns in different frames, a matter mentioned in Section 3.1.) This is, of course, a rather special type of unsteady flow, but it serves the present purpose well. Illustration of the same ideas for a truly unsteady flow requires cine-film; Ref. [141] provides a very effective example.

Figure 6.2 shows the result of a numerical solution [95] of the Navier–Stokes and continuity equations for flow past a circular cylinder at a Reynolds number of 40. (In this and subsequent figures only half the flow is shown; the pattern is, of course, symmetrical about the centre plane *PQ*.) This type of flow was the topic of Chapter 3, where we saw that 40 is about the highest Reynolds number at which there is no unsteadiness due to wake instability. In Fig. 6.2 the cylinder is at rest and the fluid far from it moves from left to right at speed u_0. The figure shows streamlines, which, since the flow pattern is steady, are also particle paths and streaklines. The closed streamlines in the attached eddies behind the cylinder are thus regions where fluid particles are moving on closed paths; the eddies always consist of the same fluid.

Detailed experimental comparison with this computed pattern is difficult. In practice, a Reynolds number as low as 40 can be achieved only by working with a small length-scale, at which observation of the flow details is not readily achievable. However, the overall features of the flow are in agreement with the observations described in Chapter 3. In addition, agreement between the value of the drag coefficient given by the computations and the observed value suggests that the details are correct.

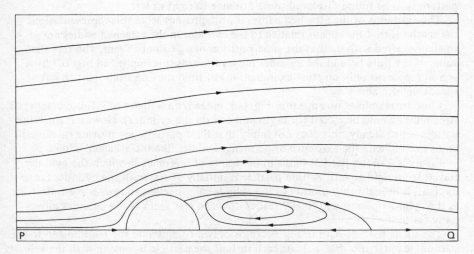

Figure 6.2   Flow past a circular cylinder at Re = 40. Ref. [95].

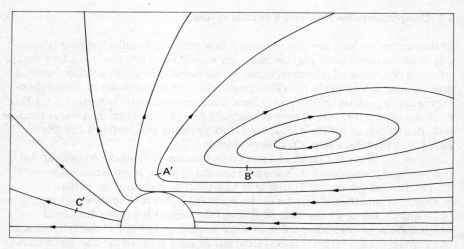

Figure 6.3   Streamlines for cylinder moving through stationary ambient fluid.

Figure 6.3 shows the corresponding streamline pattern in the frame of reference in which the cylinder moves from right to left at speed u_0, the fluid far from it being at rest. It is thus related to Fig. 6.2 by the transformation of Fig. 3.1. The regions where the fluid is now (Fig. 6.3) moving from left to right correspond to regions where it was previously (Fig. 6.2) moving downstream faster than u_0; regions where it is now moving from right to left are those where it was previously moving downstream more slowly than u_0. The motion in the perpendicular direction is the same at corresponding points of the two figures.

The pattern of Fig. 6.3 is an instantaneous one; at any other time the same pattern is to be found displaced some distance to right or left.

The existence of the attached eddies is not apparent from this representation; the reason is that the speeds relative to the cylinder in the attached eddies are so small compared with u_0 that the superposition of u_0 swamps them. The fact that some of the fluid behind the cylinder moves towards it is implied in Fig. 6.3 by a region (apparent only on close examination) of fluid moving from right to left at speeds slightly above u_0.

Closed streamlines do appear in Fig. 6.3; indeed, on a figure of infinite extent, all streamlines would be closed (or begin and end on the cylinder). However, since the pattern is not steady, this does not imply that fluid particles are moving on closed paths nor indicate the existence of permanent eddies like the attached eddies.

Figure 6.4 shows particle paths in the frame of reference in which the cylinder travels from right to left. A fluid particle is initially at rest with the cylinder far to its right, is brought into motion as the cylinder approaches, follows some trajectory as the cylinder passes, and finally settles down to rest again as the cylinder moves away far to the left.

The single particle path in Fig. 6.4(a) is drawn to illustrate the relationship to the streamline pattern of Fig. 6.3. At each instant the particle is moving with the velocity indicated by the appropriate point on the streamline pattern. For example, when the particle has reached point A, the cylinder is directly below it (in the position

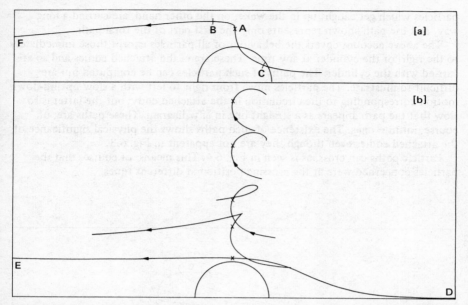

Figure 6.4 Particle paths for cylinder moving through stationary ambient fluid. See text for significance of parts (a) and (b).

shown); the particle is thus at point A' of Fig. 6.3. The particle path at A is seen to be parallel to the streamline through A'. At a later instant, the particle is at point B. This corresponds to point B' of the streamline pattern, because, during the time in which the particle has moved from A to B, the cylinder and the whole streamline pattern have moved to the left a distance of $1.5d$ (d being the cylinder diameter). Similarly, when the cylinder was a distance $1.5d$ to the right of its illustrated position (in Fig. 6.4(a)), the particle was at position C; it was thus at position C' of the streamline pattern, and was moving accordingly.

Figure 6.4(b) shows a number of other particle paths for particles starting at different distances from the plane of symmetry. Different particles, initially the same distance from the plane of symmetry but separated in the direction of the cylinder's motion, follow paths of similar shapes but at different times and in different places. The paths in Fig. 6.4 have been drawn so that the particles concerned are all immediately above the cylinder at the same instant (which we may call $t = 0$); i.e. they are at the positions marked with crosses when the cylinder is in the position shown.

These particle paths are of finite length. However, computation of their complete length would require information extending outside the region for which the flow pattern has been computed. Hence, the paths shown correspond to tu_0/d (i.e. time in units of the time in which the cylinder moves one diameter) extending from -10 to 10. (For the cases where the edge of the diagram is reached first, points D, E, F correspond to values of tu_0/d of respectively $-6.0, 3.7$, and 7.3.) The motion before $tu_0/d = -10$ would be very slow and, for the particle paths near the top of the diagram, the motion after $tu_0/d = 10$ would be similarly very slow. Those particles which get caught up in the wake, on the other hand, are carried a long way, and the path shown represents only the first part of the total path.

The above account covers the behaviour of all particles except those immediately to the right of the cylinder at any time. These are in the attached eddies and so are carried with the cylinder. The paths of such particles can be computed but are difficult to illustrate. The particles move from right to left with a slow up-and-down motion corresponding to the circulation in the attached eddy; but the latter is so slow that the path appears as a straight line in any diagram. These paths are, of course, infinite ones. The existence of such paths shows the physical significance of the attached eddies even though they are not apparent in Fig. 6.3.

Particle paths can cross, as is seen in Fig. 6.4. This means, of course, that the particles concerned were at the crossing position at different times.

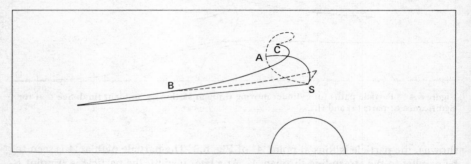

Figure 6.5   Streaklines for cylinder moving through stationary ambient fluid (and related particle paths, shown as broken lines).

Figure 6.5 exhibits two streaklines (the two solid lines). Dye is supposed to have been emitted continuously from a point S at a distance d from the plane of symmetry since $tu_0/d = -10$ ($t = 0$ being the instant at which the cylinder is in the position illustrated with its centre directly below the source). The lines show the computed distributions of that dye at $t = 0$ (curve SA) and at $tu_0/d = 10$ (curve SBC). Each streakline consists of particles that have passed through S at various times – the further along the streakline from S, the earlier the time.

To demonstrate the relationship between streaklines and particle paths, Fig. 6.5 also shows – broken lines – two trajectories of particles originating at the source. Line SAC originates at $tu_0/d = -10$, reaches A at $t = 0$ and C at $tu_0/d = 10$. Line SB originates at $t = 0$ and reaches B at $tu_0/d = 10$. These particle trajectories can be seen to be segments of paths like those in Fig. 6.4.

For reasons indicated above, these results are not of much value for direct comparison with observation. They do demonstrate, however, the complexity of the relationships between the various flow features in unsteady flow. They point out the need for care in interpreting flow visualization experiments and illustrate the type of reasoning that enters such interpretation.

6.3 The stream function

Since, for incompressible flow,

$$\text{div } \mathbf{u} = 0 \tag{6.5}$$

one can put

$$\mathbf{u} = \text{curl } \mathbf{A} \tag{6.6}$$

where $\mathbf{A}$ may be called a vector velocity potential. Since this replaces one vector variable, $\mathbf{u}$, by another vector variable, $\mathbf{A}$, this is not in general very useful. It is useful, however, in a two-dimensional or axisymmetric flow, where only one component of $\mathbf{A}$ is non-zero.

In a two-dimensional flow, for example, equation (6.5) becomes

$$\frac{\partial u}{\partial x} + \frac{\partial v}{\partial y} = 0 \tag{6.7}$$

and this can always be satisfied by introducing ψ such that

$$u = \frac{\partial \psi}{\partial y}, \quad v = -\frac{\partial \psi}{\partial x}. \tag{6.8}$$

ψ is known as the stream function, because it is constant along a streamline — verified as follows:

$$d\psi = \frac{\partial \psi}{\partial x} dx + \frac{\partial \psi}{\partial y} dy = -v dx + u dy \tag{6.9}$$

On a streamline

$$dx/u = dy/v \tag{6.10}$$

and so

$$d\psi = 0 \tag{6.11}$$

6.4 Vorticity

The vorticity, $\boldsymbol{\omega}$, of a fluid motion is defined as

$$\boldsymbol{\omega} = \text{curl } \mathbf{u} \tag{6.12}$$

It is thus a vector quantity defined at every point within the fluid. We shall see in later chapters that some flow configurations are most readily understood through a consideration of the vorticity.

The definition of curl by

$$\hat{n} \cdot \text{curl } \mathbf{u} = \lim_{S \to 0} \frac{1}{S} \oint \mathbf{u} \cdot d\mathbf{l} \tag{6.13}$$

(where $\hat{n}$ is the unit vector normal to the surface S, round the edge of which the line integral is taken) indicates that vorticity corresponds to rotation of the fluid; the line integral is non-zero only if fluid is going round the point under consideration. Flow without vorticity is called irrotational flow.

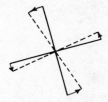

Figure 6.6   Example of change of orientation (with translation subtracted out) in short time interval of two material lines instantaneously at right angles.

The physical meaning of 'rotation' and thus of vorticity when fluid particles can change shape (Section 5.6) requires some consideration. A convenient way of seeing how one may meaningfully talk about the rotation of a fluid particle in the presence of deformation is the following. Consider a flow, such as a two-dimensional flow, in which only the z-component of the vorticity is non-zero

$$\omega_z = \frac{\partial v}{\partial x} - \frac{\partial u}{\partial y} \tag{6.14}$$

and consider two short material lines instantaneously at right angles to one another in a plane perpendicular to z (Fig. 6.6). A short time later these lines of fluid may have changed their orientation as shown. (We ignore the effect of second velocity derivatives in making them curved, as we are concerned with the first order effect at a point.) The rate at which the two lines are turning will not in general be the same, and it would not be sensible to define the rotation rate of a fluid particle in terms of the angular velocity of one such line. However, the average angular velocity of any two such lines at right angles is the same and is equal to $\omega_z/2$. This may be seen from the case in which the lines are parallel to the x- and y-axes; then the angular velocity of the former is $\partial v/\partial x$ and that of the latter is $-\partial u/\partial y$. Since the definition of curl is not related to any particular set of axes, the result is valid for other pairs of perpendicular lines in an xy-plane.

For further discussion of the physical significance of vorticity, it is convenient to refer to three examples:

(i) The first is a fluid rotating as if it were a rigid body with angular velocity $\mathbf{\Omega}$. The velocity field is

$$\mathbf{u} = \mathbf{\Omega} \times \mathbf{r} \tag{6.15}$$

giving

$$\mathbf{\omega} = 2\mathbf{\Omega} \tag{6.16}$$

The vorticity is the same at every point and equal to twice the angular velocity. For comparison with the next example we write this also in cylindrical polar coordinates:

$$u_\phi = \Omega r, \qquad u_r = u_z = 0 \tag{6.17}$$

$$\omega_z = 2\Omega, \qquad \omega_r = \omega_\phi = 0 \tag{6.18}$$

(ii) The second example again has every fluid particle moving on a circular path about the z-axis, but with a different radial distribution of azimuthal velocity:

$$u_\phi = \frac{K}{r}, \qquad u_r = u_z = 0 \tag{6.19}$$

This gives

$$\omega_\phi = 0, \qquad \omega_r = 0$$

$$\omega_z = \frac{1}{r} \frac{\partial}{\partial r}(ru_\phi) = 0 \qquad \text{for} \quad r \neq 0 \tag{6.20}$$

but leaves ω_z indeterminate on the axis. In fact, ω_z becomes infinite on the axis, as can be seen from Stokes's theorem

$$\oint u \cdot dl = \int (\text{curl } u) \cdot dS = \int \omega \cdot dS \tag{6.21}$$

Carrying out the line integration round a circular path at constant r makes the left-hand side equal to $2\pi K$ independently of r. Hence, there must be a singularity in ω_z such that the contribution $\omega_z \, dS_z$ from the element at $r = 0$ to the surface integral is $2\pi K$. Hence, this case corresponds to irrotational motion everywhere except on the axis. Obviously, exactly this flow cannot occur in practice; however, there are situations in which the vorticity is very high over a narrow linear region and practically zero elsewhere.

(iii) The third example is the simple shear-flow

$$u = u(y) \qquad v = w = 0 \tag{6.22}$$

(in Cartesian co-ordinates) considered previously for different reasons (Sections 1.2 and 2.2). This has

$$\omega_x = \omega_y = 0, \qquad \omega_z = -\partial u/\partial y \tag{6.23}$$

Examples (ii) and (iii) illustrate an important distinction. Rotation, as specified by vorticity, corresponds to changing orientation in space of the fluid particle and *not* to motion of the particle on a closed path. In example (ii) each fluid particle moves round a circular path, but its vorticity is zero. In example (iii) each fluid particle moves in a straight line but it has vorticity. The concept of an isolated rigid particle moving on a circular path without rotating is readily illustrated, Fig. 6.7. It is here contrasted with rigid body rotation in which the particle both moves on a circular path and changes its orientation in space, so that the same side of it always faces the axis of rotation. A fluid particle in the flow of example (i) behaves like

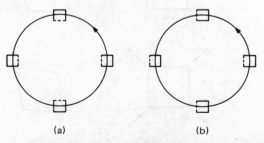

(a)   (b)

Figure 6.7 Successive positions of solid particle in (a) rigid body rotation and (b) circulation without rotation. One side of particle is shown dotted to indicate its orientation.

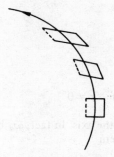

Figure 6.8   Successive positions and shapes of initially square fluid particle circulating without vorticity (size of particle exaggerated relative to radius of circle).

the particle in Fig. 6.7(a); its vorticity corresponds to its changing orientation. The behaviour of a fluid particle in example (ii) is less closely analogous to that of the particle in Fig. 6.7(b), because it is also being deformed. Successive configurations of an initially rectangular fluid particle are shown in Fig. 6.8. For small displacements, one can see the meaning of the statements that the particle is not changing its orientation and that perpendicular sides are rotating in opposite senses to give zero vorticity.

Figure 6.9 illustrates the interpretation of example (iii), where rotational flow in straight lines occurs. Subsequent configurations of an initially square fluid particle are parallelograms. Similar geometries may be reached by a non-rotational distortion, stretching along one diagonal and compressing along the other (corresponding mathematically to the principal axes of the rate-of-strain tensor). Rotation is then necessary, however, to give the actual orientation. Considering small displacements, we see that one of two instantaneously perpendicular sides is rotating, the other is not, thus the average is non-zero and there is vorticity.

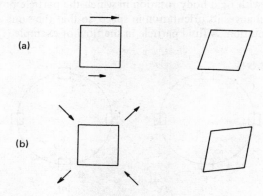

Figure 6.9   Square in (a) shear flow, equation (6.22), and (b) non-rotational distortion.

6.5 Vorticity equation

An equation for the vorticity in incompressible flow is obtained by applying the curl operation throughout the Navier–Stokes equation (5.22) (with $\mathbf{F} = 0$). We have, as a vector identity,

$$\nabla \times (\mathbf{u} \cdot \nabla \mathbf{u}) = \mathbf{u} \cdot \nabla (\nabla \times \mathbf{u}) - (\nabla \times \mathbf{u}) \cdot \nabla \mathbf{u} + (\nabla \cdot \mathbf{u})(\nabla \times \mathbf{u}) \tag{6.24}$$

The continuity equation (5.10) makes the last term zero, and so

$$\frac{\partial \boldsymbol{\omega}}{\partial t} + \mathbf{u} \cdot \nabla \boldsymbol{\omega} - \boldsymbol{\omega} \cdot \nabla \mathbf{u} = \nu \nabla^2 \boldsymbol{\omega} \tag{6.25}$$

The pressure has disappeared because it occurs in a conservative term, but, to offset this simplification, the equation involves the velocity itself as well as the vorticity. Equation (6.25) may be rewritten

$$\frac{D\boldsymbol{\omega}}{Dt} = \boldsymbol{\omega} \cdot \nabla \mathbf{u} + \nu \nabla^2 \boldsymbol{\omega}, \tag{6.26}$$

giving an expression for the rate of change of the vorticity of a fluid particle. The second term on the right-hand side shows that the action of viscosity produces diffusion of vorticity down a vorticity gradient, like it produces diffusion of momentum down a momentum gradient. This might be expected from the fact that rigid body rotation with its uniform distribution of vorticity (example (i) above) involves no viscous action.

The first term on the right-hand side of equation (6.26) represents the action of velocity variations on the vorticity. The precise physical interpretation of this term varies with the details of the velocity field, but may be illustrated as follows. Consider a particle with its vorticity (instantaneously) in the z-direction and of magnitude ζ. Then the z-component of the term under discussion

$$(\boldsymbol{\omega} \cdot \nabla \mathbf{u})_z = \zeta \frac{\partial w}{\partial z} \tag{6.27}$$

Positive $\partial w/\partial z$ indicates that the fluid particle is elongating in the direction of its vorticity. To conserve mass it contracts in the x- and/or y-direction (notice that the continuity equation entered into the derivation of equation (6.26)). It thus rotates faster, as does a solid body of decreasing moment of inertia (e.g. a ballet dancer who brings in her arms, or the Earth as its denser materials settle to the centre). The vorticity increases. This process is often referred to as vortex stretching.

Just as one can draw streamlines everywhere in the direction of the local velocity, so one can draw vortex lines everywhere in the direction of the local vorticity. An important result, that will form the basis of some of the physical arguments in subsequent chapters, is that for an inviscid fluid (see Section 8.3 and Chapter 10) a vortex line always consists of the same fluid particles.

This may be shown by considering a short segment AB of length ϵ of a vortex line instantaneously in the z-direction (Fig. 6.10)

$$\boldsymbol{\omega}_{t=0} = (0, 0, \zeta) \tag{6.28}$$

For an inviscid fluid, the development of the vorticity field is governed by the

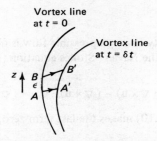

Figure 6.10   Successive positions of vortex line and two points on it.

equation

$$\frac{D\boldsymbol{\omega}}{Dt} = \boldsymbol{\omega} \cdot \nabla \mathbf{u} \tag{6.29}$$

$$= \zeta \frac{\partial \mathbf{u}}{\partial z} \tag{6.30}$$

and so, after a small time δt, the vorticity of the same fluid is

$$\boldsymbol{\omega}_{t=\delta t} = \left(\zeta \frac{\partial u}{\partial z} \delta t, \, \zeta \frac{\partial v}{\partial z} \delta t, \, \zeta + \zeta \frac{\partial w}{\partial z} \delta t \right) \tag{6.31}$$

We now enquire about the orientation of $A'B'$, A' being the position at $t = \delta t$ of the fluid that was at A at $t = 0$ and B' being similarly related to B. If the velocity components at A are (u, v, w), those at B are

$$\left(u + \frac{\partial u}{\partial z} \epsilon, \, v + \frac{\partial v}{\partial z} \epsilon, \, w + \frac{\partial w}{\partial z} \epsilon \right)$$

Thus

$$AA' = (u\delta t, v\delta t, w\delta t) \tag{6.32}$$

$$BB' = \left[\left(u + \frac{\partial u}{\partial z} \epsilon \right) \delta t, \, \left(v + \frac{\partial v}{\partial z} \epsilon \right) \delta t, \, \left(w + \frac{\partial w}{\partial z} \epsilon \right) \delta t \right] \tag{6.33}$$

and

$$A'B' = \left(\frac{\partial u}{\partial z} \epsilon \delta t, \, \frac{\partial v}{\partial z} \epsilon \delta t, \, \epsilon + \frac{\partial w}{\partial z} \epsilon \delta t \right) \tag{6.34}$$

The components of (6.34) are in the same ratios to one another as those of (6.31); the new orientation of the segment of vortex line is the same as that of the material line. Applying this result at each point along the vortex line, one concludes that it always consists of the same fluid particles.

6.6 Circulation

The circulation round any arbitrary closed loop in the fluid is defined as

$$\Gamma = \oint \mathbf{u} \cdot d\mathbf{l} \tag{6.35}$$

This differs from the definition of the vorticity in equations (6.12) and (6.13) in that the loop is now a finite one. The circulation is non-zero in example (ii) of Section 6.4 as well as in examples (i) and (iii).

The circulation is related to the vorticity by Stokes's theorem, equation (6.21). There must be vorticity within a loop round which circulation occurs.

7
Dynamical Similarity

7.1 Introduction

In only a minority of fluid dynamical situations can one determine the flow as an exact solution of the equations of motion. The necessary mathematical methods often do not exist. Even when an exact solution can be obtained it may not be unique and so may not correspond to what actually occurs. Hence, much of fluid mechanics concerns the development of both experimental and theoretical procedures for elucidating flows that cannot be rigorously calculated.

A useful starting point for this development is the following question: under what conditions do similar flow patterns occur in two geometrically similar pieces of apparatus? When these conditions are fulfilled, the two flows are said to be dynamically similar.

It is easier to think in terms of a specific system and we choose the example shown in Fig. 7.1. An elliptical obstacle of dimensions a and b as shown is placed in a channel of width c through which fluid moves. Other lengths may be necessary to specify the dimensions in the third direction. We consider two such pieces of apparatus, which are geometrically similar; i.e. one is just a scaled up version of the other, so that

$$a_2/a_1 = b_2/b_1 = c_2/c_1 \tag{7.1}$$

(where the suffixes refer, of course, to apparatus 1 and apparatus 2). The two fluids in the two sets of apparatus may be different; ρ and μ are parameters of the problem. Given geometrical similarity, there is then the possibility that the two flow patterns will be similar; that is

$$u_{P2}/u_{P1} = v_{P2}/v_{P1} = w_{P2}/w_{P1} = u_{Q2}/u_{Q1} = v_{Q2}/v_{Q1} = w_{Q2}/w_{Q1} \tag{7.2}$$

for all pairs of geometrically similarly located points $P1$, $Q1$, $P2$, $Q2$ in the two pieces of apparatus. However, this dynamical similarity will occur only if further conditions are fulfilled, and we have to investigate what these are.

Although the discussion will refer to this example, the analysis to be given applies to all steady situations governed by the incompressible continuity equation and the Navier–Stokes equation without a body force. The same general method is applied with appropriate modifications to situations where other terms and/or other equations come in, as we shall be seeing in later chapters.

There are several ways in which this question of dynamical similarity is important. It is evidently of practical importance for experiments with models. Tests of, say, an aeroplane or a ship using a small-scale model in a wind-tunnel or a towing tank will not be useful if the flow in the model experiment is quite different from that

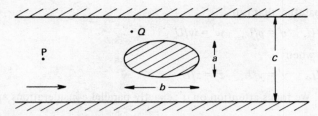

Figure 7.1 Example of situation to which ideas in text can be applied.

which occurs on the full scale. To take an extreme example, they will be useless if the flow with the model is laminar and that on the full scale is turbulent; less extreme differences, such as two laminar flows with different streamline patterns, are also undesirable. Dynamical similarity is likewise important in more fundamental experimental work. If one has observed a certain flow behaviour, one needs to know when this behaviour will occur and whether further experiments are necessary to investigate the full range of behaviour. Dynamical similarity also plays an important role in the theoretical development; it leads to useful approximations to the equations of motion (see Chapter 8).

7.2 Condition for dynamical similarity: Reynolds number

The derivation of the condition for dynamical similarity starts by introducing length and velocity scales, L and U. These are typical measures of the size of the apparatus and the rate at which the fluid is moving in it. In our example, a possible choice of L would be the width of the obstacle, $L = a$, and a possible choice of U would be the speed at the centre of the channel well upstream of the obstacle, $U = u_P$. However, the choices are arbitrary and the conclusion does not depend on the details of them. No pressure difference scale is introduced as the pressure differences cannot be varied independently of the velocity field. It would be possible to introduce a pressure difference scale instead of a velocity scale, but again this would alter only the form in which the conclusion is expressed, not the conclusion itself.

No time scale is introduced, because we are restricting attention to steady imposed conditions. The analysis will include time-variation of the flow, because, as we have seen in Chapters 2—4, unsteadiness can arise spontaneously. When this happens, the unsteadiness does not provide any time scale of its own; the rapidity of the fluctuations is related to the length and velocity scales. A flow that is inherently unsteady because of variations in the imposed conditions does involve an independent time scale, indicating the rapidity of these variations; this case is not covered by the following analysis.

There are two routes by which we may reach the conclusion. We will consider each in turn. The first is the quicker. The second perhaps shows better what underlies the conclusion and illustrates the method used in more complicated problems where the first route is less easy to apply.

Dynamical similarity pertains if the ratio of each of the velocity components at geometrically similar points of the flow to the velocity scale is the same in both pieces of apparatus; that is if

$$u' = u/U, \quad v' = v/U, \quad w' = w/U \qquad (7.3)$$

are the same when

$$x' = x/L, \quad y' = y/L, \quad z' = z/L \qquad (7.4)$$

are the same. We focus attention on u'; exactly parallel considerations apply to v' and w'.

u' is a dimensionless quantity. In any expression for it, dimensional quantities must appear in non-dimensional combinations. We can thus write

$$u' = f\left(\frac{b}{L}, \frac{c}{L}, \ldots, x', y', z', \frac{\rho U L}{\mu}\right) \qquad (7.5)$$

The quantities on the right-hand side are all the independent non-dimensional combinations of the physical parameters on which u' can depend. Any further non-dimensional combinations, for example $\rho U b/\mu$, are also combinations of the above and are thus implicitly included.

If all the quantities on the right-hand side of (7.5) are the same for two systems, then u' is the same. Equality of $b/L, c/L$, etc. in the two cases is a restatement of geometrical similarity. Equality of x', y' and z' indicates that geometrically similar points are being considered. Hence, equality of $\rho U L/\mu$ is the significant criterion.

Dynamical similarity of two geometrically similar systems of the type under consideration exists if they have the same value of the Reynolds number

$$\text{Re} = \frac{\rho U L}{\mu} = \frac{U L}{\nu} \qquad (7.6)$$

The second route to this result starts with the governing equations, in this case equation (5.10) and equation (5.22) with $\mathbf{F} = 0$. The argument is clearer if we expand these in Cartesian co-ordinates,

$$\frac{\partial u}{\partial x} + \frac{\partial v}{\partial y} + \frac{\partial w}{\partial z} = 0 \qquad (7.7)$$

$$\frac{\partial u}{\partial t} + u\frac{\partial u}{\partial x} + v\frac{\partial u}{\partial y} + w\frac{\partial u}{\partial z} = -\frac{1}{\rho}\frac{\partial p}{\partial x} + \nu\left(\frac{\partial^2 u}{\partial x^2} + \frac{\partial^2 u}{\partial y^2} + \frac{\partial^2 u}{\partial z^2}\right) \qquad (7.8)$$

with similar equations for v and w. Length and velocity scales, L and U, are introduced as before and are used to give non-dimensional forms (denoted by primes) of the variables:

$$x' = x/L \quad y' = y/L \quad z' = z/L \quad t' = tU/L$$
$$u' = u/U \quad v' = v/U \quad w' = w/U \quad (\Delta p)' = \Delta p/\rho U^2 \qquad (7.9)$$

(Δp being the difference between the pressure and some reference pressure.) Separate time and pressure difference scales are not introduced for the reasons discussed earlier. This means that t and Δp are non-dimensionalized using appropriate combinations of the other scales. The ways chosen are not unique (e.g. $\mu U/L$ has the dimensions of pressure as well as ρU^2); however, different choices would make no difference to the final conclusion. Substituting (7.9) into equations (7.7) and (7.8) gives

$$\frac{U}{L}\left(\frac{\partial u'}{\partial x'} + \frac{\partial v'}{\partial y'} + \frac{\partial w'}{\partial z'}\right) = 0 \tag{7.10}$$

$$\frac{U^2}{L}\frac{\partial u'}{\partial t'} + \frac{U^2}{L}\left(u'\frac{\partial u'}{\partial x'} + v'\frac{\partial u'}{\partial y'} + w'\frac{\partial u'}{\partial z'}\right)$$

$$= -\frac{U^2}{L}\frac{\partial (\Delta p)'}{\partial x'} + \frac{\nu U}{L^2}\left(\frac{\partial^2 u'}{\partial x'^2} + \frac{\partial^2 u'}{\partial y'^2} + \frac{\partial^2 u'}{\partial z'^2}\right) \tag{7.11}$$

with similar equations for v' and w'. Hence,

$$\nabla'\cdot\mathbf{u}' = 0 \tag{7.12}$$

$$\frac{\partial \mathbf{u}'}{\partial t'} + \mathbf{u}'\cdot\nabla'\mathbf{u}' = -\nabla'(\Delta p)' + \frac{1}{\mathrm{Re}}\,\nabla'^2\mathbf{u}' \tag{7.13}$$

where

$$\nabla' = \hat{x}\frac{\partial}{\partial x'} + \hat{y}\frac{\partial}{\partial y'} + \hat{z}\frac{\partial}{\partial z'} \tag{7.14}$$

$$\mathbf{u}' = \mathbf{u}/U \tag{7.15}$$

and Re is the Reynolds number, UL/ν. The boundary conditions can be similarly converted to conditions in the non-dimensional variables. We see that if the Reynolds number is the same for two geometrically similar situations, then the equations for the non-dimensional variables are the same. Hence, they have the same solutions and the same flow patterns occur. If the Reynolds number is different, the equations are different and there is no reason to expect the same flow behaviour. We have the same result as before that the condition for dynamical similarity is equality of the Reynolds number.

This conclusion greatly reduces the amount of work needed to obtain full information about a situation such as that in Fig. 7.1. Whereas it might seem that one would need to investigate separately the effect of varying each of L, U, ρ and μ, in fact one need investigate only the variations with Reynolds number.

7.3 Dependent quantities

One may need to know the value of some quantity dependent on the flow. One would expect that when dynamical similarity pertains, then information about such quantities can be transferred between systems; for instance, model experiments can give information not only about the flow on full scale but also about quantities associated with it.

We may use, as an example of such a quantity, the force acting on an obstacle like that in Fig. 7.1. We denote this by D (treated as a scalar on the assumption that its direction is known from symmetry; if not the argument can apply to each component). The drag coefficient, defined as

$$C_D = D/\tfrac{1}{2}\rho U^2 L^2 \tag{7.16}$$

is a non-dimensional form of this (the $1/2$ is irrelevant but introduced for consistency with conventional notation – see also Chapter 3).† It is not the only non-dimensional form, but a different choice would give an equivalent conclusion.

The drag coefficient depends only on the Reynolds number

$$C_D = f(\text{Re}) \tag{7.17}$$

There are again two routes to this conclusion. The first is a direct dimensional argument: one says that the only dimensionally satisfactory expressions of

$$D = f(L, b, c, \ldots, U, \rho, \mu) \tag{7.18}$$

are of the form

$$C_D = f\left(\frac{b}{L}, \frac{c}{L}, \ldots, \text{Re}\right) \tag{7.19}$$

and when there is geometrical similarity (7.19) becomes (7.17).

The second route starts with the fact that forces acting on the obstacle are pressure forces of Δp per unit area and viscous forces of the form $\mu \partial u/\partial y$ per unit area. In the non-dimensional variables, these are $\rho U^2 (\Delta p)'$ per unit area and $(\rho U^2/\text{Re})\partial u'/\partial y'$ per unit area. When Re is the same in two cases the solutions for the primed variables are the same and the forces per unit area are proportional‡ to ρU^2. The total forces are thus proportional to $\rho U^2 L^2$. Hence, when Re is the same, $D/\rho U^2 L^2$ is the same; and one has equation (7.17).

This relationship enables information about forces to be transferred from one apparatus to another geometrically similar apparatus. If Re is the same, C_D is the same; one can then infer the force in one apparatus from measurements in the other. We now have the full justification for the viewpoint adopted in Chapter 3 that Fig. 3.14 contains complete information about the drag on a circular cylinder in steady incompressible flow.

It is well known that dimensional analysis sometimes gives a more explicit expression for a dependent quantity than a relationship of the type of (7.17). This occurs when the number of dimensional quantities involved is smaller. For example, we shall see in Section 8.2 that when the Reynolds number is low, the equation of motion simplifies to a form (equation (8.7)) not involving ρ. Thus ρ drops out of (7.18) and so out of the relationship between Re and C_D. This requires

$$C_D \propto 1/\text{Re} \tag{7.20}$$

When the other quantities are fixed this corresponds to the drag being directly proportional to the speed.

If μ drops out instead of ρ, similar reasoning gives

$$C_D = \text{const. w.r.t. Re} \tag{7.21}$$

corresponding to the drag being proportional to the square of the speed. This result relates in a rather complex way to the behaviour at high Reynolds numbers (Sections 8.3 and 11.5).

---

†The appearance of L^2 in the denominator of (7.16) compared with d in (3.3) is because D is now the total force on the obstacle whereas, in Chapter 3, it was the force per unit length.
‡As one goes from one case to the other: *not* as one varies U.

Although this section has been almost entirely concerned with drag, the discussion has been intended to illustrate general principles applying to any dependent quantity. Another example is the frequency of a vortex street. We see now how the statement (equation (3.2)) that the Strouhal number is a function of the Reynolds number is a consequence of dynamical similarity.

7.4 Other governing non-dimensional parameters

The above discussion of the Reynolds number illustrates a general procedure. When other equations or other terms in the equations are applicable, other dimensionless combinations of the parameters may be formulated in addition to or instead of the Reynolds number. An early stage of the investigation of a new configuration is usually the formulation of the governing non-dimensional parameters, which determine the dynamical similarity. The use of the Rayleigh and Prandtl numbers to specify the convection problem in Chapter 4 arises from such considerations. This and other cases will be considered in detail in later chapters, but we look straightaway at a few simple examples to illustrate further the principles:

(i) The first is a situation similar to that considered in Sections 7.1–7.3 but with a free surface on which waves can develop. In certain circumstances, important in the dynamics of ships, these waves are dominantly gravitational and in addition to U, L, ρ and ν, the acceleration due to gravity, g, is a parameter of the flow. There are two independent non-dimensional combinations of these

$$\text{Re} = UL/\nu \quad \text{and} \quad \text{Fr} = U/(gL)^{1/2} \tag{7.22}$$

the Reynolds number and the Froude number. Dynamical similarity requires that

$$\text{Re}_1 = \text{Re}_2 \quad \text{and} \quad \text{Fr}_1 = \text{Fr}_2 \tag{7.23}$$

(suffixes 1 and 2 referring to the two geometrically similar systems being compared). The drag coefficient, for example, has the dependence

$$C_D = f(\text{Re}, \text{Fr}) \tag{7.24}$$

(ii) Sometimes one is concerned primarily with effects of the gravitational waves and the viscous flow below the surface is unimportant. The Froude number is then the only relevant governing non-dimensional quantity, and

$$C_D = f(\text{Fr}) \tag{7.25}$$

(This applies, more precisely, when nearly all the energy, generated by the work done by force D is carried away by the waves rather than dissipated by viscosity.)

(iii) For a situation again similar to our main example but with a speed high enough for the fluid to be compressible, dynamical similarity requires equality between systems of both the Reynolds number and the Mach number, $\text{Ma} = U/a$ (a is the speed of sound; see Section 5.8). Thus

$$C_D = f(\text{Re}, \text{Ma}) \tag{7.26}$$

(iv) When the flow is unsteady as a result of changes in the imposed conditions, these changes will have a time scale Ψ associated with them. In problems such as the above there is then the additional non-dimensional parameter $U\Psi/L$, and dynamical similarity throughout the development of the flow requires equality of this in addition to the Reynolds number.

It should be noted that, in the context of model testing, the above discussion of dynamical similarity is the statement of an ideal. It is often not possible in practice to make all the governing non-dimensional parameters the same as on the full scale. In ship model testing, for instance, a reduction in L requires an increase in U to keep the Reynolds number the same but a reduction in U to keep the Froude number the same (since there is little manoeuvreability of ρ, ν and g). Hence, tests have to be made without full dynamical similarity, and special attention must be given to the errors arising in the transfer of information to the full scale.

8

Low and High Reynolds Numbers

8.1 Physical significance of the Reynolds number

The Reynolds number — introduced in the last chapter in the context of dynamical similarity — can be given a physical interpretation. This is useful in gaining an understanding of the dynamical processes that are important in different Reynolds number ranges, and in formulating corresponding approximations to the equations of motion.

To discuss this we need a name for each of the terms in the dynamical equation of steady incompressible flow

$$\rho \mathbf{u} \cdot \nabla \mathbf{u} = -\nabla p + \mu \nabla^2 \mathbf{u} \tag{8.1}$$

The second and third terms are given the obvious names, pressure force and viscous force. The first term is called the inertia force. Physically, it is not a force, but it has the dimensions of force per unit volume and it is sometimes convenient to think of the dynamical equation in terms of a static balance between forces. The procedure is analogous to the more familiar use of the term centrifugal force to represent the acceleration involved in circular motion. No new idea is involved here, just a new name.

In the non-dimensional form of equation (8.1)

$$\mathbf{u}' \cdot \nabla' \mathbf{u}' = -\nabla'(\Delta p)' + \frac{1}{\mathrm{Re}} \nabla'^2 \mathbf{u}' \tag{8.2}$$

(cf. equation (7.13)), the primed quantities (possibly excepting $(\Delta p)'$) may be expected to be of order unity in magnitude. We shall see later that there are important qualifications to that statement. However, as a starting point it is justified so long as the length and velocity scales, U and L, have been chosen as typical quantities. Then a general speed will be of order U and $|\mathbf{u}'| \sim 1$; a general distance over which quantities vary significantly will be of order L and $\partial/\partial x'$ etc. will be of order unity.

Hence the ratio of the first term to the third in equation (8.2) is of order Re. The corresponding terms in equation (8.1) are in the same ratio. This indicates a physical interpretation of the Reynolds number as

$$\mathrm{Re} \sim \frac{\text{inertia forces}}{\text{viscous forces}} \tag{8.3}$$

An alternative (entirely equivalent) formulation of this result, cited because we shall proceed in this way in subsequent chapters, is to write

$$|\mathbf{u} \cdot \nabla \mathbf{u}| \sim U^2/L, \quad |\nu\nabla^2\mathbf{u}| \sim \nu U/L^2 \tag{8.4}$$

Hence

$$\frac{|\mathbf{u} \cdot \nabla\mathbf{u}|}{|\nu\nabla^2\mathbf{u}|} \sim \frac{UL}{\nu} = \text{Re} \tag{8.5}$$

The Reynolds number thus indicates the relative importance of two dynamical processes. At a general point within the flow, the ratios of these two terms will not be exactly equal to the Reynolds number, but their characteristic magnitudes will be in this ratio.

8.2 Low Reynolds number

When the Reynolds number is much smaller than unity the viscous force dominates over the inertia force so much that the latter plays a negligible role in the flow dynamics. One may use an approximate form of the equation of motion with the inertia term dropped. Equation (8.2) becomes

$$0 = -\nabla'(\Delta p)' + \frac{1}{\text{Re}} \nabla'^2\mathbf{u}' \tag{8.6}$$

these terms being of order $1/\text{Re}$ and the neglected term of order 1. The pressure term must be retained since it is necessary to match the number of variables to the number of equations (Section 5.6). Physically, this means that the size of the pressure term is always governed by the other dynamically important terms — in this case by the viscous term.

Reverting to the dimensional form, equation (8.6) is

$$\nabla p = \mu \nabla^2\mathbf{u} \tag{8.7}$$

At every point in the fluid there is an effective balance between the local pressure and viscous forces. Equation (8.7) is known as the equation of creeping motion. It is evidently much simpler than the full Navier–Stokes equation, and solutions have been found for many cases for which the full equation has not yielded a solution. One case will be discussed in Section 9.4. Such solutions are found to agree well with the observed behaviour at low Reynolds number (see, e.g., Fig. 9.3), thus justifying the procedure leading to the approximation.

It is a characteristic feature of low Reynolds number flows that viscous interactions extend over large distances. For example, particles sedimenting at low Reynolds number affect each other's motion even when their separation is large compared with their size. Figure 8.1 illustrates this long range viscous action for flow past a circular cylinder. It re-presents the information of Fig. 3.2 to show the velocity distribution across the mid-plane at a Reynolds number of 0.1. In the next section we shall be looking at the corresponding figure for high Reynolds number flow; comparison of the two provides a good illustration of the way in which different dynamical processes dominate in different Reynolds number ranges.

Apart from Section 9.4, we shall give little further attention to low Reynolds number flows. There are nevertheless many interesting low Reynolds number phenomena, as is particularly well illustrated by the film of Ref. [42].

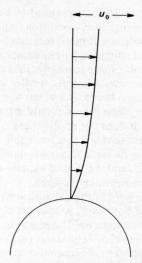

Figure 8.1 Velocity distribution on centre plane in flow past circular cylinder at Re = 0.1.

8.3 High Reynolds number

Corresponding arguments for high Reynolds number flow indicate that the viscous force is so small compared with the inertia force that it can be neglected. Equation (8.2) then approximates to

$$\mathbf{u'} \cdot \nabla' \mathbf{u'} = - \nabla'(\Delta p)'$$

(8.8)

or dimensionally

$$\rho \mathbf{u} \cdot \nabla \mathbf{u} = -\nabla p$$

(8.9)

This is Euler's equation of inviscid motion. When it applies, the fluid at each point has an acceleration directly related to the pressure gradient.

The argument applies also to unsteady flow ($\mu \nabla^2 \mathbf{u}$ being negligible compared with $\rho \mathbf{u} \cdot \nabla \mathbf{u}$ regardless of the size of $\rho \partial \mathbf{u}/\partial t$), and a more general form of Euler's equation is

$$\rho \frac{D\mathbf{u}}{Dt} = -\nabla p$$

(8.10)

The relationship of this equation to the actual behaviour at high Reynolds numbers is much more complex than the relationship of the creeping motion equation to low Reynolds number flow. Comparing Euler's equation with the Navier–Stokes equation, we see that the discarded term is the highest order differential term — the only one involving second space derivatives. The approximation thus reduces the order of the differential equation. A corresponding reduction must be made in the number of boundary conditions.

We saw in Section 5.7 that the no-slip boundary condition is a consequence of the action of viscosity. One may thus expect that this is the condition that should be discarded for mathematical consistency with the inviscid equation. This is indeed the case; we shall see in Chapter 10 that solutions of Euler's equation are obtained by matching only to the impermeability condition (equation (5.33)). Imposition of the no-slip condition also would result in no solution being obtainable.

We now have a paradoxical situation. The statement that Euler's equation applies at high Reynolds number means, more precisely, that as the Reynolds number is increased the viscous term becomes relatively smaller and smaller, although never absolutely zero; Euler's equation becomes a better and better approximation. A boundary condition, however, cannot be similarly relaxed as the Reynolds number increases. It either applies or it does not apply; there is no meaning to the statement that the no-slip condition is present but to a negligible extent. On the other hand, one would not expect there to be some Reynolds number at which the no-slip condition suddenly 'switches off', and it is found experimentally that it continues to apply no matter how high the Reynolds number.

Consequently, the viscous term in the dynamical equation must always remain significant in the vicinity of a boundary, so that the equation remains of the order appropriate to the boundary conditions. The region in which this happens is known as the boundary layer. The reasoning (equations (8.2)–(8.5)) that the viscous force should be negligible breaks down in the boundary layer because the flow develops an internal length scale much smaller than the imposed length scale, L. This is the boundary layer thickness, δ. We shall see below, and in more detail in Chapter 11, that the size of the viscous term can be determined by δ whilst the size of the inertia term is still determined by L:

$$| \mathbf{u} \cdot \nabla \mathbf{u} | \sim U^2/L \qquad | \nu \nabla^2 \mathbf{u} | \sim \nu U/\delta^2 \qquad (8.11)$$

Inertia and viscous forces can thus remain of comparable order of magnitude if

$$U^2/L \sim \nu U/\delta^2 \qquad (8.12)$$

that is if

$$\frac{\delta}{L} \sim \left(\frac{UL}{\nu} \right)^{-1/2} = \mathrm{Re}^{-1/2} \qquad (8.13)$$

The difference between the two length scales must become more marked as the Reynolds number increases.

We consider first the simplest example of a boundary layer. Suppose that a flat plate of negligible thickness is placed in a uniform stream, speed u_0, parallel to it (Fig. 8.2). Then, for a theoretical situation governed by Euler's equation and without the no-slip condition, the flow could obviously continue as if the plate were not there (Fig. 8.2(a)). The speed would be u_0 everywhere. In a real fluid, at large Reynolds number, the speed remains very close to u_0 over most of the flow. Close to and behind the plate, however, there are regions in which a large change occurs (Fig. 8.2(b)). These are the boundary layers on either side of the plate and the wake behind it. We shall not consider the wake further at the moment, but it can be thought of as the extension of the boundary layers downstream.

The rapid variation of speed in the boundary layer gives rise to much larger values of $\partial^2 u/\partial y^2$ than would otherwise exist. This makes the viscous force much larger and so makes it appropriate to use (8.11), rather than (8.4), for the orders of magnitude.

It is often useful to have a precise definition of the boundary layer thickness, δ (shown in Fig. 8.2(b)). There is, of course, no line beyond which the presence of

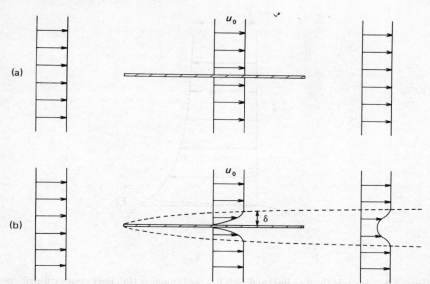

Figure 8.2   Velocity profiles in flow past thin plate: (a) imagined inviscid flow; (b) real fluid at high Reynolds number. Dotted lines indicate edges of boundary layer and wake.

the plate has absolutely no effect; the velocity still asymptotes to u_0, but very rapidly. A common procedure is to choose δ such that

$$u = 0.99u_0 \quad \text{at} \quad y = \delta \tag{8.14}$$

(y is distance from plate); the boundary layer is taken to be the region in which the velocity differs by more than 1 per cent from the free-stream velocity.

The longitudinal length scale L is provided in this example by the distance from the leading edge. We shall see in Section 11.3 (equation (11.29)) that

$$\frac{\delta}{x} \propto \left(\frac{u_0 x}{\nu} \right)^{-1/2} \tag{8.15}$$

— as expected from relationship (8.13).

The edge of the boundary layer is *not* a streamline. The only significance of the line, $y = \delta$, shown in Fig. 8.2(b) is that indicated by equation (8.14). Fluid crosses this line. In the present example, fluid just outside the boundary layer at one value of x is inside it at larger x.

For any obstacle other than a flat plate parallel to the free-stream, the situation is more complicated. The fluid is diverted past the obstacle and the solution of Euler's equation is not just a uniform flow (which would not satisfy the impermeability boundary condition). It would thus be meaningless to define the boundary layer and wake as the regions in which the velocity departs significantly from u_0. They are defined instead as the regions in which the action of viscosity significantly affects the velocity distribution. Suppose one has found a solution of Euler's equation for the flow past such an obstacle (which we may call the inviscid flow solution). This will not satisfy the no-slip condition. Close to the wall of the

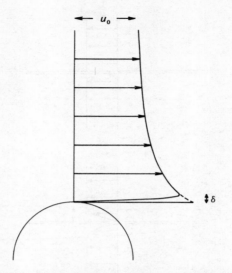

Figure 8.3   Inviscid (broken line) and high Reynolds number (full line) velocity distributions across centre plane in flow past circular cylinder (neglecting effects of boundary layer separation).

obstacle, viscous action will modify the flow so that the no-slip condition is obeyed. The region in which this happens is the boundary layer.

We can thus generalize the specification of a boundary layer implied by equation (8.14): the boundary layer is the region in which the velocity differs by more than 1 per cent from the inviscid flow solution.

Figure 8.3 shows an example (cf. Fig. 8.1 for the corresponding example at low Reynolds number). The inviscid flow solution for flow past a circular cylinder gives a velocity profile across the mid-plane as shown by the broken curve. The speed at the wall is twice the free-stream speed. The full curve shows a high Reynolds number velocity profile, satisfying the no-slip condition. The boundary layer is the region in which the two profiles differ significantly.†

Chapter 10 will describe the elements of inviscid flow theory. Chapter 11 will discuss boundary layers. We can now see the role of these two aspects in the development of our understanding of flow at high Reynolds numbers. The first stage in tackling a new problem is usually a solution of the inviscid flow problem. This will, subject to qualifications made below, describe most of the flow. It does so, however, only because the region in which it applies is separated off from the no-slip condition by the boundary layer. One of the pieces of information obtained from

†We know from Chapter 3 that Fig. 8.3 involves some oversimplification. In the first place, over a wide Reynolds number range, the separation of the flow from the wall leading to the formation of attached eddies occurs upstream of the station shown. Secondly, even when it occurs downstream, the existence of the separation will modify the inviscid flow solution — not directly through the extension of the viscous region but indirectly through a change of the pressure distribution that makes a different solution of Euler's equation applicable. (See Section 11.4.)

the inviscid flow solution is the pressure distribution over the boundaries. This is part of the input to the second stage, a treatment of the boundary layer. If this indicates that the boundary layer undergoes separation (see Section 11.4), some modification to the inviscid solution will be required; in principle an iterative procedure is then needed, though in practice it may be difficult.

Historically, Euler's equation is older than the Navier–Stokes equation, and it was puzzling that it described some aspects of fluid behaviour very well whilst failing totally to describe others. We can now see the reason: those aspects described well were those unaffected by the presence of boundary layers. An important feature that does depend on boundary layers is the force on an obstacle, and we shall see that it was with this that failure of Euler's equation was particularly dramatic. The introduction of the concept of boundary layers, by Prandtl in 1904, was a landmark in the history of fluid dynamics; a very high proportion of subsequent developments stem directly from it.

We have seen in Chapters 2 and 3 that flow at high Reynolds number is prone to instability. Above we have been thinking mainly of laminar flow. The discussion is, however, by no means academic. Transition to turbulence occurs in regions such as boundary layers and wakes, whilst laminar flow continues in inviscid regions. Hence, the division into the two regions is still useful.

It is apparent that a much wider range of phenomena occur at high Reynolds number than at low. For this reason alone one would wish to give the former situation much more extensive consideration in a book of this sort. However, it is worth noting that this emphasis coincides to a large extent with the type of situation one meets most frequently in practical situations. The values of the kinematic viscosity for water and air (at common values of the temperature and pressure) are respectively 1.0×10^{-6} m^2 s^{-1} and 1.5×10^{-5} m^2 s^{-1}. In either fluid one needs only an object of a few centimetres in size moving at a speed of a few centimetres per second to reach a moderately high Reynolds number.

$$\frac{UL}{1.5 E-5} =$$

$$10^5 \frac{UL}{1.5} = 3E5$$

$$UL = 4.5$$

$$U = 300$$

$$L = 1.5 E^{-2} = 1.5 \text{ cm}$$

9
Some Solutions of the Viscous Flow Equations

9.1 Introduction

An obvious aim, once the equations of motion have been set up (in either the full form of Chapter 5 or in an approximate form such as those in Chapter 8) is to find solutions of them. Fluid dynamics thus constitutes an important branch of applied mathematics, although there are severe limitations to what can be learned by theory alone because of mathematical complexity, non-uniqueness, and instability. In this book, the mathematical aspects are somewhat underplayed to leave room for a full development of the experimental aspects. In this chapter we do look briefly at a few solutions of the Navier–Stokes equation and of the equation of creeping motion, both to illustrate the mathematical aspects of the subject and to provide information required elsewhere. For more systematic mathematical treatment see Refs. [12, 13, 14, 15].

Incidentally, in the solutions considered in this chapter, the non-linear terms play either no role at all or a secondary role. They are unimportant either for geometrical reasons or, in the case of creeping motion, for the reasons discussed in Section 8.2. These solutions are, in this respect, untypical of much of fluid dynamics where non-linearity is responsible for both the mathematical difficulties and for the distinctive phenomena. The solutions of the boundary layer equations in Chapter 11 will provide examples of the mathematical handling of such problems.

9.2 Poiseuille flow

We have already looked in Chapter 2 at solutions for flow through a channel and through a pipe. For completeness we need to see that the equations set up there from first principles are indeed special cases of the full continuity and Navier–Stokes equations.

The assumption that there is only one non-zero component of the velocity reduces the continuity equation (5.10) to

$$\partial u / \partial x = 0 \tag{9.1}$$

which accords with the velocity profile being the same at all values of x. It also means that only one component of the Navier–Stokes equation is significant and this is

$$\rho u \frac{\partial u}{\partial x} = -\frac{\partial p}{\partial x} + \mu \nabla^2 u \tag{9.2}$$

The left-hand side is zero from (9.1), and the equation takes the form of either (2.6) or (2.14) for respectively Cartesian and cylindrical co-ordinates. Equations (2.8) and (2.17) are thus solutions of the equations of motion that we have now established.

9.3 Rotating Couette flow

Another simple case of some importance (as the principle of a device for measuring viscosity, amongst other applications) is rotating Couette flow. Fluid is contained in the annulus between two long concentric cylinders of radii a_1 and a_2 rotating about their common axis with angular velocities Ω_1 and Ω_2 (Fig. 9.1). We want to know the velocity distribution within the annulus (and, in viscosity measurements, the torque acting on the cylinders). A solution of the equations of motion may be obtained by assuming that the velocity is everywhere in the azimuthal (ϕ) direction and that the velocity and pressure are independent of ϕ and z (cylindrical polar co-ordinates shown in Fig. 9.1). These assumptions are the obvious ones suggested by the geometrical symmetry, but, as we shall consider in detail in Section 17.5, instability can produce a changeover to a flow with a more complex structure, to which the following theory does not apply.

The continuity equation $\partial u_\phi / \partial \phi = 0$ is automatically satisfied by these assumptions, and the azimuthal and radial components of the Navier–Stokes equation become

$$0 = \mu \left(\frac{d^2 u_\phi}{dr^2} + \frac{1}{r} \frac{du_\phi}{dr} - \frac{u_\phi}{r^2} \right) \tag{9.3}$$

$$-\frac{\rho u_\phi^2}{r} = -\frac{dp}{dr} \tag{9.4}$$

with the boundary conditions

$$u_\phi = \Omega_1 a_1 \quad \text{at} \quad r = a_1; \quad u_\phi = \Omega_2 a_2 \quad \text{at} \quad r = a_2 \tag{9.5}$$

The first equation can be solved to give u_ϕ and this is then put into the second equation to give p. Thus, the distribution of the azimuthal velocity across the

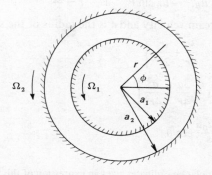

Figure 9.1 Definition sketch for rotating Couette flow (z-axis is normal to paper).

annulus is determined by the balance of viscous stresses, whilst the pressure
distribution is determined by the balance between a radial pressure gradient and the
centrifugal force associated with the circular motion.

The solution for u_ϕ (obtained by working in terms of the variable u_ϕ/r) is

$$u_\phi = Ar + B/r \qquad \qquad (9.6)$$

where

$$A = (\Omega_2 a_2^2 - \Omega_1 a_1^2)/(a_2^2 - a_1^2), \qquad B = (\Omega_1 - \Omega_2)a_1^2 a_2^2/(a_2^2 - a_1^2) \qquad (9.7)$$

The torque Σ_1 acting on the inner cylinder (per unit length in the z-direction) is
given by the viscous stress† $\mu[r\,\partial(u_\phi/r)/\partial r]_{r=a_1}$ multiplied by the area $2\pi a_1$ and by
the radius a_1; i.e.

$$\Sigma_1 = 4\pi\mu a_1^2 a_2^2 (\Omega_2 - \Omega_1)/(a_2^2 - a_1^2) \qquad (9.8)$$

Similarly, the torque on the outer cylinder

$$\Sigma_2 = -4\pi\mu a_1^2 a_2^2 (\Omega_2 - \Omega_1)/(a_2^2 - a_1^2) \qquad (9.9)$$

We notice that Σ_1 and Σ_2 are equal and opposite, as they must be since the total
angular momentum of the fluid is not changing.

9.4 Stokes flow past a sphere

The most famous solution of the equation of creeping motion (8.7) applies to low
Reynolds number flow past a sphere. It leads to the relationship between the
velocity and the drag used to determine viscosity in the familiar procedure of observing the rate of fall of a sphere through a viscous fluid. This is often known as
Stokes flow.

In spherical polar co-ordinates with $\theta = 0$ in the flow direction in the frame of
reference in which the sphere is at rest (Fig. 9.2) the equations are obtained from
equations (5.29)–(5.32) with the inertia terms (the left-hand sides of equations
(5.30)–(5.32)) and the body force terms put equal to zero, and with $u_\phi = 0$,
$\partial/\partial\phi = 0$ by symmetry. The boundary conditions are

$$u_r = u_\theta = 0 \quad \text{at} \quad r = a \qquad (9.10)$$

$$u_r \to u_0 \cos\theta, \quad u_\theta \to -u_0 \sin\theta \quad \text{as} \quad r \to \infty \qquad (9.11)$$

where u_0 is the free-stream velocity and a is the radius of the sphere. The solution is

$$u_r = u_0 \cos\theta \left[1 - \frac{3a}{2r} + \frac{a^3}{2r^3}\right] \qquad (9.12)$$

$$u_\theta = -u_0 \sin\theta \left[1 - \frac{3a}{4r} - \frac{a^3}{4r^3}\right] \qquad (9.13)$$

$$p - p_0 = -\frac{3}{2}\frac{\mu u_0 a}{r^2} \cos\theta \qquad (9.14)$$

---

†That transformation to polar co-ordinates gives an expression of this form is to be expected
from the fact that there will be no stress in rigid body rotation, $u_\phi \propto r$.

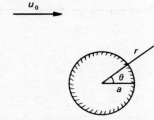

Figure 9.2   Definition sketch for Stokes flow past a sphere (ϕ is azimuthal angle about $\theta = 0$ axis).

p_0 being the ambient pressure. This may readily be shown by substituting the solution into the equations; for the forward integration the reader is referred to other sources (e.g. Refs. [12, 15]).

The force per unit area in the flow direction acting at a point on the surface of the sphere is the sum of the appropriate components of the viscous and pressure forces; that is[†]

$$\sigma = -\mu \left(\frac{\partial u_\theta}{\partial r} \right)_{r=a} \sin \theta - (p - p_0)_{r=a} \cos \theta \tag{9.15}$$

Substituting the solution into this gives

$$\sigma = 3\mu u_0 / 2a \tag{9.16}$$

Since this happens to be independent of θ the total force on the sphere is just σ multiplied by the surface area of the sphere;

$$D = 4\pi a^2 \sigma = 6\pi\mu a u_0 \tag{9.17}$$

In terms of a drag coefficient defined by (7.16) with $L = 2a$, this is

$$C_D = 6\pi / \text{Re} \tag{9.18}$$

(cf. (7.20)).

Equation (9.17) is the well-known result, due to Stokes, used in falling sphere viscometry. Figure 9.3 shows a comparison of this result with experimental observations. The good agreement is important, not only for viscometry, but also because it demonstrates the validity of the reasoning leading to the equation of creeping motion and so encourages one to apply similar reasoning to other problems.

Figure 9.3 also shows the departures from Stokes's law that occur when the Reynolds number is too high for the creeping flow equation to apply. It is important to remember that equation (9.17) can be used only when Re is less than about 0.5. (It is not sufficient, as is sometimes said, that the flow should be laminar.)

In applying this result it should also be remembered that, as remarked in Section 8.2, the viscous effects extend a long way at low Reynolds numbers. Distant boundaries may thus have a disturbingly large effect. In a falling sphere viscometer, the container diameter must be more than one hundred times the sphere diameter for the error to be less than 2 per cent [123].

[†] The viscous stress in spherical polar co-ordinates reduces to this simple form for a boundary at rest.

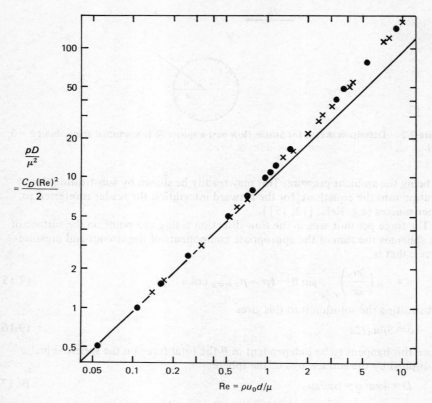

Figure 9.3   Drag on a sphere at low Reynolds numbers. Experimental points from Refs. [161] (x) and [221] (•), both using the falling sphere method. The line represents equation (9.17).

9.5 Low Reynolds number flow past a cylinder

Although the equation of creeping motion generally describes flow at low Reynolds number very satisfactorily, there is a complication that arises in two-dimensional flow, such as the flow past a circular cylinder. No solution of the equation can be found that matches to the boundary conditions both at the surface of the cylinder and at infinity (for mathematical details see, e.g., Ref. [12]). This fact is sometimes referred to as Stokes's paradox. Its resolution again involves the fact that the effect of a boundary on the velocity field extends to very large distances from that boundary. If we consider a moving cylinder in stationary ambient fluid, the fluid velocity remains comparable with the cylinder velocity to distances so large compared with the cylinder radius that the Reynolds number based on the flow lengthscale is of order unity. There is thus a region in which inertia forces are significant. The lower the Reynolds number the more remote this region is from the cylinder, but it always exists.

A low Reynolds number theory allowing for the existence of this region has been developed [7]. It gives, for the dependence of the drag coefficient on Reynolds number for a circular cylinder, the expression (in the notation of Section 3.4)

$$C_D = 8\pi/\text{Re}(2.002 - \ln \text{Re}) \tag{9.19}$$

This provides the low Reynolds number end of the curve in Fig. 3.14 (the rest of which is compiled from experimental data). There is always a small departure from (7.20).

In real situations, of course, it may be other boundaries rather than a remote inertial region that should be considered in resolving Stokes's paradox.

10
Inviscid Flow

10.1 Introduction

The relationship of inviscid flow theory to actual flow at high Reynolds number has been considered in Section 8.3. We now look at some of its features. Although Euler's equation is non-linear, we shall see that in many important cases it reduces to a linear equation. Consequently, it yields solutions much more readily than the full Navier–Stokes equation. This is one of the most mathematically developed branches of fluid mechanics in which experimental work plays a more minor role. It is very fully treated in many books e.g. Refs. [7, 10, 179, 262]. Consequently, we shall confine attention here to the important basic ideas, without developing the methods of application of these ideas to particular cases.

10.2 Kelvin circulation theorem

It may be shown that, for any flow governed by Euler's equation, the circulation round a loop consisting continuously of the same fluid particles is conserved. One may write this

$$\frac{D}{Dt} \oint \mathbf{u} \cdot d\mathbf{l} = 0 \tag{10.1}$$

This result is known as the Kelvin circulation theorem.

10.3 Irrotational motion

A related, less general but for present purposes more useful, result concerns the vorticity. The vorticity equation corresponding to Euler's equation is equation (6.29). This has the property that

$$\text{if} \quad \boldsymbol{\omega} = 0, \quad \text{then} \quad \frac{D\boldsymbol{\omega}}{Dt} = 0 \tag{10.2}$$

If a fluid particle has no vorticity at some initial instant then it can never acquire any.

This result is known as the permanence of irrotational motion. It corresponds physically to the fact that, when Euler's equation applies, the only stresses acting on a fluid particle are the pressure stresses. These act normally to the particle surface and so cannot apply a couple to the particle to bring it into rotation. (Once it is rotating, its vorticity can change through the vortex stretching action described in Section 6.5, but this cannot produce the initial rotation.)

Many interesting flows are initially irrotational — for example, a uniform flow approaching an obstacle. Hence, the study of inviscid motion may for many purposes be reduced to the study of irrotational motion. This does not cover all solutions of Euler's equation, but in the others, the vorticity would have to be introduced initially by some other process.

In irrotational motion

$$\boldsymbol{\omega} = \text{curl } \mathbf{u} = 0 \tag{10.3}$$

throughout the flow. Hence, one may introduce ϕ such that

$$\mathbf{u} = \text{grad } \phi \tag{10.4}$$

ϕ is known as the velocity potential (by analogy with other potentials; it is not, however, associated with energy in the way electrostatic and gravitational potentials are).

From continuity

$$\text{div } \mathbf{u} = 0 \tag{10.5}$$

and so

$$\nabla^2 \phi = 0 \tag{10.6}$$

the velocity potential obeys Laplace's equation.

Two parenthetic comments about this theory are worth making. Firstly, the boundary condition corresponding to the impermeability condition at a stationary wall is

$$\partial \phi / \partial n = 0 \tag{10.7}$$

where n is the direction normal to the boundary. We can now see that if we had also a condition on ϕ corresponding to the no-slip condition, the problem would be over-specified and no solution would be available.

Secondly, the analysis leading to equation (10.6) applies to both steady and unsteady flow. Yet any time variation does not appear explicitly in (10.6). This means that the instantaneous flow pattern depends only on the instantaneous boundary conditions and not on the history of the flow. Every point of the flow responds immediately to any change in the boundary conditions (a change, for example, in the speed at which an object is moving through a fluid). The physical mechanism by which this response is brought about is a change in the pressure distribution. Evidently there must be an upper limit to the rate at which a pressure change can actually transmit through the fluid, and so a limit to the applicability of the present theory. Small pressure changes transmit at the speed of sound; larger ones transmit at a speed of the same order of magnitude. Hence, the criterion for validity of the theory is closely related to the low Mach number criterion. If

$$L/a\Psi \ll 1 \tag{10.8}$$

(where L is the length scale, Ψ is the time scale introduced in example (iv) of Section 7.4 and a is the speed of sound), then pressure changes transmit a distance large compared with L in the time in which significant changes in the flow pattern occur. Hence, the response can be effectively instantaneous.

Techniques for solving Laplace's equation are highly developed as a result of its importance in a variety of other physical contexts. The problem of inviscid flow past an obstacle is directly analogous to that of the flow of electric current around a cavity in a conductor, or to that of the electric field distribution in a region of high dielectric constant around a cavity of low dielectric constant. However, we shall see in Section 11.4 that, because of the phenomenon of boundary layer separation, many simple solutions do not correspond closely to real flows. The most important solutions are for cases, such as the flow past an aerofoil, that have no physically significant counterpart in other branches of physics. Consequently, there has been a lot of work on solutions of Laplace's equation in fluid dynamical contexts. The special methods developed are described in the references mentioned above.

10.4 Bernoulli's equation

As well as the velocity distribution, derivable straightaway from a solution for ϕ, one may also want to know the pressure distribution. In deriving an equation for this, we will now confine attention to steady flow. However, we will derive it in the first place for any steady inviscid flow, irrotational or rotational. Then Bernoulli's equation relates the variation of speed and variation of pressure along a streamline. For steady flow we have a fixed streamline pattern. We consider one streamline and denote the distance along it by l. At any point on it the component of Euler's equation in the streamline direction is

$$\rho q \frac{\partial q}{\partial l} = -\frac{\partial p}{\partial l} \tag{10.9}$$

q is the magnitude of the velocity, $q = |\mathbf{u}|$. Integrating equation (10.9),

$$\tfrac{1}{2}\rho q^2 + p = \text{constant along a streamline} \tag{10.10}$$

This is called Bernoulli's equation.

At positions along the streamline where the velocity is high the pressure is low and vice versa. $\tfrac{1}{2}\rho q^2$ is the kinetic energy per unit volume, and the equation may be interpreted in the following way. When the pressure is increasing in the flow direction, a fluid particle is doing work against the pressure gradient and so loses kinetic energy. When the pressure is decreasing it gains kinetic energy.

When the flow is irrotational, Bernoulli's equation can be extended. We start with the vector identity

$$\mathbf{u} \cdot \nabla \mathbf{u} = \tfrac{1}{2}\nabla(\mathbf{u} \cdot \mathbf{u}) - \mathbf{u} \times (\nabla \times \mathbf{u}) \tag{10.11}$$

For irrotational flow, the second term is zero and

$$\mathbf{u} \cdot \nabla \mathbf{u} = \tfrac{1}{2}\nabla q^2 \tag{10.12}$$

Euler's equation is then

$$\nabla(\tfrac{1}{2}\rho q^2 + p) = 0 \tag{10.13}$$

and so

$$\tfrac{1}{2}\rho q^2 + p = \text{constant throughout the flow} \tag{10.14}$$

The Bernoulli constant is the same for every streamline. The relationship between high velocity and low pressure and its converse apply throughout the flow.

We may see the physical significance of this result by referring to two simple examples in which q is constant. If, further, **u** is constant — the flow is entirely uniform — there can be no pressure variations between streamlines as there is nothing to balance the pressure gradient. The Bernoulli constant is constant throughout the flow. The other example is flow in circular streamlines with u_ϕ independent of r (a case intermediate between examples (i) and (ii) in Section 6.4, but more difficult to generate in practice than either of those). This involves vorticity. The pressure varies with radius, the pressure gradient balancing the centrifugal force of the circular motion. The Bernoulli constant is thus a constant only on each streamline.

10.5 Drag in inviscid flow: d'Alembert's 'paradox'

Bernoulli's equation indicates the pressure distribution over the surface of an obstacle placed in a stream and thus the force that would act on that obstacle if the boundary layers could be ignored. We consider this for an obstacle that is symmetrical upstream and downstream, as in Fig. 10.1, If the flow were from right to left instead of from left to right, the streamline pattern would be the mirror image pattern about the plane of symmetry AB. However, equation (10.6) has the property that, if $\phi = \phi_1$ is a solution, then so is $\phi = -\phi_1$. Thus the streamline pattern for the flow from right to left is the same as that for the flow from left to right; just the direction of flow along the streamlines is reversed. Hence, considering now just the flow from left to right, the flow pattern downstream of the plane of symmetry is the mirror image of that upstream. The speed q is the same at symmetrically placed points such as C and D (Fig. 10.1). From Bernoulli's equation the pressure is also the same. The pressure distribution around the rear half of the obstacle is the same as that round the front half, and there is thus no net force on the obstacle. The drag is zero.

This result is actually true whether or not the obstacle is symmetrical (although

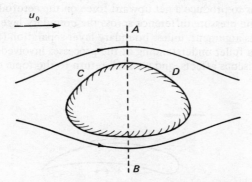

Figure 10.1 Inviscid flow past a symmetric body, considered in discussion of d'Alembert's paradox.

it is not demonstrated so quickly in the latter case [12]). Irrotational flow calculations give zero drag on any obstacle placed in a fluid stream.

At one time it was thought that theory of this type ought to produce the correct
drag. Hence, the above result became known as d'Alembert's paradox. This name
lingers today, although the result ceases to be paradoxical once one knows that the
region of applicability of the theory is separated from the surface of the obstacle by
a boundary layer. (See also Section 11.5.)

Indeed it would be more paradoxical if completely inviscid theory did give a
drag. We can see this most readily by switching attention to the frame of reference
in which the obstacle is moved through stationary fluid. Work would then be done
against any drag and energy would be fed into the fluid. But, in the absence of
viscous action, there is no process by which this energy could be dissipated, and no
steady state would exist. (Arguments of this character require some caution. They
do not apply when there are waves present which can carry energy away 'to
infinity'.)

The result that inviscid motion produces no drag applies only for steady flow.
In unsteady flow, although the velocity distribution is the same as that for the
instantaneously corresponding steady flow, the pressure distribution is different.
The work done against the drag as an obstacle is accelerated through a fluid provides
the change in the kinetic energy of the fluid.

10.6 Applications of Bernoulli's equation

Although, in steady flow, inviscid theory predicts no force on an obstacle in the
direction of relative motion between it and the fluid, it can predict a force at right
angles to this direction. Such a force is called a lift. Lift generation is obviously of
great practical importance; Bernoulli's equation can be used to understand in a
general way why an aeroplane can fly. Consider an aerofoil such as that shown in
Fig. 10.2. We use the frame of reference in which the aerofoil is fixed, so that the
flow is steady. Above the convex upper surface the streamlines are pushed together
and the fluid moves faster than the free-stream speed; the pressure is therefore
reduced, as indicated in the figure. Similarly, the speed is reduced below the concave lower surface, and the pressure is increased. One sees that these pressure
changes are such as to produce a net upward force on the aerofoil. In Section 11.2
we shall see that the pressure difference across the boundary layers is small, and so
does not affect this argument, unless boundary layer separation (Section 11.4)
occurs. However, a fuller understanding of the processes involved does require
consideration of viscous effects, and we shall return to the topic of lift in Chapter 12.

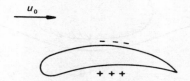

Figure 10.2   Pressure changes associated with Bernoulli's equation around an unsymmetrical
aerofoil.

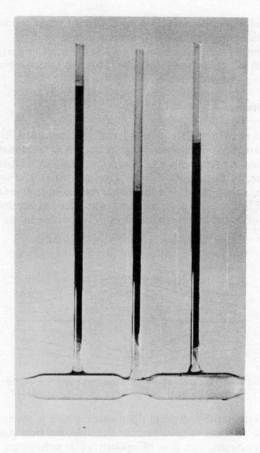

Figure 10.3   Venturi demonstration. (Flow is from left to right; fluid in side-tubes is dyed.)

   Another system that is readily understood in terms of Bernoulli's equation is the
Venturi tube. Indeed, this provides the simplest convenient demonstration of the
relationship between speed and pressure. A pipe with a fluid passing through at high
Reynolds number (thin boundary layers) has a constriction in it — a short length of
reduced diameter. Because of continuity, the speed increases at the constriction
and so the pressure is reduced. This is demonstrated by the apparatus shown in
Fig. 10.3; the height the water rises up the vertical open side tubes is a measure of
the pressure. The pressure is seen to drop markedly at the constriction and to rise
again after it. According to Bernoulli's equation, the pressures on either side of the
constriction should be the same, but, because of some viscous effects (notably those
to be described in Section 11.4), the downstream pressure is a little lower.
   The Venturi tube is of importance not merely as a demonstration device. For a
carefully designed constriction, the pressure differences can be related quantitatively
to the flow rate; this thus provides one method of measuring flow rates through
pipelines. The Venturi is also a convenient simple way of obtaining pressures below

atmospheric; for example, the suction pumps, fitted to taps and used by chemists to speed up filtration, operate on the Venturi principle.

Bernoulli's equation is also the basis of one of the most important instruments for measuring fluid velocities, the Pitot tube. This will be described in Section 23.2.

10.7 Some definitions

Since all the terms in Bernoulli's equation have the dimensions of pressure, the following nomeclature has developed. $\frac{1}{2}\rho q^2$ is known as the dynamic pressure and $(\frac{1}{2}\rho q^2 + p)$ as the total pressure or sometimes (for reasons indicated below) as the stagnation pressure. To distinguish it from these quantities, p is sometimes called the static pressure, although this is a somewhat misleading name (and it is quite different from the hydrostatic pressure to be introduced in Section 13.2). The static pressure is, of course, the pressure physically existing in the fluid.

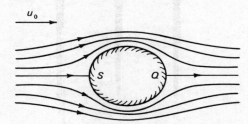

Figure 10.4   Inviscid flow past an obstacle showing front and rear stagnation points, S and Q.

The total pressure has the physical significance that it is the pressure at which the fluid comes to rest. Let us consider, for example, the flow past an obstacle placed in an otherwise uniform flow of velocity u_0 at pressure p_0 (Fig. 10.4). The streamlines pass on different sides of the obstacle. One streamline, in the middle, ends on the obstacle at point S and the fluid at this point is at rest. According to inviscid flow theory, this and a corresponding point Q at the rear of the obstacle are the only points at which the velocity is zero. S and Q are known as the forward and rear stagnation points. Applying Bernoulli's equation to the streamline ending there shows that the pressure at S is

$$p_S = \frac{1}{2}\rho u_0^2 + p_0 \qquad\qquad (10.15)$$

i.e. it is the total pressure associated with the undisturbed flow. In theory, the same pressure exists at Q, but in practice the action of the boundary layer almost always greatly alters this. At the forward stagnation point, however, the effect of the boundary layer is slight, and the pressure p_S is actually observed. This is the highest pressure anywhere in the flow.

11
Boundary Layers and Related Topics

11.1 Boundary layer formation

The reason for the occurrence of boundary layers and their role in high Reynolds number flows have been considered in Section 8.3. However, the fact that flow outside the boundary layers is irrotational (Section 10.3) provides another way of viewing the process of boundary layer formation. Fluid particles can acquire vorticity only by viscous diffusion (i.e. through the action of the term $\nu\nabla^2\boldsymbol{\omega}$ in equation (6.26)). The action of viscosity comes in at the boundary through the need to satisfy the no-slip condition. As a result vorticity is introduced into the flow at the boundary, and then diffuses away from it. The boundary layer can be defined as the region of appreciable vorticity. The boundary layer is long and thin ($L \gg \delta$) when the fluid travels a long distance downstream during the time that the vorticity diffuses only a small distance away from the boundary. This happens when the Reynolds number is large.

11.2 The boundary layer approximation [22]

Because of the difference in length scales in different directions, certain terms in the equations of motion play a negligible part in the dynamics of boundary layers. We now see in a systematic way how this can be used to formulate an appropriate approximation to the equations. This will provide further justification for the ideas introduced in Section 8.3. Also, the resulting equations can sometimes be solved when the exact equations cannot. We shall be looking (Sections 11.3 and 11.8) at a couple of solutions both for their own interest and as our examples of the mathematical methods used for fully non-linear problems.

From the outset we confine attention to steady, two-dimensional boundary layers — a severe restriction from a practical point of view, but one that still allows us to see the general principles involved. We suppose that the boundary layer is forming on a flat wall (with the x co-ordinate in the flow direction and y normal to the wall). A free-stream velocity outside the boundary layer is prescribed as a function of x. This could be achieved by making the wall one side of a channel of variable width as in Fig. 11.1 (with the channel width always large compared to the boundary layer thickness). In fact, however, it makes negligible difference if the surface is curved, so long as there are no sharp corners — more precisely, so long as the radius of curvature of the surface is everywhere large compared to the boundary layer thickness. Thus, the prescribed free-stream velocity could be a solution of

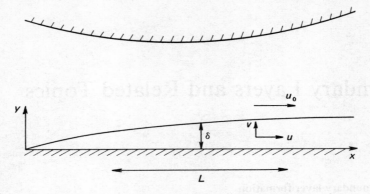

Figure 11.1   Boundary layer on flat wall of channel: definition sketch.

Euler's equation for flow past an obstacle (x then being a curvilinear co-ordinate in the surface).

We denote the free-stream velocity by u_0 and the pressure associated with it by p_0.

We take the boundary layer to have length scales L and δ in the x- and y-directions, as in Section 8.3. We may expect that the velocity scales will also be different in different directions and we denote the scales of u and v by U and V. Similarly the order of magnitude of the pressure differences across the boundary layer in the y-direction may not be the same as the order of magnitude of the imposed pressure differences outside the boundary layer; we denote the scale of the former by Υ and the scale of the latter by Π. We now consider each of the equations in turn, labelling the terms with their orders of magnitude.

The continuity equation is

$$\frac{\partial u}{\partial x} + \frac{\partial v}{\partial y} = 0 \tag{11.1}$$

$$\frac{U}{L} \qquad \frac{V}{\delta}$$

The two terms must be of the same order of magnitude; fluid entering or leaving the boundary layer at its outer edges must be associated with variations in the amount of fluid travelling downstream within the boundary layer. Hence,

$$V \sim U\delta/L; \tag{11.2}$$

the velocity component normal to the wall is small compared with the rate of downstream flow when the boundary layer is thin.

The x-component of the Navier–Stokes equation is

$$u\frac{\partial u}{\partial x} \ + \ v\frac{\partial u}{\partial y} \ = \ -\frac{1}{\rho}\frac{\partial p}{\partial x} + \nu\frac{\partial^2 u}{\partial x^2} + \nu\frac{\partial^2 u}{\partial y^2} \tag{11.3}$$

$$\frac{U^2}{L} \qquad \frac{VU}{\delta} \sim \frac{U^2}{L} \qquad \frac{\Pi}{\rho L} \qquad \frac{\nu U}{L^2} \qquad \frac{\nu U}{\delta^2}$$

The second expression for the order of magnitude of $v\, \partial u/\partial y$ has been written using relationship (11.2). The two parts of the inertia term are comparable with one another, the smallness of V/U compensating for the more rapid variation of u with y than with x. The two parts of the viscous term are however of different sizes when δ/L is small, and $v\, \partial^2 u/\partial x^2$ may be neglected.

The y-component of the Navier–Stokes equation is

$$u\,\frac{\partial v}{\partial x} \;+\; v\,\frac{\partial v}{\partial y} \;=\; -\frac{1}{\rho}\,\frac{\partial p}{\partial y} \;+\; v\,\frac{\partial^2 v}{\partial x^2} \;+\; v\,\frac{\partial^2 v}{\partial y^2} \tag{11.4}$$

$$\frac{UV}{L}\sim\frac{U^2\delta}{L^2} \qquad \frac{V^2}{\delta}\sim\frac{U^2\delta}{L^2} \qquad \frac{\Upsilon}{\rho\delta} \qquad \frac{vV}{L^2}\sim\frac{vU\delta}{L^3} \qquad \frac{vV}{\delta^2}\sim\frac{vU}{L\delta}$$

In both equation (11.3) and equation (11.4) the pressure term will be of the same order of magnitude as the largest of the other terms. Hence,

$$\Pi/\rho L \sim U^2/L \sim vU/\delta^2 \tag{11.5}$$

$$\Upsilon/\rho\delta \sim U^2\delta/L^2 \sim vU/L\delta \tag{11.6}$$

and so

$$\Upsilon/\Pi \sim \delta^2/L^2 \tag{11.7}$$

The pressure differences across the boundary layer are much smaller than those in the x-direction. Hence, at any value of y the difference between $(1/\rho)\partial p/\partial x$ and $(1/\rho)\mathrm{d}p_0/\mathrm{d}x$ is much smaller than the significant terms in equation (11.3) and we may replace the former by the latter, giving

$$u\,\frac{\partial u}{\partial x}+v\,\frac{\partial u}{\partial y}=-\frac{1}{\rho}\,\frac{\mathrm{d}p_0}{\mathrm{d}x}+v\,\frac{\partial^2 u}{\partial y^2} \tag{11.8}$$

Outside the boundary layer there is no variation with y and

$$u_0\,\frac{\mathrm{d}u_0}{\mathrm{d}x}=-\frac{1}{\rho}\,\frac{\mathrm{d}p_0}{\mathrm{d}x} \tag{11.9}$$

a result which could also be obtained from Bernoulli's equation. Hence

$$u\,\frac{\partial u}{\partial x}+v\,\frac{\partial u}{\partial y}=u_0\,\frac{\mathrm{d}u_0}{\mathrm{d}x}+v\,\frac{\partial^2 u}{\partial y^2} \tag{11.10}$$

This equation together with

$$\frac{\partial u}{\partial x}+\frac{\partial v}{\partial y}=0 \tag{11.11}$$

constitute the boundary layer equations — two equations in the two variables u and v. $u_0(x)$ must be known for a solution to be found.

11.3 Zero pressure gradient solution

The simplest, and in a sense most fundamental, solution of the above equations is the zero-pressure gradient boundary layer;

$$\mathrm{d}p_0/\mathrm{d}x = 0 \tag{11.12}$$

and so

$$u_0 = \text{constant} \tag{11.13}$$

Such a boundary layer is readily observed on a thin flat plate set up parallel to the free-stream; one wall of an empty wind-tunnel or water-channel is sometimes used.
    The equations for this case are

$$u\frac{\partial u}{\partial x} + v\frac{\partial u}{\partial y} = v\frac{\partial^2 u}{\partial y^2} \tag{11.14}$$

$$\frac{\partial u}{\partial x} + \frac{\partial v}{\partial y} = 0 \tag{11.15}$$

with boundary conditions

$$u = v = 0 \quad \text{at} \quad y = 0$$

$$u \to u_0 \quad \text{as} \quad y \to \infty \tag{11.16}$$

    We look for a solution of the form

$$u = u_0 g(y/\Delta) \tag{11.17}$$

where Δ is a function of x. That the solution should be of this form is an assumption. It corresponds to the velocity profile having the same shape at all values of x, although with a different scale in the y-direction, and is thus physically plausible. Δ is directly proportional to the boundary layer thickness, but it is convenient to define it slightly differently from δ.
    Equation (11.15) can be satisfied by introducing a stream function ψ such that

$$u = \partial\psi/\partial y \quad v = -\partial\psi/\partial x \tag{11.18}$$

as in Section 6.3. Equation (11.17) is then

$$\psi = u_0\Delta f(y/\Delta) \quad (g = f') \tag{11.19}$$

    Substituting this in equation (11.14) gives

$$\frac{u_0^2}{\Delta}\frac{d\Delta}{dx}ff'' + \frac{vu_0}{\Delta^2}f''' = 0 \tag{11.20}$$

where the prime indicates differentiation with respect to

$$\eta = y/\Delta \tag{11.21}$$

If this is to reduce to a total differential equation in f as a function of η, as it must if the solution is of the assumed form, then one must have

$$\frac{u_0^2}{\Delta}\frac{d\Delta}{dx} \propto \frac{vu_0}{\Delta^2} \tag{11.22}$$

and so

$$\Delta^2 \propto vx/u_0 + \text{const.} \tag{11.23}$$

It is convenient to choose the constant of proportionality and the origin of x so that

$$\Delta = (vx/u_0)^{1/2} \tag{11.24}$$

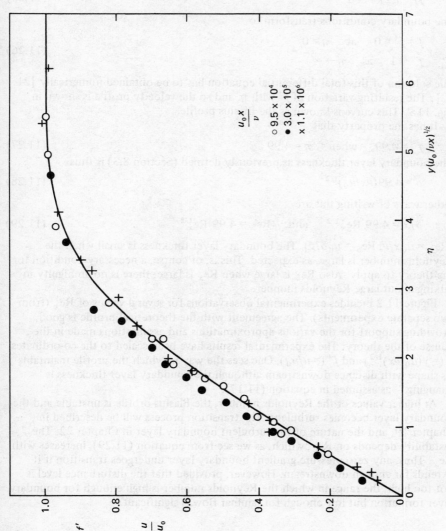

Figure 11.2 Theoretical Blasius profile and experimental confirmation from Refs. [96] and [162].

It is found experimentally that this choice of the origin of x corresponds fairly closely to the leading edge of a flat plate set up in an otherwise unobstructed flow. Equation (11.24) is essentially the same result as equation (8.13).

Equation (11.20) now becomes

$$ff'' + 2f''' = 0 \qquad\qquad (11.25)$$

The boundary conditions transform to

$$f = f' = 0 \quad \text{at} \quad \eta = 0$$
$$f' \to 1 \quad \text{as} \quad \eta \to \infty \qquad\qquad (11.26)$$

The solution of this total differential equation has to be obtained numerically [21, 22]. The resulting variation of f' with η, and so the velocity profile is shown in Fig. 11.2. This curve is known as the Blasius profile.

It has the property that

$$f' = 0.99 \quad \text{when} \quad \eta = 4.99 \qquad\qquad (11.27)$$

The boundary layer thickness as previously defined (Section 8.3) is thus

$$\delta = 4.99(\nu x/u_0)^{1/2} \qquad\qquad (11.28)$$

Other ways of writing this are

$$\delta/x = 4.99 \, \mathrm{Re}_x^{-1/2} \quad \text{and} \quad \mathrm{Re}_\delta = 4.99 \, \mathrm{Re}_x^{1/2} \qquad\qquad (11.29)$$

($\mathrm{Re}_x = u_0 x/\nu$; $\mathrm{Re}_\delta = u_0 \delta/\nu$). The boundary layer thickness is small when the Reynolds number is large, as expected. This is, of course, a necessary condition for the theory to apply. Also Re_δ is large when Re_x is large; there is no ambiguity in talking about large Reynolds number.

Figure 11.2 includes experimental observations for several values of Re_x (from two separate experiments). The agreement with the theoretical profile is good, providing support for the various approximations and assumptions made in the course of the theory. The experimental results have been scaled to the co-ordinates $\eta \, (= y(u_0/\nu x)^{1/2})$ and $f' \, (= u/u_0)$. One sees the way in which the profile maintains its shape with distance downstream although the boundary layer thickness is changing — as assumed in equation (11.17).

At higher values of the Reynolds number, the Blasius profile is unstable and the boundary layer becomes turbulent. The transition process will be described in Chapter 19, and the nature of the turbulent boundary layer in Chapter 22. The instability depends on Re_δ, which, as we see from equation (11.29), increases with Re_x. Thus, any zero pressure gradient boundary layer undergoes transition if it extends far enough downstream. However, provided that the disturbance level is not too high, the range in which the Reynolds number is high enough for boundary layer formation but low enough for laminar flow is significant.

11.4 Boundary layer separation

We shall not enter into a discussion of the very large amount of work that has been done to extend the ideas of the last section to less simple distributions of $u_0(x)$ (and to three-dimensional and unsteady boundary layers). There is, however, an important phenomenon, known as boundary layer separation, which we must consider physically, if not mathematically. It can occur when the pressure is increasing with distance downstream; that is when

$$dp_0/dx > 0 \qquad (11.30)$$

and so

$$du_0/dx < 0 \qquad (11.31)$$

A pressure gradient of this sort is called adverse (the opposite is called favourable). The phenomenon may thus occur, for example, on the walls of a diverging channel and on the rear part of an obstacle placed in a flow.

In an adverse pressure gradient, all fluid particles are losing kinetic energy as they travel downstream. Those close to the wall have less energy initially than those in the free stream as a result of viscous action. The pressure gradient can thus bring them to rest at a distance downstream where u_0 is still appreciable. Further downstream the pressure gradient pushes fluid close to the wall in the opposite direction from the mainstream. The result is a sequence of velocity profiles of the general form shown in Fig. 11.3(a). The corresponding pattern of streamlines is shown in Fig. 11.3(b). The point marked S in each figure is known as the separation point.

Figure 11.4 is a photograph of two streamlines (streaklines in steady flow) in a region of separation, for comparison with Fig. 11.3(b). The streamlines originate at dye sources close to the wall on either side of the separation point.

If the wall has a sharp corner, separation will normally occur there. Otherwise, it occurs at a position without special characteristics; the wall on which the separation was occurring in Fig. 11.4 was flat, the adverse pressure gradient being produced by a protuberance some distance downstream (out of the picture to the right).

Both laminar and turbulent boundary layers can separate. (In the latter case, the velocity profiles and streamlines in Fig. 11.3 must be interpreted as means.) Laminar layers usually (depending on the initial velocity profile) require only a relatively short region of adverse pressure gradient to produce separation. Turbulent layers separate less readily.

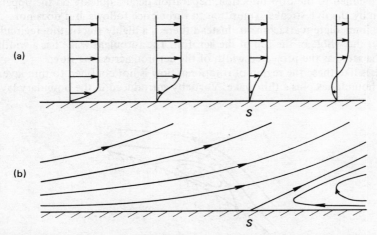

Figure 11.3 (a) Velocity profiles during boundary layer separation; (b) corresponding streamline pattern.

Figure 11.4   Streamlines in separating flow.

The overall flow pattern, when separation occurs, depends greatly on the particular flow. The upstream flow behind the separation point is normally fed by recirculation of the separating fluid, but little can be said in general beyond this. In some cases of laminar separation, the consequences are only local. The separated boundary layer is much more unstable than the previous attached one and transition to turbulence may occur very quickly after separation. The turbulent region may then reattach to the wall (for reasons to be discussed in Section 22.7). The result is a *mean* streamline pattern of the form shown in Fig. 11.5. Downstream the boundary layer is turbulent. We saw in Chapter 3 (Fig. 3.12) that there is a Reynolds number range — 3×10^5 to 3×10^6 — in which this sequence of events occurs on a circular cylinder.

When local reattachment does not occur, the consequences of separation are much more extensive. Chapter 3 has again provided an example — the formation of attached eddies at all values of the Reynolds number above about 4 (although at the lower Reynolds number end it is hardly a boundary layer that is separating). Figure 11.6 shows another example — the flow past an aerofoil (see Chapter 12) sharply inclined to the flow direction. Separation occurs quickly on the upper side, as shown by the dye streaks. Transition to turbulence follows, but does not produce immediate reattachment. Instead there is a highly fluctuating recirculating flow over the whole of the top of the aerofoil. The turbulent wake has a width about the same as the projected width of the aerofoil across the flow.

In cases like these the region of rotational flow is not confined to thin layers next to boundaries plus a thin wake. Vorticity introduced in the boundary layers is

Figure 11.5   Mean streamline pattern in laminar separation followed by turbulent reattachment.

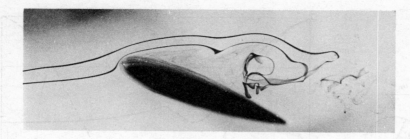

Figure 11.6   Flow over an aerofoil at large angle of attack (view is slightly oblique from above and front).

carried by the separated flow into regions that one would suppose to be irrotational in obtaining the inviscid flow solution. The presence of separation thus significantly modifies the inviscid flow, and the assumption that the inviscid flow can be analysed without reference to the boundary layers (except as a reason for ignoring the no-slip condition) breaks down. As an example, consider the observation that, over a wide Reynolds number range, separation on a circular cylinder occurs upstream of the maximum width (Fig. 3.12). On the inviscid flow solution for flow past a circular cylinder this is a region of favourable pressure gradient (Fig. 11.7). Inviscid flow is still occurring outside the boundary layer and wake, but not that particular inviscid flow solution.

11.5 Drag on bluff bodies

Figure 11.7 includes a measured pressure distribution over the surface of a cylinder. It can be seen that, as a result of the boundary layer separation, the rear region (around $\theta = 180°$) is at a much lower pressure than indicated by the inviscid flow solution. The difference between this pressure and that at the front (around $\theta = 0°$) produces a drag on the cylinder. At high Reynolds numbers, this drag is much larger than the one produced by the viscous stress over the surface. Thus for bluff bodies, such as a circular cylinder, the inapplicability of d'Alembert's 'paradox' arises primarily from the indirect effect of viscous action on the pressure distribution and only secondarily from direct viscous stresses.

Over a wide range of high Reynolds number, the drag coefficient for a bluff body varies little. One example is Fig. 3.14, and it is a useful general rule in a variety of situations that the drag is roughly proportional to the square of the speed. We have seen in Section 7.3 (equation (7.21)) that constancy of the drag coefficient is predicted by dimensional considerations if one assumes that the viscosity is not a relevant parameter. At first sight, d'Alembert's paradox renders this result useless. However, we can now see how it relates to observation. Over the Reynolds number range concerned, the separation point moves little. The pressure distribution, like that shown in Fig. 11.7, is thus always much the same. The pressure differences are proportional to the square of the speed, and, since these generate most of the drag, that has the same proportionality. The drag coefficient is not completely constant because of small changes in the pressure distribution and

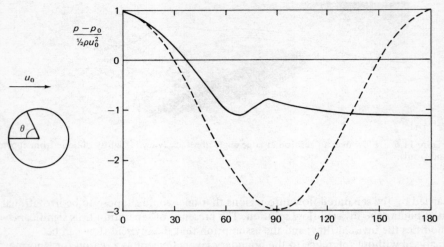

Figure 11.7 Pressure distribution on a circular cylinder. Broken line: inviscid flow solution. Solid line: distribution measured at Re = 1.9×10^5 (data obtained by Flachsbart, given in Ref. [8]).

because of the small contribution of the viscous stress. When the separation point moves substantially, as when the boundary layer becomes turbulent, the pressure distribution is changed markedly and equation (7.21) breaks down completely — as already discussed in Section 3.4.

11.6 Streamlining

The fact that the drag on an obstacle at high Reynolds number is primarily due to the redistribution of the pressure from the inviscid flow distribution, as a result of separation, has important practical implications. If separation can be delayed till near the rear, or eliminated altogether except right at the rear where boundary layers from opposite sides meet, the drag will be very low; the pressure forces on the front and rear will almost balance. This can be achieved with two-dimensional and axisymmetric shapes such as that shown in Fig. 11.8. Such shapes are said to be streamlined. The drag on a two-dimensional streamlined body can be as low as 1/15 of that on the cylinder of the same thickness. The most important feature is the slowly tapering tail. This is the reason why streamlining of a railway engine with a train behind it makes only marginal difference. On the other hand, it is essential

Figure 11.8   Streamlined body.

to their performance that the wings and fuselage of an aeroplane and the parts of a submarine should have streamlined profiles. It is also apparent that Fig. 11.8 resembles the shape of many marine creatures — fish, dolphins, etc.

11.7 Wakes

The fluid that has become rotational in a boundary layer retains this property as it travels downstream. The flow past an obstacle thus departs from irrotational theory not only around the obstacle but also behind it. The latter region of rotational flow is called the wake.

Behind a flat plate or a streamlined body the initial width of this wake is the thickness of the boundary layers at the downstream end of the body (Fig. 11.9). Behind a body on which separation occurs the initial wake width is governed by the separation process and is much more related to the width of the body itself rather than to the boundary layer thickness. Beyond these remarks, the structure of the wake immediately behind the obstacle (the near-wake) depends too much on the details of the particular obstacle for any general discussion to be useful.

After some distance, the velocity profile always develops into the general shape shown in Fig. 3.13, regardless of the geometry of the obstacle. As we saw in Section 3.4 the reduction of momentum transport is related to the drag. The properties of far-wakes can be considered in terms of the properties of this profile. Many of the features of the flow behind cylinders described in Chapter 3 are observed also in the wakes of other obstacles; as an example, Fig. 11.10 shows a vortex street in the wake of a flat plate.

When the Reynolds number is high, a wake is long and thin — for the same reason as before that the fluid travels a long distance downstream whilst the vorticity diffuses only a small distance sideways. The boundary layer equations can thus be applied to wakes — a fact that we shall use when considering turbulent wakes in Section 22.4. The solution for steady laminar flow will not be considered; the procedure is similar to that for jets described below [22].

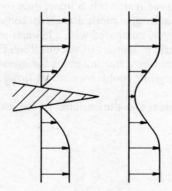

Figure 11.9 Boundary layer and wake velocity profiles at trailing edge of streamlined body (schematic).

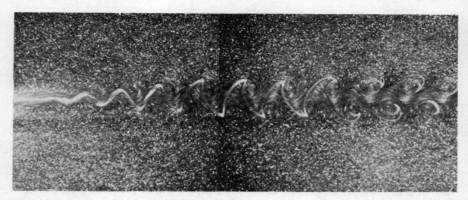

Figure 11.10   Vortex street behind flat plate at zero incidence with Reynolds number based on plate length of 6600. Flow visualization is combination of dye released from plate and aluminium powder suspended in fluid. From Ref. [246].

11.8 Jets

A jet is produced when fluid is ejected from an orifice. We are concerned here with the case when the ambient fluid into which the jet emerges is the same fluid as the jet itself. Because of their simplicity, the geometries that have been most investigated are a circular orifice giving an axisymmetric jet and a long thin slit giving a two-dimensional jet. The former is obviously the easier experimental configuration, but experiments with the latter have been performed; care is needed to make the jet nearly uniform along its length.

At low Reynolds numbers, the fluid from an orifice spreads out in all directions. At high Reynolds numbers, with which we are concerned here, a jet, like a wake, is long and thin; the equations of motion may be used in the form of the boundary layer approximation.

Jets become unstable at too low a Reynolds number for the laminar flow solution of these equations to be observed. We will, however, take a look at the solution for a two-dimensional jet for three reasons: it is interesting to see a solution like the Blasius solution but not requiring numerical analysis; some results for turbulent jets (Section 22.2) may usefully be compared with a laminar jet; and in Section 11.9, we can illustrate certain basic properties of viscous flows in this context. Nor is the result wholly academic; it can be a starting point for investigations of the instability. What actually happens in high Reynolds number jet flows will be considered in Section 19.2.

The equations for a laminar two-dimensional jet are just as for the Blasius boundary layer

$$\frac{\partial u}{\partial x} + \frac{\partial v}{\partial y} = 0 \tag{11.32}$$

$$u\,\frac{\partial u}{\partial x} + v\,\frac{\partial u}{\partial y} = \nu\,\frac{\partial^2 u}{\partial y^2} \tag{11.33}$$

(with x in the jet direction and y across the slit from which it emerges). There is no pressure gradient for reasons parallel to those considered in Section 11.2; on the boundary layer approximation the effective pressure gradient is that imposed from outside and this is zero since the ambient fluid is at rest. The ejection of the fluid from the orifice will normally have been achieved by maintaining a higher pressure behind it. This will provide the fluid with its momentum, but the pressure variations do not extend significantly downstream of the orifice.

The difference from the boundary layer solution lies in the boundary conditions, which are

$$u \to 0 \quad \text{as} \quad y \to \infty$$

$$\partial u / \partial y = 0 \quad \text{and} \quad v = 0 \quad \text{at} \quad y = 0 \tag{11.34}$$

expressing the facts that the ambient fluid is at rest and the jet is symmetrical about its centre plane. (See also footnote to Section 11.9, p. 116.)

The procedure for solution closely follows that for the boundary layer. It is again assumed that the velocity profile is a similar shape at different distances downstream. However, the velocity scale, as well as the jet width, can now vary with x; the form of successive velocity profiles is shown schematically in Fig. 11.11. Hence, the velocity profile is taken to be of the form

$$u = u_{\max} g(y/\Delta) = u_{\max} g(\eta) \tag{11.35}$$

where both the maximum speed $u_{\max}$ and Δ (proportional to the jet-width δ) are functions of x. Drawing on our experience with the boundary layer solution we take them to be proportional to powers of x:

$$u_{\max} \propto x^m, \quad \Delta \propto x^n \tag{11.36}$$

One relationship between m and n is obtained from the requirement that the inertia term and the viscous term must vary in the same way with x.

$$u \partial u / \partial x \propto x^{2m-1}; \quad \nu \partial^2 u / \partial y^2 \propto x^{m-2n} \tag{11.37}$$

and so

$$2m - 1 = m - 2n \tag{11.38}$$

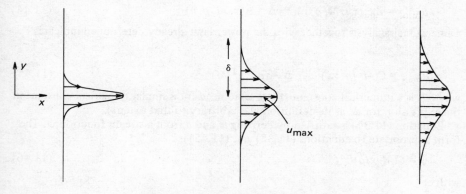

Figure 11.11   Development of a jet.

(This is entirely parallel to the derivation for the boundary layer that $\Delta \propto x^{1/2}$, but presented in a somewhat different way.)

A second relationship is obtained from the fact that the total momentum per unit time passing every cross-section of the jet must be the same. This is a statement of momentum conservation for the jet as whole, which must apply since the jet does not exert any force on any external body. (Its relationship to equation (11.33) for the momentum of individual fluid particles will be discussed in Section 11.9.) Since the jet is two-dimensional we consider the momentum per unit length in the z-direction. The momentum per unit volume is ρu and the rate at which it is being transported downstream is u. Hence, the total rate of momentum transport at any x is

$$M = \int_{-\infty}^{\infty} \rho u^2 \, dy \tag{11.39}$$

M is conveniently used as a measure of the strength of the jet. Conservation of momentum indicates that

$$dM/dx = 0 \tag{11.40}$$

Substituting (11.35) in (11.39),

$$M = \rho u_{max}^2 \Delta \int_{-\infty}^{\infty} g^2 \, d\eta \propto x^{2m+n} \tag{11.41}$$

Hence,

$$2m + n = 0 \tag{11.42}$$

From equations (11.38) and (11.42) together we have

$$m = -\frac{1}{3}, \quad n = \frac{2}{3} \tag{11.43}$$

The ways in which the maximum velocity and the jet-width vary with x have been determined.

The parameters determining the velocity profile at any x are x itself, the jet momentum, and the properties of the fluid:

$$u_{max} = u_{max}(x, M, \rho, \nu); \quad \Delta = \Delta(x, M, \rho, \nu) \tag{11.44}$$

Dimensional analysis together with the power laws already determined indicates that

$$u_{max} = C(M^2/\rho^2 \nu x)^{1/3}; \quad \Delta = (\rho \nu^2 x^2/M)^{1/3} \tag{11.45}$$

where C is a numerical constant (there is no need for a similar numerical constant in the expression for Δ, as its definition was arbitrary to that extent).

Equation (11.32) is satisfied by deriving u and v from a stream function ψ. The form appropriate to equations (11.35) and (11.45) is

$$\psi = C(M\nu x/\rho)^{1/3} f \tag{11.46}$$

with

$$f' = g \tag{11.47}$$

Substituting in equation (11.33) gives

$$\frac{3}{C}f''' + ff'' + f'^2 = 0 \tag{11.48}$$

with the boundary conditions

$$
\begin{aligned}
f = f'' = 0 \quad &\text{at } \eta = 0 \\
f' \to 0 \quad &\text{as } \eta \to \infty
\end{aligned}
\tag{11.49}
$$

This can be integrated directly to give

$$f = A \tanh(AC\eta/6) \tag{11.50}$$

and so

$$g = \frac{1}{6}A^2 C \operatorname{sech}^2(AC\eta/6) \tag{11.51}$$

A appears as an arbitrary constant, but substitution in equation (11.39) indicates that

$$(AC)^3 = 9/2 \tag{11.52}$$

Hence the solution for the velocity profile is

$$u = \left(\frac{3M^2}{32\rho^2 vx}\right)^{1/3} \operatorname{sech}^2\left[y\left(\frac{M}{48\rho v^2 x^2}\right)^{1/3}\right] \tag{11.53}$$

Although, as remarked before, this flow is not observable because of instability, it may be supposed that this result is to be interpreted in the following way. $u_{\max} = \infty$ at $x = 0$, and the solution will not be valid in this region. A real jet starts off with a finite velocity but a velocity profile different from that given by the theory. As it travels downstream, the profile tends to the theoretical one, which will occur asymptotically with an origin of x displaced from the jet orifice (either upstream or downstream depending on the initial profile). The solution has the property that

$$\frac{d}{dx}\int_{-\infty}^{\infty} \rho u\,dy > 0 \tag{11.54}$$

Hence, the amount of fluid being transported downstream by the jet increases with distance downstream. The jet draws fluid into itself from the sides — a process known as entrainment. Far enough downstream, only a small proportion of the fluid in the jet is fluid that came out of the orifice. We shall see in Section 11.9 that this result follows from rather general considerations and is thus not a property of the particular solution.

It is for this reason that M, and not the rate of efflux from the orifice, is used as a measure of the jet strength.

The reader may have noticed that no boundary condition on v at large y was applied. Once one knows about the entrainment the reason is apparent; such a boundary condition would overconstrain the system.

11.9 Momentum and energy in viscous flow

The foregoing theory of a laminar jet provides a convenient context for a few
further remarks about the basic properties of the equations of viscous flow.

Equation (11.40) was established by applying the principle of momentum
conservation to the jet as a whole, a different type of procedure from those
used so far. Although the equation follows directly from the laws of mechanics,
one would expect it to be related to the equation for the momentum of a fluid
particle and we now see how it is derived from this.

$$\frac{dM}{dx} = \frac{d}{dx} \int_{-\infty}^{\infty} \rho u^2 \, dy = 2\rho \int_{-\infty}^{\infty} u \frac{\partial u}{\partial x} \, dy \tag{11.55}$$

From equation (11.33)

$$\int_{-\infty}^{\infty} u \frac{\partial u}{\partial x} \, dy + \int_{-\infty}^{\infty} v \frac{\partial u}{\partial y} \, dy = \nu \int_{-\infty}^{\infty} \frac{\partial^2 u}{\partial y^2} \, dy = \nu \left[\frac{\partial u}{\partial y} \right]_{-\infty}^{\infty} = 0 \tag{11.56}$$

since the velocity gradient is zero far outside the jet. Also

$$\int_{-\infty}^{\infty} v \frac{\partial u}{\partial y} \, dy = [uv]_{-\infty}^{\infty} - \int_{-\infty}^{\infty} u \frac{\partial v}{\partial y} \, dy = 0 + \int_{-\infty}^{\infty} u \frac{\partial u}{\partial x} \, dy \tag{11.57}$$

using continuity. The two terms on the left-hand side of equation (11.56) are thus
equal to one another, and so

$$dM/dx = 0 \tag{11.58}$$

This result is thus shown to be an integrated form of (an approximation to)
the Navier–Stokes equation.† Such integrated forms are used in a variety of contexts. In general (e.g. when the boundary layer approximation does not apply or
when there is a boundary on which the flow exerts a force), they are more complicated, but we shall not consider the general case in this book.

It is interesting to discuss kinetic energy similarly. An equation for the energy of
a fluid particle is obtained in general by taking the scalar product of the Navier–
Stokes equation with **u**. In a case such as the jet (where the two-dimensional
boundary layer approximation applies and there is no pressure gradient), only one
velocity component contributes significantly to the energy; the equation is obtained
by multiplying equation (11.33) by u:

$$\frac{1}{2} u \frac{\partial (u^2)}{\partial x} + \frac{1}{2} v \frac{\partial (u^2)}{\partial y} = \nu u \frac{\partial^2 u}{\partial y^2} = -\nu \left(\frac{\partial u}{\partial y} \right)^2 + \frac{1}{2} \nu \frac{\partial^2 (u^2)}{\partial y^2} \tag{11.59}$$

The left-hand side is the rate of change of kinetic energy (per unit mass) following
a fluid particle. The right-hand side has two parts: one is essentially negative and so
represents dissipation of energy; the other can have either sign and has the nature of
a diffusion of energy down the energy gradient.

---

†It may be thought surprising that the laminar jet solution uses both equation (11.33) and an
integrated form of it. The extra information involved in the latter is the boundary condition
$\partial u/\partial y \to 0$ as $y \to \infty$. The solution, equation (11.53), satisfies this, although it was not used
explicitly. Equation (11.40) could be omitted if this condition were used explicitly, but the
procedure adopted much simplifies the determination of the exponents m and n.

We can learn more from the integrated form. The rate of transport of kinetic energy in the x-direction by the jet is

$$E = \frac{1}{2}\rho \int_{-\infty}^{\infty} u^3 \, dy \tag{11.60}$$

By a procedure similar to that for dM/dx, it can be shown that

$$\frac{dE}{dx} = -\mu \int_{-\infty}^{\infty} \left(\frac{\partial u}{\partial y}\right)^2 dy \tag{11.61}$$

and thus is negative, as could have been anticipated.

Alternatively the argument can be turned round to show that since dE/dx must be negative, μ must be positive. A fluid with a negative viscosity coefficient could gain mechanical energy from heat in a way that would violate the second law of thermodynamics.

The discussion has been formulated in terms of a two-dimensional jet, but, from their physical significance, we expect the results to apply generally. For a jet of arbitrary cross-section, the momentum and energy transports are

$$M = \int \rho u^2 \, dS, \quad E = \frac{1}{2} \int \rho u^3 \, dS \tag{11.62}$$

dS is an element of cross-sectional area perpendicular to the main flow direction, and the integrations are carried out over the whole cross-section. M and E are respectively constant and decreasing with distance downstream.

These results enable us to make some general remarks about the action of viscosity on momentum and energy. The jet illustrates these points well because the complicating effects of boundaries and of a pressure gradient are absent. Viscous action tends towards equalizing the momentum of different fluid particles. This is a redistribution of the momentum which conserves the total. The effect on the kinetic energy consists partly of a dissipation that reduces the energy at every point and partly of a redistribution, similar to the momentum redistribution, with no net effect. Some parts of the fluid can be gaining kinetic energy by viscous action, the redistribution more than counteracting the dissipation, but on average there is a loss. The situation is analogous to the collision of inelastic bodies: conservation of total momentum together with a redistribution such that the momentum of different bodies is more nearly equal results in a loss of total kinetic energy.

From the facts that

$$\frac{d}{dx} \int u^2 \, dS = 0 \tag{11.63}$$

and

$$\frac{d}{dx} \int u^3 \, dS < 0 \tag{11.64}$$

one may infer that

$$\frac{d}{dx} \int u \, dS > 0 \tag{11.65}$$

This is a rigorous argument if the profiles are similar at different x (as in equation (11.35)), a plausibility argument otherwise. Hence, the fact that a jet entrains ambient fluid is a consequence of the combination of momentum conservation and energy dissipation.

12
Lift

12.1 Introduction

We have seen that the drag on an obstacle placed in a flow arises essentially from viscous action (Sections 10.5, 11.5 and 11.6), whereas the generation of lift on a suitably shaped obstacle can be understood, at least in a general sense, from inviscid theory (Section 10.6). In fact viscous action also enters into the process of lift generation in an essential, although more subtle, way. We now look at the reasons for and consequences of this.

Lift can be obtained either by appropriate asymmetrical shaping as discussed in Section 10.6, or by having a symmetrical body inclined to the flow direction, or, of course, by a combination of asymmetry and inclination (Fig. 12.1).

The curvature of the centre line in Fig. 12.1(a) and (d) is called the camber. The inclination angle α is called the angle of attack. The simplest geometry giving lift is an inclined flat plate (Fig. 12.1(b)). However, boundary layer separation at the sharp leading edge results in a 'stalled' flow configuration (see below) except for very small values of α and this does not provide a good context for a discussion of the important ideas. We turn instead to those shapes (known as aerofoils) that have been developed specially to produce high lift; our understanding of the subject has been strongly influenced by the obvious application to aircraft wings. An aerofoil is a slender body with a rounded leading edge and a sharp trailing edge (Fig. 12.1(a), (c) and (d)); we shall see that these features help to provide a good lifting behaviour as well as helping to reduce drag (Section 11.6). A well-designed aerofoil can produce a much larger lift than drag, as is illustrated by Fig. 12.2.

It will be convenient in the following discussion to use the standard names for the different dimensions of an aerofoil, as shown in Fig. 12.3. It will also be convenient to talk of the top and bottom of the aerofoil with the lift thought of as upwards, although the direction of the vertical does not enter into the dynamics; in

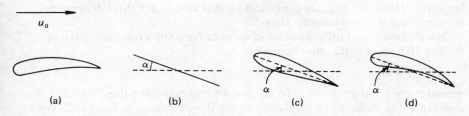

Figure 12.1 Examples of lifting configurations.

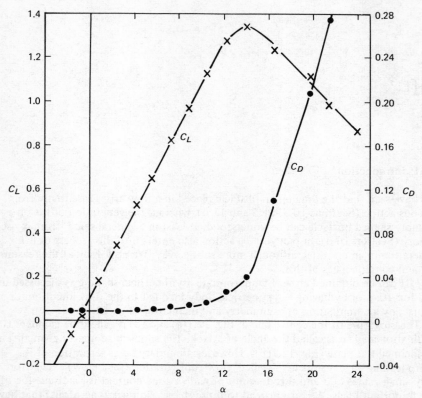

Figure 12.2   Example of variation with angle of attack of lift coefficient and drag coefficient for an aerofoil. Note different scales for C_D and C_L. (Aerofoil type RAF 34 at Re based on chord of 4.5×10^6; measurements by Relf, Jones, and Bell, given in Ref. [8].)

general, a lift is any force perpendicular to the direction of relative motion between a body and a fluid.

12.2 Two-dimensional aerofoils

The first part of the following discussion applies to strictly two-dimensional flow. This should obviously be relevant to the motion around a body, such as a wing, of large span. However, there are complications that arise in *any* three-dimensional system, which we must consider later.

The explanation of lift generation in terms of Bernoulli's equation, given in Section 10.6, implies that the circulation

$$\Gamma = \oint \mathbf{u} \cdot d\mathbf{l} \tag{12.1}$$

around the aerofoil is non-zero. To see this, we may consider a thin (thickness ≪ chord) aerofoil inclined at a small angle to the flow direction, so that nearly every point of the surface is nearly parallel to the flow direction (Fig. 12.4). The upward

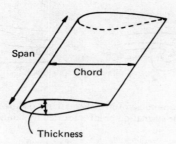

Figure 12.3   Aerofoil terminology.

force (per unit length in the spanwise direction) on the element dx is $(p_B - p_T)\,dx$, where p_B and p_T are the pressures below and above the aerofoil at this station along the chord. Bernoulli's equation gives

$$p_B - p_T = \tfrac{1}{2}\rho(u_T^2 - u_B^2) = \tfrac{1}{2}\rho(u_T + u_B)(u_T - u_B) \tag{12.2}$$

For a thin aerofoil, the variations of the velocity from the free-stream velocity u_0 will be small, and we may approximate this by

$$p_B - p_T = \rho u_0(u_T - u_B) \tag{12.3}$$

Hence the total lift per unit span,

$$L = \rho u_0 \int_0^c (u_T - u_B)\,dx \tag{12.4}$$

The circulation round a contour following the surface of the aerofoil (physically round a contour just outside the boundary layer) may be approximated by

$$\Gamma = \int_0^c u_B\,dx + \int_c^0 u_T\,dx = -\int_0^c (u_T - u_B)\,dx \tag{12.5}$$

Thus

$$L = -\rho u_0 \Gamma \tag{12.6}$$

Γ is the circulation round any loop enclosing the aerofoil (since the circulation $\oint \mathbf{u}\cdot d\mathbf{l} = \int \boldsymbol{\omega}\cdot d\mathbf{S}$ round any loop not enclosing it is zero for irrotational flow).

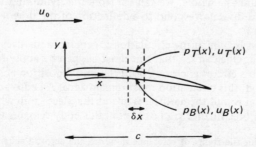

Figure 12.4   Definition sketch for discussion of lift and circulation of a thin aerofoil.

Figure 12.5 Inviscid flow around aerofoil (schematic): (a) flow without circulation; (b) flow with circulation, in which rear stagnation point is located by boundary layer separation.

This is an example of a general exact result of inviscid irrotational flow theory, the Kutta–Zhukovksii (or Joukovski) theorem. The force per unit length on any two-dimensional body in relative motion to the ambient fluid with velocity u_0 and with circulation Γ round it is

$$L = -\rho u_0 \Gamma \tag{12.7}$$

acting at right angles to the direction of u_0. (The sign corresponds to the convention that u_0 is positive when the fluid moves past a stationary obstacle from left to right or the obstacle moves through stationary ambient fluid from right to left; Γ is positive when the circulation is anticlockwise; and L is positive upwards.)

This much can be said without reference to viscosity. However, the generation of the circulation in the first place requires viscous action. This is apparent from the Kelvin circulation theorem (Section 10.2) if we consider an aerofoil started from rest in stationary fluid – so that there is no initial circulation. There is always a solution of the inviscid flow equations with no circulation. For a cambered and/or inclined aerofoil that would normally generate lift, this solution has the rear stagnation point some distance ahead of the trailing edge on the upper surface (Fig. 12.5(a)). This is the flow pattern† which actually occurs immediately after motion starts and which would necessarily occur at all subsequent times in a truly inviscid fluid. However, boundary layer processes change it. The boundary layer on the lower side separates at the trailing edge; the eddy so produced interacts with the inviscid flow to make its stagnation point coincide with the separation point (Fig. 12.5(b)). The new inviscid flow, outside the boundary layers, now involves circulation, of an amount determined by the geometry of the aerofoil in conjunction with the requirement that the rear stagnation point is at the trailing edge.

Any force on an obstacle must be balanced by a rate of momentum change integrated over the fluid as a whole. We can see from the figure that the movement of the stagnation point does correspond to a deflection of the flow in the appropriate direction.

The starting process by which the circulation is generated involves discharge of vorticity into the fluid. One can see that this must happen by applying the Kelvin circulation theorem to a circuit enclosing both the initial position and the present position of the aerofoil; this circulation must remain zero. An eddy, of opposite sense to the circulation round the aerofoil is left at the place from which it started. In principle, if one ignores further viscous action, this eddy remains there for ever.

---

†The pattern is drawn for the frame of reference in which the aerofoil is at rest, although the simplest way of producing the effects described is to start the aerofoil moving.

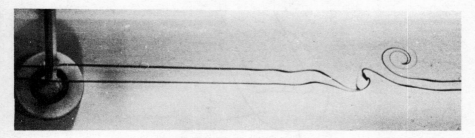

Figure 12.6   Eddy produced by changing angle of attack of aerofoil. Flow visualization: two dye lines originating far upstream.

Figure 12.6 shows a demonstration of this effect. Instead of starting the motion, the aerofoil is fixed in a steady flow but its angle of attack is suddenly changed (actually from one sign to the other to produce a large effect). The resulting change in lift corresponds to a change in the circulation and a 'starting eddy' must be generated as described above. The photograph, taken when the disturbance produced by the rotation of the aerofoil has travelled some distance downstream, shows that the pattern, although somewhat complicated, is dominated by an eddy circulating in the opposite sense to the change in circulation round the aerofoil. (The Reynolds number was comparatively low to avoid complications due to wake instability.)

We return now to considering an aerofoil in steady motion. When the angle of attack becomes large, boundary layer separation occurs on the upper surface close to the leading edge, giving a flow pattern like that shown in Fig. 11.6. The flow is said to have stalled. The pressure in the separated region is less than that below the aerofoil (around the front stagnation point). There is thus still some lift, but much less than before stalling; there is also a sharp increase in the drag (Fig. 12.2).

12.3 Three-dimensional aerofoils

The relationship between lift and circulation gives rise to further complications in three-dimensional situations, i.e. for an aerofoil of finite span. The existence of circulation in combination with Stokes's theorem,

$$\oint \mathbf{u} \cdot d\mathbf{l} = \int \boldsymbol{\omega} \cdot d\mathbf{S} \tag{12.8}$$

implies that there must be vorticity generated in the vicinity of the aerofoil (but outside the boundary layer); the surface over which the right-hand integral is carried out can extend over an end of the aerofoil as shown in Fig. 12.7. In other words, the concept of circulation in an entirely irrotational motion is meaningful only for a multiply-connected geometry.

The vorticity is generated near the ends of the aerofoil. Because of the pressure difference, $p_B - p_T$, fluid flows around each end from bottom to top. Vorticity is produced in the boundary layers associated with this motion and is then carried into the wake by the main-stream, giving the pattern shown in Fig. 12.8.

The fact that div $\boldsymbol{\omega} \equiv 0$ is in principle satisfied by the longitudinal vortices from

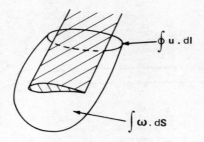

Figure 12.7   Loop and surface integrals at end of aerofoil.

the two ends of an aerofoil extending back to the position where the aerofoil started and there joining up through the starting vortex, as shown in Fig. 12.8. However, as they go back a long distance, the vortices become so diffuse and weak, through the action of viscosity, that there is no appreciable motion associated with them.

Usually, an aerofoil tapers towards its ends and the circulation drops gradually to zero; the longitudinal vorticity in the wake is then more spread out in the spanwise direction. Lift on a body of which the span is not long compared with the thickness cannot, of course, be discussed in these terms at all. The detailed dynamics of the boundary layer must then be considered, the generation of a wake with longitudinal vorticity again being an important part of the process.

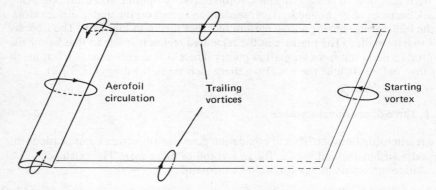

Figure 12.8   Schematic diagram of circulation, trailing vortices, and starting vortex.

12.4 Spinning bodies

It is well known that a spinning ball is deflected sideways. Studies have been made of the lift force generated both on rotating cylinders (the Magnus effect) and rotating spheres (the Robins effect) [57].

A cylinder rotating about its axis and moving through a fluid in a direction perpendicular to its axis experiences a force perpendicular to both the direction of motion and the axis. Like the lift on an aerofoil, this phenomenon can be under-

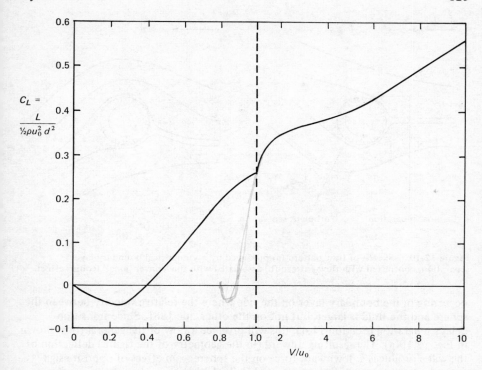

Figure 12.9 Experimental variation of lift coefficient with relative rotation rate for spinning sphere. Note change in abscissa scale by factor of 8 at $V/u_0 = 1$. Curve is average of data in Reynolds number range $1.5 \times 10^3 - 1.1 \times 10^5$ from Refs. [57, 88, 173].

stood through Bernoulli's equation — by working in a frame of reference in which the axis is at rest and so the flow is steady. On the side on which the cylinder moves in the same direction as the flow, the fluid velocity is increased and so the pressure is reduced; on the other side the velocity is decreased and the pressure increased. There is thus a force acting on the cylinder from the latter to the former. But, again as with the aerofoil, it is necessary to invoke viscous action to understand why the rotation of the cylinder should produce a corresponding circulation of fluid. Indeed, but for the no-slip condition the flow would make no distinction between a rotating cylinder and a stationary one. At relatively low rotation rates, complications, like those described below for a sphere, can occur.

A rotating sphere also experiences a force perpendicular to both the rotation axis and its motion. As for an aerofoil, the three-dimensional problem is inherently more complicated than the two-dimensional. Figure 12.9 shows observations of the variation of the lift coefficient with the ratio of the circumferential speed of the sphere (V) to the flow speed (u_0). At large V/u_0, the behaviour can be understood qualitatively in the way described for a rotating cylinder, but any quantitative information must come from experiment.

At low V/u_0, the force reverses in direction (although this may not occur for all Reynolds numbers). This effect is probably the result of transition to turbulence

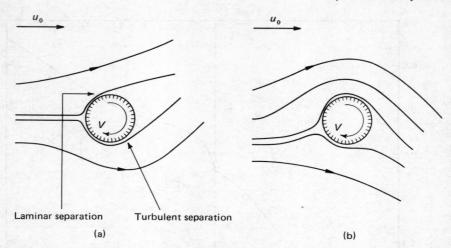

Figure 12.10   Sketch of flow pattern (a) produced by asymmetrical boundary layer separation, contrasted with flow pattern (b) associated with the 'conventional' Robins effect.

occurring in the boundary layer on the side where the relative velocity between the sphere and the fluid is larger, but not on the other side [88]. Since transition delays separation (Section 11.4), this will produce a flow of the general form shown in Fig. 12.10(a). The resulting upward (in the geometry of the figure) deflection of the wake produces a downward force on the sphere — an effect of opposite sign from the 'conventional' Robins effect (Fig. 12.10(b)).

13
Thermal Flows: Basic Equations and Concepts

13.1 Introduction

We turn now from the isothermal flows that we have been considering in previous chapters to flows in which temperature variations are introduced. The practical importance of such flows needs little illustration. The use of moving fluids to transport or remove heat is well known, ranging from the circulation of coolant through a nuclear reactor to the mounting of a power transistor on a block with cooling fins. Equally apparent is the importance of thermal processes in meteorology and other branches of geophysics; indeed, the ultimate source of energy for almost all atmospheric motions and much of the oceanic circulation is solar radiation.

In these examples, and in the more fundamental situations to be considered in this book, the temperature variations are introduced by some process independent of the flow dynamics. We are not concerned here with flow induced temperature variations, arising from adiabatic expansion or compression or from viscous dissipation. (The conditions in which such effects are negligible are considered in Section 5.8 and in the appendix to Chapter 14.) Most commonly, the temperature variations are introduced through temperature differences between boundaries, or between a boundary and ambient fluid. Occasionally, they are produced by internal heat generation, which can arise from a variety of causes such as radioactivity, absorption of thermal radiation, and release of latent heat as water vapour condenses. Heating and cooling at either the boundaries or within the fluid results in the temperature being a continuous function of position.

The name convection is given to this general category of flows. The same name is sometimes used for more specific processes occurring within such flows; however, we shall use it in this book only in the general sense. Another name for the general topic is heat transfer, used particularly of course when the effect of the flow in transporting heat is of importance.

A closely related topic is that of flow with concentration variations or mass transfer. We shall not be considering this systematically in this book, but brief discussion of the analogy will be given in Section 13.5.

13.2 Equations of convection [8, 33]

The temperature variations within a convective flow give rise to variations in the properties of the fluid, in the density and viscosity for example. An analysis including the full effects of these is so complicated that some approximation becomes essential. The equations are commonly used in a form known as the Boussinesq approximation. Here, we shall make this approximation without considering just when it is valid or demonstrating the fact that its different parts are internally self-consistent. These matters will be considered in some detail for the particular case of free convection in the appendix to Chapter 14; this will illustrate the procedure. In part, the Boussinesq approximation is the counterpart for convection of the incompressibility approximation for the flows considered hitherto.

In the Boussinesq approximation, variations of all fluid properties other than the density are ignored completely. Variations of the density are ignored except insofar as they give rise to a gravitational force. Thus the continuity equation is used in its constant density form

$$\nabla \cdot \mathbf{u} = 0 \qquad (13.1)$$

Similarly, $\rho D\mathbf{u}/Dt$ is replaced by $\rho_0 D\mathbf{u}/Dt$, with ρ_0 constant — chosen, for example, as the density at one typical position. However, a body force term is included to allow for the effect of gravity; that is in equation (5.21) one puts

$$\mathbf{F} = \rho \mathbf{g} \qquad (13.2)$$

We may anticipate that the density variations will be important here and write

$$\rho = \rho_0 + \Delta\rho \qquad (13.3)$$

Also the gravitational acceleration is derivable from a potential

$$\mathbf{g} = -\nabla \Phi \qquad (13.4)$$

(In most cases $\mathbf{g} = -g\hat{\mathbf{z}}$ and $\Phi = gz$, where z is taken vertically upwards, but this is, of course, not true on a global scale.) Hence

$$\mathbf{F} = -(\rho_0 + \Delta\rho)\nabla\Phi = -\nabla(\rho_0\Phi) + \Delta\rho\mathbf{g} \qquad (13.5)$$

If we introduce

$$P = p + \rho_0\Phi \qquad (13.6)$$

the Navier–Stokes equation (5.21) becomes

$$\rho_0 \frac{D\mathbf{u}}{Dt} = -\nabla P + \mu\nabla^2\mathbf{u} + \Delta\rho\mathbf{g} \qquad (13.7)$$

If $\Delta\rho = 0$, this is the same as the Navier–Stokes equation without a body force except that P has replaced p. Provided that the pressure does not appear explicitly in the boundary conditions, this change makes no difference. We have thus verified the conclusion considered more physically in Section 5.6, that the gravitational force is unimportant if the density is uniform. One merely has to correct for the hydrostatic pressure (the difference between p and P) if the actual pressure is required.

We are now concerned with cases in which $\Delta\rho \neq 0$, because of the temperature variations. As a further part of the Boussinesq approximation, the dependence of ρ on T is linearized,

$$\Delta\rho = -\alpha\rho_0\Delta T \qquad (13.8)$$

α is the coefficient of expansion of the fluid. Hence, the Boussinesq dynamical equation is

$$\frac{Du}{Dt} = -\frac{1}{\rho}\nabla p + \nu\nabla^2 u - g\alpha\Delta T \tag{13.9}$$

(where we have reverted to writing ρ and p for the quantities temporarily denoted by ρ_0 and P).

One requires in addition an equation for the temperature. In the spirit of the Boussinesq approximation, it is supposed that the fluid has a constant heat capacity per unit volume, ρC_p; then $\rho C_p DT/Dt$ is equal to the rate of heating per unit volume of a fluid particle. (The choice of C_p, the specific heat at constant pressure, is physically sensible, since the pressure is not free to respond directly to the heating process; for a proper justification, however, one needs to look at the detailed nature of the Boussinesq approximation — see the appendix to Chapter 14.) This heating is brought about by transfer of heat from neighbouring fluid particles by thermal conduction and sometimes also by internal heat generation. The corresponding terms in the thermal equation are analogous respectively to the viscous term and the body force term in the dynamical equation. The conductive heat flux

$$\mathbf{H} = -k \text{ grad } T \tag{13.10}$$

where k is the thermal conductivity of the fluid. Thus

$$\rho C_p DT/Dt = -\text{div } \mathbf{H} + J \tag{13.11}$$

where J is the rate of internal heat generation per unit volume. Taking k to be constant, equation (13.11) may be rewritten

$$\frac{\partial T}{\partial t} + \mathbf{u}\cdot\nabla T = \kappa\nabla^2 T + \frac{J}{\rho C_p} \tag{13.12}$$

where

$$\kappa = k/\rho C_p \tag{13.13}$$

κ is known as the thermal diffusivity or sometimes as the thermometric conductivity.

Equations (13.1), (13.9), and (13.12) constitute the basic equations of convection in the Boussinesq approximation. They are one vector and two scalar equations for the one vector and two scalar variables $\mathbf{u}$, p and ΔT. (Since T appears differentiated throughout equation (13.12) this is effectively an equation in ΔT, thus matching up with equation (13.9).)

It is useful to have names for the new terms. The additional term in the dynamical equation, $-g\alpha\Delta T$, is known as the buoyancy force† (even when ΔT is negative and the term represents the tendency for heavy fluid to sink). The two terms on the right-hand side of equation (13.12) have obvious names: the conduction term and the heat generation term. $\mathbf{u}\cdot\nabla T$, which represents the transport of heat by the motion, may be called the advection term. (It is often called the convection term, but it is convenient to have a separate name from the processes represented by the equations as a whole.)

---

† For a perfect gas $\alpha = 1/T$, and in texts concerned primarily with gases, the buoyancy term is often written $-g\Delta T/T$.

Equation (13.12) requires boundary conditions for the temperature field. The commonest type specifies the temperature of a boundary wall; the fluid right next to the wall must then also be at that temperature. There are, however, other types. As an example, we may mention the case in which the heat transfer through a wall is specified; the temperature gradient in the fluid is then fixed at the wall.

It is worth noting that thermal conduction plays an integral role in convection. For example, when heat is introduced into a fluid by heating a boundary wall, there is no advection of heat through the boundary; the fluid first gains heat entirely by conduction, although further from the wall advection may be the principal process. The traditional division of heat transfer processes into radiation, conduction, and convection is not completely sharp. Whenever convection occurs, it and conduction become parts of a single process.

13.3 Classification of convective flows

Evidently a wide range of dynamical behaviours is to be expected, depending on the importance of the buoyancy force relative to the other terms in equation (13.9). The extreme cases are the least complicated and have been most extensively studied.

One extreme is represented by situations in which the fluid would be at rest in the absence of the temperature variations; the buoyancy force is the sole cause of motion. This is known as free convection, or sometimes as natural convection. A whole variety of new phenomena arise, and these form the topic of Chapter 14.

The other extreme corresponds to the buoyancy force being negligible. Temperature variations are introduced into a flow originating from some other cause, but they are not large enough to modify the flow significantly. This is called forced convection. For example, at high Reynolds number, forced convection will occur if the buoyancy force is small compared with the inertia force; that is if

$$g\alpha\Theta L/U^2 \ll 1 \qquad\qquad\qquad (13.14)$$

where L is a length scale, Θ a temperature difference scale, and U a velocity scale introduced independently of Θ. (Anticipating the nomenclature to be introduced in Section 16.1, relationship (13.14) says that the Richardson number must be low, or the internal Froude number high, for forced convection.) Forced convection is frequently of importance in heat transfer applications. However, no new flow phenomena arise and the only matter needing consideration is the temperature distribution resulting from the flow. This will be discussed briefly below.

Intermediate cases are known as mixed convection. We shall not be considering these in general. However, an important special case occurs when the imposed flow is predominantly horizontal so that the buoyancy force acts perpendicularly to it. This situation is known as stratified flow and will be considered in Chapter 16.

13.4 Forced convection

In forced convection, the velocity field is unaffected by the temperature field and can be determined in the same ways as before. Once the velocity field is known, equation (13.12) determines the temperature field. But, of course, it is frequently necessary to turn to experiment to get required results. The transfer of information from one system to another requires not only dynamical similarity — i.e. that the flow patterns should be the same — but also thermal similarity — i.e. that the temperature fields should have the same patterns. The former is guaranteed by equality of the Reynolds number, but the latter gives rise to an extra condition.

We will confine attention to steady convection without internal heat generation. Equation (13.12) becomes

$$\mathbf{u} \cdot \nabla T = \kappa \nabla^2 T \tag{13.15}$$

Analysis of this equation along the lines of the analysis of the Navier–Stokes equation in Section 7.2 shows that there will be thermal similarity when the two systems have the same value of

$$\mathrm{Pe} = UL/\kappa \tag{13.16}$$

Pe is called the Péclet number. It may be interpreted as a measure of the relative importance of the two terms in equation (13.15), analogously with the interpretation of the Reynolds number as the ratio of inertia forces to viscous forces:

$$\mathrm{Pe} \sim \frac{\text{advection of heat}}{\text{conduction of heat}} \tag{13.17}$$

When Pe is small, equation (13.15) approximates to

$$\kappa \nabla^2 T = 0 \tag{13.18}$$

the flow is having negligible effect on the temperature distribution, which is determined by the same equation as in a material at rest. At high Pe, equation (13.15) approximates at first to

$$\mathbf{u} \cdot \nabla T = 0 \tag{13.19}$$

but now conduction can be important in thermal boundary layers for reasons analogous to the origin of viscous boundary layers.

Full similarity of forced convection situations requires equality of both Re = UL/ν and Pe = UL/κ. An equivalent statement is that it requires the equality of both the Reynolds number and

$$\mathrm{Pr} = \nu/\kappa \tag{13.20}$$

This non-dimensional parameter, called the Prandtl number, is a property of the fluid, not of the particular flow. Hence, there is a restriction on the transfer of information from experiments with one fluid to those with another.

The Prandtl number is the ratio of two diffusivities, ν being the diffusivity of momentum and vorticity and κ that of heat. The meaning of this can be illustrated by considering irrotational fluid at a uniform temperature entering a pipe of which the walls are maintained at a higher temperature. Both the Reynolds number and the Péclet number are taken to be significantly above 1. We know from Section 11.1 that vorticity is introduced into the flow in a viscous boundary layer that increases in thickness with distance downstream. Similarly, heat spreads into the flow in a thermal boundary layer of increasing thickness, leaving a diminishing core of fluid that is still effectively at its initial temperature. Figure 13.1 shows schematically the relative thicknesses of the two boundary layers for values of the Prandtl number significantly greater than 1, around 1, and significantly less than 1. The relatively

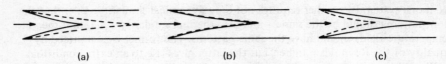

Figure 13.1   Relative positions of edges of velocity boundary layer (solid lines) and thermal boundary layer (broken lines) in pipe flow entry: (a) Pr significantly above 1; (b) Pr ~ 1; (c) Pr significantly below 1.

more rapid diffusion of heat than vorticity as the Prandtl number is decreased can be seen.

Gases have values of the Prandtl number around (but a little less than) 1. Most liquids have values greater than 1 but by widely varying amounts. Water is typical of the low end of the range with Prandtl number (at room temperature) around 6. In general, the kinematic viscosity varies much more widely than the thermal diffusivity, so the high Prandtl number liquids are very viscous ones. The important exception to these statements is liquid metals with high thermal diffusivities, produced by the free electrons, giving low Prandtl numbers; for example mercury has a value around 0.025.

A quantity of frequent practical importance in convection problems is the heat transfer through a surface into or out of the fluid. If we denote the rate of transfer per unit area by H, a non-dimensional form of this is

$$\text{Nu} = HL/k\Theta \tag{13.21}$$

where k is the thermal conductivity and L and Θ are length and temperature difference scales (e.g. Θ might be the temperature difference between the surface under consideration and the ambient fluid). Nu is the Nusselt number. The Nusselt number may have both local and overall meanings depending on whether H is the local heat transfer or an average value over the whole surface. We shall look at this distinction in more detail in the context of free convection (Section 14.5). For the moment we are concerned principally with the latter meaning.

For forced convection, dimensional considerations indicate that

$$\text{Nu} = f(\text{Re}, \text{Pr}) \tag{13.22}$$

Neither Re nor Pr involves Θ. Hence, when all other quantities are being held constant,

$$H \propto \Theta \tag{13.23}$$

the heat transfer is proportional to the imposed temperature excess. This result, which comes essentially from the linearity in ΔT of equation (13.15), is Newton's law of cooling. We shall see in Section 14.5 that it does not apply to free convection; nor, in general, does it apply to mixed convection. The familiar statement that Newton's law of cooling applies in a strong draught can be made more precise: it applies when the forced convection approximation is valid.

13.5 Flow with concentration variations (mass transfer)

We turn now to situations in which, in place of the temperature variations, there is a variable amount of some substance mixed with, dissolved in, or otherwise carried by the fluid. The variable salinity (salt concentration) of the oceans can be dynamically important; air pollution studies require understanding of the processes determining pollutant concentration; chemical engineering processes often involve the mixing of different substances. The interaction between concentration variations and a velocity field is closely analogous to that between temperature variations and a velocity field; the two situations are governed by very similar equations. Thus many of the ideas to be described in this and subsequent chapters can be applied also to mass transfer problems.

The amount of a substance carried by a fluid may be expressed by a concentration c — say, the mass of the substance per unit volume. c is a continuously variable function of position. The presence of the substance increases the density by an amount $\Delta\rho$ above its value ρ_0 corresponding to $c = 0$. One may take a linear relationship between concentration and density,

$$\Delta\rho = \rho_0\alpha_c c \tag{13.24}$$

where α_c is a coefficient. ($\rho_0\alpha_c = 1$ if the substance is absorbed into the fluid without increase in volume, but that is not necessarily the case. α_c can be negative, as in the case of a lighter gas mixing in the flow of a heavier gas.) Thus the dynamical equation may be taken as

$$\frac{Du}{Dt} = -\frac{1}{\rho}\nabla p + \nu\nabla^2 u + g\alpha_c c \tag{13.25}$$

The distribution of c is determined by its advection by moving fluid particles and by its diffusion between fluid particles. Hence,

$$\frac{Dc}{Dt} = \kappa_c \nabla^2 c \tag{13.26}$$

where κ_c is a diffusion coefficient depending both on the fluid and on the diffusing substance.

The correspondence between equations (13.25) and (13.26)† and equations (13.9) and (13.12) (with, of course, the continuity equation (13.1) applying to both systems) allows one to transfer ideas and results between convective systems and mass transfer systems.

The point at which the analogy is most likely to break down is in the boundary conditions. Ways of introducing concentration variations are usually not the counterparts of the commonest ways of introducing temperature variations as considered in Section 13.1. In particular, it is difficult to maintain the concentration at a fixed value at a boundary, the counterpart of the common fixed temperature boundary condition. An example of a more likely way of introducing concentration variations — one that is more readily achieved in the laboratory — is for two meeting streams to have different concentrations.

Consequently, the mass transfer counterparts of most of the convection problems considered in this book are not of much interest. The general ideas are, however, applicable and, in particular, the classification of convective flows in Section 13.3 has its mass transfer counterpart depending on the relative importance of the gravitational term in equation (13.25). The non-dimensional parameters governing mass

---

† In the absence of chemical reactions, equation (13.26) contains no counterpart to the internal heat generation term in (13.12).

transfer problems are analogues of those for convection. We may mention in particular the Schmidt number, ν/κ_c, which corresponds to the Prandtl number, and
which is a property of the substances involved and not of the flow. One is usually
concerned either with Schmidt number around 1 (the case for one gas mixed in
another) or with very large Schmidt number (most other cases, such as aqueous
solutions of electrolytes or small solid particles carried by a liquid or gas flow).

One further point about the equations may now be made — partly to relate the
present approach to that sometimes adopted elsewhere. It is sometimes permissible
to ignore mass diffusion and so to approximate equation (13.26) by

$$Dc/Dt = 0 \qquad\qquad\qquad (13.27)$$

Two considerations are involved here: the fact that diffusivities are frequently very
small, that is the Schmidt number is frequently large; and the fact that concentration
differences are often introduced in a way that does not give the diffusivity an essential role at boundaries. When equation (13.27) applies, each fluid particle always
consists of the same material and thus conserves its density; that is

$$D\rho/Dt = 0 \qquad\qquad\qquad (13.28)$$

Substituting this into the general form of the continuity equation (5.9) reduces
that to

$$\nabla \cdot \mathbf{u} = 0 \qquad\qquad\qquad (13.29)$$

without further approximation. This fact is useful because the Boussinesq approximation applied to concentration variations does not have so many aspects as the
Boussinesq approximation applied to thermal convection. There are no counterparts
of the neglected thermodynamic processes, such as viscous dissipation and density
changes in the pressure field (see appendix to Chapter 14). In fact, the only approximations in using the set of equations (13.25), (13.27), and (13.29) are the neglect
of diffusivity and the assumption that the viscosity does not vary with the concentration (although it is usually necessary to make the further approximation, $\rho = \rho_0$
in handling equation (13.25)).

We shall not be considering specific mass transfer topics in this book. The matter
has been introduced because useful general remarks can be made by analogy with
convection. In the somewhat different context of stratified flow (Chapter 16), we
shall be referring again to the fact that temperature variations and concentration
variations have similar effects.

14
Free Convection

14.1 Introduction [33]

A free convection flow is one produced by buoyancy forces. Temperature differences are introduced, for example through boundaries maintained at different temperatures, and the consequent density differences induce the motion; hot fluid tends to rise, cold to fall.

Such flows have already been placed in the context of general thermal flows in Section 13.3, and the introductory remarks to Chapter 13 have indicated their importance. Figure 14.1 shows one example of free convection, the flow produced by a horizontal heated cylinder in a large expanse of cooler fluid, illustrating the complexity of the phenomena that can arise from the simple fact that hot fluid rises. One sees that the cylinder is surrounded by a boundary layer of hot fluid; from this a relatively narrow column (or 'plume') of hot fluid emerges, becoming unstable and ultimately turbulent as it rises.

In this chapter we shall be examining the basic principles of the study of free convection, and then applying these to several situations, which, because of their geometrical simplicity, have been extensively investigated.

We shall use the Boussinesq approximation (Section 13.2). (An appendix to this chapter considers the conditions in which this is valid and Section 14.3 describes a method of extending its applicability − important in geophysical contexts.) Thus for steady convection without internal heat generation, we are dealing with the equations

$$\nabla \cdot \mathbf{u} = 0 \tag{14.1}$$

$$\mathbf{u} \cdot \nabla \mathbf{u} = -\frac{1}{\rho} \nabla p + \nu \nabla^2 \mathbf{u} - g\alpha \Delta T \tag{14.2}$$

$$\mathbf{u} \cdot \nabla T = \kappa \nabla^2 T \tag{14.3}$$

Equations (14.2) and (14.3) must now be considered simultaneously, as both involve both $\mathbf{u}$ and T. The velocity distribution is governed by the temperature distribution, but the temperature distribution depends through the advection of heat on the velocity distribution. There is no possibility of determining one independently of the other, as could be done in forced convection. For this reason, free convection is hard to treat theoretically and much of our information about it comes from experimental investigations.

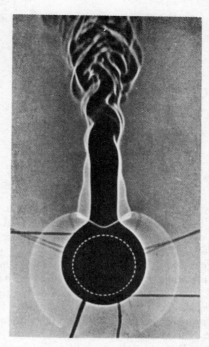

Figure 14.1   Shadowgraph of convection around a heated horizontal cylinder (in position indicated by dotted line – cf. Fig. 4.16); approximately, dark regions are those of hot fluid. From Ref. [220].

14.2 The governing non-dimensional parameters

In such experimental investigations one needs to know when dynamical similarity pertains. No velocity scale is provided by the specification of a free convection situation. Hence, one cannot define a Reynolds number using only parameters involved in setting the problem up. Instead, a temperature difference scale, Θ, will govern how vigorous the motion is. If equations (14.1) to (14.3) are analysed by the methods introduced in Chapter 7, it is found that the dynamical similarity depends on two non-dimensional parameters:

$$\text{Gr} = g\alpha\Theta L^3/\nu^2 \tag{14.4}$$

$$\text{Pr} = \nu/\kappa \tag{14.5}$$

These are respectively the Grashof number and the Prandtl number. Only when both of these are the same in two geometrically similar situations can the same flow patterns be expected. As already mentioned in the context of forced convection (Section 13.4), Pr is a property of the fluid and the transfer of information from one fluid to another is restricted. A full investigation of a given situation requires ranging of the Grashof number for fluids of a variety of values of the Prandtl number and thus is inherently longer than an investigation of a situation governed by a single non-dimensional parameter such as the Reynolds number.

For a given fluid, the Grashof number indicates the type of flow to be expected – which dynamical processes are dominant, whether the flow is laminar or turbulent, and so on – as the Reynolds number does for forced flow. The Grashof number cannot be given a general simple interpretation as the ratio of two dynamical processes. Nevertheless it indicates the relative importance of inertia and viscous forces, as the following discussion shows.

Either the inertia force or the viscous force, or both, must be of the same order of magnitude as the buoyancy force. The motion can reach a steady state only when other terms balance the buoyancy force; on the other hand, since the buoyancy force is the cause of the motion, these other terms cannot become large compared with it. We suppose in the first place that the inertia force is of the same order of magnitude as the buoyancy force.

$$| \mathbf{u} \cdot \nabla \mathbf{u} | \sim | g\alpha\Delta T | \tag{14.6}$$

that is

$$U^2 / L \sim g\alpha\Theta \tag{14.7}$$

This enables a velocity scale to be written down indicating typically how fast the fluid will move as a result of the temperature variations

$$U \sim (g\alpha L\Theta)^{1/2} \tag{14.8}$$

We can now compare the orders of magnitude of the inertia and viscous forces:

$$\frac{| \mathbf{u} \cdot \nabla \mathbf{u} |}{| \nu\nabla^2 \mathbf{u} |} \sim \frac{UL}{\nu} \sim \left(\frac{g\alpha\Theta L^3}{\nu^2} \right)^{1/2} = Gr^{1/2} \tag{14.9}$$

This tells us that, when the Grashof number is large, the viscous force is negligible compared with the buoyancy and inertia forces (subject to qualifications discussed below). On the other hand, it tells us nothing in the case of small Grashof number as the apparent prediction that the inertia force is small is in contradiction with the original assumption that the inertia force is comparable with the buoyancy force.

To deal with that case, we start with the alternative assumption that the viscous force is comparable with the buoyancy force

$$| \nu\nabla^2 \mathbf{u} | \sim | g\alpha\Delta T | \tag{14.10}$$

The corresponding procedure gives

$$U \sim g\alpha\Theta L^2 / \nu \tag{14.11}$$

and so

$$\frac{| \mathbf{u} \cdot \nabla \mathbf{u} |}{| \nu\nabla^2 \mathbf{u} |} \sim Gr \tag{14.12}$$

This analysis indicates that small Grashof number implies negligible inertia forces, but is irrelevant to the case of high Grashof number.

Hence, in general, the Grashof number is a measure of the relative importance of viscous and inertial effects; but, because of the different powers to which Gr appears in relationships (14.9) and (14.12), one cannot write a general expression for Gr as a ratio of effects.

In convection problems, one needs to know not only which dynamical processes are important but also which processes are important in determining the temperature distribution.

$$\frac{\text{Advection}}{\text{Conduction}} \sim \frac{|\mathbf{u} \cdot \nabla T|}{|\kappa \nabla^2 T|} \sim \frac{UL}{\kappa} \tag{14.13}$$

and so, when Gr is large,

$$|\mathbf{u} \cdot \nabla T| / |\kappa \nabla^2 T| \sim \text{Gr}^{1/2} \text{Pr} \tag{14.14}$$

and, when Gr is small,

$$|\mathbf{u} \cdot \nabla T| / |\kappa \nabla^2 T| \sim \text{GrPr} \tag{14.15}$$

When the Prandtl number is around 1 (as it is for gases and for some liquids, see Section 13.4), dominance of advection over conduction always occurs simultaneously with dominance of inertial forces over viscous forces. When the Prandtl number is small (as in liquid metals) or large (as in viscous oils and many other liquids), this correspondence does not apply.

The quantity

$$\text{Ra} = \text{GrPr} = g\alpha\Theta L^3 / \nu\kappa \tag{14.16}$$

appearing in relationship (14.15) plays a special role in studies of convection in horizontal layers (see Chapter 4 and Section 14.7) and is called the Rayleigh number.

The quantities UL/ν and UL/κ appearing in (14.9) and (14.13) can, of course, be identified as a Reynolds number and a Péclet number. Their role, however, is different from that in forced flows, since they involve U which is a dependent scale, not an independent one. Hence, Re (and similarly Pe) is a dependent non-dimensional parameter and one can write

$$\text{Re} = f(\text{Gr}, \text{Pr}) \tag{14.17}$$

Another important dependent parameter is the Nusselt number, indicating the heat transfer as for forced convection (Section 13.4). From dimensional analysis

$$\text{Nu} = f(\text{Gr}, \text{Pr}) \tag{14.18}$$

The form of this dependence will be considered further in the context of particular examples later in this chapter.

Large values of the Grashof number occur much more frequently than small ones. For example, the comparatively small temperature difference and length scales of $1°C$ and 10^{-2} m give Gr $\sim 10^3$ in water and $\sim 10^2$ in air. This is related to the fact that quite vigorous convection currents often arise as a result of stray temperature differences in any large volume of fluid left standing (and can be a nuisance if one is trying to investigate something else!).

When Gr is large (and Pr is not too small), relationships (14.9) and (14.14) imply the dominance of inertia forces over viscous and of advection over conduction. However, this is based on the assumption that the only length scale is the imposed one, L. This assumption will be invalidated by boundary layer formation for reasons similar to those explained in Section 8.3. (Notice that the conduction term is the highest order differential term in equation (14.3) just as the viscous term is in the Navier—Stokes equation.) In the commonest situation where the flow is produced by maintaining the temperature differences between impermeable boundaries, thermal conduction is responsible for the introduction of temperature differences into the fluid. Without thermal conduction the fluid next to a wall could remain at a different temperature from the wall (a state of affairs analogous to the theoretical possibility of a velocity difference between fluid and wall in the absence of viscosity). Omitting the action of conductivity would thus remove the convection problem altogether. The correct inference when $Gr^{1/2}$ and $Gr^{1/2} Pr$ are large is that the flow will have a boundary layer character. The flow considered in Section 14.5 will illustrate more explicitly the nature of such boundary layers.

14.3 The adiabatic temperature gradient

We digress here to consider a matter of little significance for laboratory fluid dynamics but of importance in the application of laboratory results to almost any geophysical situation. The matter concerns the effect of the hydrostatic pressure on the convection: as fluid rises, it expands and so cools; as fluid falls, it is compressed and so warms. This effect is ignored in the Boussinesq approximation, but it is both useful and possible to make allowance for it. (The point is discussed more systematically in the appendix to this chapter.)

The matter is not confined to free convection, but is conveniently considered in this context. Indeed, we consider it first in the context of the particular type of free convection, already introduced in Chapter 4, in which the imposed temperature differences are vertical. Considering such a situation on the basis of the Boussinesq approximation, a first requirement for instability to bring the fluid into motion is that the temperature should decrease with height. This is inferred by considering a fluid particle displaced a small distance vertically — upwards, say. Ignoring interactions with other fluid particles, the particle will be lighter than its new environment when the temperature decreases upwards and heavier when it increases upwards. In the former case, it will tend to move further upwards and the displacement is amplified; in the latter case, it tends to be restored to its original level. (When interactions, such as heat conduction between particles, are taken into account, additional requirements for instability come in.)

This argument is valid when the effect of changes in hydrostatic pressure can be neglected. If it cannot, then the criterion for instability must be modified to allow for the cooling of an upward moving fluid particle. Only if the particle's new temperature exceeds that of its new environment will it continue to be displaced upwards. There is a certain vertical temperature distribution for which a fluid particle moving vertically always has just the local temperature. For instability, the temperature must decrease with height more rapidly than this. We denote this distribution by $T_a(z)$.

To determine it, we again consider a fluid particle displaced vertically in an ideal inviscid non-heat-conducting fluid. Thermodynamically irreversible processes and heat transfer between particles involve the action of viscosity and conductivity. Hence, the displacement occurs at constant entropy, and

$$\frac{\mathrm{d}T_a}{\mathrm{d}z} = \left(\frac{\partial T}{\partial p}\right)_S \frac{\mathrm{d}p}{\mathrm{d}z} \tag{14.19}$$

The vertical pressure gradient is produced by the weight of the fluid. Hence,

$$\frac{dp}{dz} = -g\rho \tag{14.20}$$

Also, in conventional thermodynamic notation (with $\rho = 1/V$)

$$\left(\frac{\partial T}{\partial p}\right)_S = \left(\frac{\partial V}{\partial S}\right)_p = \left(\frac{\partial T}{\partial S}\right)_p \left(\frac{\partial V}{\partial T}\right)_p = \frac{\alpha T}{\rho C_p} \tag{14.21}$$

and so

$$\frac{dT_a}{dz} = -\frac{g\alpha T_a}{C_p} \tag{14.22}$$

The temperature gradient given by (14.22) is known as the adiabatic gradient, or, in geophysical usage, the adiabatic lapse rate.

The criterion for instability, $-\partial T/\partial z > 0$, is thus more correctly written

$$-\frac{\partial T}{\partial z} > \frac{g\alpha T}{C_p} \tag{14.23}$$

The distinction is frequently important in geophysical situations, although rarely in the laboratory. We may illustrate this by considering the adiabatic temperature gradient for air, which, at $T \sim 300$ K is approximately 10^{-2} K m^{-1}. A Rayleigh number of 10^4 (see Chapter 4) in a layer of 3×10^{-2} m (typical in the laboratory) corresponds to a temperature gradient of around 10^2 K m^{-1} whereas over a depth of 10 m (the small end of atmospheric scales) it corresponds to 10^{-8} K m^{-1}. In natural situations it is thus usually the temperature gradient criterion (14.23) that governs whether convection occurs. The Rayleigh number criterion (Section 4.2) is rarely relevant.

We saw (Fig. 4.13) that, for situations in which the adiabatic gradient is negligible, high Rayleigh number convection has a negligible temperature gradient except in thin boundary layers. Correspondingly, vigorous convection in natural situations reduces the temperature gradient to the adiabatic gradient. For this reason, regions occur in which the temperature distribution is governed by an equation of the form of (14.22) – a fact of particular importance in the theories of both stellar and planetary interiors.

The foregoing considerations suggest that problems of convection may usefully be treated in terms of

$$\theta = T - (T_a - T_0) \tag{14.24}$$

a quantity known as the potential temperature. This is indeed the case, not only for the above type of stability consideration but quite generally. When temperature changes due to motion in the hydrostatic pressure field are taken into account, the equations become the same as those derived ignoring such changes, provided that T is replaced by θ. (The justification for this statement and the conditions in which it is true are both indicated in the appendix to this chapter.) The main body of our discussion of free convection is being developed in terms of laboratory situations for which the distinction between T and θ is insignificant. However, the applicability of these ideas is greatly extended by the concept of potential temperature.

Because of the adiabatic temperature gradient, it is not always satisfactory to describe flows without buoyancy forces as 'isothermal'. The alternative term is 'barotropic'. Flows with buoyancy forces are conversely described as 'baroclinic'. In general, a barotropic situation is one in which surfaces of constant pressure and surfaces of constant density coincide; a baroclinic situation is one in which they intersect. When the principal cause of pressure variation is the hydrostatic effect, barotropy implies that constant density surfaces are horizontal and thus that buoyancy forces are absent.

14.4 Free convection as a heat engine

A free convective flow is thermodynamically a heat engine. Heat enters the fluid at hot boundaries, is transported by the flow, and leaves it at colder boundaries; during the transport, forces are generated which feed kinetic energy into the flow. The fact that this energy is usually dissipated again within the fluid, rather than becoming available as work done externally, complicates the overall thermodynamics but does not change the character of the kinetic energy generation process. (One can do a 'thought experiment' in which the action of viscosity is simulated by a large number of tiny propellers which do deliver external work.) One might expect therefore that considerations involving the laws of thermodynamics would enter more explicitly into the analysis of free convection. The aim of this section is to clarify this point.

From equations (14.1) to (14.3) one can derive expressions for the rate of kinetic energy generation and for the rate of heat transfer. In order of magnitude the ratio of these quantities is†

$$W/Q_1 \sim g\alpha L/C_p \qquad (14.25)$$

where L is the length scale of the convecting system and the notation of the left-hand side corresponds to conventional thermodynamic usage as in Fig. 14.2. This ratio is always very small in any situation to which the Boussinesq approximation

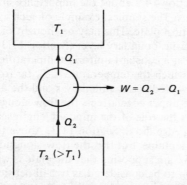

Figure 14.2 Definition diagram for heat engine, drawing heat Q_2 from thermal reservoir at temperature T_2 and delivering heat Q_1 to thermal reservoir at temperature T_1 and doing external work W.

---

†The derivation of this result involves methods outside the scope of this book. They are somewhat similar to those mentioned in Section 11.9. The result is also closely related to equation (14.78).

applies (see appendix); that is such situations have very low 'efficiency',

$$W \ll Q_1, \quad Q_2 \approx Q_1 \tag{14.26}$$

This fact has two consequences. Firstly, the kinetic energy generation is a negligible perturbation in the first law of thermodynamics. This therefore reduces to a heat conservation law (strictly an enthalpy conservation law, corresponding to the appearance of C_p, not C_V, in the equations). Such a law is expressed by an integrated form of equation (14.3). (Note – this does not mean that mechanical effects on the heat transfer are in every way negligible; the heat transfer is usually much larger than it would be if the fluid remained at rest.)

Secondly, the efficiency is so low compared with the Carnot efficiency, $(T_2 - T_1)/T_1$, that the constraints imposed by the second law of thermodynamics are automatically fulfilled and do not need explicit consideration. (It might be remarked that the efficiency in (14.25) is, in order of magnitude, independent of $(T_2 - T_1)/T_1$, and that one could thus envisage a very weak convection produced by very small temperature differences in which the actual efficiency did apparently exceed the Carnot efficiency. The resolution of this apparent paradox lies in the fact that such temperature differences would be smaller than those associated with the adiabatic temperature gradient – which, from equation (14.22), have order of magnitude $g\alpha TL/C_p$. The existence of the latter provides a Carnot efficiency at least as large as the actual efficiency.)

Situations to which the Boussinesq approximation does not apply do require much more explicit thermodynamic formulation than the situations being considered here.

14.5 Convection from a heated vertical surface

We now start looking at particular free convective flows, bearing in mind the remarks at the end of Section 14.2 about the importance and character of high Grashof number situations. The simplest example of such a flow is that produced by an isolated heated vertical plate. This may be thought of as the counterpart in free convection of the Blasius boundary layer (Section 11.3) in forced flow.

The plate, maintained at a constant uniform temperature T_1 is on one side of a large expanse of fluid of which the temperature is T_0 far from the plate (Fig. 14.3). The distance from the lower edge is denoted by x and the distance from the plate by y. The presence of the upper edge affects the flow alongside the plate only very near the top. x thus plays the role of the imposed length scale in the way that the distance from the leading edge did in Section 11.3. Above the upper edge the hot fluid continues to rise in a plume, but it is the flow alongside the plate with which we are concerned here. We are supposing that the plate is wide enough in the z-direction for the motion to be considered as two-dimensional.

The fluid next to the plate is heated by thermal conduction. As a result it rises up the plate. When the Grashof number, now defined as

$$\mathrm{Gr} = g\alpha(T_1 - T_0)x^3/\nu^2 \tag{14.27}$$

is large enough (and considering at the moment a fluid with $\mathrm{Pr} \sim 1$), the speed generated in this way is large enough that the heat is carried off in the x-direction before it has penetrated far in the y-direction. The convection occurs

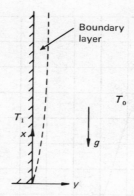

Figure 14.3   Definition diagram for free convection from a heated vertical surface.

entirely in a thin boundary layer (Fig. 14.4). Outside this the fluid remains almost at rest at temperature T_0. It does drift slowly towards the plate, as the boundary layer entrains fluid, the amount of fluid moving up the plate increasing with x.

The temperature is T_1 at the wall and T_0 outside the boundary layer. The velocity is zero both at the wall and outside the boundary layer. Their profiles must

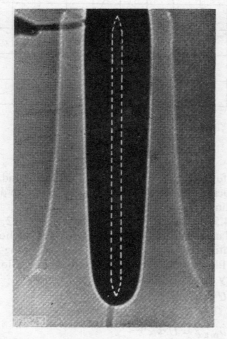

Figure 14.4   Shadowgraph of convection around a heated vertical plate — cf. Fig. 4.16. Inner bright lines are produced by closest negligibly refracted light and indicate edge of boundary layers; outer bright lines are produced by strongly refracted light at plate surface and indicate temperature gradient there. From Ref. [220].

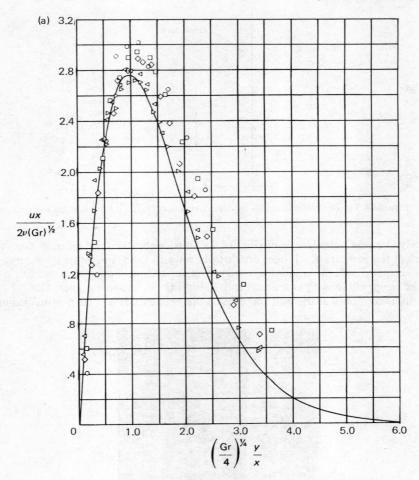

(a)

$\dfrac{ux}{2\nu(\mathrm{Gr})^{\frac{1}{2}}}$

$\left(\dfrac{\mathrm{Gr}}{4}\right)^{\frac{1}{4}}\dfrac{y}{x}$

thus be of the general forms shown in Fig. 14.5. Both the boundary layer thickness and the maximum velocity vary with x, whilst the temperature difference across the boundary layer is of course fixed at $(T_1 - T_0)$.

The lines on Fig. 14.5 are actually the solution for $\mathrm{Pr} = 0.72$, on the assumption that the flow remains laminar. This is obtained by making the boundary layer approximation to equations (14.1) to (14.3) and then following a procedure closely similar to that for the Blasius boundary layer described in Section 11.3 (see Refs. [8, 22]). The boundary layer thickness and velocity scales are

$$\Delta = x\,\mathrm{Gr}^{-1/4}, \quad U = \nu\,\mathrm{Gr}^{1/2}/x \tag{14.28}$$

Thus in a given flow

$$\delta \propto \Delta \propto x^{1/4}, \quad u_{\max} \propto U \propto x^{1/2} \tag{14.29}$$

and the total amount of fluid moving up the plate is proportional to $x^{3/4}$. A local Reynolds number can be defined on the maximum velocity and the boundary layer thickness and this is proportional to $\mathrm{Gr}^{1/4}$.

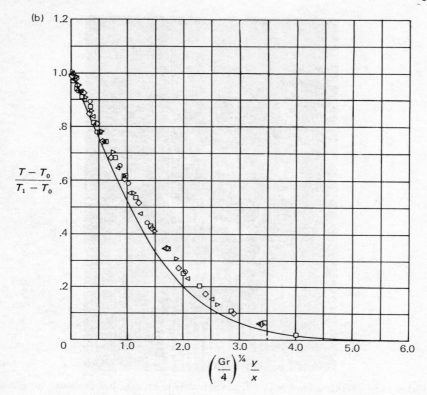

Figure 14.5 Velocity (a) and temperature (b) profiles for laminar free convection on a vertical plate. ○ $Gr^{1/3} = 20.5$, □ 41, ◇ 82, ◁ 143, ▷ 225. Co-ordinates are scaled to allow representation by a single curve for all Gr. Experimental data in air (due to Schmidt and Beckmann) for constant conditions; $Gr^{1/3}$ is proportional to distance from lower edge. From Ref. [192].

Similar results can be obtained for other values of the Prandtl number [192]. When the Prandtl number is large, the velocity boundary layer is thick compared with the temperature boundary layer (as in forced convection, Fig. 13.1). The heat diffuses only slowly away from the wall, but the buoyancy of the thin hot layer drags much more fluid into motion through the action of viscosity. On the other hand, when the Prandtl number is small, the velocity and temperature boundary layers are of similar thicknesses (in contrast to the behaviour in forced convection). Any fluid that is heated by thermal conduction moves under the action of buoyancy, even if viscous effects have not spread that far from the wall [177].

Laminar flow is observed over the lower part of a vertical heated plate. In this region, good agreement is found between the calculations of boundary layer theory and experimental measurements (with the origin of x taken close to the lower edge), as is illustrated by the data included in Fig. 14.5.

Further up the plate, the laminar flow becomes unstable and undergoes a transition process which results ultimately in a fully turbulent boundary layer (Fig.

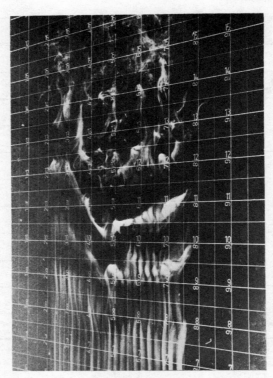

Figure 14.6   Transition in free convection boundary layer, exhibited by smoke introduced through a row of holes close to the lower edge. From Čolak—Antić, P. 'Dreidimensionale Instabilitätserscheinungen des laminarturbulenten Umschlags bei freier Konvektion längs einer vertikalen geheizten Platte', Sitzungsberichte der Heidelberger Akademie der Wissenschaften, Mathem.-naturw. Klasse. Jahrg. 1962/64, 6. Abhandlung. Berlin-Heidelberg-New York. Springer 1964.

14.6) [81, 112, 244]. It is difficult to give a value for the Grashof number at which the transition starts, for several reasons: it will vary with Prandtl number; it is sensitive to disturbances; and, perhaps most important, the disturbances grow slowly at first, so there may be a considerable length in which the transition process has started but has not significantly altered the laminar flow. For fluids with Pr around 1, substantially laminar flow can be observed up to a Grashof number of an order of magnitude of 10^9, even though it becomes unstable, in the sense to be explained in Chapter 18, at a Grashof number [187] between 10^5 and 10^6. (Such high Grashof numbers do not require an enormous system, since x appears to a high power in Gr. For the same reason, the difference between 10^6 and 10^9 represents only a factor of 10 in distance up the plate, but it is nevertheless a striking difference.)

There are two mechanisms by which this type of boundary layer can become unstable [187]. One is essentially the same process as initiates transition in other shear flows (see Section 17.6). Its onset after some distance up the plate is associated with the increase of the local Reynolds number. The buoyancy force plays no direct role in this instability, although it does, of course, produce the flow in the first place. The other instability involves the buoyancy force directly; that is to say, it would not be exhibited by a similar velocity profile produced in a different way. The buoyancy of a displaced fluid particle modifies the velocity field in a way that accentuates the displacement.

The relationship of the two instability mechanisms to the transition to turbulence is uncertain. However, the second type of instability starts lower down the plate (except at very low Pr), but amplifies only slowly, so that probably the first type actually gives rise to transition [111] (except perhaps at very high Pr). The later stages of transition involve the growth and spreading of turbulent spots [276] as described for other flows in Chapters 2 and 19.

We shall not be considering the structure of the fully turbulent flow for this configuration, but it is, of course, investigated by methods like those described in Chapters 20 and 22.

The heat transfer per unit area from the plate by the combination of conduction and convection is, of course, a function of the distance up the plate, $H(x)$. The local Nusselt number is

$$\text{Nu}_L = Hx/k(T_1 - T_0) \tag{14.30}$$

The total heat transfer per unit area from a plate of length l is

$$H_T = \int_0^l H \, dx/l \tag{14.31}$$

and the Nusselt number based on this is

$$\text{Nu}_T = H_T l/k(T_1 - T_0) \tag{14.32}$$

If the dependence of the heat transfer can be represented by a power law

$$\text{Nu} = C \, \text{Gr}^n \tag{14.33}$$

(corresponding to

$$H \propto x^{3n-1} \tag{14.34}$$

in a given flow), the total Nusselt number has a similar power law dependence on the Grashof number based on the total plate length,

$$\text{Nu}_T = \frac{C}{3n} \left[\frac{g\alpha(T_1 - T_0)l^3}{\nu^2} \right]^n \tag{14.35}$$

In laminar flow, both theory and experiment show a power-law dependence of this sort with $n = 1/4$; C depends on the Prandtl number.

In turbulent flow [76, 288], a similar power-law representation, usually with $n = 1/3$ (corresponding to uniform heat-flux), is often used to summarize the experimental data. In this case, however, it may be only an approximate representation of a more complicated dependence.

It is interesting to note the implications of these results for the dependence of the total heat transfer from a given plate on the temperature elevation $(T_1 - T_0)$. If the plate is short enough for the flow to remain laminar over it,

$$H_T \propto (T_1 - T_0)^{5/4} \tag{14.36}$$

If the plate is long enough for most of the flow to be turbulent, then approximately

$$H_T \propto (T_1 - T_0)^{4/3} \tag{14.37}$$

Intermediate cases are more complicated because the transition region will move as the temperature elevation is changed.

These results are typical of free convection in general. In contrast with forced convection, Newton's law of cooling does not apply. The heat transfer always increases more rapidly than direct proportionality to the temperature elevation. This is because of the dual role of the heating. The larger the temperature elevation, the greater is the rate of heat transfer by a particular flow rate; but also the larger the temperature elevation, the greater is the flow rate.

14.6 Thermal plumes [27, 33, 280]

In the same sense that the flow considered above is the counterpart of the Blasius boundary layer, a thermal plume is the counterpart of a jet. It is produced by a local source of heat with a large expanse of fluid above it. A column of hot fluid rises above the source and further fluid is drawn in and heated. When $Gr^{1/2}$ and $Gr^{1/2}Pr$ are large (as is almost always the case), this column or plume extends vertically much further than it extends horizontally. Readily observable examples are the plumes over fires and chimneys.

Just as a jet far enough from its orifice can be considered to originate from a point (or line) source of momentum, so a plume can be considered to originate from a point (or line) source of heat (sometimes displaced vertically from the actual source). The quantity conserved with distance along the plume (analogous to momentum in a jet, equations (11.39) and (11.40)) is the heat transport;

$$\frac{d}{dz} \int w \Delta T \, dS = 0 \tag{14.38}$$

z being vertical. The momentum flux increases with distance up the plume through the action of the buoyancy force. The mass flux also increases; the plume entrains ambient fluid.

As with jets, laminar plumes are very unstable [112] and it is the turbulent ones that are of most physical interest. The top part of Fig. 14.1 is, of course, a plume and a further picture will be shown in Section 22.7 (Fig. 22.23), where we shall be using plumes to illustrate the Coanda effect.

14.7 Convection in fluid layers

Convection in thin layers of fluid has already been considered in Chapter 4, with particular reference to horizontal layers. The purpose of the present section is to place that chapter in context and to extend the discussion to vertical layers.

A layer of fluid is confined between two parallel plates at different temperatures, T_1 and T_2, and a distance d apart. The other dimensions of the layer are large compared with d. It is usual to specify dynamical similarity in terms of the Rayleigh number (= GrPr) and Prandtl number. This originates from the special role of the Rayleigh number when the layer is horizontal, but, in general, it is simply an equivalent alternative to the Gr and Pr specification.

If the length scale L is taken to be d, the Nusselt number

$$\text{Nu} = Hd/k(T_2 - T_1) \tag{14.39}$$

has a special interpretation for this particular geometry. It is the ratio of the actual heat transfer through the layer to the heat transfer that would occur by conduction alone if the fluid remained at rest. (Figure 4.4 illustrated the use of the increase of Nu above 1 as an indication of the onset of motion.)

Convection in fluid layers has a special interest as the simplest example of the fact that a fluid may come into motion for two alternative reasons. Either there is no equilibrium configuration (i.e. putting $\mathbf{u} = 0$ in the equations does not result in a balance of the remaining terms); or there is an equilibrium configuration, but it is unstable. (There is a third possibility, although it does not arise in the present context: that there is a stable equilibrium configuration and also a dynamic solution of the equations, the latter occurring if sufficient initial disturbance is present.)

When the two plates are horizontal, with T_1 the temperature of the upper, then equations (14.1) to (14.3) are satisfied by

$$\mathbf{u} = 0, \quad T = T_2 + (T_1 - T_2)z/d, \quad p = \rho g \alpha (T_2 - T_1) z^2/2d \tag{14.40}$$

where z is measured vertically upwards from the lower plate (and the reference density ρ_0 used in subtracting out the hydrostatic pressure has been chosen as the density at T_2). When $T_1 > T_2$, this solution is always stable and the fluid remains at rest. When $T_2 > T_1$, the stability depends on whether the Rayleigh number is below or above its critical value. As will be seen in Section 18.2, this value is independent of the Prandtl number, although for all other developments Pr is a parameter of the problem. The flow patterns that result from this instability have been considered in Section 4.3.

When the layer is not horizontal, there is no equilibrium solution. For the remainder of this section we consider the layer between two vertical plates. The smaller gravitational force on the fluid close to the hot wall (T_2, say) cannot be balanced by the same vertical pressure gradient as would balance the larger force on the fluid close the cold wall; but, with the fluid at rest, there can be no horizontal pressure gradient. Mathematically, if the fluid were at rest, the temperature distribution would be

$$T = T_2 - (T_2 - T_1)x/d \tag{14.41}$$

where x is the distance from the hot wall. The buoyancy force, $g\alpha\Delta T$, then has non-zero curl in the other horizontal direction, $g\alpha(T_2 - T_1)/d$. $(1/\rho)\nabla p$ has zero curl and so these two terms cannot be in balance.

The simplest consequence of this non-equilibrium is a simple circulation of the sort shown in Fig. 4.2. However, this flow can break up into more complicated patterns, and we now look briefly at these.

Because the same circulation can extend from bottom to top as in Fig. 4.2, the height h of the layer is a relevant parameter even when it is large compared with d. (The other horizontal dimension should remain unimportant provided it is large enough.) There are thus three governing non-dimensional parameters, Ra, Pr, and h/d. Moreover, fewer experiments have been performed for this configuration than for horizontal layers. It is unlikely that the full range of phenomena has been observed [115]. Also, a summary of the principal observations must be rather vague about the quantitative conditions in which the different flows may occur. The following account is probably most accurate at high Prandtl number (around 10^3) [101, 102]. When the Prandtl number is lower (e.g. around 1), the second development (formation of boundary layers) is probably not to be observed because

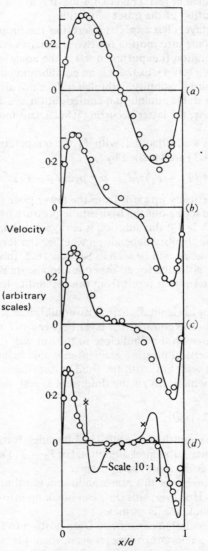

Figure 14.7   Distribution of vertical velocity at midheight across a vertical slot containing paraffin for various values of the Rayleigh number: (a) 3.1×10^4; (b) 2.95×10^5; (c) 6.6×10^5; (d) 3.6×10^6. From Ref. [101].

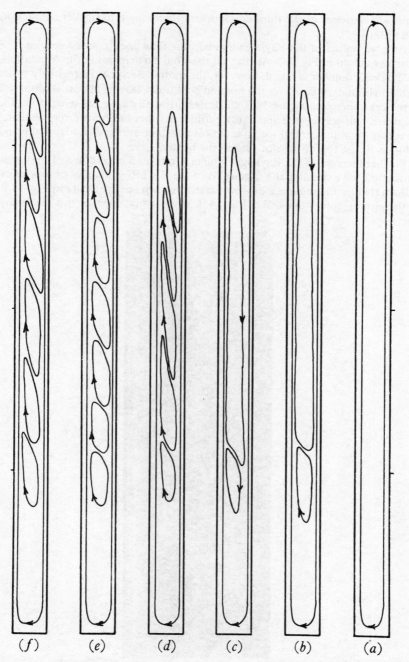

Figure 14.8   Sketches of streamlines for convection of silicone oil of Pr $\approx$ 900 in a vertical slot for various values of the Rayleigh number: (a) 3.0×10^5; (b) 3.6×10^5; (c) 4.0×10^5; (d) 4.9×10^5; (e) 5.8×10^5; (f) 6.8×10^5. From Ref. [101].

of prior occurrence of the third development (break up into smaller convection cells) [286].

At lower values of the Rayleigh number, the flow does have the general character shown in Fig. 4.2. At first, all the fluid participates in the circulation. As the Rayleigh number is raised, however, the motion becomes increasingly concentrated in boundary layers on the hot and cold walls, leaving almost stationary fluid in the central region. Figure 14.7 illustrates this with a series of velocity profiles measured half-way up the apparatus; profiles at other heights are very similar. The temperature in the central region is almost constant over each horizontal plane but is higher at the top of the slot than at the bottom.

Further increase of the Rayleigh number produces a breakdown of the single convection cell extending the full height of the slot into a number of shorter cells, as is illustrated by the sequence of flow patterns shown schematically in Fig. 14.8 and by the photograph of one cell in Fig. 14.9. When it first appears, this secondary

Figure 14.9   Convection cell in vertical slot (Ra $\approx$ 4.5 x 10^5, Pr $\approx$ 900, h/d = 20); aluminium powder flow visualization (see Section 23.4). From Ref. [286].

flow is weakly superimposed on the primary circulation, but at higher Rayleigh numbers, the two interact strongly.

In each of the cells, the fluid is travelling up the hot wall and down the cold one. The sense of circulation is the same in neighbouring cells (in contrast to the behaviour in horizontal layers) and large shear must occur between them. The next development is presumably a consequence of this. Smaller cells of reverse circulation, not extending to the hot and cold walls appear between the main cells, giving a flow pattern of the form shown in Fig. 14.10. The small cells act in a sense as 'idling wheels' reducing the shear between the main convecting cells.

Figure 14.10   Sketch of streamlines for convection of silicone oil in vertical slot at Ra ≈ 3 x 10⁶. Based on Ref. [101].

At the highest values of the Rayleigh number the flow ceases to be steady. Waves are generated in the lower part of the hot upgoing boundary layer and the upper part of the cold downgoing boundary layer. These break down into turbulent motion in a way similar to transition on a single heated surface. The result is a disruption of the previous cellular motion and the production of a turbulent core in the centre of the slot. Thus the general structure of the flow is as shown in Fig. 14.11.

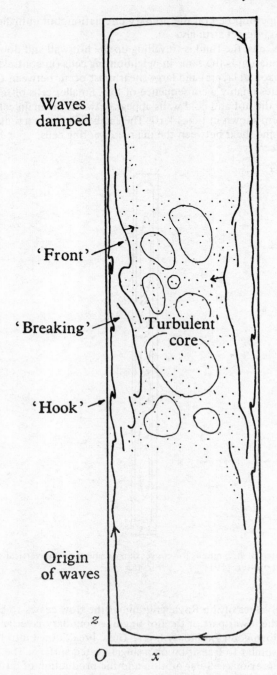

Figure 14.11 Schematic representation of principal features of high Rayleigh number ($>\sim 10^6$) convection in a vertical slot. From Ref. [102].

Appendix: The Boussinesq approximation in free convection

In this appendix we examine systematically the conditions for the Boussinesq approximation to be a good approximation in the specific context of steady free convection. This is not the only context in which the matter is important (indeed, some of the points, such as the effect of the hydrostatic pressure on the density, should in principle be considered even for barotropic flows) but a general discussion becomes too complicated. The following analysis may serve as the principal demonstration in this book of the methods used in such considerations. Some of the discussion that follows the analysis has wider application. On the other hand, particular examples of free convection may involve complexities not covered by the general discussion — for example, through having more than a single length scale.

We have not made extensive use of the Boussinesq equations in this book. However, it should be remembered that the Boussinesq approximation underlies the statement that dynamical similarity of free convective flows depends on the Grashof and Prandtl numbers. When the approximation fails, other non-dimensional parameters come in. Thus, the considerations of this section are important not only for the mathematical formalism but also for the whole question of the transfer of results from one situation to another. This is of particular relevance to attempts to model geophysical situations in the laboratory.

We suppose that the flow is produced by the introduction of temperature differences of order Θ into a system of length scale L. It is important for some of the following considerations that the vertical dimension of the system should be of order L, but we shall not usually make a distinction between scales in different directions.

The principal criteria for the applicability of the Boussinesq approximation are

$$A = \alpha\Theta \ll 1 \tag{14.42}$$

$$B = g\rho\beta L \ll 1 \tag{14.43}$$

$$C = g\alpha L/C_p \ll 1 \tag{14.44}$$

(β = isothermal compressibility; other symbols as before). There are some supplementary criteria connected with the constancy of fluid properties.

If in addition to the above,

$$D = g\alpha L T_0/C_p\Theta \ll 1 \tag{14.45}$$

(where T_0 is the absolute temperature), the Boussinesq equations apply directly. If (14.42)–(14.44) are fulfilled but not (14.45), they apply with the variable T replaced by the potential temperature θ (equation (14.24)). In this case Θ is the scale of the imposed variations in θ.

We shall consider the significance of relationships (14.42)–(14.45) after we have examined their roles in the Boussinesq approximation. We may remark, however, that relationships (14.43), (14.44) and (14.45) are likely to be violated only in large-scale geophysical situations and it is for these that the following considerations are most important.

We choose the two independent thermodynamic variables in terms of which other thermodynamic quantities may be expressed as the pressure and temperature, and write

$$p = p_0 + p_h + p' \tag{14.46}$$

$$T = T_0 + T' \tag{14.47}$$

p_0 and T_0 are the absolute pressure and temperature at some arbitrarily chosen reference point. p_h is the hydrostatic variation of the pressure and is thus a function only of the vertical co-ordinate. p' and T' are the variations associated with the motion, and are thus general functions of position. T' encompasses all variations in T, whether associated with the boundary conditions or arising from internal effects such as viscous dissipation or adiabatic volume change.

The density may now be written

$$\rho = \rho_0 + \rho_h + \rho' \tag{14.48}$$

where ρ_0 is the density at p_0 and T_0, ρ_h is the departure from this in hydrostatic conditions, and ρ' is the further departure associated with the flow.

We now consider how the more general equations of motion reduce to the Boussinesq approximation. For steady flow, the continuity equation is

$$\mathbf{u} \cdot \nabla \rho + \rho \, \nabla \cdot \mathbf{u} = 0 \tag{14.49}$$

The orders of magnitude of the two terms are $(\rho_h + \rho')U/L$ and $(\rho_0 + \rho_h + \rho')U/L$. To write the equation in its incompressible form (14.1) we require

$$\rho_h/\rho_0 \ll 1, \quad \rho'/\rho_0 \ll 1 \tag{14.50}$$

When these are true (we may assume them and look for self-consistency), ρ_h and ρ' may be expressed

$$\rho_h = \rho_0 \beta p_h, \quad \rho' = \rho_0(-\alpha T' + \beta p') \tag{14.51}$$

and (14.50) is equivalent to

$$\beta p_h \ll 1 \tag{14.52}$$

$$\alpha T' \ll 1 \tag{14.53}$$

$$\beta p' \ll 1 \tag{14.54}$$

Taking these in turn, condition (14.52) depends on the size of p_h, which may be estimated from the hydrostatic balance

$$\nabla p_h = (\rho_0 + \rho_h)\mathbf{g} \approx \rho_0 \mathbf{g} \tag{14.55}$$

giving

$$p_h \sim \rho_0 g L \tag{14.56}$$

Hence, (14.52) is fulfilled when B is small.

One requirement for condition (14.53) is evidently that A should be small. However, it is not at this stage apparent that this is the only requirement as we have yet to examine flow-induced temperature variations.

We shall see below that condition (14.54) is a much weaker condition than (14.52) and (14.53) and so does not need separate consideration.

Turning to the dynamical equation, the conditions in (14.50) enable us to replace $\rho \mathbf{u} \cdot \nabla \mathbf{u}$ by $\rho_0 \mathbf{u} \cdot \nabla \mathbf{u}$, and when equation (14.1) applies the viscous term may be reduced to $\mu \nabla^2 \mathbf{u}$ (for constant μ) as considered in Section 5.6. Hence, for steady flow

$$\rho_0 \mathbf{u} \cdot \nabla \mathbf{u} = -\nabla p' + \rho' \mathbf{g} + \mu \nabla^2 \mathbf{u} \tag{14.57}$$

where the hydrostatic balance of equation (14.55) has been subtracted out as in Section 13.2.

To put equation (14.57) into the form used in the Boussinesq approximation (equation (14.2)) one also writes

$$\rho' = -\rho_0 \alpha T' \tag{14.58}$$

which will be valid if

$$\beta p' \ll \alpha T' \tag{14.59}$$

The order of magnitude of p' is indicated by equation (14.57); the second term in this will be of the same order of magnitude as the largest of the other terms. For free convection

$$p'/L \sim g\rho_0 \alpha T' \tag{14.60}$$

Hence, criterion (14.59) is equivalent to (14.43) (small B).

In circumstances in which (14.42) and (14.59) are fulfilled, (14.54), of which we postponed consideration above, will be much more strongly fulfilled.

The starting point for the development of the temperature equation (14.3) is the first law of thermodynamics in the form

$$dE = dQ - p dV \tag{14.61}$$

where E is the internal energy (conventionally denoted by U in texts on thermodynamics), dQ is the heat supplied, and V is the volume. If the thermodynamic quantities are taken to apply to unit mass

$$V = 1/\rho \tag{14.62}$$

Applying (14.61) to a fluid particle

$$\frac{DE}{Dt} = \frac{DQ}{Dt} - p \frac{DV}{Dt} \tag{14.63}$$

From the considerations in Section 13.2, the heat supplied to a fluid particle per unit mass is

$$\frac{DQ}{Dt} = \frac{1}{\rho}(k \nabla^2 T + J + \Phi) \tag{14.64}$$

where J is the internal heat generation per unit volume due to external causes, and Φ is the heating due to viscous dissipation of mechanical energy.

Using relationships derived by standard thermodynamic procedures we may write

$$\frac{DE}{Dt} = \left(\frac{\partial E}{\partial T}\right)_p \frac{DT}{Dt} + \left(\frac{\partial E}{\partial p}\right)_T \frac{Dp}{Dt} = \left(C_p - \frac{\alpha p}{\rho}\right) \frac{DT}{Dt} + \frac{\beta p - \alpha T}{\rho} \frac{Dp}{Dt} \tag{14.65}$$

$$\frac{DV}{Dt} = \left(\frac{\partial V}{\partial T}\right)_p \frac{DT}{Dt} + \left(\frac{\partial V}{\partial p}\right)_T \frac{Dp}{Dt} = \frac{\alpha}{\rho} \frac{DT}{Dt} - \frac{\beta}{\rho} \frac{Dp}{Dt} \tag{14.66}$$

Substituting (14.64), (14.65) and (14.66) into (14.63) gives

$$C_p \frac{DT}{Dt} - \frac{\alpha T}{\rho} \frac{Dp}{Dt} = \frac{1}{\rho} (k \nabla^2 T + J + \Phi) \tag{14.67}$$

This becomes the Boussinesq equation (14.3) if the terms $(\alpha T/\rho)Dp/Dt$ and Φ/ρ can be neglected.

The first of these has two contributions, from the variation of the hydrostatic pressure p_h and from that of the hydrodynamic pressure p'. The ratio of the former to the first term of equation (14.67) is

$$\frac{\alpha T \mathbf{u} \cdot \nabla p_h}{\rho C_p \mathbf{u} \cdot \nabla T} \sim \frac{\alpha T_0 p_h}{\rho_0 C_p T'} \sim \frac{g\alpha L T_0}{C_p T'} \tag{14.68}$$

Hence, the term may be neglected when (14.45) is fulfilled (i.e. when D is small). (14.45) is often a much more severe criterion than (14.44), and it is therefore fortunate that this criterion can be dispensed with by working in terms of the potential temperature

$$\theta = T - (T_a - T_0) \quad \text{where}\dagger \quad \frac{dT_a}{dz} = -\frac{g\alpha T_0}{C_p} \tag{14.69}$$

We see this as follows. p_h and T_a vary vertically only. Hence,

$$\frac{\alpha T}{\rho} \frac{Dp_h}{Dt} = \frac{\alpha T w}{\rho} \frac{dp_h}{dz} = -g\alpha w T$$

$$= C_p \frac{DT_a}{Dt} - g\alpha w T' \tag{14.70}$$

But

$$\frac{g\alpha w T'}{C_p DT/Dt} \sim \frac{g\alpha L}{C_p} \tag{14.71}$$

and the second term of the last expression of (14.70) can be neglected when (14.44) is fulfilled. Then equation (14.67) becomes

$$C_p \frac{D\theta}{Dt} - \frac{\alpha T}{\rho} \frac{Dp'}{Dt} = \frac{1}{\rho} (k \nabla^2 \theta + J + \Phi) \tag{14.72}$$

Since T_a does not vary horizontally, this change makes no difference to the dynamic equation (14.57).

For the remaining unwanted pressure effect, the second term in (14.72), to be negligible, one requires

$$\frac{\alpha T \mathbf{u} \cdot \nabla p'}{\rho C_p \mathbf{u} \cdot \nabla T} \sim \frac{\alpha T_0 p'}{\rho C_p T'} \ll 1 \tag{14.73}$$

---

†A definition of T_a slightly different from equation (14.22) has been chosen, so that $\nabla^2 T_a = 0$ and the heat conduction term is unaffected by the change of variable; the following considerations imply that T_a is significantly different from the physical adiabatic temperature only in circumstances in which the approximation breaks down. There is also slight arbitrariness, depending on the exact definition of T_0, but this is similarly unimportant.

p' can be estimated from (14.60) and the criterion is

$$\frac{g\alpha L}{C_p} \alpha T_0 \ll 1 \tag{14.74}$$

Since αT_0 is around 1 for gases and is small for other fluids, (14.74) will be fulfilled whenever (14.44) is fulfilled.

We may note parenthetically that the above discussion provides the rigorous justification for the choice of C_p as the specific heat in Section 13.2. By using T and V as the independent thermodynamic variables one can analogously formulate an equation for $C_V \, DT/Dt$, but an extra term arises that is negligible only when the difference between C_V and C_p is itself negligible.

Finally, the reduction of (14.67) or (14.72) to the Boussinesq form requires that the viscous heating should be negligible. Viscous energy dissipation has been considered only in terms of the example of a laminar two-dimensional jet (Section 11.9). However, this indicates the essential information that we need for an order of magnitude estimate — that the dissipation per unit volume is proportional to the viscosity and to the square of the velocity gradient (see equation (11.59)). In fact, generalization of the ideas in Section 11.9 gives the result that

$$\Phi = \mu \frac{\partial u_i}{\partial x_j} \left(\frac{\partial u_i}{\partial x_j} + \frac{\partial u_j}{\partial x_i} \right) \tag{14.75}$$

(with the summation convention for repeated suffixes applying). Thus

$$\Phi \sim \mu U^2 / \delta^2 \tag{14.76}$$

where δ is the length scale appropriate to viscous effects. The distinction between L and δ is made so that the discussion applies even when there is strong boundary layer formation.

In free convection, the balance between the buoyancy force and the viscous force gives

$$\mu U / \delta^2 \sim \rho g \alpha T' \tag{14.77}$$

Hence,

$$\frac{\Phi}{\rho C_p \mathbf{u} \cdot \nabla T} \sim \frac{\rho g \alpha T' U}{\rho C_p U T'/L} \sim \frac{g \alpha L}{C_p} = C \tag{14.78}$$

The criterion for the viscous dissipation to have a negligible effect on the thermal balance is that this should be small; i.e. it is relationship (14.44). This applies whether $\delta \sim L$ (viscous flow) or $\delta \ll L$ (viscous dissipation confined to boundary layers).

We can now return to the one question that we left unsettled in connection with the continuity and dynamic equations, whether (14.42) (small A) is an adequate representation of (14.53). When the temperature equation takes the Boussinesq form it will be, but there remains the possibility that the largest temperature difference is that associated with the adiabatic gradient. The corresponding fractional density change is

$$\alpha \Delta T_a \sim \frac{g \alpha L}{C_p} \alpha T_0 \tag{14.79}$$

and, as with (14.74), this is always small when C is small.

In addition to the various effects considered above, the Boussinesq approximation, as designated in Section 13.2, requires effective constancy of the physical properties of the fluid; that is of μ, k, α, and C_p. The temperature and pressure variations must not be so large as to produce large fractional changes in these quantities. Often fulfilment of this requirement will go along with fulfilment of the requirement of small fractional density changes. However, in principle, any parameter having a much larger temperature or pressure coefficient than density needs special consideration. In practice, the temperature variation of viscosity is often the most serious problem, both in the laboratory and in studies of natural situations.

What is the physical significance of the parameters, A, B, C, and D that principally govern the applicability of the Boussinesq approximation?

The requirement of small A just says that the fractional density change produced by expansion in the imposed temperature field must be negligible.

B and C relate to the 'scale heights' of the system − the heights over which various parameters change by a fraction of order unity. For example, in an isothermal perfect gas at rest

$$dp/dz = -\rho g, \quad \rho = p/RT \tag{14.80}$$

giving

$$p = p_0 e^{-gz/RT}, \quad \rho = \rho_0 e^{-gz/RT} \tag{14.81}$$

In this case the scale heights of pressure and density are both RT/g. More generally, $1/g\rho\beta$ and $C_p/g\alpha$ are the scale heights of isothermal pressure and adiabatic temperature. B and C are the ratios of the length scale of the system to these scale heights. The Boussinesq approximation applies only to systems that are small compared with the scale heights.

Another physical interpretation of C − in terms of thermodynamic 'efficiency' − has been discussed in Section 14.4.

D is evidently related to C (although usually $D \gg C$), but it is more readily thought of as the ratio of the adiabatic temperature gradient to a typical imposed temperature gradient.

B and C (and for that matter D) are always exceedingly small on the laboratory scale. Departures from Boussinesq conditions can occur owing to variations of fluid properties − particularly temperature variation of viscosity and, in water, temperature variation of expansion coefficient − and, in experiments with gases, owing to A not being small enough.

The importance of B and C arises in large-scale geophysical systems, where they are not always small. Motions of the atmosphere extending throughout its depth, and motions in the interiors of planets and stars, for example, may involve processes that cannot be modelled in the laboratory. The foregoing analysis shows that when B is not small, one must additionally take into account (i) the effect of the hydrostatic pressure p_h throughout the equations of motion and (ii) the effect of the hydrodynamic pressure p' on the buoyancy force. When C is not small, one must take into account (iii) heat generation by viscous dissipation and (iv) other non-Boussinesq effects in the thermal balance (relationships (14.71) and (14.73)).

B and C are in principle thermodynamically independent parameters. In practice they tend to be of the same size. For a perfect gas

$$-\alpha = 1/T, \quad \beta = 1/\rho RT \tag{14.82}$$

and so

$$B/C = C_p/R = \gamma/(\gamma - 1) \qquad (14.83)$$

For real gases the ratio will similarly be of order unity. For condensed phases (liquids and solids) the ratio $\alpha/\rho\beta C_p$ is known as Grüneisen's ratio, G, giving

$$B/C = 1/G \qquad (14.84)$$

G rarely differs greatly from 1. Water is something of an exception to this (its G varies strongly with temperature but is typically 10^{-1}), but there would seem to be no application of this; the density at the bottom of the sea is increased only a small amount by the weight of the water above. On the other hand, there are applications of these ideas to condensed phases in the study of planetary interiors (see, e.g., Section 24.4).

These considerations imply that all the effects (i) to (iv) above are liable to become significant simultaneously and it is generally not useful to take one into account whilst ignoring the others. Thus situations in which the Boussinesq approximation fails become very complicated theoretically. We have already seen the problems of modelling them in the laboratory, so it is altogether difficult to ascertain the flow patterns.

15
Flow in Rotating Fluids

15.1 Introduction [35, 130, 163]

This chapter is concerned with the dynamics of fluids in rotating systems. This branch of fluid mechanics has developed rapidly in recent years as an obvious consequence of interest in geophysical flow problems. Evaluation of the parameters shows that the motions, particularly on the large scale, of the Earth's atmosphere, oceans, and core and of stars and galaxies will all exhibit the effects discussed in this chapter. The rotation gives rise to a range of new phenomena; here we consider a small selection of these.

The whole subject could be formulated as seen by an observer external to the rotation. Since, however, all boundary conditions will be specified in terms of the rotating frame of reference it is easier to modify the equations of motion so that they apply in such a frame.

If one takes a body of fluid and rotates its boundaries at a constant angular velocity Ω, then at any time sufficiently long after starting the rotation, the whole body is rotating with this angular velocity, moving as if it were a rigid body. There are then no viscous stresses acting within the fluid. Any disturbance — i.e. anything that would produce a motion in a non-rotating system — will produce motion relative to this rigid body rotation. This relative motion can be considered as the flow pattern; it is the pattern that will be observed by an observer fixed to the rotating boundaries.

15.2 Centrifugal and Coriolis forces

The effect of using a rotating frame of reference is well known from the mechanics of solid systems; there are accelerations associated with the use of a non-inertial frame that can be taken into account by introducing centrifugal and Coriolis forces. That statement may be expressed in a form appropriate to fluid systems by

$$\left(\frac{Du}{Dt}\right)_I = \left(\frac{Du}{Dt}\right)_R + \Omega \times (\Omega \times r) + 2\Omega \times u_R \tag{15.1}$$

The subscripts I and R refer to inertial and rotating frames of reference. $(Du/Dt)_I$ is thus the actual acceleration that a fluid particle is experiencing and so $\rho(Du/Dt)_I$ is the quantity to be equated with the sum of the various forces acting on the fluid particle. $(Du/Dt)_R$ is the acceleration relative to the rotating frame and can thus be expanded in the usual way:

$$\left(\frac{Du}{Dt}\right)_R = \frac{\partial u_R}{\partial t} + (\mathbf{u} \cdot \nabla \mathbf{u})_R \tag{15.2}$$

Dropping the subscript R, as all velocities will be referred to the rotating frame throughout the rest of this chapter, the equation of motion is

$$\frac{\partial \mathbf{u}}{\partial t} + \mathbf{u} \cdot \nabla \mathbf{u} = -\frac{1}{\rho} \nabla p - \mathbf{\Omega} \times (\mathbf{\Omega} \times \mathbf{r}) - 2\mathbf{\Omega} \times \mathbf{u} + \nu \nabla^2 \mathbf{u} \tag{15.3}$$

The second and third terms on the right-hand side of (15.3) are, of course, respectively the centrifugal and Coriolis forces.

In many problems the centrifugal force is unimportant. This is because it can be expressed as the gradient of a scalar quantity;

$$\mathbf{\Omega} \times (\mathbf{\Omega} \times \mathbf{r}) = -\nabla(\tfrac{1}{2}\Omega^2 r'^2) \tag{15.4}$$

where r' is the distance from the axis of rotation (Fig. 15.1). Hence replacing the pressure by $(p - \tfrac{1}{2}\rho\Omega^2 r'^2)$ reduces the problem to one that is identical except that the centrifugal force is absent. This is entirely analogous to the procedure of subtracting out the hydrostatic pressure to remove the effect of gravitational forces, as discussed in Section 13.2. The centrifugal force is balanced by a radial pressure gradient which is present whether or not there is any flow relative to the rotating frame and which does not interact with any such flow. The limitations to this statement are just the same as for the gravitational case. Firstly, the pressure must not appear explicitly in the boundary conditions. Secondly (since ρ has been taken through ∇), the density must be constant; centrifugal force variations associated with density variations do give rise to body forces that can alter or even cause a flow; such effects are outside the scope of the present discussion, although a flow in which they are present is considered briefly in Section 15.8.

Figure 15.1   Definition sketch.

It should be emphasized that the centrifugal force under discussion here is that associated with the rotation of the frame of reference as a whole. In other contexts (e.g. rotating Couette flow) it is sometimes convenient to talk about the centrifugal force associated with circular motion relative to the frame of reference (either inertial or rotating). This is then a way of discussing physically effects that are contained mathematically in one or both of $(\mathbf{u} \cdot \nabla \mathbf{u})$ and the Coriolis term.

15.3 Geostrophic flow and the Taylor–Proudman theorem

We thus see that the cause of differences between the dynamics of non-rotating and rotating fluids is the Coriolis force. It is instructive to consider flows that are dominated by the action of Coriolis forces and thus see these differences in their extreme form. Let us suppose therefore that the Coriolis effect is large compared with both the inertia of the relative motion and viscous action. Restricting attention to steady flow this means

$$|\mathbf{u} \cdot \nabla \mathbf{u}| \ll |\mathbf{\Omega} \times \mathbf{u}| \qquad (15.5)$$

and

$$|\nu \nabla^2 \mathbf{u}| \ll |\mathbf{\Omega} \times \mathbf{u}| \qquad (15.6)$$

Expressing these in terms of scales in the usual way

$$U^2/L \ll \Omega U \quad \text{and} \quad \nu U/L^2 \ll \Omega U \qquad (15.7)$$

or

$$U/\Omega L \ll 1 \quad \text{and} \quad \nu/\Omega L^2 \ll 1 \qquad (15.8)$$

The quantities $U/\Omega L$ and $\nu/\Omega L^2$ are known respectively as the Rossby number and the Ekman number; they indicate the ratios of respectively inertial to Coriolis forces and viscous to Coriolis forces. As in a non-rotating fluid, viscous effects may become important, even when simple order of magnitude considerations indicate otherwise, in boundary layers close to surfaces. We are here considering flows outside such boundary layers; that is flow in a region for which Euler's equation would apply if the system were not rotating.

When both the Rossby number and the Ekman number are small, the equation of motion becomes

$$2\mathbf{\Omega} \times \mathbf{u} = -\frac{1}{\rho} \nabla p \qquad (15.9)$$

where the pressure has been modified by the centrifugal pressure as discussed above. Flows in which this balance between Coriolis force and pressure force pertains are called geostrophic flows.

An important property of such flows is immediately evident. The Coriolis force is always perpendicular to the flow direction. Hence, the pressure gradient is also perpendicular to the flow direction. This means that the pressure is constant along a streamline — in marked contrast to the behaviour in non-rotating systems where one is accustomed to think of the pressure variations along a streamline (e.g. Bernoulli's equation).

This feature of geostrophic flows is familiar in the interpretation of weather maps. These are usually compiled primarily from information about the pressure distribution. Isobars are drawn and, because of the dominating influence of the Earth's rotation, these are then taken to be also the lines along which the wind is blowing (strictly speaking, the wind at some height rather than the wind near ground level).

Another interesting property of geostrophic flow is discovered by taking the curl of equation (15.9)

$$\nabla \times (\mathbf{\Omega} \times \mathbf{u}) = 0 \qquad (15.10)$$

This expands to

$$\mathbf{\Omega} \cdot \nabla \mathbf{u} - \mathbf{u} \cdot \nabla \mathbf{\Omega} + \mathbf{u}(\nabla \cdot \mathbf{\Omega}) - \mathbf{\Omega}(\nabla \cdot \mathbf{u}) = 0 \qquad (15.11)$$

Ω is not a function of position, so the second and third terms are zero. The continuity equation is unaltered by the rotation, so

$$\nabla \cdot \mathbf{u} = 0 \tag{15.12}$$

and equation (15.11) becomes

$$\Omega \cdot \nabla \mathbf{u} = 0 \tag{15.13}$$

If axes are chosen so that Ω is in the z-direction, this is

$$\Omega \partial \mathbf{u}/\partial z = 0 \tag{15.14}$$

i.e.

$$\partial \mathbf{u}/\partial z = 0 \tag{15.15}$$

There is thus no variation of the velocity field in the direction parallel to the axis of rotation. This result is known as the Taylor–Proudman theorem. In component form

$$\frac{\partial u}{\partial z} = \frac{\partial v}{\partial z} = \frac{\partial w}{\partial z} = 0 \tag{15.16}$$

If one is dealing with a system with solid boundaries perpendicular to the rotation axis so that $w = 0$ at some specified value(s) of z then this implies

$$\frac{\partial u}{\partial z} = \frac{\partial v}{\partial z} = 0, \quad w = 0 \quad \text{everywhere} \tag{15.17}$$

and the theorem says that the flow is entirely two-dimensional in planes perpendicular to the axis of rotation.

15.4 Taylor Columns

The Taylor–Proudman theorem has simple and striking consequences, illustrating the fact that rotating fluids exhibit a range of phenomena not found in non-rotating fluids. The principal of these is the formation of 'Taylor columns'. These occur when there is relative motion between an obstacle and the fluid in a strongly rotating system. We consider first the case in which this motion is perpendicular to the axis of rotation (giving what is called a transverse Taylor column). The fluid is deflected past the obstacle. Since the flow must be two-dimensional this deflection also occurs above and below the obstacle (visualizing the axis of rotation as vertical). There are thus columns of fluid, extending parallel to the axis from the obstacle, round which the fluid is deflected just as if the solid walls themselves extended there.

Although Taylor columns realizable in the laboratory involve complications not described by this simple explanation, prediction of their occurrence has received abundant experimental confirmation. Figure 15.2 illustrates this with a sequential pair of photographs showing the development of dye streaks originating inside and outside a Taylor column. Two features are to be noted. Firstly, the dye streak originating in the column is much shorter than those originating outside, showing that the fluid there is moving very slowly (all the dye streaks were initiated at the same instant). Secondly, the dye streaks meeting the Taylor column are deflected around it much as if it were a solid obstacle; it is important to realize that the dye lines are well above the top of the obstacle and would just pass straight over it in the absence of rotation.

Full appreciation of Fig. 15.2 requires some description of the method by which it was obtained. The basic apparatus consists of a rotating cylindrical tank, with an

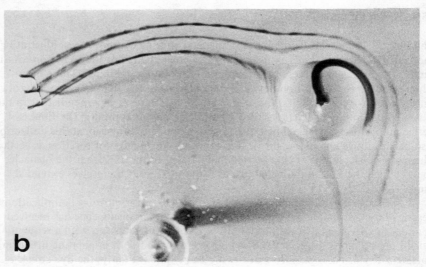

Figure 15.2   Streakline development in and around transverse Taylor column; see text for details. Photos by C. W. Titman.

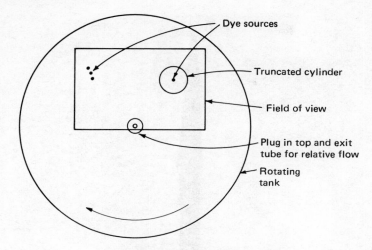

Dye sources

Truncated cylinder

Field of view

Plug in top and exit
tube for relative flow

Rotating
tank

Figure 15.3 Key to Fig. 15.2.

arrangement for pumping water in at the periphery and out on the axis. This produces the relative flow between the body of the fluid and an obstacle fixed in the
tank. Because the tank is rotating, this flow is not radial but azimuthal, fluid
particles moving round on circles concentric with the tank; the pumping can be
thought of as producing a radial pressure gradient which is balanced by the Coriolis
force associated with the azimuthal motion. The obstacle is a truncated cylinder on
the floor of the tank and extending about one-third of its depth. Dye can be
released (by the pH-technique described in Section 23.4) in four places, of which
the positions in plan are shown in the sketch (Fig. 15.3); in elevation, these dye
sources are about midway between the top of the obstacle and the top of the tank.
One source is over the obstacle and thus in the Taylor column. The other three are
placed so that the dye from them meets and passes round the Taylor column.

This experiment is, in principle, a repetition of the pioneering experiment by
Taylor [256], first demonstrating the validity of the surprising predictions of the
Taylor—Proudman theorem. Subsequent work [126, 127, 284] has provided much
information about the quite complex detailed structure of flows of this type; brief
mention of further features will be made at the end of this section.

A different type of Taylor column, a longitudinal Taylor column, arises when an
obstacle moves along or parallel to the axis of rotation. To understand this directly
in terms of the Taylor—Proudman theorem, one needs to consider the fluid as
extending to infinity in both directions parallel to the axis of rotation. Then the
obstacle pushes a column of fluid moving with its own speed ahead of it and pulls a
similar column behind it. In practice, as one might expect, Taylor columns are very
long but not infinite when the Rossby number is very small but not zero. Moreover,
for reasons connected with the local non-geostrophic regions mentioned below, part
of a Taylor column can be observed even when the apparatus is relatively short.
Experimental observation of this type of Taylor column is thus possible. Figure 15.4
gives an example. A sphere is rising along the axis of a rotating tank. Water near the
bottom of the tank is dyed, and the sphere has risen into a region of clear water

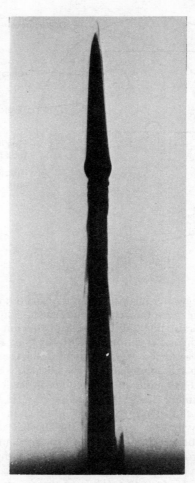

Figure 15.4   Longitudinal Taylor columns, shown by method described in text. The sphere is seen as a bulge in the column. $Ro = u_0/\Omega d = 0.136$; $Ek = \nu/\Omega d^2 = 0.00134$. From Ref. [176].

above. Dye carried into this region by the motion demonstrates the presence of Taylor columns ahead of and behind the sphere. With this technique, not all the fluid in the forward Taylor column is necessarily dyed, since some may have started above the dyed region; but the presence of dye so far ahead of the sphere clearly demonstrates the existence of the column, and is in marked contrast with what would happen in the absence of rotation.

In developing an understanding of the behaviour of rotating fluids, it is evidently going to be valuable to formulate a physical description of the processes underlying the Taylor–Proudman theorem. This is not in fact easy, just as it is not easy to develop a ready physical intuition about the behaviour of solid gyroscopes. A reading of Taylor's original papers makes it evident that he was surprised by the theoretical predictions and perhaps half expected that his experiments would not confirm them. However, some comments may be made.

As a starting point we note that the Coriolis force is independent of the actual location of the axis of rotation. The phenomena are thus not a result of rotation about a *particular* axis but rather the result of the flow occuring in the presence of uniform background vorticity of value 2Ω. At low Rossby number any vorticity associated with the relative motion is small compared with this. The relative motion cannot interact with the background vorticity in a way that would alter it so that it no longer corresponded just to a uniform rotation. It is motions that would do this that are excluded by the Taylor–Proudman theorem. (Note that the derivation of the theorem – starting with taking the curl of the momentum equation – indicates that it is a statement about the action of vorticity.)

One can say that there are two types of such motion: flows that violate

$$\partial u/\partial z = \partial v/\partial z = 0 \tag{15.16a}$$

and that would cause twisting of the background vorticity; and flows that violate

$$\partial w/\partial z = 0 \tag{15.16b}$$

and that would cause stretching of the background vorticity. (These ideas depend on the result – Section 6.5 – that vortex lines always consist of the same fluid.) The two processes are not in general independent but it is convenient to consider them separately.

Vortex twisting would occur for example if the fluid approaching an obstacle were slowed down but that approaching the region above it were not (Fig. 15.5 – the sort of flow that would occur in the absence of the background vorticity). This would produce a large vorticity component not in the z-direction, associated with which would be relative motions large compared with the original relative motion. The background vorticity thus resists the twisting and, in the case of low enough Rossby number, prevents it altogether. This is closely analogous to the action of a solid gyroscope in resisting turning, except that it is each individual vortex line that has the gyroscopic action not the system as a whole.

Vortex stretching would occur if fluid in a tank of finite depth moved from above an obstacle to some other station (Fig. 15.6). This would locally increase the vorticity (by the process described in the discussion following equation (6.27)) again causing a relative motion large compared with the original relative motion.

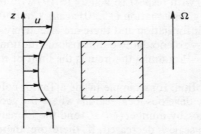

Figure 15.5 Flow violating Taylor–Proudman theorem through vortex twisting in regions of non-zero $\partial u/\partial z$.

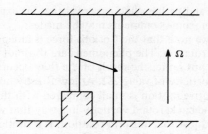

Figure 15.6   Taylor–Proudman theorem violating motion of fluid from above obstacle.

Thus this is also resisted. The analogy with a gyroscope is not quite so simple here; if a gyroscope were made of a deformable material certain deformations would be resisted by gyroscopic action. It should be noted that, although the above discussion has been given in terms of vortex stretching, it applies equally to vortex compression; a local reduction in the vorticity also corresponds to a large relative motion.

The Taylor–Proudman theorem indicates that, under circumstances specified above, the flow is two-dimensional. It is natural to enquire next about the pattern of this two-dimensional flow. For example, we have seen that, according to the theorem, there is no transfer of fluid between the inside and outside of a Taylor column; but there will be separate two-dimensional flows in each of these regions. However, no further information about these flows can be obtained from the geostrophic flow equation. This may be seen as follows. The equation now has two components:

$$-2\Omega v = -\frac{1}{\rho}\frac{\partial p}{\partial x} \tag{15.18}$$

$$2\Omega u = -\frac{1}{\rho}\frac{\partial p}{\partial y} \tag{15.19}$$

u and v are linked by the continuity equation

$$\frac{\partial u}{\partial x} + \frac{\partial v}{\partial y} = 0 \tag{15.20}$$

apparently providing three equations for the three unknowns u, v, and p. However, differentiating (15.18) with respect to y and (15.19) with respect to x and then eliminating $\partial^2 p/\partial x \partial y$ gives equation (15.20) again. Continuity, therefore, does not give any independent information and there are effectively only two equations for the three variables. Any solenoidal two-dimensional motion satisfies the geostrophic equations. The Taylor–Proudman theorem is the limit of the information to be obtained in this way.

How then is the motion, for example inside a Taylor column, determined? The answer is that the flow develops local regions where the geostrophic equations do not apply. Both the Rossby number $(U/\Omega L)$ and the Ekman number $(\nu/\Omega L^2)$ are increased if the length scale is decreased. If, therefore, there are regions in which the flow parameters vary over a distance small compared with the imposed length scales, then inertia forces and/or viscous forces may be locally important. There may be local violation of the Taylor–Proudman theorem. An obvious place for such a development to occur is between the two flows which, according to the theorem, do not interact; that is at the edge of the Taylor column. Thin shear layers are observed here. The whole structure of the detailed flow in the Taylor column (such as the slow motion seen in Fig. 15.2) is determined by these shear layers together with the boundary layer on the obstacle's surface. Because the two regions are separated by a layer in which the Taylor–Proudman theorem does not apply, there is in fact some interchange of fluid between the interior and the exterior of a transverse Taylor column. It is the shear layers also that govern the length of a Taylor column (either transverse or longitudinal) so that, although it is long at low Rossby and Ekman numbers, it does not extend to infinity as predicted by the Taylor–Proudman theorem.

A discussion of the structure of the shear layers is beyond the scope of this book [182]. However, it is interesting to note that we now have two classes of flows that spontaneously develop regions of small length scale. In boundary layer formation it happens in order that all the imposed conditions should be fulfilled; there is no solution of the equations when all terms that are small on the first approximation are neglected. Here, it happens as a process that selects a particular flow pattern; there is a multiplicity of solutions when all apparently small terms are neglected.

15.5 Ekman layers

We consider now a flow in a rotating fluid in which viscous forces are important but which is much simpler than the shear layers mentioned above. This is the Ekman layer, the boundary layer between a geostrophic flow and a solid boundary at which the no-slip condition applies. This turns out to be actually simpler than the corresponding problem in a non-rotating fluid. The results have the added interest of rather direct application to the atmosphere and the oceans.

We suppose that a body of fluid rotating about the z-axis has a boundary in the xy-plane. A geostrophic flow is occurring within the main body of the fluid and this is taken to be a uniform unidirectional flow, u_0, in the x-direction. In practice this means that the length scale of variations in the geostrophic flow must be large compared with the boundary layer thickness that emerges from the following analysis. Associated with u_0 is a uniform pressure gradient in the y-direction, the equations of motion in the geostrophic region being

$$2\Omega u_0 = -\frac{1}{\rho}\frac{\partial p_0}{\partial y} \tag{15.21}$$

$$0 = -\frac{1}{\rho}\frac{\partial p_0}{\partial x} \tag{15.22}$$

Between this geostrophic flow and the boundary is a region in which, as usual, viscous forces are brought into play by the boundary condition. We look for a solution for this boundary layer with the velocity field uniform in both the x-and y-directions. This is best justified *a posteriori*: one finds such a solution. However, it is at first sight a rather surprising procedure, since one knows that no solution of this type exists in the absence of rotation (Section 11.3). The reason for the difference is associated with the fact that a stress acts between the boundary and the fluid. Without rotation, this stress extracts momentum from the flow; in zero pressure gradient, the total flow momentum must decrease as one goes downstream, i.e. the boundary layer must grow. In a rotating fluid the stress can come into equilibrium with the integrated Coriolis force associated with the motion; once the boundary layer is formed no further growth need occur. Since the Coriolis force acts at right angles to the motion, this explanation implies that the boundary layer necessarily involves flow in both directions parallel to the wall.

Accordingly, we take u and v both non-zero but

$$\frac{\partial u}{\partial x} = \frac{\partial u}{\partial y} = \frac{\partial v}{\partial x} = \frac{\partial v}{\partial y} = 0 \tag{15.23}$$

and, as is then required by continuity,

$$w = 0 \tag{15.24}$$

The three components of the momentum equation become

$$-2\Omega v = -\frac{1}{\rho}\frac{\partial p}{\partial x} + \nu\frac{\partial^2 u}{\partial z^2} \tag{15.25}$$

$$2\Omega u = -\frac{1}{\rho}\frac{\partial p}{\partial y} + \nu\frac{\partial^2 v}{\partial z^2} \tag{15.26}$$

$$\frac{\partial p}{\partial z} = 0 \tag{15.27}$$

Equation (15.27) implies that

$$\frac{\partial p}{\partial x} = \frac{\partial p_0}{\partial x} = 0; \quad \frac{\partial p}{\partial y} = \frac{\partial p_0}{\partial y} \tag{15.28}$$

Hence, substituting (15.21), the equations to be solved are

$$-2\Omega v = \nu\frac{\partial^2 u}{\partial z^2} \tag{15.29}$$

$$-2\Omega(u_0 - u) = \nu\frac{\partial^2 v}{\partial z^2} \tag{15.30}$$

The boundary conditions are

$$u = v = 0 \quad \text{at} \quad z = 0 \tag{15.31}$$

$$u \to u_0 \quad \text{and} \quad v \to 0 \quad \text{as} \quad z \to \infty \tag{15.32}$$

Eliminating u or v gives a soluble fourth-order differential equation. However, the equation can be kept second-order by working in terms of the complex variable

$$Z = (u + iv)/u_0 \tag{15.33}$$

Multiplying equation (15.30) by i and adding it to equation (15.29) gives

$$2i\Omega(u + iv) - \nu\frac{\partial^2}{\partial z^2}(u + iv) - 2i\Omega u_0 = 0 \tag{15.34}$$

i.e.

$$\nu \frac{d^2 Z}{dz^2} - 2i\Omega(Z - 1) = 0 \tag{15.35}$$

with

$$Z = 0 \quad \text{at} \quad z = 0 \tag{15.36}$$

and

$$Z \to 1 \quad \text{as} \quad z \to \infty \tag{15.37}$$

The solution of this is

$$Z = 1 - \exp\left[\left(\frac{2i\Omega}{\nu}\right)^{1/2} z\right] \tag{15.38}$$

or, taking real and imaginary parts,

$$u = u_0\left[1 - e^{-z/\Delta}\cos(z/\Delta)\right] \tag{15.39}$$

$$v = u_0 e^{-z/\Delta}\sin(z/\Delta) \tag{15.40}$$

where

$$\Delta = (\nu/\Omega)^{1/2} \tag{15.41}$$

Figures 15.7 and 15.8 show the nature of this solution. The former shows u/u_0 and v/u_0 as functions of z/Δ. The latter presents the same information in the form of a polar diagram, known as the Ekman spiral. Different points along this correspond to different values of z/Δ (not uniformly spaced) and the velocity at each height is then given in magnitude and direction by the line from the origin to the corresponding point on the spiral. Noteworthy features are, firstly, that close to the boundary $v/u = 1$ and so the flow is at $45°$ to the geostrophic flow; and secondly, that at $z/\Delta = \pi$ the flow is in the same direction as the geostrophic flow but approximately 1.1 times as fast.

We notice that, as $\Omega \to 0$ then $\Delta \to \infty$; in the absence of rotation this solution collapses, as implied by the physical discussion above. In that case the problem of physical interest is always the growth of the boundary layer.

Laboratory verification of the above theory in full is difficult because achievable Ekman layers are rather thin. However, the main features can be demonstrated, an example being given in Fig. 15.9. This shows traverses with hot-wire anemometers (Section 23.2) in an air flow similar to the water flow discussed in connection with Fig. 15.2. The geostrophic flow is thus azimuthal, but radial motion exists in the Ekman layers on the top and bottom boundaries. Although the profile very close to the boundary is lost owing to probe size, maxima in the azimuthal and radial velocities are observed in relative positions that are in good agreement with Fig. 15.7.

A more important role of laboratory work on Ekman layers has been to reveal two types of instability [103, 253]. Both can be seen in Fig. 15.10, a dye pattern generated from crystals on the boundary. One type produces the shorter waves at the top left of the picture; the other produces the less regular, larger scale pattern in the middle.

The Ekman spiral is related to the observation that the wind at ground level and the wind aloft are commonly in different directions. At a general latitude, it is the vertical component of the Earth's rotation that is important, and the theory indicates

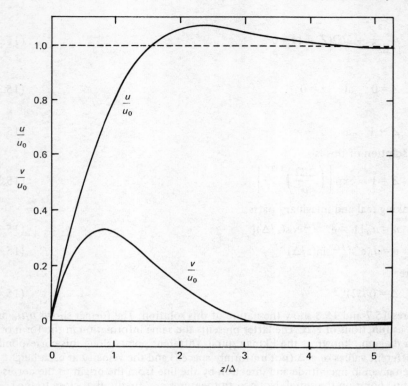

Figure 15.7   Velocity distributions in Ekman layer.

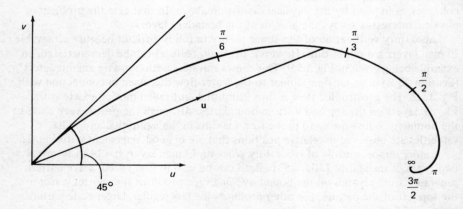

Figure 15.8   The Ekman spiral: polar diagram of velocity vector **u** in Ekman layer. Numbers along spiral are values of z/Δ.

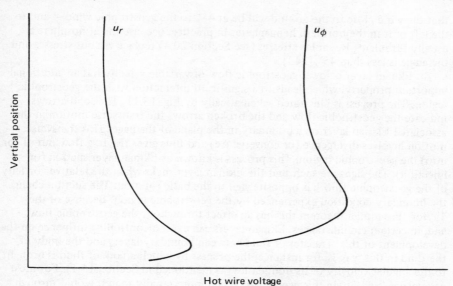

Figure 15.9   Azimuthal and radial velocity component measurements in Ekman layer below azimuthal geostrophic flow. From Ref. [253].

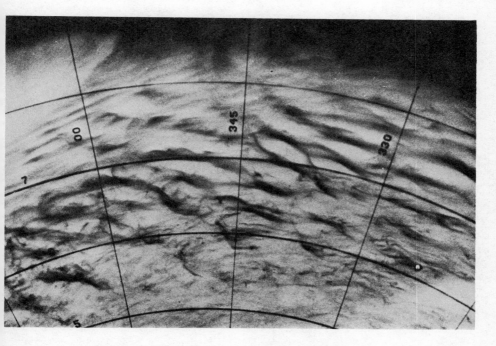

Figure 15.10   Ekman layer instabilities. From Ref. [103].

that the wind close to the ground will be at 45° to the geostrophic wind — and to the left of it in the northern hemisphere. In practice, because the atmosphere is usually turbulent, Reynolds stresses (see Section 20.4) replace viscous stresses and the angle is less than 45° [243].

An Ekman layer below a geostrophic flow of variable velocity has an additional important property, which leads to a significant interaction with the geostrophic region. The process is illustrated schematically by Fig. 15.11. The solid arrows indicate the geostrophic flow and the broken arrows the transverse motion in the associated Ekman layer on a boundary in the plane of the page. This transverse motion involves divergence (or convergence) and thus gives rise to a flow out of (or into) the geostrophic region. This process is known as Ekman layer suction (or injection). The signs are such that the Ekman layer sucks when the relative vorticity of the geostrophic flow has opposite sign to the basic rotation. The suction changes the boundary condition experienced by the geostrophic region. Because of the Taylor—Proudman theorem this has an effect throughout the geostrophic flow, and, in certain circumstances, Ekman layers can exert a controlling influence on the development of this. Transfer of fluid between boundary layers and the body of the fluid in this way is, for instance, the process by which a tank of fluid is brought to the angular velocity of its boundaries (as mentioned in Section 15.1). For most geometries 'spin-up' in this way occurs much more rapidly than it would through viscous diffusion [35].

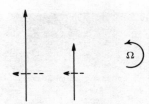

Figure 15.11   Sketch indicating reason for Ekman layer suction: see text.

15.6 Intrinsic stability and inertial waves

Rotating fluids have an intrinsic stability, in the sense that if a fluid particle is displaced there is a tendency for it to return in a way that would not occur in a non-rotating fluid. Consider an isolated particle of unit mass which, as a result of some disturbance, moves with a speed q in any direction perpendicular to the axis of rotation. (We are not, of course, considering here a genuine fluid motion or even a particular physical situation, but merely illustrating a general feature in the simplest way.) A Coriolis force of magnitude $2\Omega q$ acts on it, always at right angles to its direction of motion. It thus moves on a circular path of radius r given by

$$q^2/r = 2\Omega q \tag{15.42}$$

that is

$$r = q/2\Omega \tag{15.43}$$

It goes once round the circle in a time

$$t = 2\pi r/q = \pi/\Omega \tag{15.44}$$

independent of q. It thus returns to its original position periodically, twice during every revolution of the fluid. It is thus often said that a rotating fluid has an intrinsic angular frequency, $2\pi/t = 2\Omega$.

In a complete system, the effect of this constraining tendency acting on every fluid particle is that rotating fluids can support wave motions, known as inertial waves, that would not arise in the absence of rotation. Waves can be generated, for example, by oscillating a disc in a rotating tank (Fig. 15.12). Both theoretically and experimentally, waves are generated for any angular frequency below 2Ω.

We shall not enter into a detailed discussion of the properties of these waves. Very similar waves occur in stratified fluids and will be described in Section 16.4. Many of the features of those waves, such as the frequency being related to the orientation but not the magnitude of the wave number and the group velocity being perpendicular to the phase velocity, also apply to inertial waves [35, 200]. A consequence is the similar appearances of Figs. 15.12 and 16.11(a).

Figure 15.12   Inertial waves produced by oscillating disc in a rotating tank (lower part of pattern is produced by reflection at walls). Aluminium powder flow visualization (see Section 23.4). From Ref. [35].

15.7 Rossby waves [202]

By way of a further illustration of waves resulting from rotation of the system, we consider Rossby waves. These occur in particular geometrical arrangements. We consider them partly because they are of some meteorological importance (see Section 24.3) and partly because their origin can be seen rather directly in terms of the Taylor–Proudman theorem.

The simplest configuration in which Rossby waves occur is a layer of fluid bounded by two planes both almost perpendicular to the axis of rotation but not quite parallel to one another so that there are slight variations in the depth of the layer. Wave motions can then arise from 'twanging' the constraint produced by the Taylor–Proudman theorem. If a flow in the layer were exactly geostrophic, then it would have to follow contours of constant depth (from a line of reasoning exactly parallel to that given for the formation of Taylor columns). Correspondingly, if a fluid particle is displaced to a position of different depth, there will be a tendency for it to return to its original station. If it has inertia it will overshoot and oscillate. A complete flow pattern of such oscillations constitutes a Rossby wave.

The inertia involved here is that associated with the unsteadiness of the wave, $\partial \mathbf{u}/\partial t$. That associated with $\mathbf{u} \cdot \nabla \mathbf{u}$ is still neglected — by restricting attention to waves of small enough amplitude. Viscous effects are also assumed negligible. The dynamical equation is thus

$$\frac{\partial \mathbf{u}}{\partial t} + 2\mathbf{\Omega} \times \mathbf{u} = -\frac{1}{\rho} \nabla p \tag{15.45}$$

The nature of Rossby waves can be shown by considering the simplest case (Fig. 15.13) in which the depth, h, varies uniformly and in one direction only (chosen as the y-direction):

$$\frac{\partial h}{\partial x} = 0; \qquad \frac{dh}{dy} = \gamma, \text{ a constant} \tag{15.46}$$

γ is taken to be small.

We suppose that the waves retain the properties of geostrophic flow that

$$\partial u/\partial z = \partial v/\partial z = 0 \tag{15.47}$$

but that $\partial w/\partial z$ becomes non-zero. (This apparently arbitrary procedure can be shown, *a posteriori*, to involve no inconsistency; the pressure variation obtained by integrating the z-component of equation (15.45) produces negligible modification to the x and y components when γ is small.) Then the first two terms in the continuity equation

$$\frac{\partial u}{\partial x} + \frac{\partial v}{\partial y} + \frac{\partial w}{\partial z} = 0 \tag{15.48}$$

are independent of z and so

$$\frac{\partial w}{\partial z} = \text{const. w.r.t. } z \tag{15.49}$$

It now simplifies the analysis to choose the z-axis to be exactly normal to one of the boundaries, $z = 0$ say (Fig. 15.13). If γ is small, this makes negligible difference

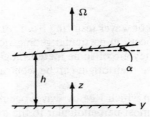

Figure 15.13   Definition diagram for simple Rossby wave theory.

to the dynamical equations. At this boundary $w = 0$. Hence

$$\partial w/\partial z = w_h/h \tag{15.50}$$

where w_h is the value of w at the top boundary, $z = h$. Here the flow must be parallel to this boundary (since it is supposed separated from the no-slip condition by a thin boundary layer). Thus

$$w_h \cosec \alpha = v_h \sec \alpha \tag{15.51}$$

$$w_h = v_h \tan \alpha = \gamma v_h = \gamma v \tag{15.52}$$

in view of equation (15.47). Combining equations (15.48), (15.50), and (15.52),

$$\frac{\partial u}{\partial x} + \frac{\partial v}{\partial y} + \frac{\gamma v}{h} = 0 \tag{15.53}$$

The Rossby waves are given by this form of the continuity equation taken in conjunction with the x and y components of equation (15.45),

$$\frac{\partial u}{\partial t} - 2\Omega v = -\frac{1}{\rho}\frac{\partial p}{\partial x} \tag{15.54}$$

$$\frac{\partial v}{\partial t} + 2\Omega u = -\frac{1}{\rho}\frac{\partial p}{\partial y} \tag{15.55}$$

From the physical ideas discussed earlier we expect to find waves involving oscillations up and down the depth gradient. We look for ones in which the velocity is constant in this direction; i.e. u and v are not functions of y. In so doing, we are losing generality even for the particular geometry considered. However, this provides an adequate context in which to see the principal properties of the waves.

The pressure must still vary in the y-direction because of the Coriolis force. Cross-differentiation of equations (15.54) and (15.55) now gives

$$\frac{\partial^2 v}{\partial x \partial t} + 2\Omega \frac{\partial u}{\partial x} = 0 \tag{15.56}$$

Substituting from equation (15.53) (in which the second term is now zero),

$$\frac{\partial^2 v}{\partial x \partial t} - \frac{2\Omega \gamma}{h} v = 0 \tag{15.57}$$

For scales over which the depth variation is small enough, $2\Omega\gamma/h$ may be treated as a constant, and we have a linear equation for which we may look for a solution of the form

$$v = v_0 e^{i(\omega t - kx)} \tag{15.58}$$

If this can be found with real ω and k, the flow can be described as a wave motion. Substituting gives

$$\omega k v_0 - 2\Omega \gamma v_0/h = 0 \tag{15.59}$$

and thus

$$k = 2\Omega\gamma/h\omega \tag{15.60}$$

The phase and group velocities are respectively

$$c_p = \omega/k = h\omega^2/2\Omega\gamma \tag{15.61}$$

$$c_g = d\omega/dk = -h\omega^2/2\Omega\gamma \tag{15.62}$$

These waves have the following properties:

(i) they are linear (the properties are independent of the amplitude so long as this is small enough for the equations to apply);
(ii) they are dispersive (c_p is a function of ω);
(iii) they are essentially progressive (the solution applies for only one sign of c_p, and so there can be no superposition to give standing waves);
(iv) $\partial u/\partial x$ and v are in phase (equation (15.53) with $\partial v/\partial y = 0$) and so u and v are $\pi/2$ out of phase.

The most direct experimental method of checking a theory of this sort is to introduce a mechanical oscillator into an appropriate configuration. Such experiments have been performed [132], although not in a geometry to which the above simplest theory can be applied, and show good agreement between theoretical and observed properties of Rossby waves.

Spontaneously occurring Rossby waves arise when an otherwise geostrophic flow is deflected in a way that violates the Taylor–Proudman theorem. Figure 15.14 shows schematically the pattern produced when a Rossby wave of the type analysed above is superimposed on a uniform bulk flow (speed U) in the x-direction. The wave causes the flow to meander up and down the depth variations. The wavy lines represent the instantaneous streamline pattern produced by the combination of the bulk flow and the instantaneous Rossby wave motions — indicated by the short arrows. The streamlines have the same spacing at the crests and at the troughs; the greater speed when u has the same sign as U is associated with each streamline then being at its minimum depth.

The whole pattern in Fig. 15.14 progresses in the x-direction with the phase velocity c_p relative to the bulk flow. If $U = -c_p$, the pattern remains stationary.

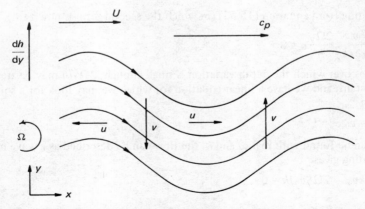

Figure 15.14   Diagram summarizing the properties of a Rossby wave superimposed on a mean flow.

This is what happens in flow past an obstacle in the appropriate direction in a rotating fluid of variable depth. The fluid is disturbed by the obstacle in a way that 'twangs' the Taylor–Proundman theorem and then oscillates as its travels downstream. The waves select the wavelength such that $c_p = -U$, and so the pattern is a steady flow relative to the obstacle (which could be analysed as a steady flow by replacing $\partial/\partial t$ by $U\partial/\partial x$ in the above treatment). The waves propagate downstream despite the 'freezing' by the bulk flow because the group velocity is different from the phase velocity; they propagate at a speed c_g relative to the fluid and thus at a speed $c_g + U = 2U$ relative to the obstacle.

Figure 15.15 shows a wave pattern produced in this way. This again is a situation

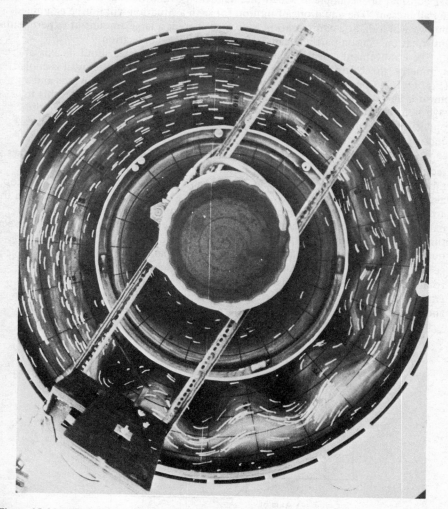

Figure 15.15 Train of Rossby waves produced by flow past a bump – see text – and shown by trajectories over a short time interval of suspended particles. Photo by A. J. Faller from Ref. [202].

to which the above simple analysis is not really applicable, but the processes
occurring are similar to those described above. The rotating annulus contains fluid
of greater depth at the outer wall than at the inner. The obstacle is at the bottom
left of the picture, obscured by its support, and the relative flow generating the
waves was produced as a transient effect by a sudden small change in the rotation
rate.

15.8 Convection in a rotating annulus [108, 128]

We consider one example in which thermal density variations, gravity, and rotation
are all present. The equations of motion for such a situation will not be examined,
but we will look at a configuration for which there is a large amount of experimental
information — again partly because of meteorological application.

The arrangement consists of an annulus of fluid that rotates about its axis of
symmetry, this being vertical; the outer wall is heated and the inner wall is cooled
(Fig. 15.16). Convection sets up a flow in which hot fluid moves upwards and
inwards and cold moves downwards and outwards. Coriolis forces act on this to
give an azimuthal flow in the same sense as the rotation near the top and in the
opposite sense near the bottom. This becomes dominant when the rotation is fast
enough.

This flow can then develop instabilities, such as that in Fig. 15.17, which shows
sections through the same flow at three different depths. The development of a
number of regular cells (three in Fig. 15.17) causes the azimuthal flow near the top
and bottom to meander in a wavelike fashion. As a non-linear development when the
amplitude of the instability becomes large, this circulation is concentrated into a
narrow fast meandering stream with rather slow closed eddies in the regions between
this and the walls (as can be seen in the first and third pictures of Fig. 15.17). The
number of waves round the annulus varies with the parameters concerned — the
geometry and the non-dimensional forms of the temperature difference and
rotation rate. The waves can also develop less regular and/or less steady forms,
either because the flow region is close to the transition from one wave number to
another or because the whole wave pattern itself becomes unstable.

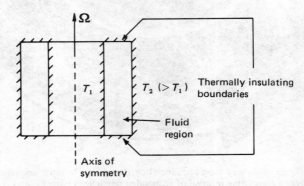

Figure 15.16   Arrangement for convection in a rotating annulus.

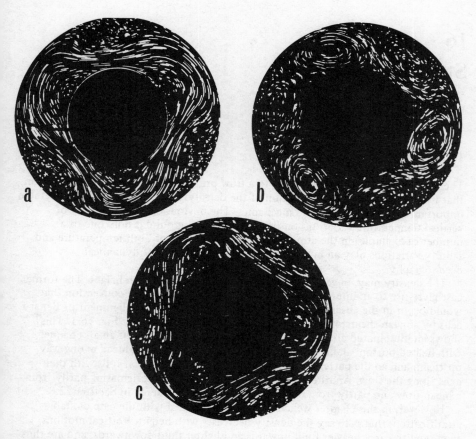

Figure 15.17 Patterns produced by suspended particles at three levels in rotating convecting annulus: (a) near top, (b) in middle, (c) near bottom. From Ref. [99].

16
Stratified Flow

16.1 Basic Concepts [33, 34]

The name, stratified flow, is applied to a flow primarily in the horizontal direction that is affected by a vertical variation of the density. Such flows are of considerable importance in geophysical fluid mechanics. The obvious case of the effect of vertical temperature variations on the wind near the ground is only one of a number of examples in the atmosphere, and the effects of both temperature and salinity variations play an important role in many aspects of dynamical oceanography.

The density may, in general, either increase or decrease with height. The former case gives rise to an interaction between the mean flow and the convection that would occur in the absence of mean flow. One example is the alignment of Bénard cells by a mean shear [49, 184], illustrated in the laboratory by Fig. 16.1. This shows an illuminated cross-section, perpendicular to the flow, of an air channel with heated bottom and cooled top; the smoke has been introduced a long way upstream and so the pattern indicates the occurrence of regular rolls with their axes along the flow. Another example — turbulent motion originating partly from a mean flow and partly from convection — will be considered in Section 22.8.

However, in this chapter we are primarily concerned with the case of stable stratification, that is to say the density decreases with height. Vertical motions then tend to carry heavier fluid upwards and lighter fluid downwards, and are thus inhibited. This inhibition may take the form of modifying the pattern of the laminar motion or of preventing or modifying its instability.

We require a quantitative criterion for this to be a strong effect. Since most of the experiments on stratified flows have used salt rather than heat as the stratifying agent (cf. Section 13.5) we shall retain the density variations explicitly, rather than relating them to temperature variations. We consider the case of flow outside boundary layers at high Reynolds and Péclet† numbers, so that both viscous and diffusive processes are negligible. Thus we write the momentum and density equations (for steady flow)

$$\rho \mathbf{u} \cdot \nabla \mathbf{u} = -\nabla p + \rho \mathbf{g} \tag{16.1}$$

$$\mathbf{u} \cdot \nabla \rho = 0 \tag{16.2}$$

---

†For brevity, we retain the names, Péclet number and (subsequently) Prandtl number, although, when salt is the stratifying agent these now refer to UL/κ_c and ν/κ_c (the Schmidt number), where κ_c is the diffusivity of the salt.

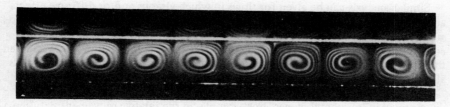

Figure 16.1 Cross-section of convection cells in channel flow; Ra = 4.16 x 10³, Re = 8.3. (Note: patterns at top are reflection of cells in channel roof.) From Ref. [49].

We take z vertically upwards and suppose that the basic stratification consists of a uniform density gradient $(-d\rho_0/dz)$. Because ρ_0 does not vary horizontally, the balance between $\rho_0 g$ and the hydrostatic pressure can be subtracted out from equation (16.1) just as it can for an entirely uniform density (Section 13.2).

We now consider, superimposed on this basic configuration, a flow with length and velocity scales L and U, produced, for example, by moving an obstacle of size L horizontally through the fluid at speed U. This will produce a modification of the density field which we denote by ρ', related to the stratification by equation (16.2) in the form

$$\mathbf{u} \cdot \nabla \rho' + w d\rho_0/dz = 0 \tag{16.3}$$

In order of magnitude

$$\rho' \sim \frac{WL}{U} \left| \frac{d\rho_0}{dz} \right| \tag{16.4}$$

W is now restricted by the fact that the flow cannot produce buoyancy forces associated with ρ' that are larger than the other forces involved. Since the buoyancy force does not contribute directly to the horizontal components of equation (16.1) it is convenient to work in terms of the vorticity form of this equation:

$$\rho(\mathbf{u} \cdot \nabla \boldsymbol{\omega} - \boldsymbol{\omega} \cdot \nabla \mathbf{u}) = -g \left(\hat{\mathbf{x}} \frac{\partial \rho'}{\partial y} - \hat{\mathbf{y}} \frac{\partial \rho'}{\partial x} \right) \tag{16.5}$$

Since the order of magnitude of $\boldsymbol{\omega}$ is U/L this indicates that the order of magnitude of ρ' must remain not greater than

$$\rho' \sim \rho_0 U^2/gL . \tag{16.6}$$

Comparison of this with (16.4) indicates that

$$W/U \sim \rho_0 U^2 \Big/ gL^2 \left| \frac{d\rho_0}{dz} \right| = (Fr)^2 \tag{16.7}$$

When $(Fr)^2$ is small the horizontal motion has only much weaker vertical motion associated with it.

Fr is called the internal Froude number, or, when as at present, there is no danger of confusion with the Froude number associated with free surface effects (Section 7.4), simply the Froude number. $1/(Fr)^2$ is sometimes known as the Richardson number (see also Section 22.8).

Similar analysis can be given for flows in which viscous and/or diffusive effects are strong. This is a matter of some complexity, since different detailed treatments are appropriate for low, intermediate and high Prandtl number. Thus we omit consideration of it; when we talk below of low Froude number flows, it is assumed that any other criterion for the flow to be strongly constrained by stratification is also fulfilled.

Often low Froude number motion can be considered to be entirely two-dimensional in horizontal planes. For example, in the relative movement between a spherical obstacle and a stratified fluid, nearly all the fluid is deflected to the sides of the sphere, little above and below it. Thus the flow pattern in a horizontal plane has a closer resemblance to unstratified flow past a cylinder than to unstratified flow past a sphere.

This is illustrated by Fig. 16.2, showing patterns produced by dye originating on a sphere in this type of flow. The view from above (Fig. 16.2(a)) is very similar to patterns observed in flow past cylinders (e.g. Figs. 3.4 and 3.8). In contrast the sideview (Fig. 16.2(b)) shows none of the structure of such patterns; for it to do so, there would have to be marked vertical motions.

An indirect consequence of this is that the instability in the wake of a sphere in a stratified fluid also resembles that in the wake of a cylinder, as is illustrated by Fig. 16.3 (cf. Fig. 3.5).

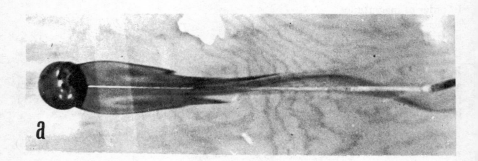

Figure 16.2   Plan-view (a) and side-view (b) of flow past a sphere in a stratified fluid; Fr = 0.21, Re = 164. From Ref. [92].

Figure 16.3   Wake of a sphere in a stratified fluid; Fr = 0.8, Re = 377. Photo by W. R. Debler. Reproduced by permission from 'Periodic Flow Phenomena', by E. Berger and R. Wille, *Ann. Rev. Fluid Mechanics*, Volume 4. Copyright © 1972 by Annual Reviews Inc. All rights reserved.

16.2 Blocking

Clearly a geometry for which the motion is two-dimensional in *vertical* planes will lead to radical differences between strongly stratified and unstratified flow. Consider, for example, relative motion between the fluid and a horizontal cylinder which extends right across the flow. No fluid can be deflected round the cylinder without vertical motion. If this is prevented, all the fluid in front of or behind the cylinder must be at rest relative to the cylinder no matter how far upstream or downstream one goes. Formally, if $v = 0$ because of two-dimensionality and $w = 0$ because of strong stratification, the continuity equation becomes

$$\partial u/\partial x = 0; \tag{16.8}$$

then for any z at which u is zero at one value of x, u is zero at all x.

There is an evident similarity between this phenomenon, known as blocking, and a longitudinal Taylor column (Section 15.4). Indeed a fairly detailed analogy can be drawn between two-dimensional motion in stratified and rotating fluids, the gravitational and gyroscopic constraints producing a range of comparable phenomena [285]. The analogy is closest when the stratified fluid has a Prandtl number around unity.

Figure 16.4 shows an experimental demonstration of the blocking effect. A cylinder was traversed slowly from right to left through a very long channel containing salt-stratified water. A dyed region was introduced initially ahead of the cylinder, but at a position that, when the photograph was taken, was far to the right. The interpretation is thus similar to that of Fig. 15.4. Not all the blocked region is necessarily dyed, but the presence of dye far to the left of the cylinder does demonstrate strong blocking action.

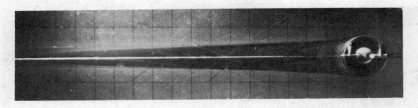

Figure 16.4   Blocking ahead of a cylinder in a stratified fluid; see text for experimental procedure. From Ref. [73].

As with Taylor columns, the simple theory provides a useful understanding of why the phenomenon occurs but little information about the detailed motion. In fact, low Froude number flows past obstacles observed in the laboratory often show marked asymmetry. Blocking occurs strongly ahead of the obstacle, as seen in Fig. 16.4, giving rise to a region sometimes known as an upstream wake, but the downstream effect may be much weaker. Almost certainly this difference has been particularly noticed because most experiments have been performed with salt in water as the stratifying agent. This has a very low diffusivity, giving a very high Prandtl (Schmidt) number. We can understand the behaviour for such a fluid in the following way [73, 117].

In any real situation, the disturbance produced by relative motion of fluid and an obstacle can extend only a finite, even if very large, distance ahead of the obstacle. Fluid initially far ahead of the obstacle must ultimately pass above or below it into the downstream region. This requires terms neglected in the simple prediction of blocking to become significant. We may anticipate that this comes about through the common process of a difference in length scales in different directions. Ahead of the obstacle it is not in fact necessary to have a small length scale appearing; the required effect can come about through the difference between the height of the obstacle, L, and the length of the blocked region, λ, as sketched in Fig. 16.5. For the same reason as with equation (16.5), we work in terms of the vorticity equation; we make the simplifications appropriate to two-dimensional flow, but, for a reason which will become apparent, we now include the viscous term.

$$\mathbf{u} \cdot \nabla \eta = \nu \nabla^2 \eta + \frac{g}{\rho} \frac{\partial \rho}{\partial x} \quad (\boldsymbol{\omega} = \hat{\mathbf{y}} \eta) \tag{16.9}$$

Because we are considering high Prandtl number, it is consistent to continue to

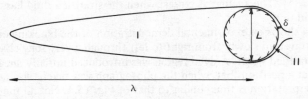

Figure 16.5   Length scales L, λ, and δ in stratified flow past an obstacle (see text). I – blocked region ahead of obstacle; II – boundary layer region behind obstacle.

neglect diffusion of the stratifying agent. Then every fluid particle conserves its density throughout its motion (the meaning of equation (16.2)). The horizontal density differences produced by some fluid particles rising a distance $\sim L$ will be $\sim L \mid d\rho_0/dz \mid$. Remembering also that $\eta \sim U/L$, we can write down the orders of magnitude of each of the terms in equation (16.9); using the same method as for the analysis of boundary layers in Section 11.2, the three terms are respectively $\sim U^2/\lambda L$, $\sim \nu U/L^3$ and $\sim gL \mid d\rho_0/dz \mid/\rho\lambda$. These are in the ratios $(\text{Fr})^2 : \lambda(\text{Fr})^2/\text{Re}L : 1$ (where Fr is defined by equation (16.7) and Re is the Reynolds number UL/ν). We see that no matter how large λ/L is, the inertia force remains small compared with the buoyancy force when Fr is small. But the viscous force can become comparable with the buoyancy force if

$$\lambda/L \sim \text{Re}/\text{Fr}^2 \qquad (16.10)$$

This result serves two purposes. Firstly, it provides a quantitative estimate of the length of the blocked region. As expected it is long compared with the obstacle size when Fr is small (provided Re is not too small).

Secondly, it indicates the physical mechanism by which fluid particles pass the obstacle. Small viscous effects come into play far ahead of the obstacle and very

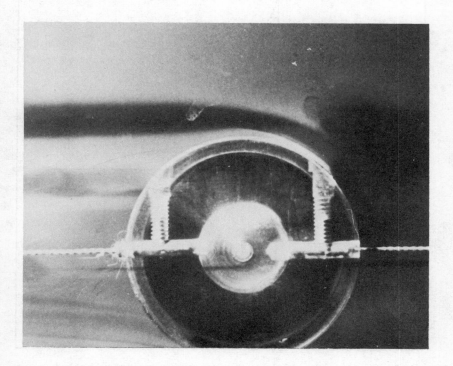

Figure 16.6 Flow around a cylinder in a stratified fluid. The dark band from top left is a streakline originating well ahead of cylinder and above blocked region; the rapid dropping down of this fluid immediately behind the cylinder can be seen. From Ref. [73].

gradually lift fluid particles (or lower them in the case of fluid particles starting below the centre plane) so that, by the time they reach the obstacle, they are able to pass over it.

The downstream behaviour can now be understood. The particles coming over the obstacle have retained their original density, which is markedly different from that appropriate to the level they now occupy. They thus tend to drop back to their original level very rapidly, an effect that can be seen in Fig. 16.6 (a close-up of the cylinder in the flow previously shown in Fig. 16.4). Inertia and/or viscous forces come into play here; the argument leading to equation (16.8) breaks down here through the appearance of a local length scale δ, small compared with L (Fig. 16.5). The subsequent downstream development will be referred to in Section 16.3.

This sequence of events depends on density diffusion being weak. For a fluid with Prandtl number around unity, for example, diffusion acts on the density whilst viscous action is lifting fluid, and particles passing over the obstacle differ in density only slightly from other particles at the same level. The dropping-back process does not then occur. The analogy with Taylor columns leads one to expect the downstream region to be much more like the upstream.

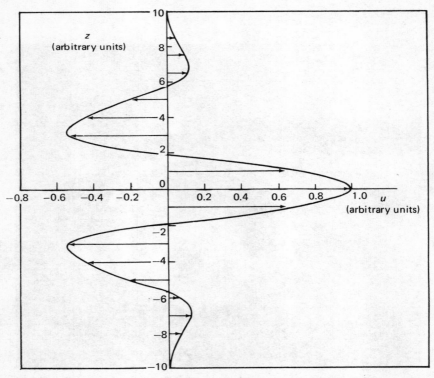

Figure 16.7   Example of theoretical velocity distribution in upstream wake of body moving from left to right. Reproduced, with permission, from 'Finite Amplitude Disturbances in the Flow of Inviscid Rotating and Stratified Fluids over Obstacles', by R. R. Long, *Ann. Rev. Fluid Mechanics*, Volume 4. Copyright © 1972 by Annual Reviews Inc. All rights reserved.

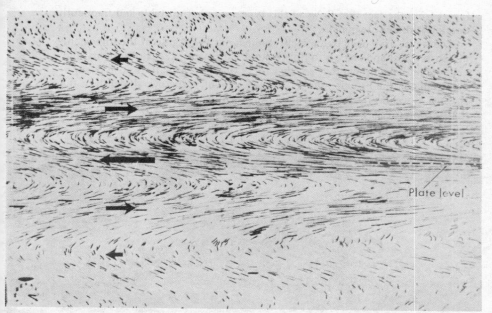

Figure 16.8   Pattern produced by suspended particles in region ahead of a zero-incidence flat plate (out of picture to right) moving through a stratified fluid. From Ref. [195].

The minimum Prandtl number at which there is negligible downstream blocking and the maximum at which there is effectively upstream–downstream symmetry both depend in complex ways on the other parameters [106]. By appropriate choice of obstacle size and speed, it has been possible to observe nearly symmetrical flows in a salt-stratified system [155]. There is not, however, so much experimental information available as for the asymmetric flow described above.

The detailed structure of upstream blocked regions has been the subject of several investigations. An interesting feature is the appearance of alternations in the flow direction, giving a velocity profile of the form shown in Fig. 16.7 and illustrated experimentally in Fig. 16.8.

16.3 Lee waves

The dropping-down process illustrated by Fig. 16.6 will (except at low Reynolds number) be inertial. Overshoot and oscillations about the equilibrium position may then occur.

A similar process may occur at any Prandtl number when inertial and stratification effects interact; that is at values of the Froude number around unity. The result is a pattern of waves, known as lee waves, downstream of the obstacle. An example is shown in Fig. 16.9; the obstacle in this case is on the floor of the channel. Although each fluid particle is oscillating up and down as it travels downstream, the overall flow pattern is steady in the frame of reference of the obstacle (apart from the fact that flows of this type are rather unstable and frequently develop turbulent regions).

Lee waves have been extensively studied, partly because of the important meteorological application to flow behind hill ranges [27]. Both theory and experiment have shown that a wide variety of different patterns can occur depending on the Froude number and the geometry; the overall depth of the channel as well as the height of the obstacle influences the structure of flows like that shown in Fig. 16.9 [34, 90].

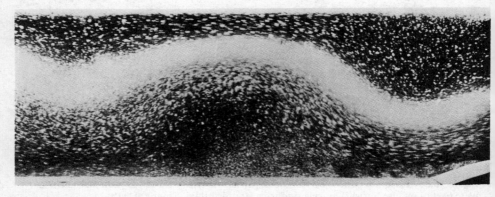

Figure 16.9   Example of lee waves produced by towing obstacle (from left to right) along floor of tank of stratified fluid; the camera moves with the obstacle to give approximately steady flow pattern. From Ref. [170].

16.4 Internal waves

The tendency for a displaced fluid particle in a stably stratified fluid to return to its original level means that waves can be generated in a variety of situations, of which the lee wave phenomenon is just one example. In this section, we examine some of the properties of these internal waves in the simplest context of a small-amplitude wave in an expanse of fluid that is otherwise at rest.

An important parameter associated with this situation may be introduced (and its physical significance illustrated) by considering first the behaviour of a small fluid particle that is displaced vertically. Suppose its density — which it conserves — is $\rho_0(0)$. If it is displaced a distance Δz upwards, the density of the fluid surrounding it is $\rho_0(0) + \Delta z \, d\rho_0/dz$ and the net gravitational force on it is $-g\Delta z \, d\rho_0/dz$. Hence, its motion is governed by the equation

$$\rho_0 \frac{d^2\Delta z}{dt^2} = g \frac{d\rho_0}{dz} \Delta z \tag{16.11}$$

and it oscillates about its original position with an angular frequency,

$$N = \left(-\frac{g}{\rho_0} \frac{d\rho_0}{dz} \right)^{1/2} \tag{16.12}$$

($d\rho_0/dz$ being negative).

N is called the Brunt–Väisälä frequency. When the density variations are due to temperature variations

$$N = (g\alpha \, dT_0/dz)^{1/2} \tag{16.13}$$

When, in addition, the adiabatic temperature gradient (Section 14.3) is significant

$$N = \left[g\alpha \left(\frac{dT_0}{dz} + \frac{g\alpha T_0}{C_p} \right) \right]^{1/2} \tag{16.14}$$

The above analysis does not, of course, describe any actual fluid dynamical situation. For that we must turn to the full equations of motion. We consider a wave of small amplitude in an inviscid, non-diffusive fluid. Hence, we require the equations of unsteady motion, but we omit the non-linear terms on the basis that these must be negligible when the amplitude is small enough:

$$\rho_0 \partial \mathbf{u}/\partial t = -\nabla p + \mathbf{g}\Delta\rho \tag{16.15}$$

$$\nabla \cdot \mathbf{u} = 0 \tag{16.16}$$

$$\partial \Delta\rho/\partial t + w \, d\rho_0/dz = 0 \tag{16.17}$$

$\Delta\rho$ is the departure of the density from its basic distribution, $\rho_0(z)$, and p is the corresponding departure from the hydrostatic pressure. We note that, although the problem is linearized, the term $\mathbf{u} \cdot \nabla\rho$ in the density equation still enters through the interaction between the vertical velocity component and the basic stratification.

We look for wavelike solutions, periodic in both space and time:

$$\mathbf{u} = \mathbf{U} \exp i(\omega t + k_x x + k_y y + k_z z) \tag{16.18}$$

$$p = P \exp i(\omega t + k_x x + k_y y + k_z z) \tag{16.19}$$

$$\Delta\rho = Q \exp i(\omega t + k_x x + k_y y + k_z z) \tag{16.20}$$

(where, of course, the real parts correspond to the physical quantities). Substitution of these into equations (16.15) to (16.17) gives

$$i\omega\rho_0 U = -ik_x P \tag{16.21}$$

$$i\omega\rho_0 V = -ik_y P \tag{16.22}$$

$$i\omega\rho_0 W = -ik_z P - gQ \tag{16.23}$$

$$ik_x U + ik_y V + ik_z W = 0 \tag{16.24}$$

$$i\omega Q + \frac{d\rho_0}{dz} W = 0 \tag{16.25}$$

where (U, V, W) are the components of $\mathbf{U}$. Elimination of U, V, W, P and Q from these homogeneous equations shows that they are consistent when and only when

$$\omega = N \left(1 - \frac{k_z^2}{k_x^2 + k_y^2 + k_z^2} \right)^{1/2} \tag{16.26}$$

This may also be written

$$\omega = N(k^2 - k_z^2)^{1/2}/k \tag{16.27}$$

or

$$\omega = N \mid \sin \theta \mid \tag{16.28}$$

where θ is the inclination to the vertical of the vectorial wave number
$k = \hat{x}k_x + \hat{y}k_y + \hat{z}k_z$ and $k = \mid k \mid$.

Thus waves exist for any value of the angular frequency from zero up to the
Brunt–Väisälä frequency N. Above N there are no wavelike solutions. (Since, in an
unstratified fluid, $N = 0$, this gives confirmation that the waves are essentially a
consequence of the stratification.) When $k_z = 0$, corresponding to a wave pattern
without vertical variation, $\omega = N$; an array of vertical columns, with the velocity
varying in the horizontal direction, oscillates at the Brunt–Väisälä frequency – as
might be expected from its simple derivation above. When $k_x = k_y = 0$, corresponding to a wave pattern without horizontal variation, $\omega = 0$; this corresponds to the
blocking phenomenon in steady flow discussed in Section 16.2.

The phase velocity of the waves is a vector in the direction of k with magnitude
ω/k.

Of greater physical importance is the group velocity, indicating the speed and
direction with which kinetic and potential energy are transmitted through the
fluid. The waves are dispersive in a rather unusual way; the frequency does not
depend on the magnitude of the wave number but it does depend on its direction.
The standard result that for a wave in one dimension the group velocity is $d\omega/dk$
may be extended to three dimensions giving

$$c_g = \hat{x} \frac{\partial \omega}{\partial k_x} + \hat{y} \frac{\partial \omega}{\partial k_y} + \hat{z} \frac{\partial \omega}{\partial k_z} \tag{16.29}$$

For the present situation

$$c_g = \frac{Nk_z}{k^3(k^2 - k_z^2)^{1/2}} [\hat{x}k_x k_z + \hat{y}k_y k_z - \hat{z}(k^2 - k_z^2)] \tag{16.30}$$

Since the properties of the waves are obviously axisymmetric about the vertical, we
discuss them in terms of the case for which there is no variation in the y-direction;
that is $k_y = 0$. Then

$$c_g = \frac{N \cos \theta}{k} (\hat{x} \cos \theta - \hat{z} \sin \theta) \tag{16.31}$$

It is interesting to compare this with the corresponding phase velocity:

$$c_p = \frac{N \sin \theta}{k} (\hat{x} \sin \theta + \hat{z} \cos \theta) \tag{16.32}$$

The group and phase velocities are mutually perpendicular. Energy is thus transmitted along lines in the planes of the wavefronts. It is this that gives the waves their
rather unfamiliar character – although, as noted in Section 15.6, analogous waves
can occur in a rotating fluid.

The other direction that is of interest in providing an understanding of the
structure of the wave motion is the direction of motion of the fluid particles.
Equation (16.24), which may be written

$$\mathbf{U} \cdot \mathbf{k} = 0 \tag{16.33}$$

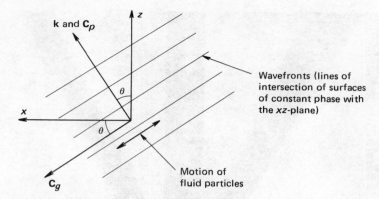

Figure 16.10   Summary of properties of internal wave in stratified fluid.

shows that this motion is always perpendicular to the wave number and thus to the phase velocity. The waves are essentially transverse. Moreover, since when $k_y = 0$, then $V = 0$ (equation (16.22)), the motion is along the same line as the group velocity. (More generally, equations (16.21), (16.22) and (16.30) show that the x and y components of U and c_g are in the same ratio k_x/k_y.)

Figure 16.10 summarizes the above properties of the waves.

The applicability of this theory has been demonstrated experimentally. Equation (16.31) shows that the group velocity is directed at an angle θ to the horizontal, independently of k. Since θ is directly related to ω, the angular frequency (equation (16.28)), all energy associated with a single frequency is transmitted at this angle. In the experiments a long horizontal cylinder was oscillated in a stratified fluid in the horizontal direction perpendicular to its axis. This produced a two-dimensional wave pattern which was observed by a schlieren optical method (Section 23.4) working on the refractive index changes associated with the density changes. (A special system was used to eliminate the effect associated with the basic stratification and to show only the changes produced by the wave perturbation.) Since the source is localized and the frequency fixed, energy radiates from the cylinder only in four narrow bands at angle θ (above and below) to the horizontal. This expectation was confirmed by the experiments, as is illustrated by Fig. 16.11(a). Experimental confirmation of the relationship between the oscillation frequency and the orientation of the rays, as given by equations (16.28) and (16.31), is shown in Fig. 16.12. When ω exceeds N, no waves are produced, as is shown by the contrast between Fig. 16.11(a) and (b).

The light and dark bands in Fig. 16.11(a) are lines of constant density perturbation and thus, in an instantaneous photograph, lines of constant phase. These are seen to run along the ray as in Fig. 16.10. Observations of the changing pattern showed that they moved across the ray in agreement with the theoretical direction of the phase velocity.

No prediction about the wave numbers present is given by the theory. For a single ω, all values of k are possible and all transmit in the same direction. In the experiments, there will have been a range of wave numbers present that Fourier

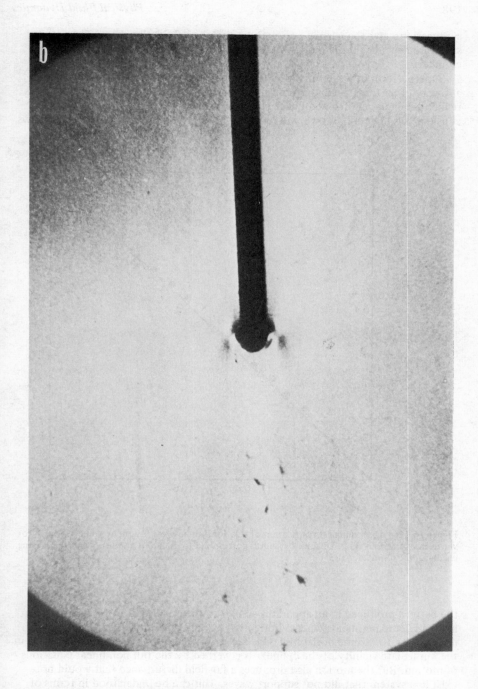

Figure 16.11   Waves produced by vibrating cylinder in a stratified fluid (dark vertical line is cylinder support). (a) $\omega/N = 0.90$; (b) $\omega/N = 1.11$. Ref. [185].

synthesize to give the narrow rays with undisturbed fluid elsewhere. The detailed structure depends on the motion in the immediate vicinity of the oscillating cylinder.

Superposition of waves of various frequency and wave number can give rise to a variety of patterns. Such patterns may be observed so long as the fluid velocities remain small enough for non-linear interactions to be negligible. We shall not consider this in detail, but we will look briefly at one example. Figure 16.13 shows

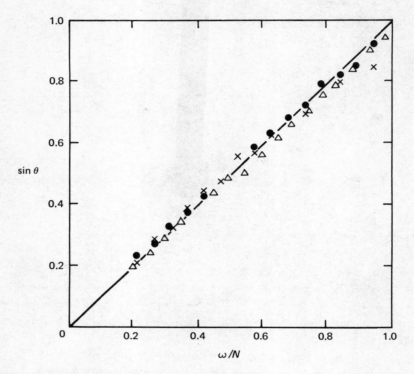

Figure 16.12 Experimental verification of relationship between frequency and ray angle for waves in a stratified fluid. Different symbols correspond to different amplitudes of the driving oscillation. From Ref. [185].

the pattern produced in an apparatus similar to the one used for the above oscillating cylinder experiments when a horizontal cylinder was moved uniformly in a direction at $10°$ to the horizontal. One sees a wake and a wave pattern. The flow in the immediate vicinity of the cylinder is governed by the full non-linear equations of motion. But the motion also produces a far-field disturbance that would not exist in a system that did not support waves. This can be understood in terms of the above linear wave theory.

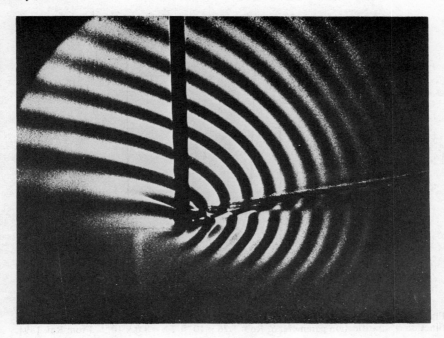

Figure 16.13   Pattern produced by motion of a horizontal cylinder through a stratified fluid (dark vertical line is cylinder support). Ref. [238].

16.5 Stratification and rotation

It is clear that the frequencies 2Ω and N, in respectively a rotating fluid and a stratified fluid, play analogous roles. Both can be shown by a crude argument to be the angular frequency with which a displaced particle oscillates; and both are the upper limit of the angular frequency range for which waves can occur. The relationship between the role of the Rossby number in a rotating fluid and that of the Froude number in a stratified fluid is readily seen if we write the latter in the form

$$\text{Fr} = U/LN \qquad\qquad (16.34)$$

When both rotation and stratification are present, their relative importance is indicated by the parameter

$$S = N/2\Omega \qquad\qquad (16.35)$$

Such situations arise in various geophysical contexts, and although we shall not consider them in any detail, it is useful to have a criterion that indicates the type of problem. A value of S around 1 indicates that rotation and stratification have comparable influences; when S is small, one is dealing essentially with a rotating flow modified by stratification, and when S is large it is the other way round.

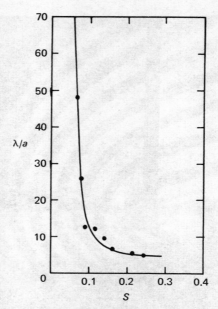

Figure 16.14 Length λ of a Taylor column (non-dimensionalized by sphere radius a) as a function of stratification parameter S. Ro = 1.76×10^{-2}, Ek = 8.0×10^{-4}. From Ref. [89].

Nevertheless the modifications can be substantial even when S is not close to 1. For example, it is found that Taylor column formation in a rotating fluid is strongly reduced as S is changed from 0 to around 0.1, as may be seen in the experimental results in Fig. 16.14. This shows the length of the transverse Taylor column on a sphere as a function of S (the length being defined as the distance in which an average fluid velocity in the column relative to the ambient fluid falls to $1/e$ of the sphere's velocity).

17
Instability Phenomena

17.1 Introduction

Frequent mention has been made in foregoing chapters of transitions from one type of flow to another (or from a state of rest to a state of motion) occurring as a result of instability of the former. We now come to a systematic consideration of such phenomena.

This chapter collects together a variety of examples of instability, emphasizing the experimental observations. Sections 17.2, 17.3 and 17.4 concern instabilities of rest configurations; that is they are cases where the instability is the cause of motion. Sections 17.5 and 17.6 concern flow instabilities causing transition from one type of motion to another. In most cases, instability leads not to a single new flow pattern but a whole sequence. Some of the further developments, after the initial instability, are also described in this chapter, but the amount of detail varies, depending partly on whether the topic is considered elsewhere in the book.

Often one can formulate a physical argument indicating the basic dynamical processes involved in an instability. Where appropriate, such arguments are given in the present chapter; they can add greatly to one's understanding of the phenomena. However, they do not give any quantitative indication of when the instability occurs. The next chapter will introduce the type of theory that has been developed for that purpose.

17.2 Surface tension instability of a liquid column

The first example is taken from a branch of fluid mechanics — flows with free surfaces — generally outside the scope of this book. It is included because it relates to familiar observations and because the instability has a simple physical explanation.

The basic state is a cylindrical column of liquid held together by the action of surface tension. As time proceeds, such a column develops corrugations in its shape and ultimately breaks into discrete drops [116, 120].

Theoretically, one may consider the column to be initially stationary; we are dealing with the instability of a rest configuration. In practice, of course, such a column cannot be supported. The instability is investigated experimentally in jets of liquid emitted from a circular hole. If the stress exerted on the jet by its surroundings is negligible its velocity is uniform both across and along the jet. The instability develops as the fluid travels away from the hole, resulting in a break up some distance downstream. (Such jets differ from those considered in Section 11.8,

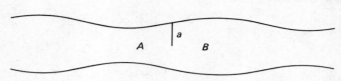

Figure 17.1   Instability of water column – schematic.

in that we were there concerned with jets emerging into the same ambient fluid –
for example air into air, or water into water – whereas we are now concerned with
jets emerging into surroundings with which there is negligible interaction – for
example water into air.)

The destabilizing mechanism may be understood in terms of Fig. 17.1, showing
the type of disturbance that grows. The column retains its circular cross-section but
with diameter varying along its length. The changed surface curvature will produce
a change in the pressure within the jet needed to balance the action of surface
tension. Provided that the wavelength is long enough the azimuthal curvature
dominates over the longitudinal curvature; i.e. the radius of curvature is
effectively the local radius a. Hence, the pressure is a maximum where the radius is
a minimum (at, e.g., A in Fig. 17.1) and a minimum where the radius is a maximum
(at, e.g., B). The pressure gradient thus pushes fluid in directions that amplify the
original disturbance. (More precisely, in an inviscid situation, it accelerates fluid in a
direction that increases the velocity associated with the disturbance. In a viscous
situation it works against the viscous force in a way that increases the displacement
associated with the disturbance.)

An alternative, equivalent, formulation of the physical cause of the instability
may be made in terms of the fact that a disturbance of sufficiently long wavelength
that conserves the volume of the jet decreases its surface area, and thus its surface
energy.

Figure 17.2 shows an instability of this type developing in a water jet. The highly
regular wavelength has been achieved in this laboratory investigation of the
instability by deliberately introducing a disturbance, periodic in time, at the orifice.

The break up of the jet into discrete drops, when the instability amplitude has
become large, can be seen at the right-hand side of Fig. 17.2. The drops can form
various quite complicated, but repeatable, patterns, of which an example is shown
in Fig. 17.3.

Although, in these pictures, the instability was promoted by a periodic disturbance, this is not an essential feature; break up of any such jet will occur
spontaneously. This relates to the break up of a column of water from a tap (even
when the flow is fast enough for the fractional changes in velocity produced by

Figure 17.2   Initial development of capillary instability of water jet. From Ref. [116].

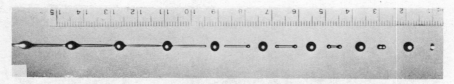

Figure 17.3   Example of subsequent development of instability in Fig. 17.2. From Ref. [116].

gravitational acceleration to be negligible) and to the familiar observation that the surface of water poured from a kettle is wavy. (In many 'domestic' examples, the situation is complicated by the jet not having an initially circular cross-section, in which case one does not start with an equilibrium configuration. However, the flow from a laboratory tap — with for example a nozzle for fitting rubber tubing — may correspond fairly closely to the ideal situation.)

17.3 Convection due to internal heat generation

Since the most important example of instability of a rest configuration, Bénard convection, has been extensively described in Chapter 4, we consider a related situation to represent this type of instability in this chapter. A horizontal layer of fluid of large horizontal extent is contained between a thermally insulating bottom boundary and a constant temperature top boundary. Heat is generated uniformly throughout the volume of the fluid. In laboratory experiments an approximation to this may be achieved through the ohmic dissipation of an alternating electrolytic current.

The heat so released is extracted from the layer through the top boundary and the temperature decreases upwards. The fluid is thus liable to the same sort of instability as a fluid layer heated from below — as in Bénard convection. Motion occurs when a modified Rayleigh number $g\alpha Jd^5/\nu\kappa k$ (in the notation of Section 13.2) exceeds a critical value. As the Rayleigh number is increased above this, the flow goes through a sequence of changes of comparable complexity to, but different in detail from, that described in Chapter 4. As examples, Figs. 17.4 and 17.5 show plan and cross-sectional views of cellular convection at Rayleigh numbers far above critical. The former illustrates a tendency for the horizontal size of the cells to become large compared with the depth of the layer. The latter shows that the falling regions become much smaller, and consequently faster moving than the rising regions. (The horizontal elongation is also apparent in this figure, but is more difficult to interpret because the section cuts different polygons of the plan view in different ways.)

One can see why differences from Bénard convection must arise at these high Rayleigh numbers. The Bénard flow involves some fluid particles travelling on closed paths at constant temperature (e.g. Fig. 4.12). This cannot occur when every fluid particle is being internally heated. The changes in cell geometry shown in Figs. 17.4 and 17.5 allow every fluid particle to lose heat by conduction during each circuit, the elongation by increasing the time for a circuit to the same order as the conduction time [273], the narrow downgoing region by bringing all fluid particles into the thermal boundary layer. That it should be the downgoing currents that are narrow and the upgoing that are broad is, of course, due to the

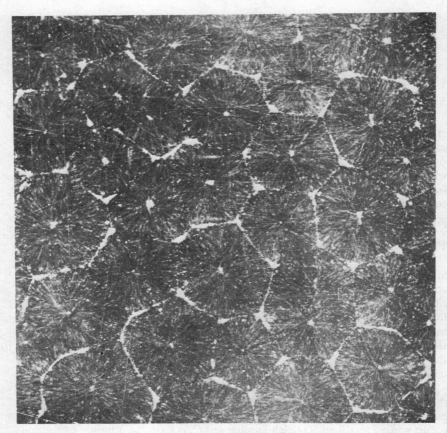

Figure 17.4   Cells in internally heated convection. Ra = 4 × 10⁴, Pr = 6. Note: field of view is about 35*d* square, where *d* is the layer depth. Flow visualization using beads that drop out of hot fluid and rise out of cold fluid (owing to difference in expansion coefficient from water); edges of polygons are regions of upward flow, centres downward flow; streaks due to beads still in suspension can also be seen. Ref. [278].

asymmetry between heating over a volume and cooling over a surface; only cold thermal boundary layers are formed (again a contrast with Fig. 4.12).

17.4 Convection due to surface tension variations

Figure 17.6 shows a cellular pattern that looks superficially similar to those considered in Sections 4.3 and 17.3. In fact, the flow is produced by a different instability mechanism, operative in a fluid layer with a free surface and depending on the temperature variation of the surface tension.

Figure 17.7 illustrates the process. A layer of liquid is bounded by a solid wall from which it receives heat and a free surface at which it loses heat. The surface tension of a liquid decreases with increasing temperature. Consequently, if part of

Figure 17.5 Vertical section through internally heated convection. Ra = 2.5 x 10⁵. Flow visualization using suspended particles illuminated only in one plane. Ref [93].

the free surface should become locally hotter than the rest, as a result of some small disturbance, fluid is drawn away from the region by the action of surface tension. Other fluid comes in from below the surface to replace it. This fluid has been closer to the hot solid boundary and will thus be hotter than the fluid at the surface. The original disturbance in the temperature distribution is thus amplified.

A steady state can be established with hot fluid moving towards the free surface, losing heat as it travels parallel to and close to the surface and then moving away again as cold fluid. In this way a distribution of surface tension can be maintained that drives the motion against the retarding action of viscous forces. It is found

Figure 17.6 Hexagonal cells arising in surface tension driven convection; aluminium powder flow visualization (see Section 23.4). From Ref. [144].

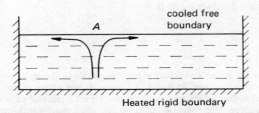

Figure 17.7 Mechanism of surface tension instability; effect of local increase in temperature at A.

experimentally (e.g. Fig. 17.6) that this process can produce an array of hexagonal cells of much greater regularity than is observed in gravitational convection. The fluid moves towards the surface at the centre of each of the hexagons and away from it around their peripheries.

Bénard's original experiments on cellular convection actually mostly showed surface tension driven patterns (cf. Section 4.1) [228]. This led to the belief — now discarded — that a hexagonal array was the primary type of convection.

Of course, one can get systems in which both surface tension and gravitational effects are significant, but we shall omit consideration of these [190].

17.5 Instability of rotating Couette flow

We return to the flow between two concentric cylinders rotating at different rates, considered in Section 9.3. There we looked at the solution applicable when the flow remains entirely azimuthal. However, this simple flow does not always occur; instability may lead to a more complex pattern developing.

Although this is the instability of a flow, not of a rest configuration, there is a significant similarity between it and Bénard type instability (Chapter 4 and Section 17.3), with centrifugal force† replacing buoyancy force as the destabilizing mechanism. The analogy extends to some features of the full mathematical treatment as well as to the physical ideas being discussed here [91].

The cause of the instability may be understood by considering a toroidal element of fluid (i.e. in cylindrical polar co-ordinates, the fluid between r and $r + dr$ and between z and $z + dz$ but at all values of ϕ). Suppose this is displaced to a slightly larger radius. If it is now rotating faster than its new environment, the radial pressure gradient associated with the basic flow will be insufficient to balance the centrifugal force associated with the displaced element. The element will then tend to move still further outwards. Similarly, an element displaced to a slightly smaller radius will tend to move still further inwards. There is thus an instability associated with some distributions of angular velocity. (The argument cannot be applied to a fluid particle localized in the ϕ-direction, as the displacement of this would introduce azimuthal pressure variations.)

The argument may be put into a quantitative form to indicate the condition for instability in the absence of the stabilizing action of viscosity; i.e. the condition analogous to the requirement for Bénard instability that the temperature must decrease with height. An elemental toroid, initially at radius ζ, and circulating at angular velocity Ω_ζ, is supposed displaced to radius η without interacting with the remainder of the fluid. Its angular momentum is then conserved and its angular velocity after displacement is

$$\Omega_\zeta' = \Omega_\zeta \zeta^2 / \eta^2 \tag{17.1}$$

---

†Only if $|\Omega_1 - \Omega_2| \ll \Omega_1$ is this a problem in rotating fluids in the sense of Chapter 15. The following discussion is thus phrased in terms of a non-rotating frame of reference. The centrifugal force considered is that acting on a particle moving on a circular path relative to this frame. The case of small relative rotation could be discussed using a rotating frame, in which case the action attributed here to the centrifugal force would appear as the action of the Coriolis force.

Its centrifugal force will exceed that of undisturbed fluid at η, circulating with angular velocity Ω_η if

$$|\Omega'_\zeta| > |\Omega_\eta| \tag{17.2}$$

Hence, there is instability if

$$|\Omega_\zeta \zeta^2| > |\Omega_\eta \eta^2| \quad \text{when} \quad \eta > \zeta \tag{17.3}$$

that is if

$$\frac{d}{dr}|\Omega r^2| < 0 \tag{17.4}$$

This is known as the Rayleigh criterion for the instability of Couette flow [37].

When the two cylinders are rotating in the same sense the flow is either stable everywhere or unstable everywhere. Substituting in equation (9.6), criterion (17.4) then becomes

$$\Omega_1 a_1^2 > \Omega_2 a_2^2 \tag{17.5}$$

When the two cylinders are rotating in opposite senses, the region close to the inner cylinder is unstable and that close to the outer cylinder is stable.

The Rayleigh criterion is modified in real cases by the action of viscosity (see Section 18.4).

Figure 17.8 shows photographs of some of the phenomena that result from the instability and its subsequent developments. These phenomena are quite varied [235, 240], and a complete account of the observations is not possible here. By way of typical illustration, Fig. 17.8(a), (b) and (c) show developments for a case in which the gap between the cylinders is relatively small compared with the overall radius and in which the outer cylinder is at rest [82, 226].

The first instability (occurring when the critical curve shown in Fig. 18.5 is crossed) gives rise to an axisymmetric flow pattern, as shown schematically in Fig. 17.9. Vortices of alternate senses circulate between the two cylinders. Each vortex extends toroidally right round the annulus. These vortices are known as Taylor cells. Figure 17.8(a) shows a photograph of this flow.

Increase of the rotation rate of the inner cylinder causes the Taylor cells to become wavy in the azimuthal direction as illustrated by Fig. 17.8(b). The number of waves around the annulus varies with rotation rate, but exhibits hysteresis, the exact pattern occurring for a particular set of conditions depending on how those conditions were approached. However, the wave pattern travels round the annulus at the same angular velocity — about one-third the angular velocity of the inner cylinder — for all wave numbers.

Further speed increases lead to further complexities in and greater irregularity of the flow pattern. As in Bénard convection, there is a long range in which both the regularity of a cellular pattern and the irregularities of turbulent fluctuations can be observed (Fig. 17.8(c)). Ultimately, the latter predominates and fully turbulent motion occurs throughout the annulus.

In some circumstances, turbulent motion appears suddenly without the preceding stages of development. This occurs principally when the two cylinders are rotating in opposite senses, but the outer one faster, so that the unstable region according to the Rayleigh criterion is confined to a small fraction of the annulus

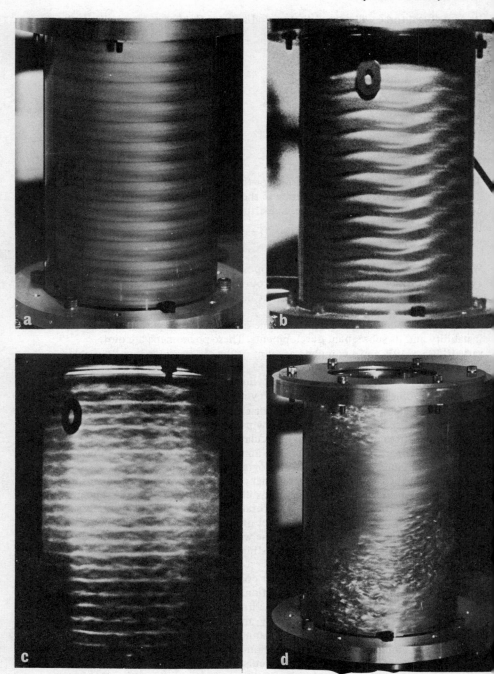

Figure 17.8   Flow patterns in rotating Couette flow − see text for details. Aluminium powder flow visualization (see Section 23.4). From Ref. [82].

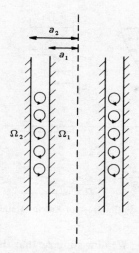

Figure 17.9   Arrangement of Taylor cells.

close to the inner cylinder. However, the turbulent region is not so confined, and it is likely that this instability is associated more with the shear in the annulus than with the action of the centrifugal forces. Its mechanics have thus more in common with the effects to be described in Section 17.6 than with the instability giving Taylor cells.

The stage preceding full turbulence is then intermittent turbulence, similar to that observed, for example, in pipe flow (Sections 2.6 and 19.3). For certain ranges of the imposed conditions, this intermittent turbulence is produced by a clearly identifiable spiral structure (Fig. 17.8(d)), [82, 283]. A spiral band of turbulent motion and a similar band of laminar motion form a pattern like the stripes on a barber's pole. This pattern rotates roughly at the mean angular velocity of the two cylinders, so that, at a fixed position, alternately laminar and turbulent motions are observed. The motion is also alternately laminar and turbulent if one follows the trajectory of a fluid particle, so that continuous transition from laminar to turbulent motion and continuous reverse transition are involved in the mechanics of the structure.

17.6 Shear flow instability

A variety of the most important cases of the instability of fluids in motion fall into the general category of the instability of shear flows. A shear flow is one in which the velocity varies principally in a direction at right angles to the flow direction (Fig. 17.10(a)). The simplest example of this, although it does not correspond immediately to a physical situation, is a flow with a finite discontinuity in the velocity as shown in Fig. 17.10(b). The fact that this is subject to instability — the Kelvin–Helmholtz instability — may be seen as follows. We consider the development of a disturbance in the frame of reference in which the two velocities are equal and opposite (Fig. 17.10(c) and (d)), so that, by symmetry, the disturbance

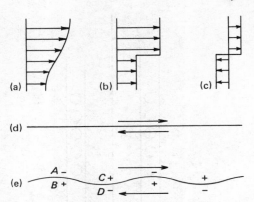

Figure 17.10   To illustrate the cause of Kelvin—Helmholtz instability — see text.

does not travel with the flow. We now suppose that the boundary between the fluid moving in one direction and that in the other becomes slightly wavy (Fig. 17.10(e)). This will make the fluid on the convex side (at, e.g., A and D) move slightly faster and that on the concave side (at, e.g., B and C) slightly slower. In a steady state, Bernoulli's equation would apply. Pressure changes indicated by the $+$ and $-$ signs in Fig. 17.10(e) will be produced by the disturbance. Thus the steady disturbed state is not possible and the pressure gradients are in directions producing amplification of the disturbance. More precisely, the fluid cannot support a pressure discontinuity and the unsteady flow must involve motions that counteract the above action of Bernoulli's equation. These are an acceleration of fluid above A and away from it and an acceleration below B and towards it. Such acclerations amplify the disturbance.

The experimental observations most closely related to this model have been made in stratified fluids (Chapter 16), primarily because the stratification provides a convenient method of producing a shear flow with little variation in the flow direction. A long horizontal channel was filled with liquid, dense at the bottom, lighter at the top. It was then tilted slightly so that the heavier fluid flowed down the sloping bottom wall and the lighter fluid up the sloping top wall, producing a steady stratified shear flow. Experiments were performed both with a sharp density discontinuity between two immiscible fluids (with surface tension acting at the interface) and with a continuous density variation in miscible fluids. Figures 17.11 and 17.12 show examples of the instability for the two cases respectively, when the destabilizing mechanism described above is strong enough to overcome the stabilizing action of the stratification. The regularity of the patterns during their development is noteworthy, but this does subsequently break down giving a turbulent motion.

Examples of shear flow instabilities in the absence of stratification appear in various places in this book. The velocity profiles (Fig. 17.13) of pipe flow, a boundary layer, a wake, a jet, and a free convection boundary layer all come into this category. In practice all such laminar flows break down when the Reynolds number based on the length scale over which the shear occurs, is high enough, although not all cases are unstable to small disturbances in the sense to be explained in Chapter 18.

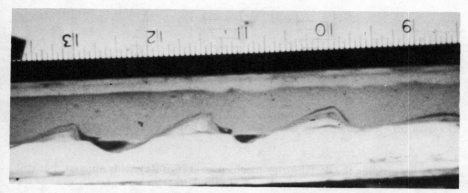

Figure 17.11 Shear instability at the interface of two immiscible liquids, the lower being denser. From Ref. [264].

The development of the instability is very sensitive to the details of the velocity profile. The critical Reynolds numbers of different flows may be widely different and, as is illustrated by Figs. 2.9, 3.5, 14.6, 14.9, 17.12, 19.5, 19.6 and 22.23(a), the consequences of the instability are very varied. Clearly, any generalizations about the physical processes must be treated with caution. However, the velocity profiles may be classified into two broad groups (Fig. 17.13): those with a point (or points) of inflection, such as a wake, a jet, or a free convection boundary layer; and those with no point of inflection, such as pipe flow or a forced flow boundary layer (in zero or favourable pressure gradient) [21, 164].

For the first group, processes broadly similar to the Kelvin–Helmholtz instability described above come into play and the flow is always unstable at high enough Reynolds number. The role of viscosity is primarily stabilizing, preventing the instability at low Reynolds numbers.

Flows of the second type are not subject to this instability, and there is the possibility (in theory rather than in practice) that they remain stable at all values of the Reynolds number. However, they frequently exhibit a different kind of instability that is essentially a consequence of viscous action. Viscosity now plays a

Figure 17.12 Shear instability in stably stratified fluid, exhibited by the lower denser fluid being dyed. From Ref. [265].

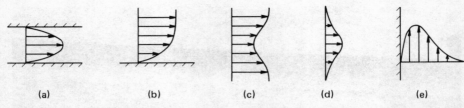

Figure 17.13   To illustrate that the velocity profiles of (a) pipe flow, (b) a boundary layer, (c) a wake, (d) a jet, and (e) a free convection boundary layer are all shear flows.

dual role, providing the destabilizing mechanism at high Reynolds number, but still damping out the instability at low Reynolds number.

The physical processes underlying these statements are subtle, and here we consider just one point. The process transferring energy from the mean flow to the disturbance to be described for turbulent flow in Section 20.4 can come into play in any shear flow for a large enough disturbance of the right structure. It may often come into play for a small disturbance, but when there is no point of inflection the disturbance can acquire the appropriate structure only through the action of viscosity.

We shall not dwell here on the consequences of the instability of shear flows. Most of the important cases are described in other chapters, with detailed discussions of pipe flow (Sections 2.6 and 19.3), the wake behind a circular cylinder (Section 3.3), boundary layer transition (Section 19.1), and transition in a jet (Section 19.2). In many cases, the final result far enough downstream is fully turbulent motion, at any Reynolds number for which the laminar flow breaks down. (There is often the complication that the Reynolds number increases with distance downstream.) A notable exception to this is the Kármán vortex street (Sections 3.3 and 11.7).

18
The Theory of Hydrodynamic Stability

18.1   The nature of linear stability theory

A large body of theoretical work has been developed in attempts to understand and predict phenomena of the sort described in the previous chapter. In most cases the cause of the instability can be formulated in a way that gives some physical understanding of the processes involved. However, this is usually opposed by some stabilizing process, such as the damping action of viscosity, and the physical argument provides no precise information about when the instability will occur. It also provides little indication of the detailed structure of the motion resulting from the instability.

This chapter describes the simplest type of theory that has been developed to make quantitative predictions about these matters — linear stability theory. We shall see that there are limitations to the information given by this and so one needs to turn to the much more difficult non-linear stability theory for further information [241]. However, that is beyond the scope of this book. Even the linear theory will be presented without mathematical detail. Thus this chapter is essentially an elementary introduction to the subject, formulated in a way that should provide those who wish to apply the results of this type of theory with some understanding of its nature and limitations.

The underlying notion is that transition from one type of flow to another results from spontaneous amplification of disturbances present in the original flow. One would then expect the occurrence of the transition to depend on the intensity and structure of disturbances present, and this is frequently found to be the case. Clearly, a theory covering all possibilities would be unmanageably complex;† moreover, comparison with experiment would be difficult since the nature of the disturbances is often not in complete experimental control.

Linear stability theory adopts a less ambitious objective — to ascertain when a flow is unstable to infinitesimal disturbances. It thus gives no prediction about transition promoted by sufficiently large disturbances; this may occur when the theory indicates stability. On the other hand, it should indicate conditions in which the flow cannot remain in its postulated form and must undergo transition to another type of motion. Infinitesimal disturbances are always present, even in the most carefully controlled experiment, and if these tend to be amplified, the flow will necessarily break down.

---

†There is also the rather vexed question of how large a 'disturbance' can be and still be regarded as a disturbance rather than a change in the basic flow.

The approach is analogous to that used to understand instability of solid mechanical systems. A pin stood on its point with its centre of gravity directly above the point is in equilibrium. This equilibrium is, however, unstable because even the smallest displacement of the pin will be amplified. Since infinitesimal disturbances can never be eliminated, the pin always falls.†

The linear stability theory for a particular flow starts with a solution (or approximate solution) of the equations of motion representing the flow. One then considers this solution with a small perturbation superimposed, and enquires whether this perturbation grows or decays as time passes. All terms involving the square of its amplitude are neglected; it is this that limits the theory to infinitesimal disturbances.

This linearization of the equations provides a means of allowing for the many different forms that the disturbance can take. Any pattern of disturbance may be Fourier analysed spatially. Because of the linearity, there are no interactions between different Fourier components. The equations may thus be broken down into separate sets of equations for each Fourier component, indicating the stability or instability of that component. All components can, of course, be treated in a single mathematical operation by retaining the wave number (indicating the particular Fourier component) as a parameter.

The theory for a single Fourier component considers a perturbation whose general form is proportional to

$$\exp[i\mathbf{k}\cdot\mathbf{r} + \sigma t] \tag{18.1}$$

The exact meaning of this statement varies from problem to problem; two examples will be considered below. In general, σ is complex

$$\sigma = \sigma_r + i\sigma_i \tag{18.2}$$

The growth or decay of the perturbation is determined by the sign of σ_r, the real part. If σ_r is positive, the Fourier component under consideration is amplified; this amplification will lead to the breakdown of the original flow. If σ_r is negative, the Fourier component dies away and the original flow can remain.

Hence, if σ_r is negative for all values of $\mathbf{k}$, the original flow is stable to all infinitesimal disturbances. This is a necessary condition for stability. If σ_r is positive for some values of $\mathbf{k}$, the corresponding perturbation will be spontaneously amplified. This is a sufficient condition for instability.

The significance of these remarks is most readily seen through particular examples.

18.2 Onset of Bénard convection [37]

The first case which we shall consider in more detail is Bénard convection — described in Chapter 4 and Section 14.7.

For an infinite expanse of fluid with the density increasing upwards, the physically evident instability is contained in the set of equations (16.15)–(16.17) for

---

† Buridan's ass — which died of starvation because it was exactly midway between a bunch of hay and an equally attractive pail of water — should have found a similar resolution to its problems.

small disturbances in a stratified fluid. The square of the Brunt—Väisälä frequency

$$N^2 = -\frac{g}{\rho}\frac{d\rho_0}{dz} = g\alpha\frac{dT_0}{dz} \tag{18.3}$$

is negative in this case. Hence the frequency ω of equation (16.28) is an imaginary quantity.

$$\omega = i\sigma \tag{18.4}$$

and the amplitude of the disturbance is proportional to $e^{\pm\sigma t}$, with σ real and positive. The case $e^{+\sigma t}$ corresponds to instability. (For instability one requires only that there should be at least one unstable solution of the equations. The existence of a second decaying solution, which would occur on its own only if one had an initially large disturbance of just the right configuration, is irrelevant.)

For the Bénard problem, one is concerned with the modification of this by viscosity and thermal conductivity, together with the boundary conditions. The previously amplifying solution may now become a decaying one (whilst the previously decaying one always remains so).

The initial condition is specified by the set of equations (14.40). A small perturbing velocity, temperature, and pressure field is superimposed. The perturbation must, of course, satisfy the continuity equation and the boundary conditions. In accordance with the ideas in Section 18.1 it is taken to be of the form

$$\mathbf{u} = U(z)\exp[i(k_x x + k_y y) + \sigma t] \tag{18.5}$$

$$\Delta T = \Theta(z)\exp[i(k_x x + k_y y) + \sigma t] \tag{18.6}$$

$$\Delta p = P(z)\exp[i(k_x x + k_y y) + \sigma t] \tag{18.7}$$

(the physical quantities being, of course, the real parts of these complex quantities). The Fourier analysis is thus performed in the two horizontal directions. It is necessary, in order to satisfy all the imposed conditions, to allow the perturbation to have general distributions in the vertical direction; $U(z)$, $\Theta(z)$, and $P(z)$ are determined as part of the solution.

The equations of motion are used to investigate the development of this perturbation with time, as indicated by σ. The results possess the following features. Firstly, they depend only on the total wave number

$$k = (k_x^2 + k_y^2)^{1/2} \tag{18.8}$$

and not on k_x and k_y individually. This is to be expected as all horizontal directions are equivalent and the choice of axes x and y is arbitrary. However, it implies that there is a variety of flow patterns all of which are simultaneously unstable.

Secondly, σ is always real,

$$\sigma_i = 0 \tag{18.9}$$

The perturbation thus either grows continuously or decays continuously. Any instability takes the form of an exponentially amplified disturbance.

The results on the sign of σ may be presented on a graph of the non-dimensional wave number,

$$\xi = kd \tag{18.10}$$

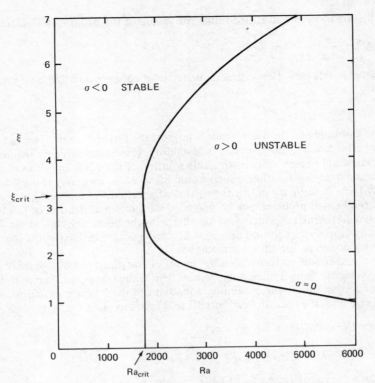

Figure 18.1   Marginal stability curve for Bénard convection.

against the Rayleigh number

$$\text{Ra} = g\alpha(T_2 - T_1)d^3/\nu\kappa \tag{18.11}$$

as in Fig. 18.1. The locus of $\sigma = 0$ separating the stable region with $\sigma < 0$ from the unstable region with $\sigma > 0$ is independent of the Prandtl number.†

For low values of Ra, σ is negative for all ξ. All disturbances tend to die away and the rest configuration is stable. For higher values of Ra there is a positive σ solution for some values of ξ. Hence, some disturbances are self-amplifying, and there is instability. A critical Rayleigh number Ra_{crit} is given by the lowest Ra at which this is true (Fig. 18.1): $\text{Ra}_{\text{crit}} = 1708$.

This is one of the successes of linear stability theory. We saw in Section 4.2 that fluid in a horizontal layer remains at rest when the Rayleigh number is less than about 1700 and convects when it is greater. There has been a number of experi-

---

†This result could have been anticipated. On this locus, $\partial u/\partial t$ is zero. $\mathbf{u} \cdot \nabla \mathbf{u}$ is also zero, because there is no mean velocity field and second-order terms in the perturbation velocity field are neglected. Hence, the whole inertia term $D\mathbf{u}/Dt$ is zero. Dynamical similarity is then governed by the Rayleigh number alone. The only balance of terms to be considered is that in the thermal equation, as indicated by (14.15) (no longer restricted to low Grashof number when the inertia term is identically zero).

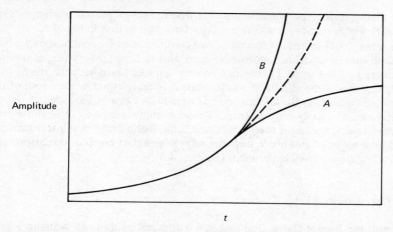

Figure 18.2 Schematic diagram of types of departure from exponential growth.

mental determinations of the Rayleigh number for the onset of motion, mostly using the heat transfer method illustrated by Fig. 4.4. Two examples of the results are: 1700 ± 50(Ref. [231]), 1790 ± 80(Ref. [263]). The agreement with the theoretical critical Rayleigh number is good and the theory can be said to explain the onset of motion.

One would hope that the theory might also make useful predictions about the flow pattern resulting from the instability. However, there are complications. The first is general to all problems in linear stability theory and concerns the relationship of a theory about exponentially amplifying disturbances to the steady or averagely steady flow pattern resulting from the instability. As the exponential growth continues, the original assumption that the perturbation was small will break down. Non-linear terms in the equations will become important and alter the exponential dependence on time. This alteration may take the form either of a levelling off (as in curve A of Fig. 18.2) or of a still faster growth (curve B). In the former case, which applies to Bénard convection, it is possible that the ultimate steady state flow pattern resembles the unstable flow pattern of linear theory. However, one cannot know whether this resemblance should exist without reference to non-linear theory. When the more catastrophic curve B applies, there must evidently be further developments before a steady state is reached and there is likely to be little resemblance between the form of the first instability and its ultimate consequence.

Returning specifically to Bénard convection, a similarity between the unstable flow patterns and the resulting convection may be expected. For values of the Rayleigh number only a little above critical, there is only a small range of unstable wave number. However, restriction to a single wave number does not uniquely specify the flow pattern, for reasons connected with equation (18.8). Not only may k_x take a whole range of values for a given k, but also linear combinations of solutions of the form (18.5) to (18.7) with different k_x but the same k are single wave-number solutions. In consequence, there are many single wave-number patterns, some of a complexity that makes them not instantly recognizable as such [239]. All occur with equal probability on linear stability theory. One has to turn to non-

linear theory or to experiment to discover that the actual pattern at slightly super-
critical Rayleigh number is a simple roll pattern such as that in Fig. 4.5.

Once the flow pattern is known one can compare the observed horizontal length
scale with that of unstable disturbances according to linear theory (i.e. that corresponding to ξ_{crit} in Fig. 18.1). The two concur — the distance between the middle of
a rising region and the middle of a falling one is roughly equal to the depth of the
layer — indicating that the application of linear theory can be extended in this way.

These remarks apply only when the Rayleigh number is just a little above critical.
At higher values, the linear theory tells one little. Again many non-linear theories,
beyond the scope of this book, have been developed, but much of our information
on this flow comes from experiment (Section 4.3).

18.3 Overstability [37]

The result for Bénard convection that $\sigma_i = 0$ does not apply to all systems. When
$\sigma_i \neq 0$, the development of the instability in time takes the form of an amplifying
sinusoid, as sketched in Fig. 18.3. Correspondingly, the resulting motion if non-
linear effects limit the growth is an oscillatory motion.

This type of behaviour is frequently known as overstability (although the name
is not a good summary of the physical processes involved).

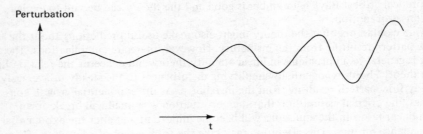

Figure 18.3   Overstability.

An example is convection in a horizontal layer rotating about a vertical axis. This
exhibits overstability when the Prandtl number of the fluid is low enough. Figure
18.4 shows an oscillogram of the temperature difference between two levels
obtained from an experiment with mercury.

In general, overstability is liable to occur whenever the system has a feature that
can give rise to wave motions. In the above example, the wave motions are those
associated with the rotation (Section 15.6).

18.4 Rotating Couette flow

We shall not discuss in any detail stability theory applied to rotating Couette flow —
which has been considered phenomenologically in Section 17.5. However, it may be
mentioned that this is another of the major successes of linear stability theory
[98, 257] and is historically important as the first case in which a detailed compa-

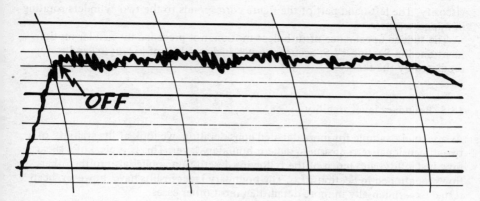

Figure 18.4 Temperature difference oscillogram in rotating Bénard convection. (Time increases from *right to left*; at start of trace system it is still warming up and at end it is switched off.) From Ref. [109].

rison was made between the theory and experiment. This was done by Taylor in 1923, observing the onset of cellular motion. Figure 18.5 shows his comparison for one value of a_2/a_1. The vertical axis corresponds to the case mainly considered in Section 17.5 of only the inner cylinder rotating. Points to the right of this correspond to both cylinders rotating in the same sense, and the dotted line represents the Rayleigh instability criterion, equation (17.5), obtained ignoring the action of

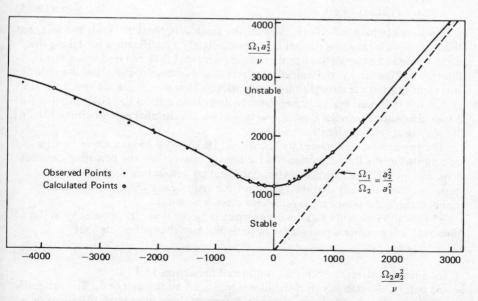

Figure 18.5 Comparison of theoretical and experimental conditions for instability of rotating Couette flow with $a_2/a_1 = 1.14$. From Ref. [257].

viscosity. The left-hand part of the figure corresponds to the two cylinders rotating in opposite senses.

The sudden appearance of turbulent motion, not preceded by cellular motion, mentioned in Section 17.5, occurs at much higher values of $| \Omega_2 a_2^2/\nu |$ and is not predicted by the theory.

18.5 Boundary layer stability

As a second example for more detailed consideration, we look at the stability of a two-dimensional zero-pressure-gradient boundary layer. This is typical of a shear flow instability, and much of the following description applies also to the other flows mentioned in Section 17.6. The boundary layer results have, however, been tested experimentally in more detail than most other cases.

The breakdown of laminar flow in the boundary layer is supposed to arise essentially from the instability of the Blasius profile (Section 11.3). This profile, with given values of the free-stream velocity u_0 and boundary layer thickness δ and thus of the Reynolds number

$$\text{Re} = u_0\delta/\nu \tag{18.12}$$

is taken as the basic flow upon which the perturbation is superimposed. The variation of δ with x is ignored for the stability calculation.

A two-dimensional disturbance of the form

$$\Delta u = U(y)\exp(ikx + \sigma t) \tag{18.13}$$

$$\Delta v = V(y)\exp(ikx + \sigma t) \tag{18.14}$$

$$\Delta p = P(y)\exp(ikx + \sigma t) \tag{18.15}$$

is considered (where the co-ordinates are the same as in Section 11.3). The fact that the basic flow is two-dimensional is not immediately a justification for taking the disturbance to be two-dimensional; a two-dimensional flow can undergo a three-dimensional transition, and indeed, the later stages of development and the resulting turbulent motion are strongly three-dimensional. However, there is a result, known as Squire's theorem, that in linear stability theory the critical Reynolds number for a two-dimensional parallel flow is lowest for two-dimensional perturbations [21,36]. We may thus restrict attention to these.

The perturbation expressed by equations (18.13)–(18.15) is a single Fourier component in the flow direction. As for Bénard convection, the perturbation must have an unprescribed form in the normal direction – a feature that might be expected from the fact that the growth of the disturbance will not extend appreciably outside the boundary layer where there is no shear.

The disturbance will be carried downstream by the flow. Its periodicity in the x direction will produce a periodicity in time. We may thus anticipate that

$$\sigma_i \neq 0 \tag{18.16}$$

– for a reason different from that considered in Section 18.3.

As before, the stability or instability is indicated by the sign of σ_r. The marginal condition is given by the locus of $\sigma_r = 0$. For shear flows in general, this locus on a Reynolds number versus non-dimensional wave number plot takes one of the forms

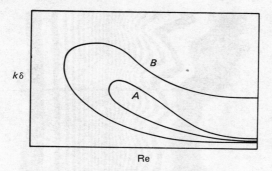

Figure 18.6   General forms of stability loops for shear flows.

shown in Fig. 18.6. There is instability inside either loop A or loop B and stability everywhere outside it. A loop of the form A, with the two limbs asymptoting towards one another as $Re \to \infty$ applies when the velocity profile has no point of inflection at which the magnitude of the vorticity is a maximum. The Blasius profile is of this kind. A loop of the form B applies for a flow, such as a jet, that does have such a point of inflection. (See Section 17.6 for a discussion of the differences in the destabilizing mechanism between these two types of flow.)

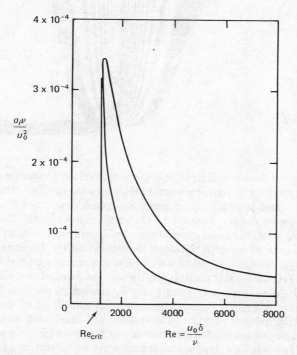

Figure 18.7   Stability loop for Blasius profile from Ref. [229]. (Note: two limbs asymptote to one another at much larger Re.)

$$\delta = 1200 \frac{1.5\,E-5}{300} = 6\,E-5$$

$$6E-5: \delta = 4.99 \left[\frac{\nu}{x}u_0\right]^{1/2}$$

$$\frac{\nu}{x}u_0 = \frac{36}{25}E-10 \qquad x = \frac{u_0\nu}{1.44\,E-10}$$

P. 106

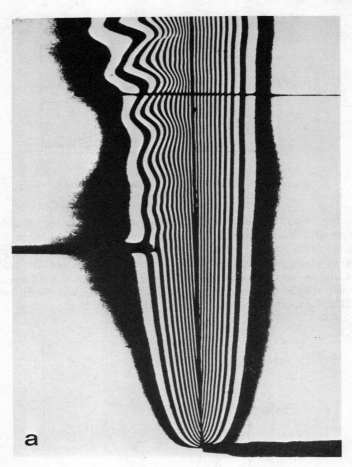

a

For comparison with experiment, it is more convenient to specify the particular Fourier component by its frequency rather than its wave number. The theory determines the speed at which each component travels downstream, so the two specifications are equivalent. Figure 18.7 shows the results for the Blasius profile in this way, $\sigma_i \nu / u_0^2$ being the most appropriate non-dimensional form of the frequency σ_i. δ is taken as the 99 per cent thickness (equation (8.14)). The curve shown gives the critical Reynolds number below which no disturbances are amplified as $\mathrm{Re}_{crit} = 1200$. (However, this result is sensitive to the detailed computational procedure and different workers' results vary by around 20 per cent [183].)

The instability of a single Fourier component, as considered by the theory, gives rise to a wave-like motion, periodic in both space and time. Such motions are called Tollmien—Schlichting waves. Their occurrence in the spontaneously occurring breakdown of laminar flow depends on the selective amplification of a particular frequency — or narrow band of frequencies. A wide range of frequencies will be present in a general disturbance. At any given Reynolds number, only a band of

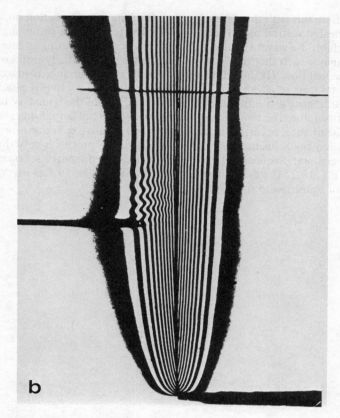

Figure 18.8 Amplified (a) and damped (b) disturbances in a free convection boundary layer. See text for details; note different horizontal and vertical scales. Disturbance is introduced in the same place in cases (a) and (b) but frequency is different. From Ref. [203].

these will be unstable according to Fig. 18.7, and within this band the amplification will vary. If a sufficiently narrow frequency range is amplified significantly more than other frequencies, a nearly sinusoidal disturbance may be observed to develop out of the initially random disturbances.

In practice, these remarks are observed to apply when the initial disturbance level is very low. Frequently when this level is not low enough, Tollmien–Schlichting waves are not observed as the first stage of boundary layer transition.

The best verification of the theory discussed above has been obtained from experiments in which a periodic disturbance is deliberately introduced [225]. The usual method in boundary layer studies is to stretch a fine metallic ribbon across the flow close to the wall. This is vibrated by passing an alternating current through it in the field of a magnet, just the other side of the wall. The resulting disturbance of the flow velocity can then be traced downstream.

It has been found that the disturbance increases or decreases its amplitude for a given frequency in good agreement with the prediction of the sign of σ_r in Fig. 18.7.

We illustrate this with the different example of the free convection boundary layer on a heated vertical plate (Section 14.5). The temperature variations make it easier to exhibit the waves visually. Figure 18.8 was obtained using an interferometric technique such that the light and dark bands are essentially isotherms of the two-dimensional flow. (It should be noted that the optical arrangement exaggerates the horizontal scale relative to the vertical by a factor of 6.4.) In this case, the periodic disturbance was introduced into the outer part of the boundary layer by a mechanical vibrator. The two parts of the figure contrast an amplifying and a decaying disturbance, occurring in the positive and negative σ_r regions for this flow.

When Tollmien—Schlichting waves are amplified, this process is only the first stage of an elaborate sequence of events. This is a case represented schematically by curve *B* of Fig. 18.2. The description is continued in Section 19.1 as part of a discussion of transition to turbulence.

19
Transition to Turbulence [21, 164, 219, 240, 249]

19.1 Boundary layer transition

Our knowledge of the development from the first instability of a boundary layer, described in Section 18.5, to the fully turbulent motion that ultimately results comes mainly from experimental investigations. Many of the experiments have used the vibrating ribbon technique (Section 18.5). Although this was originally introduced to investigate the relevance of the linear stability theory, it proved a useful way of controlling the boundary layer development and ensuring that the same features were to be observed repeatedly at the same place. Its use was thus extended to experiments on the essentially non-linear developments further downstream. The relationship of information so obtained to the processes in naturally occurring transition will be considered later in this section.

The breakdown of a Tollmien–Schlichting wave into a more complicated motion occurs when its amplitude reaches a critical value of around 0.01 to 0.02 (depending on the non-dimensional frequency of the wave) in the ratio of the root mean square velocity at its maximum position to the free-stream velocity [137].

This critical amplitude is not always reached. The Reynolds number of a laminar boundary layer increases with distance downstream, in consequence of the increasing boundary layer thickness. The linear development of a wave of a given frequency is thus indicated by a horizontal line on the stability loop, as shown in Fig. 19.1. A wave that is initially amplified may subsequently be attenuated as this line passes out of the loop. Provided that this happens before the critical amplitude is reached, the whole history of the wave is well described by the linear theory.

If, however, the critical amplitude is reached, the subsequent development of the disturbance is entirely different. The linear theory no longer applies and, regardless of whether the stability loop indicates amplification or attenuation of the initial wave, a sequence of events ensues leading finally to a fully turbulent boundary layer.

This sequence starts with the waves becoming three-dimensional; their amplitude varies in the lateral direction parallel to the wall. Simultaneously, they interact with the mean flow, so that the velocity profile also has three-dimensional variations. Figure 19.2 shows one set of measurements illustrating this development.

The growth of these three-dimensionalities continues until there are transient local regions of very high shear. Figure 19.3 indicates the variation of the velocity profile inferred from measurements with hot-wire anemometers (Section 23.2), through one cycle of the wave at the lateral position where the wave amplitude is largest. The next development is initiated in the regions of high shear, apparent in the figure for t' between 0.38 and 0.6.

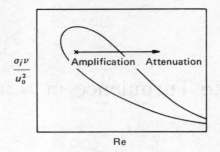

Figure 19.1   Locus on stability loop of disturbance of given frequency.

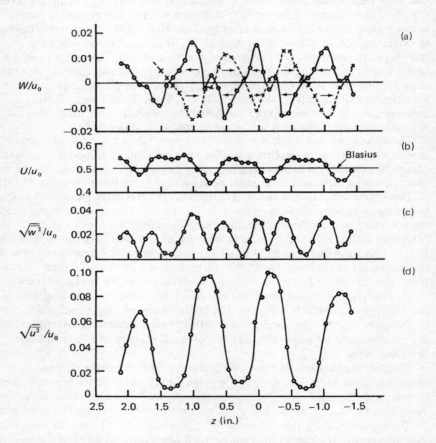

Figure 19.2   Example of variations in z-direction (where x is flow direction, y is distance from wall) of (a) mean velocity in z-direction, (b) mean velocity in x-direction, (c) r.m.s. velocity fluctuation in z-direction, and (d) r.m.s. velocity fluctuation in x-direction, in nominally two-dimensional transitional boundary layer. Solid lines: $y/\delta = 0.31$; dotted line: $y/\delta = 0.11$. From Ref. [138].

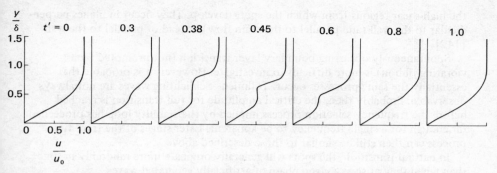

Figure 19.3 Instantaneous velocity profiles in transitional boundary layer; t' is time in units of oscillation period. From Ref. [147].

Hitherto, although the structure of the motion has become increasingly complex, the time scale of the velocity fluctuations has remained of the same order as the period of the initial wave. Now irregular fluctuations with much shorter time scales appear. A small part of the boundary layer has become turbulent.

The remainder of the transition process consists essentially of the growth of local regions of turbulent motion produced in this way, whilst they travel downstream [97]. The turbulence spreads fairly quickly over the thickness of the boundary layer. Each turbulent spot — as it is usually called — is then surrounded laterally and longitudinally by non-turbulent fluid. The motion within the spot is similar to that in a fully turbulent boundary layer. Elsewhere, the velocity fluctuations are still much slower. A spreading process then occurs, non-turbulent fluid next to the spot being continuously brought into turbulent motion. The turbulent spots have a characteristic shape — shown in Fig. 19.4 — the spreading rates in different directions being such that they retain this shape as they grow [224].

As the spots grow they merge into one another. Eventually, all the non-turbulent regions have been absorbed and the boundary layer is wholly turbulent.

The transition takes the detailed form indicated by Figs. 19.2 and 19.3 only when the boundary layer is quite closely two-dimensional. Small three-dimensional variations in the boundary layer thickness, preceding the growth of Tollmien–Schlichting waves, have been observed to change the location and orientation of

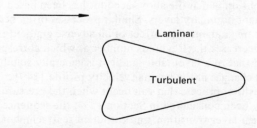

Figure 19.4 Characteristic shape (in plane parallel to the wall) of a turbulent spot in a boundary layer.

the high-shear regions from which the spots develop. They occur in planes perpendicular to the wall (and parallel to the main flow) instead of parallel to the wall [142].

Spontaneously occurring boundary layer transition (not promoted by a vibrating ribbon) is more difficult to investigate. However, it is probable that essentially the same processes occur. Tollmien—Schlichting waves are not always observable. Probably then, the critical amplitude for full transition is reached before the frequency selection process implied by the stability loop has proceeded far enough for a single frequency to be apparent. Later stages of the transition process can then still be similar to those described above.

In natural transition, the spots will generally originate more randomly in time than when they arise at a given phase of artificially generated waves.

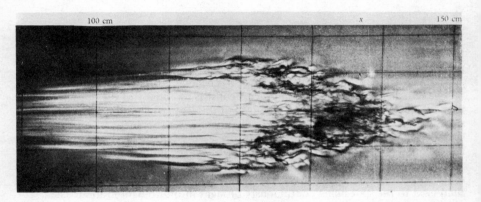

Figure 19.5   Turbulent spot generated in boundary layer in water channel by disturbance at $x = 50$ cm. Flow visualization by dye crystals sprinkled on wall upstream of picture. Note: the spot is the disturbed region at right of picture; clear patch at left is region that has been swept clear of dye by the passage of the spot. From Ref. [100].

A large localized disturbance can directly produce a turbulent spot. In experiments to investigate the growth and structure of spots, they have been generated by a rod momentarily poked into the boundary layer and by a small spark [100, 224]. Figure 19.5 shows such an artificially generated spot.

The investigations on which the above account has been based were made in zero-pressure-gradient boundary layers. Similar processes often occur in the presence of a pressure gradient. The effect of an adverse gradient is generally destabilizing — it decreases the Reynolds number at which corresponding developments occur — and that of a favourable gradient is generally stabilizing. These changes arise from changes in the laminar velocity profile [249].

A different transition process that can occur when the pressure gradient is adverse has already been considered in Section 11.4: the sequence of laminar separation, free shear layer transition, and turbulent reattachment. Although the initial attached laminar layer might be stable, the final reattached layer remains turbulent [249].

19.2 Transition in jets and other free shear flows

Some of the features of boundary layer transition, described above, occur only in shear flows adjacent to a solid boundary. We now look at the transition process in free shear flows; that is ones away from any solid boundary. As our main example we consider transition in jets (of the type introduced in Section 11.8 with the ambient fluid the same as that in the jet). We shall see that the principal differences arise in the later stages of transition.

The breakdown of a laminar jet usually starts quite close to the orifice, where the velocity profile still depends on the details of orifice geometry and the flow upstream of it. Hence, different experiments may not be directly comparable, and there may similarly be difficulties of comparison between experiment and theory. However, the broad features of the transition process are always much the same, and, if we omit quantitative detail, can be described without reference to any particular jet.

Disturbances first appear as approximately sinusoidal fluctuations, indicating a selective amplification process like that in a boundary layer. This stage can be satisfactorily related to linear stability theory — a stability loop of type B in Fig. 18.6 being relevant. Free shear flows become unstable at lower Reynolds numbers than shear flows next to walls; the order of magnitude of the critical Reynolds number for a jet is typically 10 (compared with 10^3 for a boundary layer) [218, 255].

The ability of an applied periodic disturbance in the appropriate frequency range to promote the instability can have rather spectacular results in jets — as is shown in Fig. 19.6. In such experiments, the disturbance is usually provided as a sound wave from a nearby loudspeaker. The acoustic wavelength is long compared with the wavelength of the instability, and the fluid thus experiences a periodic disturbance of negligible phase variation.†

Pictures (a)–(c) of Fig. 19.6 show a smoke-carrying jet when acoustic disturbances were minimized. Figure 19.6(a) and (b) have general illumination, (a) with a relatively long exposure so that details of the instability are blurred and (b) as a flash so that an instantaneous pattern is seen. The close-up (c) is again an instantaneous picture, but with illumination through a slit showing one part of the jet. A spontaneously arising periodic instability can be seen. Pictures (d)–(f) show the same jet with the frequency from a loudspeaker selected to have maximum

---

†The observation that jets respond to sound is an old one, first made with flames. The following introduction to an early paper on the subject, written in 1858 by J. Leconte [156], makes pleasant reading: 'A short time after reading Prof. John Tyndall's excellent article, I happened to be one of a party of eight persons assembled after tea for the purpose of enjoying a private musical entertainment. Three instruments were employed in the performance of several of the grand trios of Beethoven, namely, the piano, violin and violoncello. Two "fish-tail" gas-burners projected from the brick wall near the piano. Both of them burnt with remarkable steadiness, the windows being closed and the air in the room being very calm. Nevertheless it was evident that one of them was under a pressure nearly sufficient to make it flare. Soon after the music commenced, I observed that the flame of the last mentioned burner exhibited pulsations in height which were exactly synchronous with the audible beats. This phenomenon was very striking to everyone in the room, and especially so when the strong notes of the violoncello came in. It was exceedingly interesting to observe how perfectly even the trills of this instrument were reflected on the sheet of flame. A deaf man might have seen the harmony.'

effect; (d) and (e) are the counterparts of (a) and (b). Like (c), (f) has slit illumination, but this is stroboscopic at the same frequency as the sound. Since the exposure extends over about 1800 flashes of the stroboscope, the clarity of the picture demonstrates the extreme regularity of the pattern in its initial stages.

It is clear from Fig. 19.6 and from other similar work [50, 107] that the instability can give rise to well-developed vortices whilst it is still in the periodic

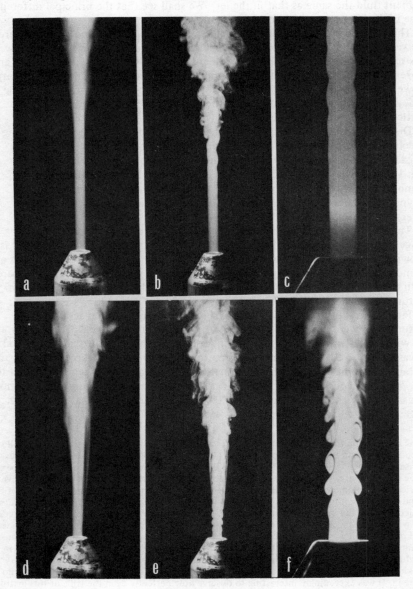

Figure 19.6   Jet instability at Re = 1690. See text for procedures for different pictures. From Ref. [59].

stage. However, the motion does not remain periodic for any great distance down-stream. Breakdown to turbulent motion occurs. The Kármán vortex street in a wake (Sections 3.3 and 11.7) appears to be the only case in which periodic motion persists to all distances downstream (and then only over a certain Reynolds number range). Presumably, this is a case in which the non-linear terms play a role of the form shown schematically as curve A in Fig. 18.2 whereas most examples of shear flow are represented by a curve of form B.

It is in the breakdown from periodic or roughly periodic motion to turbulent motion that the most significant difference between free and wall shear flows occurs. Free flows have no counterpart of turbulent spots. The randomness characteristic of turbulence develops at a roughly equal rate throughout the transition region. Correspondingly, the time scale of the fluctuations becomes continuously shorter; there is no sudden local appearance of much more rapid fluctuations.

Figures 19.7 and 19.8 show oscillograms of the velocity fluctuations at various distances downstream, for, respectively, spontaneously arising fluctuations and

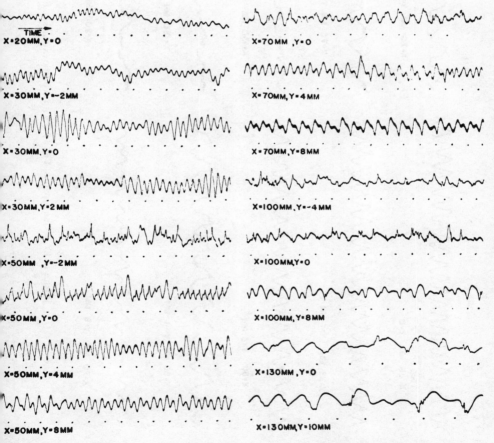

Figure 19.7 Oscillograms of naturally arising velocity fluctuations in a free shear layer. x is distance downstream from separation; y indicates position across shear layer. From Ref. [216].

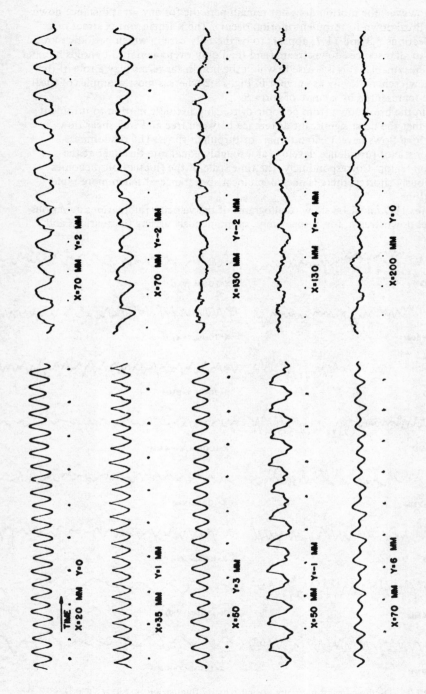

X=70 MM Y=2 MM

X=70 MM Y=-2 MM

X=130 MM Y=-2 MM

X=130 MM Y=-4 MM

X=200 MM Y=0

TIME
X=20 MM Y=0

X=35 MM Y=1 MM

X=50 MM Y=3 MM

X=50 MM Y=-1 MM

X=70 MM Y=6 MM

Figure 19.8   Counterpart of Fig. 19.7 with acoustic excitation. From Ref. [216].

acoustically stimulated ones. These were actually obtained in the free shear layer produced by boundary layer separation at a sharp corner, but essentially similar observations can be made in a jet [217]. The difference from Fig. 2.10, which is characteristic of oscillograms produced during transition involving spot growth, is apparent. The flow becomes turbulent through the continuous development of irregularities throughout the flow, instead of the sudden local appearance of irregularities which subsequently spread.

19.3 Pipe flow transition [166, 175]

We return to the topic of pipe flow; the description of transition in Section 2.6 needs filling out. Although this is in principle one of the simplest configurations and although it played such an important role in the early history of transition studies, the details of the transition process turn out to be relatively complex and are, quite possibly, not all known. Pipe flow illustrates, in a more extreme way than other flows, the limitations to linear stability theory (Chapter 18), in providing only a sufficient condition for flow breakdown, not a necessary one.

Linear stability theory applied to Poiseuille flow indicates that the parabolic velocity profile is stable at all values of the Reynolds number; $Re_{crit} = \infty$. (There is still a slight question mark, but it is only slight, against this result because there are mathematical difficulties in covering every possible type of small disturbance [242].) Nevertheless pipe flow becomes turbulent at some Reynolds number between 2×10^3 and 10^5. Almost certainly, both the departures from the parabolic profile in the entry length and the response to non-infinitesimal disturbances play a role in the interpretation of this fact.

Different geometries result in different detailed flows in the entry length, but the entering fluid will often be irrotational. Then, an annular boundary layer grows on the wall, and the flow starts approximating to Poiseuille flow when the thickness of this becomes close to the radius of the pipe (Fig. 2.5). When the thickness of this boundary layer is small compared with the pipe radius, it will resemble a Blasius boundary layer, which is known to be unstable at high enough Reynolds number. We may anticipate that there will be a stable length right at the start of the pipe (the Reynolds number based on boundary layer thickness being small here), followed by the unstable region, this being followed in turn by another stable region as the profile approaches Poiseuille flow. If disturbances are amplified sufficiently in the unstable region, then transition to turbulence may be expected.

Evidently, this description of the start of transition is consistent with a high degree of variability in the maximum Reynolds number at which laminar flow can be maintained. In the first place, small variations in the velocity profile, due to different entry geometry, may affect the extent of the unstable region. In the second place, the maximum amplitude of velocity fluctuations reached at the end of the unstable region will be sensitive to the level of small disturbances present at its start; the appearance of local regions of turbulence probably depends on a certain amplitude being reached.†

---

†The distiction between a change in entry geometry and a disturbance may be somewhat blurred, particularly if wall roughness enters the story. However, here the former is intended to imply a change in the detailed pattern of the laminar flow that would occur in the absence of any instability. The latter is intended to imply a small uncontrolled unsteadiness in the flow.

By taking great care to minimize the disturbance level, experimenters have maintained laminar flow up to values of Re $= u_{av}d/\nu$ of around 1.0×10^5 Ref. [198]. It is likely that in these experiments there was a local unstable region in the entry boundary layer, but with subsequent decay of the amplified disturbances [233, 254].

When turbulence develops at Reynolds numbers above about 10^4 the region of boundary layer instability is probably an important feature of the transition process. Turbulence has been observed [194] to appear first of all in small spots restricted laterally as well as axially and presumably forming in the boundary layer. These spots then spread in all directions and several of them merge to form a turbulent plug.

However, the lowest values of the Reynolds number (around 2×10^3) at which transition occurs are well below the minimum value (around 10^4) at which theory [233, 254] indicates the existence of an unstable region. In many experiments [64, 167, 194, 211], the entry geometry has involved sharp edges or corners and there was probably a region of separated flow. This would be unstable at a lower Reynolds number than any attached boundary layer, and rapid amplification of disturbances would occur as shown in Fig. 19.9.

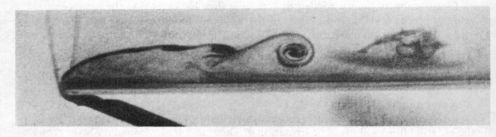

Figure 19.9   Flow at sharp entry to pipe; Re = 5240. From Ref. [152].

However, this is probably not the only way in which transition can be initiated at the lower Reynolds numbers. Observations [167, 168] have been made, some of them with an arrangement unlikely to produce separation, of transition occurring at around 3000 in a manner similar to that described above for higher Reynolds numbers — turbulent spots originating close to the wall and then spreading to give turbulent plugs. One can only say that growing turbulent plugs can originate and so transition occur at Reynolds numbers down to about 2000, provided that there are large enough disturbances. Probably there is no unique process for the origin of plugs in this range; a large disturbance can take such a variety of forms.

The triggering disturbance can be another turbulent region. Observations have been made of one turbulent spot appearing in the boundary layer a little way downstream of an older one, whose presence has caused sufficient disturbance [167, 168].

Despite these complications in the detailed mechanics of transition, it is clear what governs the lower limit in Reynolds number for transition. Once turbulent plugs are produced, the transition process is substantially the same at all values of the Reynolds number. The turbulence propagates into the neighbouring non-turbulent regions at each end of a plug. The plugs thus grow in length at the expense of the non-turbulent region. When the front interface of one plug meets the rear interface of another, the two merge to give a single plug. Thus the intermittency factor increases with distance downstream, until all the non-turbulent regions have been absorbed and fully turbulent pipe flow results. Figure 19.10 shows the rates at which front and rear interfaces travel downstream as functions of the Reynolds number. At high Re, the interface speeds are substantially constant at about 1.5 and 0.5 times the mean flow speed. The difference between them is less at lower Re and disappears when Re is about 2300. Below this plugs do not grow and fully turbulent flow is not produced at any distance downstream. There is some variability in the figure quoted for the minimum Re at which transition can be produced by large disturbances, values going down to 1800. Nevertheless, it is clear that the limiting factor is plug growth. Observations have been made of the processes leading to plug production at much lower Reynolds numbers, but transition does not then result [64].

The region of intermittently turbulent flow is often very long. This depends on the rate of plug production, which is sensitive to the disturbance level. Quantitative estimates thus relate only to particular experiments, but this region can be hundreds of diameters long.

We saw in Section 2.6 that the production of turbulent plugs can be either random or periodic in time, as illustrated by the oscillograms of Fig. 2.10. The random production might be regarded as the normal state of affairs, periodic production occurring through a rather special mechanism. Nonetheless, the latter is a phenomenon of some interest and significance and we now consider how it comes about.

The pressure gradient needed to produce a given flow rate is much larger when the flow is turbulent than when it is laminar (Fig. 2.11). Conversely, the flow rate

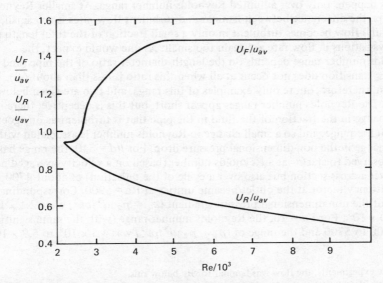

Figure 19.10 Ratios of front and rear velocities of plugs to the mean flow speed as functions of Reynolds number (based on experimental results in Refs. [169, 194, 211]).

Intake   Outlet

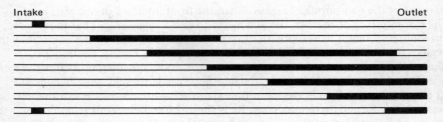

Figure 19.11 Sequence of positions of laminar and turbulent motion (shaded regions turbulent) during periodic plug formation. Length and diameter are not to the same scale (and interfaces are therefore shown plane).

produced by a given pressure difference between the ends is much higher for laminar flow than for turbulent flow. In most experimental arrangements, it is the pressure difference, not the flow rate, that is held constant. Hence, in transitional flow, as a turbulent plug grows the flow rate reduces. This inhibits the instability of the entry region, and the probability of another plug being produced becomes negligible. Only when the front of the plug passes out of the far end of the pipe does the fraction of the pipe length in laminar motion increase. The flow rate then starts to increase too. When it has increased sufficiently, another plug is produced near the entry, and the cycle recommences. Since the front of a plug travels downstream at about three times the speed of the rear (Fig. 19.10), there can be substantial variations in the fraction of the flow that is turbulent (Fig. 19.11) and thus in the flow rate. If these variations pass through the criterion for instability (such as the critical Reynolds number of the entry boundary layer), the instability can be renewed at just the same phase of each cycle and the flow will pulsate with a well-defined period.

This happens only over a limited Reynolds number range. At smaller Reynolds numbers, the difference between laminar and turbulent flow rates is too small. At higher, the flow becomes turbulent in only a small fraction of the total length and so the variations in flow rate are again too small. As one would expect, the Reynolds number range depends on the length/diameter ratio of the pipe (and periodic transition does not occur at all when this ratio is less than about 60). One can, therefore, quote only examples of this range, and two are given below [194]. The Reynolds number ranges appear short, but this is deceptive; there is a large change in the fraction of the fluid in the pipe that is turbulent as one goes through the range, and so a small change in Reynolds number is associated with a large change in the non-dimensional pressure drop. For $l/d = 540$, the range has been observed to start † at a Reynolds number (based on a velocity averaged not only over a cross-section but also over a cycle of the pulsation) of about 4700; the intermittency factor at the outlet became unity‡ at Re = 5900. Corresponding values of the non-dimensional pressure gradient $(p_1 - p_2)d^3/\rho v^2 l$ were 2.1×10^5 and 5.0×10^5. For $l/d = 78$, the Reynolds number range (with the same significance) was 5500 to 5700 and the range of $(p_1 - p_2)d^3/\rho v^2 l$ was 4.5×10^5 to 5.9×10^5.

---

† In these experiments, the flow was laminar for Re below this.
‡It is not certain whether this or a higher Re is the upper end of the pulsating regime. It is in principle possible for the pulsations to occur with fully turbulent flow at the outlet, so long as there is still a substantial fraction of the pipe length with intermittent turbulence.

In conclusion, it is now abundantly clear why the traditional view that there is a single critical Reynolds number, below which the flow is laminar, above which the flow is turbulent, cannot describe the facts. Instead we have to introduce a set of Reynolds numbers relating to different events in the transition process. We start at the high end:

(i) The theoretical linear stability limit of Poiseuille flow is Re = ∞. We may guess that a pipe flow with an artificially induced parabolic profile at the entry could remain laminar to even higher Reynolds numbers than flows with a normal entry length.

(ii) There may be a Reynolds number above which a pipe flow with a normal entry length will always become turbulent through the amplification of small disturbances. If so, this Reynolds number is at least 10^5.

(iii) Below this there is still a region of instability in the entry length but not a sufficiently large one to promote transition when the disturbances are small. The lowest Reynolds number at which this exists is somewhat uncertain but around 10^4.

(iv) When the flow is spontaneously pulsating, the Reynolds number periodically becomes larger than its average value making the entry length temporarily unstable. The lowest average Reynolds number at which this provides an instability mechanism is again uncertain but is around 5×10^3.

(v) The lower limit to transition even for very large disturbances is provided by the growth or otherwise of plugs. The critical Reynolds number for this is better defined at $(2.1 \pm 0.3) \times 10^3$.

20
Turbulence

20.1 The nature of turbulent motion

Frequent references to turbulent motion have been made in previous chapters, but detailed discussion of the nature of that motion has always been postponed. We now take this matter up [86].

No short but complete definition of turbulence seems to be possible. Perhaps the best brief summary of it is 'a state of continuous instability'. A more complete specification becomes somewhat lengthy, but, as we shall see, no definition can eliminate the borderline examples that one may or may not choose to call turbulent.

A convenient starting point for a discussion of the nature of turbulent motion is the following fact: each time a flow changes as the result of an instability, one's ability to predict the details of the motion is reduced. We examine the meaning of this statement first of all through examples in which the consequence of the instability is not (immediately) turbulent motion.

Consider the motion in a Kármán vortex street (Section 3.3) in the wake of an obstacle. The velocity at a point fixed relative to the obstacle varies periodically and roughly sinusoidally. The phase of this variation is arbitrary, depending on the small disturbances at the time the flow commenced. If, therefore, one asks for a prediction of the instantaneous velocity, without making any observations, this cannot be given within certain limits. This lack of predictability arises from the instability producing the vortex street; in the steady flow, from which the vortex street develops, such a prediction could be made. The degree of unpredictability is, however, small. One requires only a single observation indicating the phase of the fluctuations for all the details of the flow to be determined. When, with increasing Reynolds number, a further instability causes loss of regularity in the array of vortices, the unpredictability is increased. One can, for example, no longer say that, if one has made an observation of the velocity, then the velocity will be the same one period later. However, markedly systematic features may still exist — regions of high vorticity passing a point in a sequence, although not a completely periodic one. The flow can still be described with more emphasis on these systematic features rather than random ones. Each subsequent instability reduces one's ability to do this, until the random features are dominant.

Another example is provided by cellular convection (Sections 4.3, 17.3 and 17.4). In an arrangement such as Fig. 4.1, every point in a horizontal plane is *a priori* similar. There is nothing to distinguish the points at which the fluid rises from those at which it falls; one cannot predict whether it will be rising or falling at a particular place. The positions of the rising and falling currents are different on different occasions when one uses the same piece of apparatus, depending on the small disturbances present at the commencement of each experiment. Nevertheless the flow pattern can have a high degree of regularity (as is particularly exemplified by surface tension driven convection — Fig. 17.6), the *relative* location of rising and falling currents being repeatable from experiment to experiment. Further instability, in a sequence of events such as that described in Section 4.3, reduces the repeatable features of the flow and so reduces the predictability of its details. At the end of the sequence random features become dominant.

A flow may be called turbulent when the level of predictability is so reduced that it is appropriate to give a statistical description of it.

Clearly, that statement does not provide an unambiguous classification of flows into turbulent and non-turbulent. But one would not expect to be able to do this. Figure 19.8, for example, shows velocity fluctuations developing continuously from a regular form to a turbulent one. At one extreme the motion is unambiguously non-turbulent; at the other it is unambiguously turbulent; but there is no stage in between that one can identify as the start of turbulence. (Sometimes there is a sufficiently sudden development in the transition sequence that it is meaningful to say that the turbulence first occurs (locally) there. An example is the appearance of turbulent spots in boundary layer transition (Section 19.1). The difference arises through one stage of the sequence occurring on a small length scale; the time scale is correspondingly small and the developments leading to local randomness are rapid compared with the other stages of transition.)

20.2 Introduction to the statistical description of turbulent motion

A statistical description is formulated in terms of average quantities, since these are repeatable from experiment to experiment. The detailed nature of the averaging process will be considered below, but another example may indicate the general meaning of a statistical description. Consider turbulent pipe flow. A measurement of the instantaneous velocity at some point in the pipe is, on its own, of little use. It does not indicate what the velocity will be at the same point at another instant or what it will be at any other geometrically similar point (i.e. a point at the same distance from the axis). Nevertheless, one may expect a greater similarity between two geometrically similar points than between two geometrically dissimilar points. This similarity is provided by the average quantities. The mean velocity, for example, is the same at all points at the same distance from the axis, but varies with this distance.

The ideal aim of a theory of turbulent motion would be the development of a statistical mechanics analogous to those developed in the kinetic theory of gases. Such a theory would have to be based on the equations of fluid motion instead of those of the dynamics of molecules interacting only through elastic collisions. It is thus a very difficult task. Work on these lines (beyond the scope of this book) has been attempted, but various, not necessarily valid, assumptions have to be made before progress is possible.

Consequently, much of our knowledge of turbulent flows comes from experiment. Some of the quantities that enter into any statistical theory can be measured experimentally. A physical description of the principal processes occurring within a turbulent flow can be developed from these. Generally, a rather complex interaction between theory and experiment results, theory indicating which quantities

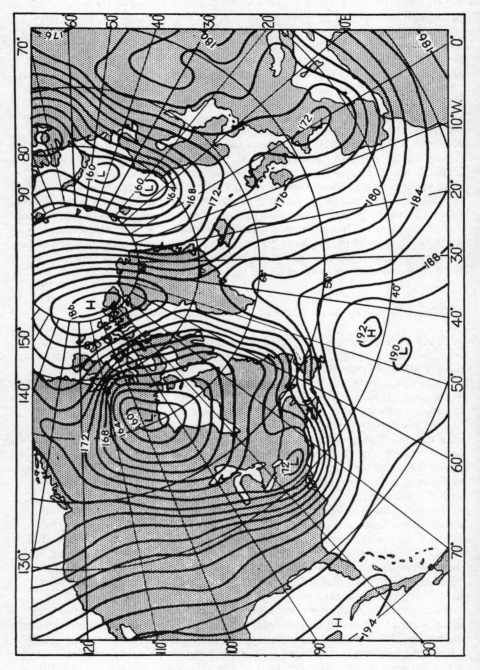
(a)

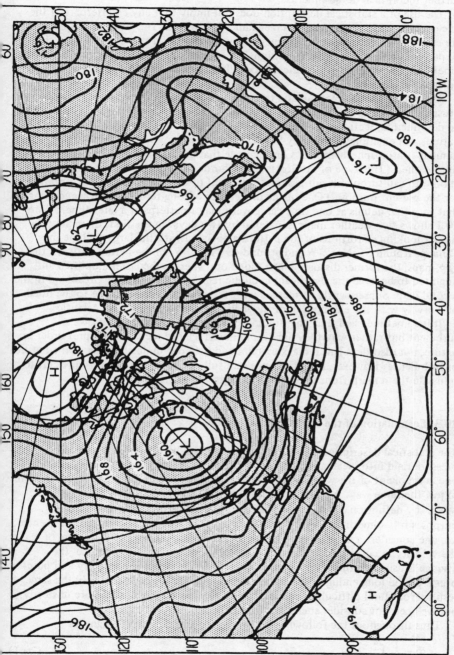

Figure 20.1 Weather maps for (a) 24 Jan 1952 (b) 26 Jan 1952. Lines are contours of the height (at intervals of 30.5 m) at which the pressure is 500 mbar (approximately half ground level pressure); contours of pressure at a fixed height of about 5.5 km would look very similar. From Ref. [234].

(b)

might usefully be measured and the experimental results pointing the way for further theoretical developments.

The use of a statistical description does not imply that any counterpart of the uncertainty principle in quantum mechanics is involved. The governing equations are essentially deterministic; in principle, every detail of a turbulent motion should be determinable if the initial conditions are completely defined. The analogy with kinetic theory is thus with classical Maxwell–Boltzmann statistics, not with quantum statistics.

The reason that a deterministic treatment of turbulent flows is not in practice possible is that important features of the motion (for example the large eddies to be described in Sections 22.4 and 22.6) develop from entirely insignificant perturbations. An example of this may be taken from a context in which it is rather familiar — atmospheric motions on the scale that governs the principal features of the weather. (This type of motion is in the borderland that one may or may not choose to call turbulent, but it shows sufficient of the characteristics of turbulence for the present purpose.) One of the difficulties of long-term weather forecasting is that very fine details at one time can govern major patterns at a later time. Figure 20.1 shows two weather maps, separated by two days. In the first, there are two similar looking distortions of the pattern associated with the large cyclone over Canada, around 55°N, 62°W and around 43°N, 75°W. In the period between the two maps, the former distortion just faded out whereas the latter amplified and migrated to become the significant cyclonic region at the south of Greenland in the second map. Subsequently, it merged with the other original cyclone to the north of Norway with the elimination of the high pressure ridge over the Atlantic.

It is sometimes said that one should not try to understand why flows are turbulent but rather why they are ever laminar; science seeks to interpret order in nature, not disorder. This remark certainly adds to our understanding of the nature of turbulence. However, in the absence of a full statistical theory, it is difficult to translate the remark from the metaphysical to the physical.

20.3 Formulation of the statistical description

The statistical description of a turbulent flow starts by dividing the velocity and pressure field into mean and fluctuating parts. We may consider the procedure for one component of the velocity; the other components and the pressure are treated in just the same way. At each point, the velocity component is written as $U + u$, where, by definition $\bar{u} = 0$ (an overbar denoting averaging). For theoretical purposes it is sometimes convenient to think of the average as an ensemble average; i.e. one considers a large number of identical systems and takes the average of the velocity at corresponding instants over all these systems. In practice, the average is usually a time average; one observes and averages the velocity at a point over a period long enough for separate measurements to give effectively the same result. Procedural difficulties can arise when the imposed conditions are unsteady, but we need not consider such situations here.

Thus throughout the following the average of any quantity Υ signifies

$$\bar{\Upsilon} = \frac{1}{2s} \int_{-s}^{s} \Upsilon dt \qquad (20.1)$$

where s is large compared with any of the time scales involved in the variations of Υ.

U indicates the mean motion of the fluid. Information about the structure of the velocity fluctuations is given by other average quantities, the first being the mean square fluctuation, $\overline{u^2}$. $(\overline{u^2})^{1/2}$ is known as the intensity of the turbulence component, and

$$\left(\overline{q^2}\right)^{1/2} = \left(\overline{u^2} + \overline{v^2} + \overline{w^2}\right)^{1/2} \tag{20.2}$$

as the intensity of the turbulence. It is directly related to the kinetic energy per unit volume associated with the velocity fluctuations,

$$\Sigma = \frac{1}{2} \rho \overline{q^2} \tag{20.3}$$

The same intensity field can in principle be produced by many different patterns of velocity fluctuation. Before we look at the average quantities most often used to examine the more detailed structure of the velocity field, we consider briefly an alternative representation. This is in a sense the most fundamental statistical representation, although it is not the most convenient for the development of models of turbulent structure based on experimental observation. The probability distribution function $P(u)$ of a velocity component at one point is defined so that the probability that the fluctuation velocity is between u and $u + \mathrm{d}u$ is $P(u)\mathrm{d}u$. One thus has

$$\int_{-\infty}^{\infty} P(u)\mathrm{d}u = 1 \tag{20.4}$$

The intensity is related to this,

$$\overline{u^2} = \int_{-\infty}^{\infty} u^2 P(u)\mathrm{d}u \tag{20.5}$$

but the probability distribution function contains more information than the intensity. Relationships between velocity fluctuations at different points (or times) are indicated by joint probability distribution functions. For example a second-order function, $P(u_1, u_2)$, may be defined so that the probability that the velocity at one point lies between u_1 and $u_1 + \mathrm{d}u_1$ and that at the other point simultaneously lies between u_2 and $u_2 + \mathrm{d}u_2$ is $P(u_1, u_2)\mathrm{d}u_1 \mathrm{d}u_2$. In principle, for a complete representation of the turbulence, this process has to be continued to all orders.

Probability distribution functions are sometimes determined experimentally, but much more frequently further average quantities are measured. Fuller information than is given by $\overline{u^2}$ about the fluctuations at a single point can be obtained by measurements of u^3, u^4, etc.

Information about velocity fluctuations at different points (or times) is given by correlation measurements. The correlation between two velocity fluctuations u_1 and u_2 is defined as $\overline{u_1 u_2}$ and the correlation coefficient as

$$R = \overline{u_1 u_2} \left/ \left(\overline{u_1^2 u_2^2} \right)^{1/2} \right. \tag{20.6}$$

u_1 and u_2 are for the moment quite general quantities; but as examples, they could be simultaneous values of the same component of the velocity at two different points, or two different components of the velocity at a single point. If the fluctuations u_1 and u_2 are quite independent of one another, then their correlation is zero. However, any turbulent flow is governed by the usual equations and these do not allow such complete independence, particularly for fluctuations at points close to one another. Hence, non-zero correlations are observed.

The concept of correlations, like that of probability distributions, can be extended to higher orders, by defining quantities such as $u_1 u_2 u_3$. A complete specification of the turbulence again requires one to consider all orders up to infinity. In practice, detailed attention is usually confined to double correlations $\overline{(u_1 u_2)}$ with briefer investigation of triple correlations.

Experimental studies of turbulent flows often involve the interpretation of correlation measurements. One of the reasons for working particularly with correlations is that those of low order lend themselves satisfactorily to physical interpretation, in ways to be discussed in Section 20.6. We shall also be introducing later (Section 20.7) the spectrum functions which are the Fourier transforms of correlation functions. However, we now have enough material to examine the way in which the equations of motion are developed for turbulent flows.

20.4 Turbulence equations

In the interests of conciseness and convention, it is necessary to use here the suffix notation for vector equations which has been avoided elsewhere in this book (except in the appendix to Chapter 5 and in equation (14.75)). For a full explanation of this notation see Refs. [23, 38, 133]. Its basic features are as follows: each suffix can take values 1, 2 or 3, corresponding to the three co-ordinate directions; a vector equation can be read as any one of its component equations by substituting the appropriate value for the suffix common to every term; and the repetition of a suffix within a single term indicates that that term is summed over the three values of that suffix.

With the velocity divided into its mean and fluctuating parts, the continuity equation (5.10) is

$$\text{div}(\mathbf{U} + \mathbf{u}) = 0 \qquad\qquad (20.7)$$

that is

$$\partial(U_i + u_i)/\partial x_i = 0 \qquad\qquad (20.8)$$

Averaging this equation (the processes of averaging and differentiation are interchangeable in order),

$$\partial U_i/\partial x_i = 0 \qquad\qquad (20.9)$$

Subtracting this result from the original equation,

$$\partial u_i/\partial x_i = 0 \qquad\qquad (20.10)$$

The mean and fluctuating parts of the velocity field thus individually satisfy the usual form of the continuity equation.

The same division applied to the Navier–Stokes equation (equation (5.22) with

$F = 0$) gives

$$\frac{\partial(U_i + u_i)}{\partial t} + (U_j + u_j)\frac{\partial(U_i + u_i)}{\partial x_j} = -\frac{1}{\rho}\frac{\partial(P + p)}{\partial x_i} + \nu\frac{\partial^2(U_i + u_i)}{\partial x_j^2} \tag{20.11}$$

Carrying out the averaging process throughout this equation

$$\frac{\partial U_i}{\partial t} + U_j\frac{\partial U_i}{\partial x_j} + \overline{u_j\frac{\partial u_i}{\partial x_j}} = -\frac{1}{\rho}\frac{\partial P}{\partial x_i} + \nu\frac{\partial^2 U_i}{\partial x_j^2} \tag{20.12}$$

which, with the aid of the continuity equation (20.10), may be rewritten

$$U_j\frac{\partial U_i}{\partial x_j} = -\frac{1}{\rho}\frac{\partial P}{\partial x_i} + \nu\frac{\partial^2 U_i}{\partial x_j^2} - \frac{\partial}{\partial x_j}(\overline{u_i u_j}) \tag{20.13}$$

where, additionally, attention has been restricted to steady mean conditions by making the first term of (20.12) zero.

Equation (20.13) for the mean velocity U_i differs from the laminar flow equation by the addition of the last term. This term represents the action of the velocity fluctuations on the mean flow arising from the non-linearity of the Navier–Stokes equation. It is frequently large compared with the viscous term, with the result that the mean velocity distribution is very different from the corresponding laminar flow.

The character of this interaction between the mean flow and the fluctuations can be seen most simply in the context of a flow for which the two-dimensional boundary layer approximation applies. The turbulent fluctuations are always three-dimensional, but if the imposed conditions are two-dimensional, there is no variation of mean quantities in the third direction and terms such as $\partial(\overline{uw})/\partial z$ (that would otherwise appear in the next equation) are zero. Omitting such terms and terms that are small on the boundary layer approximation† in equation (20.13) gives the turbulent flow counterpart of equation (11.8); that is

$$U\frac{\partial U}{\partial x} + V\frac{\partial U}{\partial y} = -\frac{1}{\rho}\frac{\partial P}{\partial x} + \nu\frac{\partial^2 U}{\partial y^2} - \frac{\partial}{\partial y}(\overline{uv}) \tag{20.14}$$

This equation is applied to turbulent boundary layers, jets, wakes, etc.

Writing the last two terms of (20.14) as

$$\frac{1}{\rho}\frac{\partial}{\partial y}\left(\mu\frac{\partial U}{\partial y} - \rho\overline{uv}\right) \tag{20.15}$$

shows that the velocity fluctuations produce a stress on the mean flow. A gradient of this produces a net acceleration of the fluid in the same way as a gradient of the viscous stress. The quantity $(-\rho\overline{uv})$, and more generally the quantity $(-\rho\overline{u_i u_j})$, is called a Reynolds stress.

The Reynolds stress arises from the correlation of two components of the velocity fluctuation at the same point. A non-zero value of this correlation implies that the two components are not independent of one another. For example, if

† The boundary layer approximation is used here to its fullest extent. In some studies of turbulent flows, some further terms (e.g. $\partial(\overline{u^2})/\partial x$) are retained because measurements indicate that they are not so very small.

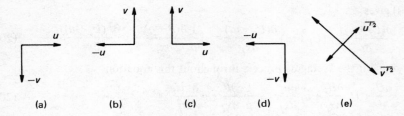

Figure 20.2   Geometrical interpretation of Reynolds stress: if patterns of velocity fluctuations shown in (a) and (b) occur more frequently than those in (c) and (d), giving negative $\overline{uv}$, then $\overline{v'^2}$ is larger than $\overline{u'^2}$ as indicated by (e).

uv is negative, then at moments at which u is positive, v is more likely to be negative than positive — and conversely when u is negative. Transferring attention to co-ordinates at $45°$ to the x and y directions shows that this corresponds to anisotropy of the turbulence—different intensities in different directions. Putting

$$u' = (u + v)/\sqrt{2} \qquad v' = (v - u)/\sqrt{2} \tag{20.16}$$

gives

$$\overline{uv} = \frac{1}{2}(\overline{u'^2} - \overline{v'^2}) \tag{20.17}$$

Figure 20.2 shows the geometrical significance of this.

One can readily see how a correlation of this kind can arise in a mean shear flow. We may consider the case of positive $\partial U/\partial y$ as shown in Fig. 20.3. A fluid particle with positive v is being carried by the turbulence in the positive y-direction. It is coming from a region where the mean velocity is smaller and it is thus likely to be moving downstream more slowly than its new environment; i.e. it is more likely to have negative u than positive. Similarly negative v is more likely to be associated with positive u. The process is in general — but not in detail — analogous to the Brownian motion of molecules giving rise to fluid viscosity.

Further understanding of the interaction between the mean flow and the fluctuations is obtained from the equation for the kinetic energy of the turbulence. Subtracting equation (20.12) from equation (20.11) gives

$$\frac{\partial u_i}{\partial t} + U_j \frac{\partial u_i}{\partial x_j} + u_j \frac{\partial U_i}{\partial x_j} + u_j \frac{\partial u_i}{\partial x_j} - \overline{u_j \frac{\partial u_i}{\partial x_j}} = -\frac{1}{\rho}\frac{\partial p}{\partial x_i} + \nu \frac{\partial^2 u_i}{\partial x_j^2} \tag{20.18}$$

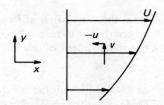

Figure 20.3   To illustrate the generation of a Reynolds stress in a mean velocity gradient.

Multiplying this by u_i and averaging

$$\frac{1}{2}\frac{\partial(\overline{u_i^2})}{\partial t} + \frac{1}{2}U_j\frac{\partial(\overline{u_i^2})}{\partial x_j} = -\overline{u_iu_j}\frac{\partial U_i}{\partial x_j} - \frac{1}{2}\frac{\partial}{\partial x_j}\overline{(u_i^2 u_j)} - \frac{1}{\rho}\frac{\partial}{\partial x_i}\overline{(pu_i)} + \nu\overline{u_i\frac{\partial^2 u_i}{\partial x_j^2}}$$

(20.19)

(where the rearrangement of terms has made use of the continuity equation (20.10)). Since the summation convention is being applied, the mathematics involves multiplying each component of the dynamical equation (20.18) by the corresponding velocity component and then adding the three resulting equations. For steady mean conditions the first term of equation (20.19) is zero, but it indicates the physical significance of the equation; in view of the summation convention

$$\overline{u_i^2} = \overline{q^2} = 2\Sigma/\rho$$

(20.20)

and so each term in the equation represents some process tending to increase or decrease the kinetic energy of the turbulence.

With the boundary layer approximation applied to a flow which is steady and two-dimensional in the mean, equation (20.19) becomes

$$\frac{1}{2}U\frac{\partial(\overline{q^2})}{\partial x} + \frac{1}{2}V\frac{\partial(\overline{q^2})}{\partial y} = -\overline{uv}\frac{\partial U}{\partial y} - \frac{\partial}{\partial y}\left(\frac{1}{2}\overline{q^2 v} + \frac{1}{\rho}\overline{pv}\right) + \nu\overline{u_i\frac{\partial^2 u_i}{\partial x_j^2}} \quad (20.21)$$

The left-hand side and the second term on the right-hand side are terms that become zero when integrated over the whole flow. They represent the transfer of energy from place to place, respectively transfer by the mean motion and transfer by the turbulence itself. As in a laminar flow (Section 11.9), the viscous term can be divided into two parts: one is essentially negative and thus represents viscous dissipation; the other (usually small) integrates to zero and so is another energy transfer process. The input of energy to compensate for the dissipation must be provided by the only remaining term, $(-\overline{uv}\partial U/\partial y)$. We have seen that $\overline{uv}$ is likely to be negative where $\partial U/\partial y$ is positive, giving this term the required sign. Although local regions of positive $(\overline{uv}\partial U/\partial y)$ can occur, they cannot occupy the majority of the flow or the turbulence cannot be maintained.†

The equation for the energy of the mean flow contains a corresponding term of opposite sign. The term thus represents a transfer of energy from the mean flow to the turbulence. One can therefore say that the Reynolds stress works against the mean velocity gradient to remove energy from the mean flow, just as the viscous stress works against the velocity gradient. However, the energy removed by the latter process is directly dissipated, reappearing as heat, whereas the action of the Reynolds stress provides energy for the turbulence. This energy is ultimately dissipated by the action of viscosity on the turbulent fluctuations. Frequently, the loss of mean flow energy to turbulence is large compared with the direct viscous dissipation.

---

†This statement need not be true for systems described by a dynamical equation with additional terms to those in (20.11); for example a buoyancy force. These can give further terms in the energy equation which may represent alternative turbulence generating mechanisms.

20.5 Calculation methods

In many practical situations, only the mean flow development is of real interest.
The structure of the turbulence is relevant only in so far as it determines the
Reynolds stress. Attempts have thus been made to relate the Reynolds stress to
the mean flow in ways that allow the mean flow development to be calculated
(for example, for boundary layers in various pressure distributions) without detailed
study of the turbulence.

A simple example of such a procedure is the concept of eddy viscosity. This
supposes that the analogy between the turbulent fluctuations and molecular
Brownian motion can be made quantitative in the form

$$-\overline{uv} = \nu_T \partial U/\partial y \tag{20.22}$$

ν_T may be taken as a constant or as a function of position — guessed from some
model of the turbulence or empirically determined. The procedure is open to the
objection that since (as we shall be seeing in Chapter 22) the turbulence normally
involves large-scale coherent motions, the Reynolds stress at any point depends on
the whole velocity profile, not just the local gradient.

More refined calculation methods have been developed [69, 70, 140] (although
we shall not be considering them here). The previously large gap between basic
studies of turbulent motion and the needs of applied scientists has diminished greatly
in recent years as a result of these methods. However, it remains true that much of
the description of turbulence of the type given in this book has not yet found application and that empirical methods with little support from fundamental studies are
still in extensive use.

20.6 Interpretation of correlations

Correlation coefficients (Section 20.3) play an important role in both theoretical
and experimental studies of turbulence. To illustrate how they can indicate the
scale and structure of a turbulent motion, we now look at typical properties of
double correlations. Some of the ideas introduced rather vaguely here will be used
more specifically in Sections 21.2, 22.4 and 22.6.

When u_1 and u_2 are velocities at different positions but the same instant, $\overline{u_1 u_2}$
is known as a space correlation. Its particulars may be specified by a diagram such
as Fig. 20.4(a). Most attention is usually given to correlations of the same

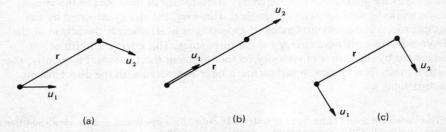

(a)   (b)   (c)

Figure 20.4   Schematic representation of double velocity correlations.

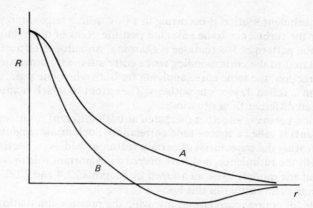

Figure 20.5   Typical correlation curves.

component of velocity at points separated in a direction either parallel to that velocity component (Fig. 20.4(b)) or perpendicular to it (Fig. 20.4(c)). We may call these respectively longitudinal and lateral correlations.

The correlation will depend on both the magnitude and direction of the separation, **r**. Different behaviours in different directions may provide information about the structure of the turbulence, a point that will be taken up again in Section 22.4. Here we pay more attention to the variation with distance, $r = |\mathbf{r}|$. When $r = 0$, $u_1 = u_2$ (provided they are in the same direction) and the correlation coefficient R of equation (20.6) is, by definition, equal to 1. At large r the velocity fluctuations become independent of one another and R asymptotes to 0. In consequence, the dependence of R on r takes typically one of the forms shown in Fig. 20.5. (R has a maximum value of 1 at $r = 0$ and so $(\partial R/\partial r)_{r=0} = 0$. However, the curvature at $r = 0$ is usually large and experimentally measured correlations often appear to have finite slope at $r = 0$.)

A negative region in the correlation curve implies that u_1 and u_2 tend to be in opposite directions more than in the same direction. For a longitudinal correlation this would imply dominant converging and/or diverging flow patterns. There is often no reason to expect such patterns and one may expect that longitudinal correlations will usually give a curve such as A (Fig. 20.5). On the other hand, lateral correlations may be expected to have a negative region, like curve B, since continuity requires the instantaneous transport of fluid across any plane (by the fluctuations) to be zero. Such expectations are not always fulfilled; but, when they fail, this may itself be informative about the structure of the turbulence.

A correlation curve indicates the distance over which the motion at one point significantly affects that at another. It may be used to assign a length scale to the turbulence; a length can be defined for example as $\int_0^\infty R\,dr$, or as the distance in which R falls to $1/e$, or, if the curve has a negative region, the value of r at which R is a minimum. We shall see in Sections 20.8, 21.3 and 22.4 that this concept is extended to associate a variety of length scales with the turbulence.

The correlation of the same velocity component at a single point at different instants is known as an autocorrelation. Such a correlation depends, of course, on the time separation s in a similar way to the dependence of a space correlation on r. It can be used to define a typical time scale of the turbulence.

When the turbulent motion is occurring in a flow with a large mean velocity, it is possible for the turbulence to be advected past the point of observation more rapidly than the pattern of fluctuations is changing. An autocorrelation will then be directly related to the corresponding space correlation with separation in the mean flow direction, the same curve applying for both when one puts $s = r/U$. This transformation is called Taylor's hypothesis. The extent to which it applies varies greatly between different flow situations.

A correlation between velocities measured at both different positions and different instants is called a space–time correlation. Such measurements are very useful in indicating the trajectories of certain features ('eddies' – Section 20.8) associated with the turbulence, and have played an important role in some of the descriptions of the motion to be mentioned in Sections 22.4 and 22.6. However, we shall not discuss them further in this book.

In principle, of course, correlations involving the pressure fluctuations as well as the velocity fluctuations may be formulated. Equation (20.21) has already involved $\overline{pv}$ – a pressure–velocity correlation. However, such quantities are difficult to measure and so have received less attention.

20.7 Spectra

Another method of discovering the time scales associated with a turbulent motion is, evidently, Fourier analysis of the velocity fluctuations into component frequencies. The reader is referred to other sources for the full theory [65]; here just sufficient theory will be given to show the result of passing a turbulence signal through a frequency filter before the usual squaring and averaging. Suppose that the velocity signal is $u(t)$. Then the output from the filter is

$$\chi(t) = \int_0^\infty u(t - t')\Psi(t')dt' \tag{20.23}$$

where $\Psi(t)$ is the response function of the filter; i.e. $\Psi(t)$ is the output at time t when the input is a delta function at $t = 0$. $\chi(t)$ is a fluctuating function and one can measure its mean square, which is

$$\overline{\chi^2} = \int_0^\infty \int_0^\infty \overline{u(t - t')u(t - t'')}\Psi(t')\Psi(t'')dt'dt'' \tag{20.24}$$

where the average is over t, by the procedure of equation (20.1), and so may be taken inside the integration with respect to t' and t''. But

$$\overline{u(t - t')u(t - t'')} = \overline{u^2}R(t' - t'') \tag{20.25}$$

where $R(s)$ is the autocorrelation coefficient for time delay s. We now introduce the the Fourier transform $\phi(\omega)$ of the autocorrelation such that

$$\overline{u^2}R(s) = \int_0^\infty \phi(\omega)e^{i\omega s}d\omega \tag{20.26}$$

($R(s)$ being an even function). Substituting in (20.24)

$$\overline{\chi^2} = \int_0^\infty \int_0^\infty \int_0^\infty \phi(\omega)\Psi(t')\Psi(t'')e^{i\omega(t'-t'')}d\omega dt'dt'' \tag{20.27}$$

But

$$\Lambda(\omega) = \int_0^\infty e^{i\omega t'} \Psi(t') dt' \tag{20.28}$$

is the amplitude of the output when the input is sinusoidal with angular frequency ω. Thus

$$\overline{\chi^2} = \int_0^\infty \phi(\omega)\Lambda(\omega)\Lambda^*(\omega)d\omega \tag{20.29}$$

If the filter is a good one, $\Lambda(\omega)\Lambda^*(\omega)$ is much larger over a narrow range of frequencies, centred on ω_0, than elsewhere and equation (20.29) reduces to

$$\overline{\chi^2} = C\phi(\omega_0) \tag{20.30}$$

where C is a calibration constant.

Thus this procedure measures the Fourier transform of the autocorrelation function. Putting $s = 0$ in equation (20.26)

$$\overline{u^2} = \int_0^\infty \phi(\omega)d\omega \tag{20.31}$$

showing that $\phi(\omega)$ may be interpreted as the contribution from frequency ω to the energy of the turbulence. (We have here considered one velocity component, but equation (20.2) provides immediate extension from the energy associated with components to the energy as a whole.) $\phi(\omega)$ is thus known as the energy spectrum.

Since $R(s)$ and $\phi(\omega)$ are Fourier transforms of one another (both real), either is in principle calculable from the other. In practice, however, much greater accuracy is obtained by a direct measurement of the quantity required than by a calculation from measurements of the other quantity. For example, the whole trend of $\phi(\omega)$ at large ω is determined by the detailed shape of the $R(s)$ curve close to $s = 0$, which, as we have seen, is difficult to determine. Hence, correlation measurements and spectrum measurements tend to make separate contributions to the understanding of a turbulent flow.

As well as the frequency spectrum, one can define wave number spectra— Fourier transforms of the space correlations . This is more complicated because one is now dealing with three dimensions, and the reader is again referred to other sources for the theory [38, 39]. Suffice it to say here that one can define a quantity $E(k)$, where k is the magnitude of the wave number, such that

$$\Sigma/\rho = \frac{1}{2}\overline{q^2} = \int_0^\infty E(k)dk \tag{20.32}$$

$E(k)$ indicates the distribution of energy over different length scales. It is an important parameter in many theoretical treatments of turbulent motion. However, it cannot be measured experimentally; one would need simultaneous information from every point of the flow.

When applicable, Taylor's hypothesis (Section 20.6) can be used to derive a spatial spectrum from an observed time spectrum. However, this is a one-dimensional spectrum with respect to the component of the wave number in the mean flow direction, and so is not in general a complete determination of the spectral characteristics or of $E(k)$.

20.8 The concept of eddies

As we shall see in the following chapters, the division of a turbulent motion into (interacting) motions on various length scales is useful because the different scales play rather different roles in the dynamics of the motion. This is usually expressed by talking of 'eddies of different sizes'. A turbulent 'eddy' is a rather ill-defined concept — but a very useful one for the development of descriptions of turbulence. On the smaller scales, one cannot identify individual eddies, and the expression 'small eddies' means no more than those parts of the motion that are coherent only over short distances. On the large scales, one can often identify characteristic features of the motion (Sections 22.4 and 22.6) and these may be called 'large eddies'.

An eddy differs from a Fourier component in the following way. A single Fourier component, no matter how small its wavelength (that is how large k), extends over the whole flow. An eddy is localized — its extent is indicated by its length scale. (The use of the word eddy does not, however, necessarily imply a simple circulatory motion.) However, small eddies contribute to larger wave-number components of the spectrum; the spectrum curve is often interpreted loosely in terms of the energy associated with eddies of various sizes.

For any separation, r, the correlation coefficient is determined by all eddies larger than $\sim r$. Only the largest eddies can thus be related directly to correlation measurements. Conversely, the observable spectrum function has a value at wave-number k_x influenced by all eddies smaller than $\sim 1/k_x$ (for reasons arising from the fact that only one-dimensional spectra can be observed [85]). Hence, it is usually most convenient to use correlation measurements to provide information about the larger scales and spectrum measurements for the smaller scales.

21
Homogeneous Isotropic Turbulence

21.1 Introduction

Many theoretical investigations of turbulence have been developed around the concept of homogeneous, isotropic turbulence — turbulence of which the statistical properties do not vary with position and have no preferred direction. An approximation to such a motion can be obtained behind a grid, such as the one shown in Fig. 21.1, in a wind-tunnel. The theories have thus been supplemented by observation. However, we will postpone consideration of experimentally based ideas about the structure of turbulence to the different contexts of Chapter 22. Here, without detail, we use the context of homogeneous isotropic turbulence to illustrate one of the basic difficulties of understanding turbulence and to develop some ideas relevant to all turbulent flows.

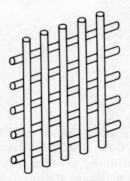

Figure 21.1 Typical turbulence generating grid.

The energy production term in equation (20.19) is zero in isotropic turbulence, and so the motion must decay through viscous dissipation. In theoretical work, the turbulence is supposed to be generated at an initial instant and then to decay as time proceeds. Behind a grid, there is strong turbulent energy production for the first ten or so grid mesh-lengths along the tunnel; the turbulence then becomes substantially isotropic and decays with distance down the tunnel. (This, in principle, implies inhomogeneity, but the decay is slow enough for this to be neglected.) We shall consider certain features of the motion applying at any stage of this decay process.

21.2 Space correlations and the closure problem

The assumption of homogeneity and isotropy much simplifies the formulation of space correlations. These depend only on the distance between the two points and not on their location or the orientation of the line joining them. Moreover, it may be shown that the general correlation, as in Fig. 20.4(a), may be expressed in terms of the longitudinal and lateral correlations of Fig. 20.4(b) and (c). Thus only these two functions of r (denoted respectively by $f(r)$ and $g(r)$) are needed for complete specification of the double velocity correlations. When, additionally, the continuity equation is introduced a relationship between these is found,

$$f + \frac{1}{2} r \mathrm{d}f/\mathrm{d}r = g \tag{21.1}$$

Hence, only a single function gives the complete specification.

The mathematics behind these statements runs as follows. The correlation coefficient between velocity component u_i at one point and component u_j at a point $\mathbf{r}$ away is a second-order tensor $R_{ij}(\mathbf{r})$. When there is isotropy [39, 133]

$$R_{ij}(\mathbf{r}) = \zeta(r) r_i r_j + \eta(r) \delta_{ij} \tag{21.2}$$

For this to take the appropriate forms in the particular cases of longitudinal and lateral correlations

$$\zeta(r) = (f(r) - g(r))/r^2 ; \quad \eta(r) = g(r) \tag{21.3}$$

Continuity gives

$$\partial u_j/\partial x_j = 0 \tag{21.4}$$

Substituting this in

$$R_{ij} = \overline{u_i(0) u_j(\mathbf{r})}\Big/ \overline{u^2} \tag{21.5}$$

gives

$$\partial R_{ij}/\partial r_j = 0 \tag{21.6}$$

which reduces to equation (21.1).

Figure 21.2 shows an experimental check of equation (21.1). Direct measurements of g are compared with ones calculated from measurements of f.

One would now like to determine f as a function of r. No use has been made so far of the dynamical equation nor of any statistical mechanical principle. These should complete the specification of the problem. However, it is at this stage that difficulties arise. We shall not consider the mathematics in any detail, but the nature of the problem will be briefly described as the simplest illustration of the difficulties encountered by theories of turbulent motion. Efforts to overcome these difficulties are still an important activity [191].

A dynamical equation for the double correlations can readily be formulated from the Navier–Stokes equation. However, because of the non-linear terms, this involves triple correlations. One form of this equation, known as the Kármán–Howarth equation, is

$$\frac{\partial}{\partial t} (\overline{u^2} f) + \frac{(\overline{u^2})^{3/2}}{r^4} \frac{\partial}{\partial r} (r^4 j) = \frac{2\nu \overline{u^2}}{r^4} \frac{\partial}{\partial r} \left(r^4 \frac{\partial f}{\partial r} \right) \tag{21.7}$$

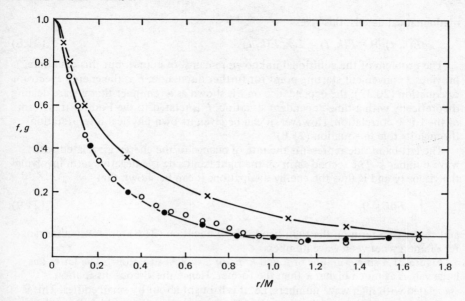

Figure 21.2 Correlations in grid turbulence: (X) $f(r)$, measured; (○) $g(r)$, calculated from $f(r)$; (●) $g(r)$, directly measured. From Ref. [258].

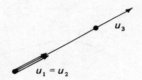

Figure 21.3 Representation of triple velocity correlation denoted by j; cf. Fig. 20.4.

j is the correlation between two velocity components at one point and one at another as shown schematically in Fig. 21.3; it contains information about all two-point triple correlations in the same way as f contains information about all double correlations. Similarly, an equation for the triple correlations involves fourth-order ones. Whatever order one goes to, there is always one more unknown than the number of equations, and the system remains insoluble. This situation is known as the closure problem in turbulence, and a variety of suggestions for an additional hypothesis to provide a solution have been advanced. However, our knowledge of f as a function of r remains primarily experimental (Fig. 21.2).

21.3 Spectra and the energy cascade

An equation in terms of spectral functions instead of correlation functions may be obtained by taking Fourier transforms throughout equation (21.7). Again omitting mathematical details, this gives

$$\partial E(k, t)/\partial t = F(k, t) - 2\nu k^2 E(k, t) \tag{21.8}$$

The problem of the additional unknown remains, of course, but this equation provides a convenient starting point for further discussion. E is the energy spectrum of equation (20.32); the dependence on t is shown as a reminder that we are dealing theoretically with a time-dependent situation. F is related to the Fourier transform of the triple correlation. However, it can be given its own physical interpretation through its role in equation (21.8).

The left-hand side represents the rate of change of the energy associated with wave number k. The second term on the right-hand side is a negative term involving the viscosity and is thus the energy dissipation. It can be shown that

$$\int_0^\infty F \, \mathrm{d}k = 0 \tag{21.9}$$

and so the first term on the right-hand side of equation (21.8) represents the transfer of energy between wave numbers.

Figure 21.4 shows graphs of E and $k^2 E$ for a typical situation.† The latter has large values at much higher k than the former. Hence the viscous dissipation is associated with high wave numbers; i.e. it is brought about by small eddies. This is a consequence of the fact that turbulent flows normally occur at high Reynolds number. The action of viscosity is slight on a length scale of the mean flow (e.g. a grid mesh-length). Yet much more dissipation occurs than in the corresponding

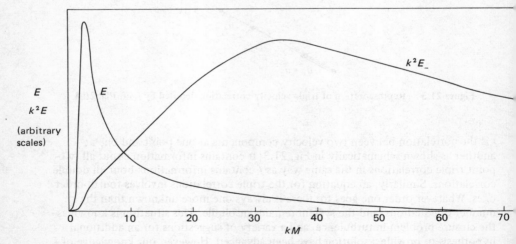

Figure 21.4   Energy and dissipation spectra in turbulence behind a grid (distance downstream from grid = $48M$, where M = grid mesh-length). Data from Ref. [282].

†Figure 21.4 is based on experimental data. For homogeneous isotropic turbulence, a relationship can be derived between $E(k)$ and the measurable one-dimensional spectrum, thus overcoming the non-measurability of $E(k)$ mentioned in Section 20.7. However, the conversion involves differentiation of experimental curves and so $E(k)$ is determined with rather poor accuracy.

laminar flow. This requires the development of local regions of high shear in the turbulence; that is the presence of small length scales.

The small dissipative eddies must be generated from larger ones. The effect of this on the energy spectrum is contained in the second term of equation (21.8); i.e. one expects the transfer of energy to be primarily from low wave numbers to high. This inference is confirmed experimentally by observations in grid turbulence of changes in the spectrum with distance downstream.

This interpretation of the behaviour of the terms of equation (21.8) allows the development of a model of turbulence which has relevance not just to homogeneous isotropic turbulence but to most turbulent flows.

Energy fed into the turbulence goes primarily into the larger eddies. (In grid turbulence this happens during the initial generation; in other flows to be considered in Chapter 22 it happens throughout the flow.) From these, smaller eddies are generated, and then still smaller ones. The process continues until the length scale is small enough for viscous action to be important and dissipation to occur. This sequence is called the energy cascade. At high Reynolds numbers (based on $(\overline{u^2})^{1/2}$ and a length scale defined in a way indicated in Section 20.6) the cascade is long; i.e. there is a large difference in the eddy sizes at its ends. There is then little direct interaction between the large eddies governing the energy transfer and the small dissipating eddies. The dissipation is determined by the rate of supply of energy to the cascade by the large eddies and is independent of the dynamics of the small eddies in which the dissipation actually occurs. The rate of dissipation is then independent of the magnitude of the viscosity. An increase in the Reynolds number to a still higher value — conveniently visualized as a change to a fluid of lower viscosity with all else held constant — only extends the cascade at the small eddy end. Still smaller eddies must be generated before the dissipation can occur. (Since, as we shall see, the total energy associated with these small eddies is small, this extension has a negligible effect on the total energy of the turbulence.) All other aspects of the dynamics of the turbulence are unaltered.

This inference, that the structure of the motion is independent of the fluid viscosity once the Reynolds number is high enough, has important implications and will be considered again in Section 22.2. It is given the (somewhat misleading) name of Reynolds number similarity.

The dynamics of the energy cascade and dissipation may be supposed to be governed by the energy per unit time (per unit mass) supplied to it at the large eddy (low wave number) end. This is, of course, equal to the energy dissipation, ϵ. This implies that for all wave numbers large enough to be independent of the energy production processes, the spectrum function E depends only on the wave number, the dissipation, and the viscosity; that is

$$E = E(k, \epsilon, \nu) \tag{21.10}$$

If the cascade is long enough, there may be an intermediate range (the inertial sub-range) in which the action of viscosity has not yet come in; that is

$$E = E(k, \epsilon) \tag{21.11}$$

Dimensional analysis then gives

$$E = A\epsilon^{2/3} k^{-5/3} \tag{21.12}$$

where A is a numerical constant.

This famous result, known as the Kolmogoroff −5/3 law, was not verified experimentally for some years, because the Reynolds numbers of turbulent flows under investigation were not high enough. Curiously, whilst experimental progress was being made towards verifying the result, doubts were arising about its theoretical validity. At any instant, energy dissipation is not occurring roughly uniformly throughout the turbulence; there are patches of intense small eddies involving high dissipation and other patches where there is little dissipation. This fits in with a model of the energy transfer process to be mentioned in Section 21.4; there is also experimental evidence that a velocity signal, filtered at a frequency corresponding to the small eddies, shows periods of activity and periods of quiescence [215]. This implies that there is a length scale − the size of the dissipating patches − that is not governed solely by ϵ and ν and thus raises doubts about the dimensional argument. The implications of this for the theory have received some discussion [122].

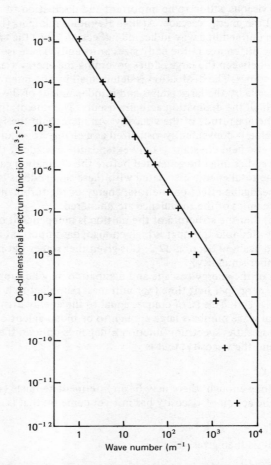

Figure 21.5   One-dimensional spectrum measured in a tidal channel; line has slope of −5/3. Data from Ref. [119].

However, there is now a body of experimental evidence supporting the $-5/3$ power spectrum. Good results were first obtained in an oceanographic channel flow, produced by tides, with a Reynolds number of 4×10^7. Figure 21.5 shows a spectrum obtained from this, plotted logarithmically, with a line of slope $-5/3$. (This is actually the measurable one-dimensional spectrum, but it can be shown that if this is proportional to k^{-n}, then so is the energy spectrum.)

21.4 Dynamical processes of the energy cascade

The discussion in Section 21.3 of the energy cascade did not consider the mechanism by which the transfer of energy from large scales to small scales occurs. It is instructive to consider first the related but more readily understood process of the mixing of a scalar contaminant [85, 86]. Suppose a blob of fluid, as shown in Fig. 21.6(1), is marked in some way, for example by being heated or dyed. If this blob is in a turbulent flow, its distribution will change with time in the way indicated schematically by successive configurations in Fig. 21.6 (see also Fig. 22.7). Its distribution in space becomes more and more contorted by the velocity fluctuations, but so long as molecular diffusion plays no role, the marked fluid is always just the same fluid. If the Péclet number is high, diffusion is negligible at first. However, the highly contorted patterns involve very steep gradients of the marker and so ultimately diffusion becomes significant, causing previously unmarked fluid to become marked. The higher the Péclet number, the more contorted the pattern must become before this happens.

This process is analogous to the cascade because it involves the appearance of smaller and smaller length scales until this is limited by molecular effects (diffusion or viscosity). However, the energy cascade is a more complicated matter because it involves the interaction of the velocity field with itself instead of with a quantity not involved in the dynamics. Any brief account of it must involve oversimplification, but three (not wholly independent) processes may be identified.

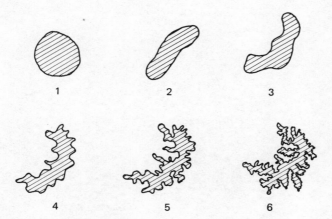

Figure 21.6 Schematic representation of successive configurations of marked blob of fluid within turbulent motion.

The first is the process of repeated instability considered in Section 20.1. Each stage may give rise to motions not only of greater complexity but also involving smaller scales than the previous stages. For example, one stage may produce local regions of high shear that can themselves be unstable.

Secondly, turbulence of a smaller scale may extract energy from larger scale motions in a way analogous to the extraction of energy from a mean flow by the turbulence as a whole (Section 20.4).

Thirdly there is vortex stretching [259]. The random nature of turbulent motion gives a diffusive action; two fluid particles that happen to be close together at some instant are likely to be much further apart at any later time. The turbulence will have carried them over different paths. This applies to two particles on the same vortex line. The process of vortex stretching, considered in Section 6.5, will thus be strongly present — although occurring in a random fashion. This increases the magnitude of the vorticity, but because of continuity also reduces the cross-section of the vortex tube. There is thus an intensification of the motion on a smaller scale; that is a transfer of energy to smaller eddies.

This process may also be seen as a cause of the patchy distribution of dissipation mentioned in Section 21.3. The vorticity intensification process will be strongest where the vorticity already happens to be large. At any instant the production of small eddies is thus occurring vigorously in some places and only weakly in others.

22
The Structure of Turbulent Flows

22.1 Introduction

Figure 22.1 shows four photographs of a turbulent boundary layer. Hydrogen bubble markers were released in small squares (as described in Section 23.4) from a fine wire parallel to the wall and perpendicular to the mean flow. The different pictures were taken with the wire at different distances from the wall, ranging from close to the wall to close to the outer edge of the boundary layer. It is apparent that the flow has considerable 'structure': different parts of the boundary layer show marked differences in the dye patterns; in each part certain features can be picked out, e.g. the longitudinal streaks in Fig. 22.1(a) and the large irregular patches into which dye has collected in Fig. 22.1 (b) and (c).

All turbulent flows exhibit structure of this kind. There is no situation in which the motion can simply be described as 'totally random'. In this chapter we look at aspects of the structure of turbulent flows, particularly of turbulent shear flows. Sections 22.2–22.6 discuss and illustrate the main concepts that have been developed to describe and interpret this structure. Much can be said that applies to all shear flows; such ideas will be illustrated by a variety of flows (depending largely on the best illustrations available). Some ideas have to be discussed in the context of a particular flow; more detailed attention is given to the turbulent wake (exemplifying shear flows away from a solid boundary — sometimes known as free shear flows) and to the turbulent boundary layer in zero pressure gradient (exemplifying shear flows next to a solid wall).

Sections 22.7–22.9 stand more on their own. Each deals with a separate aspect of turbulent flows: the tendency for flows to attach to walls or each other (the Coanda effect); the effect of stratification; and the tendency for some flows to revert to laminar motion.

22.2 Reynolds number similarity and self-preservation

As always, it is necessary to know the range of applicability of any measurement — whether it is relevant to other similar flows or whether it is peculiar to the particular situation investigated. Since the number of measurements needed for a reasonably full understanding of any turbulent flow is large, it is highly desirable to make observations of general applicability. Two ideas help here.

The first is the concept of Reynolds number similarity already introduced in Section 21.3. The larger eddies and the mean flow development are independent of the viscosity (so long as this is small enough to make the Reynolds number large).

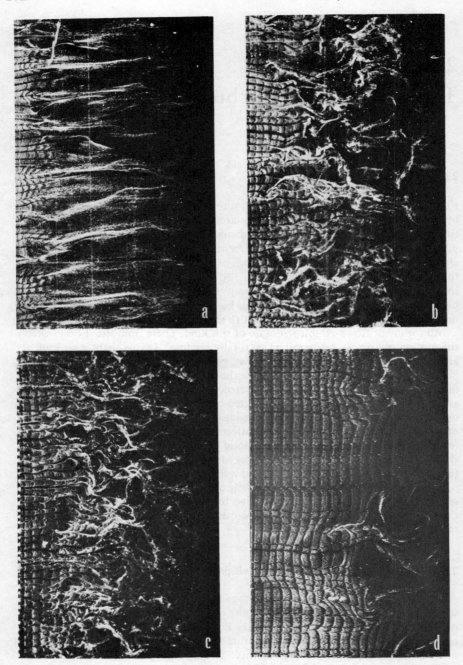

Figure 22.1   Turbulent boundary layer structure at different distances from wall. See text for procedure; flow is from left to right. (a) $yu_\tau/v = 4.5$; (b) $yu_\tau/v = 50.7$; (c) $yu_\tau/v = 101$; (d) $yu_\tau/v = 407$ ($y/\delta \approx 0.85$) (notation of Section 22.5). Ref. [139].

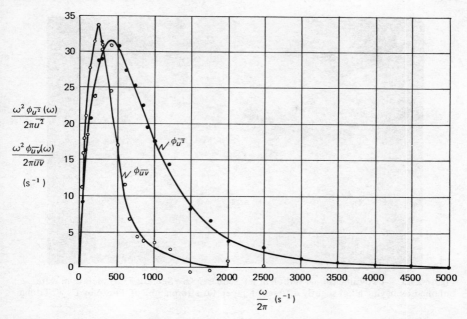

Figure 22.2 Comparison of intensity and Reynolds stress spectra in channel flow, showing former extending to much higher frequencies. (Detailed form of co-ordinates is unimportant except that ordinate is proportional to (frequency)^2 x spectrum function.) From Ref. [154].

This is true of the mean flow because the last term of equation (20.14) normally dominates the last-but-one term and because the Reynolds stress is produced by the larger eddies. (The contribution of different length-scales to the Reynolds stress may be investigated by applying spectral analysis not only to the energy as in Section 20.7, but also to the Reynolds stress [84, 154]. Figure 22.2 makes a comparison between the energy and Reynolds stress (one-dimensional) spectra in turbulent channel flow; the much more rapid fall-off of the latter at high wave numbers is apparent.) Hence, experiments at any (sufficiently high) Reynolds number provide information applicable to all values of the Reynolds number. We shall see in Section 22.5 that some qualification of this concept is needed for the motion in the vicinity of a solid boundary.

The second idea is that of 'self-preservation' [40]. This is the counterpart for turbulent flow of the occurrence of similar velocity profiles at different distances downstream in laminar flow (as discussed in Sections 11.3 and 11.8). However, self-preservation requires not only that the mean velocity distribution should be similar, but also that all the parameters associated with the turbulence should have similar distributions at different stations.

The equations of motion permit self-preservation only in particular cases. For example, it can occur in a wake only sufficiently far downstream for the mean velocity deficit at the wake centre to be small compared with the total mean velocity. The experimental evidence suggests that, when self-preservation is possible, then it occurs. This enables a description of the turbulent motion developed from measurements at one station to be applied to the whole flow.

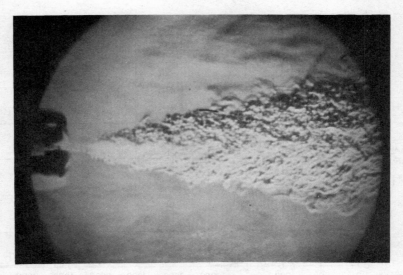

Figure 22.3   Two-dimensional turbulent jet; schlieren (see Section 23.4) picture in water, obtained by having jet at slightly different temperature from ambient. Photo by C. W. Titman.

The ideas of Reynolds number similarity and self-preservation taken in conjunction allow certain features of turbulent flows to be derived rather simply. We may illustrate this most readily by considering the development of the mean flow of a two-dimensional jet. As for a laminar flow, the jet is characterized, far enough downstream from the orifice, by M, the momentum transported per unit time over each cross-section. Ignoring a small contribution from the non-linear effects of the velocity fluctuations,

$$M = \int_{-\infty}^{\infty} \rho U^2 \, dy \tag{22.1}$$

Putting, analogously with (11.36),

$$U_{\max} \propto x^m; \quad \Delta \propto x^n \tag{22.2}$$

(the origin of x being adjustable) conservation of momentum again gives

$$2m + n = 0 \tag{22.3}$$

Secondly, the concept of Reynolds number similarity implies that ν does not enter into the counterpart of relationship (11.44) and so

$$\Delta = \Delta(x, M, \rho) \tag{22.4}$$

Dimensional requirements now imply that

$$\Delta \propto x \tag{22.5}$$

that is

$$n = 1 \tag{22.6}$$

Equation (22.3) now gives

$$m = -\frac{1}{2} \tag{22.7}$$

These results have been obtained more simply than the corresponding results for laminar flow. In contrast, however, the treatment of the laminar flow can be continued to indicate the detailed form of the velocity profile (equation (11.53)), whereas nothing more can be derived about the turbulent flow without additional assumptions or experimental observations.

Figure 22.3 shows an experiment verifying the result (equation (22.5)) that a turbulent jet spreads linearly. This result is true also of axisymmetric jets, just the same derivation applying (although now $m = -1$). Thus such jets spread out in a conical shape.

22.3 Intermittency and entrainment

In many situations turbulent motion occurs in only a limited region — that region in which high shear has been generated. Turbulent jets and wakes are usually surrounded by non-turbulent fluid; a turbulent boundary layer usually occurs beneath an inviscid irrotational flow. In such cases the interface between the turbulent and non-turbulent regions is sharp. It has however a highly irregular shape with bulges and indentations of various sizes, as shown in Fig. 22.4. The bulges and indentations are carried downstream by the flow. At the same time the detailed shape of the boundary is changing; each bulge and indentation can be identified over only a limited time.

At a fixed point (such as A in Fig. 22.4), random alternations between turbulent and non-turbulent motion occur. Figure 22.5 shows oscillograms of the velocity fluctuations at different distances from the centre line of a wake. It is possible to define quite accurately the fraction of the time that the motion is turbulent. This quantity is called the intermittency factor γ. Figure 22.6 shows its distribution in a two-dimensional wake. At the centre of the wake γ is 1; the motion is always turbulent. Outside the wake γ is 0; turbulent motion never penetrates there. But over a substantial fraction of the wake width, turbulent and non-turbulent motion alternate. Similar intermittency distributions can be determined for other flows.

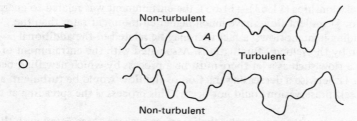

Figure 22.4   Sketch of a wake, illustrating sharp irregular interfaces between turbulent and non-turbulent fluid.

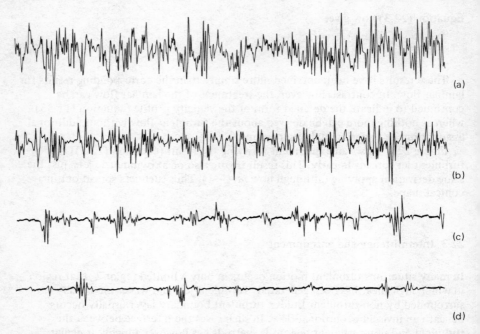

Figure 22.5   Oscillograms in turbulent wake at x/d = 28, showing increasing intermittency at edge. y/d = (a) 0.87, (b) 2.25, (c) 3.4, (d) 4.2. (Note: these traces were obtained with electronic boosting of high frequencies; this improves the contrast between laminar and turbulent periods by showing a quantity related to the vorticity.)

The effect of intermittency on flow visualization in the outer part of a boundary layer is apparent in Fig. 22.1(d). Regions can be seen where the dye patches move irregularly and are highly distorted; and others where they remain regular both in spacing and in shape.

At the interface between turbulent and non-turbulent fluid, the turbulence spreads. Fluid just in the non-turbulent region will a short time later be in turbulent motion. This spreading is part of the process of entrainment for a turbulent flow. Entrainment by laminar flows — the fact that a jet, for example, draws fluid into itself from the sides — has been discussed in Sections 11.8 and 11.9. In particular, through relationships (11.63)–(11.65), the entrainment was related to energy dissipation. Turbulent flows have much higher entrainment rates than the corresponding laminar flows, a fact that may be related to the additional dissipation by the velocity fluctuations. Associated with the entrainment of new fluid into a flow such as a jet there must be a process by which new fluid becomes turbulent. Otherwise a decreasing fraction of the flow would be turbulent, and, for example, self-preservation could not occur. This process is the spreading at the interface.

We can now see the reason why the interface is sharp. Associated with the velocity fluctuations of any turbulent motion are intense vorticity fluctuations. (The importance of vorticity in the dynamics of turbulence is apparent from the

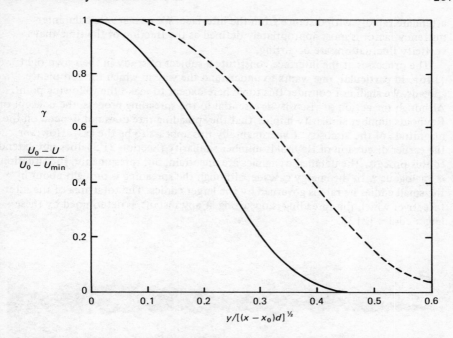

Figure 22.6 Mean velocity profile (solid line) and intermittency distribution (broken line) in a two-dimensional wake (Re = 1360; $x/d > 500$). Abscissa is distance from centre of wake, non-dimensionalized in the way appropriate to self-preservation. Both curves are experimental, although data points are not shown. From Ref. [268].

discussion in Section 21.4.) We will suppose that the flow in the non-turbulent region is irrotational, as is usually the case in the examples that have been mentioned. The acquisition of vorticity by initially irrotational fluid can only be brought about through the action of viscosity (Section 10.3). Thus the spreading of the turbulence at the interface involves the action of viscosity and must be effected by those eddies for which viscosity is significant: i.e. the small eddies. The length scale over which the change from turbulent to non-turbulent (rotational to irrotational) motion occurs is the size of these eddies, and so the interface appears very sharp on the scale of the flow as a whole.

The shape of the interface is, on the other hand, influenced by eddies of all sizes. The irregular and changing corrugations occur with a wide range of length scales. In particular, the largest bulges and indentations are produced by the large eddies to be described in Sections 22.4 and 22.6; these eddies are responsible for the fact that the region in which γ is non-zero but less than 1 extends over a sizeable fraction of the flow (see, e.g., Fig. 22.6).

The flow outside the interface, although called non-turbulent, does involve velocity fluctuations [199]. These are produced by the neighbouring turbulent region. Evidently the motion of a bulge in the interface changes the pattern of irrotational motion outside it. However, these velocity fluctuations are entirely irrotational and are dynamically quite different from turbulent fluctuations. They

attenuate rapidly with distance from the interface. We now see that the intermittency factor is most appropriately defined as the fraction of the time that
vorticity fluctuations are occurring.

The processes at the interface constitute a subject of study in their own right
[146]. In particular, one wants to understand the way in which the turbulence
spreads. We shall not consider this topic here except to make the following point.
Although the action of viscosity is essential to the spreading process, the concept of
Reynolds number similarity implies that the spreading rate does not depend on the
magnitude of the viscosity. Experimentally this appears to be the case. However,
the earlier discussion of Reynolds number similarity (Section 21.3) does not extend
to this process. The detailed dynamics are uncertain, but, presumably, the situation
is analogous with the energy cascade; although the spreading is brought about by
the small eddies its rate is governed by the larger eddies. The total area of the interface, over which the spreading is occurring at any instant, is determined by these
larger eddies [212].

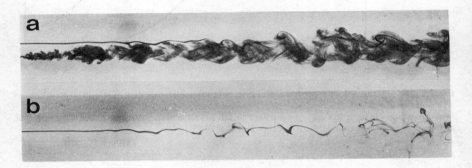

Figure 22.7   Jet in concurrent flow and neighbouring dye streak: (a) jet also dyed; (b) jet
not dyed.

Figure 22.7 illustrates and summarizes the entrainment process described in this
section. Two sources, side by side, emit water into the uniform flow in a water
channel. The water from the lower source is emitted sufficiently faster than the
main flow that it forms a turbulent jet. The water from the upper source is
emitted at the same speed as the main flow; there is thus no shear and no
turbulence generation. This source merely provides a way of marking fluid with
minimum dynamical effect. In Fig. 22.7(a), both sources emit dyed water. The jet
is visible (it has a rather different structure from jets considered elsewhere in this
book because of the motion of the surrounding fluid). The way in which its
spreading brings the dye from the other source into turbulent motion can be seen.
In Fig. 22.7(b), only water from the passive source is dyed, although the jet is still
present; this shows more clearly the effect of entrainment on the initially laminar
fluid. The figure also illustrates the processes shown schematically in Fig. 21.6; the
longer the dye streak has been inside the turbulent region, the wider is the range of
length scales on which it has been distorted.

22.4 The structure of a turbulent wake

The understanding of the dynamics of turbulence in shear flows depends primarily on the measurement and interpretation of the parameters introduced in Chapter 20. Further discussion thus has to focus attention on particular flows, and we consider the two-dimensional wake to exemplify the procedures and the ideas that come from them. Nevertheless we shall frequently refer in this section to ideas that have more general applicability.

As usual the Cartesian co-ordinate system used to specify directions has x in the mean flow direction, y across the wake, and z parallel to the axis of the body producing the wake.

Obvious first measurements are $\overline{q^2}$, the separate contributions to this ($\overline{u^2}$, $\overline{v^2}$, and $\overline{w^2}$), and the Reynolds stress $-\overline{uv}$. Figure 22.8 shows the distributions of these across a wake; Fig. 22.9 shows the same quantities divided by the inter-mittency factor, indicating approximately (not exactly, because of the irrotational fluctuations mentioned in Section 22.3) the average values during the intervals when the point of observation is inside the turbulent region.

The Reynolds stress is zero right at the middle of the wake, by symmetry, and,

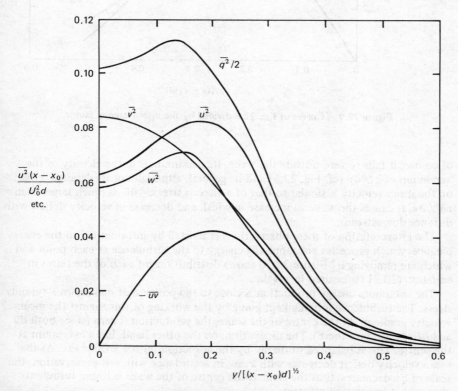

Figure 22.8 Distributions of intensities and Reynolds stress in a two-dimensional wake ($Re = 1360$, $x/d > 500$). Co-ordinates are normalized in the way appropriate to self-preservation; $y = 0$ corresponds to wake centre. All curves represent experimental data (Ref. [268]).

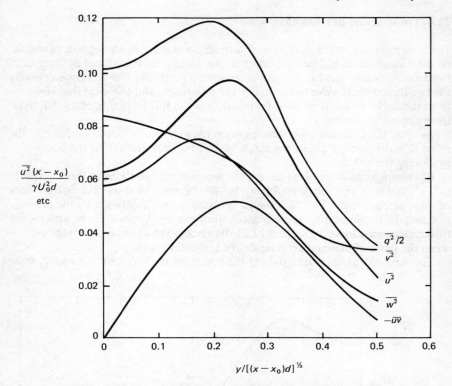

Figure 22.9   Curves of Fig. 22.8 divided by the intermittency factor.

of course, it falls to zero outside the wake. Its maximum is in the vicinity of the maximum of $\partial U/\partial y$ (cf. Fig. 22.6) and its general, although not its detailed, effect on the mean velocity is similar to that of a viscous stress. $-\overline{uv}$ is much larger than $\nu\partial U/\partial y$. It causes the wake to increase in width and decrease in velocity deficit with distance downstream.

The interpretation of these observations is assisted by information on the energy balance; which processes are supplying energy to the turbulence at each point and which are removing it? Figure 22.10 shows distributions of each of the terms in equation (20.21) measured in a wake.

The maximum energy production is close to the position of maximum Reynolds stress. The turbulence is being kept going by the working of this against the mean velocity gradient. At the centre of the wake, the production is zero (since both $\overline{uv}$ and $\partial U/\partial y$ are zero there). The dissipation, on the other hand, has a maximum at the centre. This is balanced primarily by the advection term $-\frac{1}{2}U\partial\overline{q^2}/\partial x$. As the mean velocity deficit decreases with x, so, in accordance with self-preservation, the scale of $\overline{q^2}$ decreases; thus the fluid at the centre of the wake is losing turbulent energy as it travels downstream.

At the outer edge of the wake, on the other hand, the advection term has the opposite sign. This corresponds to the supply of turbulent energy to previously non-turbulent fluid as the wake spreads. Figure 22.10 shows that this energy is supplied by the outward transport of energy by the fluctuations themselves from the region where the production is large.

When measurements such as those described above are supplemented by measurements of correlations and spectra and by flow visualization experiments, some ideas may be developed about the role of eddies of different sizes in the dynamics of the turbulence. We have already seen that the smaller eddies contribute relatively less to the Reynolds stress than to the energy (illustrated for a different flow by Fig. 22.2). More generally, the smaller eddies have a structure that is less characteristic of the particular flow than the larger eddies and the description of their behaviour developed from observations in grid turbulence (Chapter 21) may be applied. The later stages of the energy cascade are similar in all flows. It is because of this that observations in shear flows may be used for experimental investigations of the Kolmogoroff law, equation (21.12).

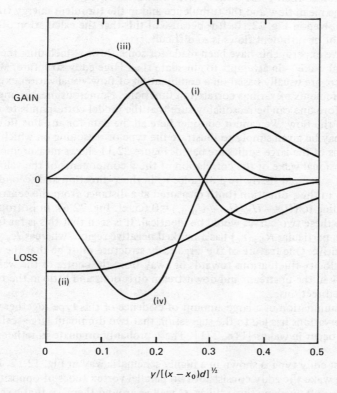

Figure 22.10 Experimentally determined turbulent energy balance in a two-dimensional wake. Abscissa scale as in previous graphs, ordinate scale arbitrary (Re = 1360, $x/d > 500$). (i) Production, $-\overline{uv}\partial U/\partial y$ (ii) dissipation, $\nu\overline{u_i\partial^2 u_i/\partial x_j^2}$ (iii) advection, $-\tfrac{1}{2}U\partial\overline{q^2}/\partial x$ (note $\tfrac{1}{2}V\partial\overline{q^2}/\partial y$ is negligible in a wake); (iv) turbulent transport, $-\partial(\tfrac{1}{2}\overline{q^2}\,v + \overline{pv}/\rho)/\partial y$. From Ref. [268].

The larger eddies, that do play a role in the generation of the Reynolds stress, must be more characteristic of the particular flow, since the Reynolds stress distribution necessarily varies from flow to flow. So long as the eddies are still relatively small compared with the length scale of the mean flow (e.g. wake width), their features are adequately described by the considerations of Section 20.4. The anisotropy associated with Reynolds stress production (Fig. 20.2) arises essentially in the way summarized by Fig. 20.3. Usually, the largest contribution to the energy of the turbulence is made by eddies large enough to be oriented in this way but small enough to be within one part of the mean velocity profile.

Still larger eddies extend across much of the flow and there will be appreciable variation of the mean shear within their length scale. The ideas of Fig. 20.3 are then too great an oversimplification. One can identify certain patterns in the turbulence on this scale that occur over and over again; one says that the large eddies have a rather definite structure and orientation. This structure varies between different flows much more than the motion on smaller scales. The large eddies play a role out of proportion to their contribution to the turbulent energy, both in the interaction between the mean flow and the turbulence and in the turbulent energy transfer process involved in Fig. 22.10. It is because of this that the calculation of the development of turbulent flows is so difficult.

Extensive experiments have been made for some flows — including the two-dimensional wake — in attempts to elucidate their large eddy structure. Models of the structure are usually based on a combination of flow visualization experiments and measurements of various correlation functions. Numerous measurements are needed before one can be reasonably sure that the model corresponds to real features of the flow. We cannot consider here all the data for any one flow, but an example may be given simply to illustrate the type of reasoning on which descriptions of the large eddies are based. Figure 22.11 shows measurements in a two-dimensional wake of the correlation of the y-components of the velocity at two points separated firstly by a distance r_x in the x-direction and secondly by a distance r_z in the z-direction (both measured at a distance from the centre plane corresponding to $(U_0 - U)/(U_0 - U_{min}) = 0.65$, cf. Fig. 22.6). In isotropic turbulence these two curves would be identical. It is seen that this is far from the case; in particular $R_{yy}(r_x)$ has a marked negative region, whereas $R_{yy}(r_z)$ is always positive. One feature of the large eddy structure must be that the return flow for velocity fluctuations towards or away from the centre of the wake occurs dominantly in the upstream and downstream directions and little in the transverse (z and $-z$) directions.

The accumulation of a large amount of evidence of this type together with visual observations has led to the suggestion that two dominant large-scale structures occur in wakes [118, 271]. These probably originate in rather different ways.

The first eddy type is shown in a highly schematic way in Fig. 22.12. In each half of the wake the eddy consists of two parallel vortex tubes of opposite sense. There is some flow along these tubes, as well as around them, so that a spiralling motion results. The tubes may not be straight, but one does not have sufficient information to assign any other shape to them. Each tube has its axis in an xy-plane, with the part near the edge of the wake further downstream than the part near the centre, and the two tubes are separated in the z-direction. Such motions occur

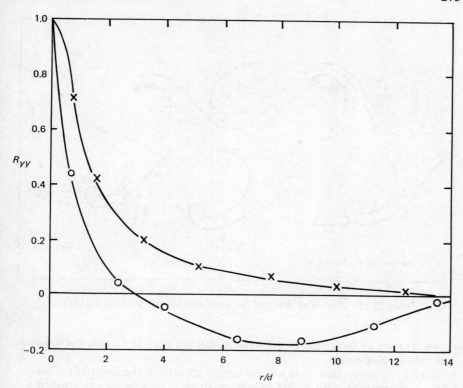

Figure 22.11   Correlation curves in a two-dimensional wake for the y-component of the velocity fluctuation and points separated in the $x(\circ)$ and $z(\times)$ directions (Re = 1300, x/d = 533, y/d = 4). Data from Ref. [118].

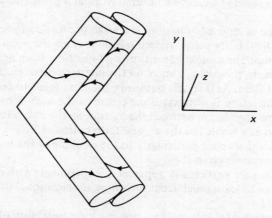

Figure 22.12   Schematic representation of double roller eddy in a wake.

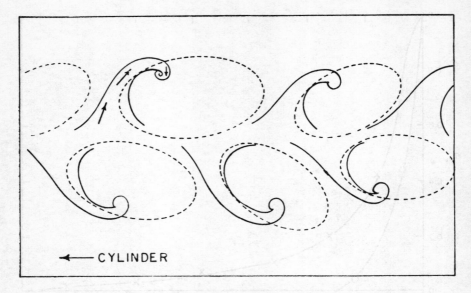

← CYLINDER

Figure 22.13   Sketch of 'jet-type' large eddies in a wake. From Ref. [118].

simultaneously on both sides of the wake so that the eddy as a whole has the shape indicated in the figure.

It has been shown that motions of this type can arise as the result of the action of the mean shear on initially isotropic fluctuations – these being generated, it is assumed, in the process of non-turbulent fluid becoming turbulent at the interface. One can readily see that shear will have a selective action on different fluctuational vorticity components, some vortex lines being stretched and the vorticity intensified, others being shortened and the vorticity reduced. However, the details of the structure so selected cannot be inferred without a mathematical theory [271].

The second type of large eddy motion in a wake occurs simultaneously at several (typically five) fairly evenly spaced positions along the wake in the streamwise direction. The motion consists of a jet-like flow from near the centre of the wake outwards, producing a bulge on the interface between the turbulent and non-turbulent fluid. As it travels outwards, the fluid tends to curve round in the flow direction. The return flow towards the centre of the wake is more diffuse. Again there is some correlation between the motion on the two sides of the wake, so that the motion as a whole has the general form indicated by Fig. 22.13.

It is these eddies that relate particularly to the example of the interpretation of correlation measurements given above.

Also, these eddies are particularly apparent in experiments with dyed wakes. One needs cine-film to learn much from such flow visualization, but the eddies can be seen in Fig. 3.11.

The probable origin of this type of motion is a local instability of the mean velocity profile, somewhat analogous to the instability of a laminar wake that produces a Kármán vortex street (Section 3.3). There is a major difference in the result of the instability in that the large eddies are of very limited extent in the third direction. Also, because it is probably triggered by the intense smaller-scale fluctuations, the occurrence of the instability is intermittent and irregular.

22.5 Turbulent motion near a wall [40, 212]

The general ideas of the last section, although made specific in the context of wake flow, apply to all turbulent shear flows. However, they provide a very incomplete story when the flow is adjacent to a solid boundary.

At such a boundary (at rest), the boundary condition that the fluid velocity is zero applies at every instant. Thus it applies to the mean velocity and to the fluctuations separately,

$$U_i = 0; \qquad u_i = 0 \tag{22.8}$$

The fact that the fluctuations drop to zero at the wall has the particular implication that the Reynolds stress is zero

$$-\overline{uv} = 0 \tag{22.9}$$

The only stress exerted directly on the wall is the viscous one.

Away from the wall, on the other hand, the turbulence generates a Reynolds stress, large compared with the viscous stress, in the usual way. The total stress

$$\tau = \mu \partial U/\partial y - \rho \overline{uv} \tag{22.10}$$

(we are still considering a two-dimensional flow for which the boundary layer equations apply). This cannot vary rapidly with y without producing a very large mean acceleration and thus requiring an improbable mean flow distribution. (For example, in channel flow with no variation of mean quantities in the x-direction, τ varies linearly across the channel as it does for laminar motion — the first integral of equation (2.6).) Consequently, the viscous stress close to the wall must match up with the Reynolds stress further out. Although τ varies only slowly, $\mu \partial U/\partial y$ and $-\rho \overline{uv}$ each vary rapidly, the former being much larger at the wall than in laminar flow but becoming very small away from the wall, the latter being large away from the wall and zero at the wall.

Figure 22.14 illustrates this by showing distributions of τ and of its two contributions measured in a zero-pressure-gradient boundary layer. The region where the viscous stress makes a large contribution is a small fraction of the total boundary layer thickness (note the change in abscissa scale). To generate this distribution of viscous stress, the mean velocity profile must rise steeply at the wall and then become comparatively flat. Figure 22.15 compares a typical turbulent boundary layer profile with a corresponding laminar one.

Parallel considerations apply to turbulent pipe flow. Figure 22.16 compares laminar and turbulent mean velocity profiles, firstly for the same flow rate and secondly for the same pressure gradient.

It is now clear that the presence of the wall causes the fluid viscosity to enter in a much more important way into the dynamics of turbulent motion than it does for free flows. The concept of Reynolds number similarity is no longer so useful.

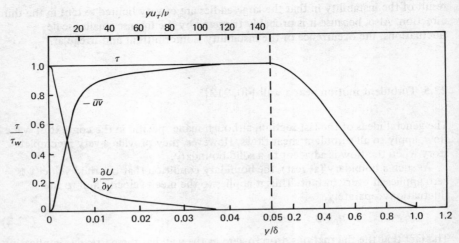

Figure 22.14 Distributions of the total stress, Reynolds stress, and viscous stress across a boundary layer ($Re_\delta = 7 \times 10^4$). Note 30-fold change in abscissa scale at $y/\delta = 0.05$. Based on data in Refs. [136, 223].

This effect extends to the fluctuations as well as to the mean flow. Figure 22.17 shows distributions of $\overline{q^2}$ and of its components $\overline{u^2}$, $\overline{v^2}$, and $\overline{w^2}$ across a boundary layer. (The reason for the alternative co-ordinates will be seen later.) Large variations are to be observed with strong maxima close to the wall. (Figure 22.17 shows also the distribution of the intermittency factor and it is evident that division by this — as was considered for wake flow, Figs. 22.8 and 22.9 — would affect only the shape of the tails at the larger values of y/δ.)

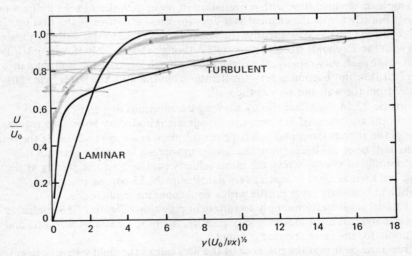

Figure 22.15 Comparison of laminar and turbulent boundary layer velocity profiles. (Laminar: Blasius profile; turbulent: experimental profile at $Re_x = 9.2 \times 10^5$, with tripping at $x = 0$ to promote transition.)

This observation can be interpreted in connection with the turbulent energy balance, Fig. 22.18. The rate of energy production, $-\overline{uv}\,\partial U/\partial y$, also has a large peak close to the wall. The reason is related to the above discussion of the stress. Very close to the wall $-\overline{uv}$ is small and so there is little energy production; far from it, $\partial U/\partial y$ is small with the same consequence. Mathematically,

$$-\overline{uv}\,\frac{\partial U}{\partial y} = \frac{1}{\rho}\left(\tau - \mu\frac{\partial U}{\partial y}\right)\frac{\partial U}{\partial y} \qquad (22.11)$$

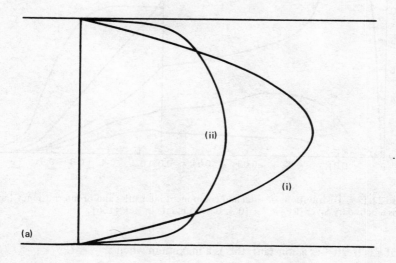

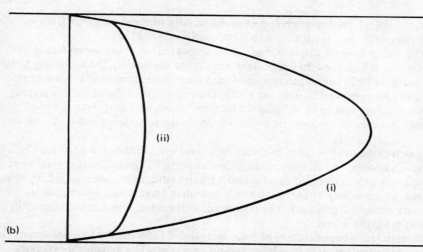

Figure 22.16 Comparison of (i) laminar and (ii) turbulent velocity profiles in a pipe for (a) the same mean velocity and (b) the same pressure gradient. (The diagrams correspond to a turbulent flow Reynolds number of about 4000; for higher Re the contrast is more marked — cf. Fig. 2.11.)

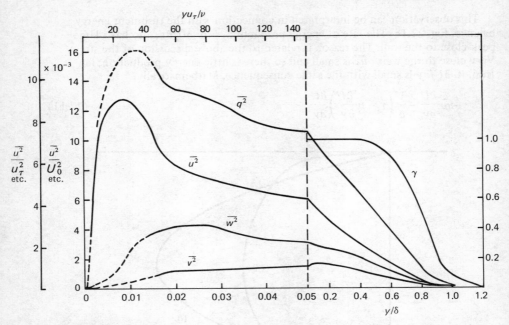

Figure 22.17   Distributions of total and component intensities and of intermittency factor across a boundary layer ($Re_\delta = 7 \times 10^4$). Based on data in Ref. [136].

and, if τ is treated as a constant, this is a maximum when

$$\mu \partial U/\partial y = \tau/2 \tag{22.12}$$

Thus the energy production is largest in the vicinity of the changeover from a predominantly viscous stress to a predominantly turbulent one.

The energy balance diagram, Fig. 22.18, shows that over the region where the production is high the other important term is the dissipation; the remaining terms in equation (20.21) are much less significant (apart from some rather complicated transfer processes very close to the wall). The inner part of the boundary layer is thus sometimes said to be in 'local equilibrium' — meaning that there is a local balance between the process supplying energy to the turbulence and that removing it.

Towards the outer edge of the boundary layer the quantities in equation (20.21) are much smaller, but all the terms are now important. The dissipation somewhat exceeds the production and there is also a loss by advection — corresponding, as in a wake, to the supply of energy to newly turbulent fluid. These losses are compensated by turbulent transport. The turbulence in the outer region is maintained by that in the inner region.

More detailed consideration of these and related ideas has led to a division of the turbulent boundary layer into inner and outer regions. The dynamical processes occurring in the latter are not dissimilar from those in a wake, but the inner region requires its own model. The ideas that have been developed for this region can be applied to most turbulent flows adjacent to a wall — for example, to turbulent

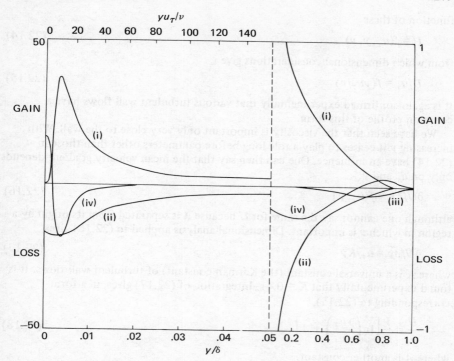

Figure 22.18 Energy balance diagram (principal features) for a turbulent boundary layer ($\mathrm{Re}_\delta = 7 \times 10^4$). (i) Production; (ii) dissipation; (iii) advection; (iv) transport across boundary layer (primarily by turbulence, but including viscous contribution at low y/δ). (Inner part based on Ref. [212]; outer part based on Ref. [136] but modified to reduce discrepancies with Ref. [212] and with requirement that integrated transport should be zero.)

channel and pipe flow (although not, for example, to a boundary layer close to separation). Because of the local equilibrium, the structure of the inner region is substantially independent of the outer flow.

We thus want to specify the flow in the 'wall-region' by a velocity scale characteristic of this region. This is provided by τ_W, the value of τ at the wall, which has the dimensions of density $\times$ (velocity)^2. Hence we define

$$u_\tau = (\tau_W/\rho)^{1/2} \tag{22.13}$$

as our velocity scale. u_τ depends on the flow as a whole, but once it is specified, the structure of the wall region is specified. It is confirmed experimentally that the turbulent intensity distributions scale with u_τ. For example, the maximum value of $\overline{u^2}$ is always about $8u_\tau^2$.

The relationship between u_τ and the external velocity U_0 for a boundary layer depends (rather weakly) on the Reynolds number. Under typical laboratory conditions, u_τ/U_0 is in the range 0.035 to 0.05.

Conditions in the wall region are now specified by the three parameters: u_τ, the distance from the wall y, and the kinematic viscosity ν. The mean velocity U is a function of these

$$U = f(u_\tau, y, \nu) \tag{22.14}$$

from which dimensional considerations give

$$U/u_\tau = f(yu_\tau/\nu) \tag{22.15}$$

It is again confirmed experimentally that various turbulent wall flows have a common profile of this form.

We have seen that the viscosity is important only very close to the wall. With increasing y it ceases to play a role long before parameters other than those in (22.14) have an influence. One can then say that the mean velocity gradient depends only on u_τ and y,

$$\partial U/\partial y = f(u_\tau, y) \tag{22.16}$$

although one cannot say the same for U because it is separated from its origin by a region in which ν is important. Dimensional analysis applied to (22.16) gives

$$\partial U/\partial y = u_\tau/Ky \tag{22.17}$$

where K is a universal constant (the Kármán constant) of turbulent wall flows. It is found experimentally that $K = 0.41$. Integration of (22.17) gives, in a form corresponding to (22.15),

$$\frac{U}{u_\tau} = \frac{1}{K}\left[\ln\left(\frac{yu_\tau}{\nu}\right) + A\right] \tag{22.18}$$

where A is another constant.

This logarithmic profile is one of the most famous results in the study of turbulent flows. In Fig. 22.19, the velocity profile of Fig. 22.15 is plotted with log–linear co-ordinates and the straight line corresponding to equation (22.18) is evident.

The profile departs from the logarithmic form when $yu_\tau/\nu < 30$, because of the importance of viscosity in this region. Very close to the wall viscous action is dominant. At the wall

$$u = v = w = 0 \tag{22.19}$$

and, taken in conjunction with the continuity equation

$$\frac{\partial u}{\partial x} + \frac{\partial v}{\partial y} + \frac{\partial w}{\partial z} = 0 \tag{22.20}$$

this gives

$$\partial v/\partial y = 0 \quad \text{at} \quad y = 0 \tag{22.21}$$

Hence,

$$\frac{\partial(\overline{uv})}{\partial y} = \frac{\partial^2(\overline{uv})}{\partial y^2} = 0 \quad \text{at} \quad y = 0 \tag{22.22}$$

and treating τ as a constant in equation (22.10)

$$\frac{\partial^2 U}{\partial y^2} = \frac{\partial^3 U}{\partial y^3} = 0 \quad \text{at} \quad y = 0 \tag{22.23}$$

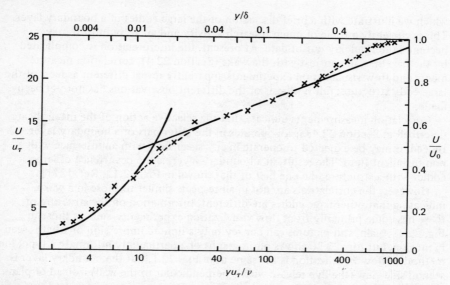

Figure 22.19 Example of a turbulent boundary layer mean velocity profile plotted on log-linear co-ordinates ($Re_\delta = 2.3 \times 10^4$). Solid lines correspond to equations (22.18) and (22.24); broken line shows trend of data.

We thus expect there to be a significant region right next to the wall in which the velocity profile is linear

$$U/u_\tau = yu_\tau/\nu \qquad (22.24)$$

The curve corresponding to this is included in Fig. 22.19 (the logarithmic plotting now serving to expand this region) and it is seen that the experimental points fall on it for $yu_\tau/\nu < 8$.

This thin region is known as the viscous sub-layer. Sometimes it is called the laminar sub-layer, but that is less accurate as it contains large velocity fluctuations; $\overline{u^2}$ and $\overline{w^2}$ are free to rise more rapidly from the wall than $\overline{uv}$. Although the viscous sub-layer is very thin, a substantial fraction of the total mean velocity change across the boundary layer occurs within it.

The upper limit in y of the logarithmic profile occurs where dynamical processes relating to the boundary layer as a whole become significant — where, for example, the large eddy structure (see Section 22.6) is influenced by the outer part of the layer. This is observed experimentally to occur around $y/\delta = 0.2$, where δ is the total boundary layer thickness (defined, say, so that $U = 0.99U_0$ at $y = \delta$). The corresponding value of yu_τ/ν (about 200 in Fig. 22.19) depends on the Reynolds number $U_0\delta/\nu$.

22.6 Large eddies in a boundary layer

The fact that any turbulent flow involves large eddies with a structure characteristic of that flow was introduced in Section 22.4. Wall flows have some special features, which we illustrate with a brief discussion of the large eddies of a boundary layer. This is currently a topic of much research activity and an account of it may become rather quickly out of date. At present, the interpretation is complicated by the fact that, in contrast with the wake (Section 22.4), correlation measurements and flow visualization experiments apparently reveal different aspects of the large eddy structure; full synthesis of the different observations has not yet been made.

Correlation measurements indicate that the selective action of the mean shear, described in Section 22.4, again operates in the outer part of a boundary layer. Indeed, it may be expected to operate in any shear flow with an interface with non-turbulent fluid. The result, in a boundary layer, is the occurrence of large eddies with a structure like one half of that shown in Fig. 22.12. Ref. [271].

However, the correlations are not in all respects similar to those in a wake, indicating that other large eddies are different. Information on the structure of these has come primarily from flow visualization experiments, such as those in Fig. 22.1. Again, still pictures can convey only a limited impression of what is seen in motion, but Fig. 22.20 shows photographs of a particularly informative type; the method of flow visualization is the same as in Fig. 22.1, but the boundary layer is seen in side-view (the dye release wire is perpendicular to the wall) instead of plan-view.

Two types of large-scale motion are apparent in such experiments, an eruption of slow moving fluid away from the wall and an inrush of rapidly moving fluid towards the wall.

The former originates in the viscous sub-layer close to the wall. The streaky structure seen there (Fig. 22.1(a)) is produced by regions, separated in the z-direction, of fluid moving faster than average downstream and of fluid moving more slowly than average. Fluid in the latter regions intermittently erupts, in a motion with a highly repeatable structure [134], into the main body of the boundary layer. The sub-layer appears to 'burst', and, for this reason, large eddies of this type are often known as bursts. Figure 22.20(a) shows a boundary layer during this process; the motion away from the wall is apparent and the spacing of the dye patches shows also that this fluid is moving downstream more slowly than average. The eruptions vary in size, but some of them penetrate right through the boundary layer to contribute to the intermittency at its outer edge.

The second type of motion — the inrush — is in its main features just the reverse of an eruption. Fluid moving faster than average downstream is carried in towards the wall. This gives it an even more marked excess longitudinal velocity and this structure is particularly apparent in the inner half of a boundary layer. Figure 22.20(b) was taken during an inrush; the slight variation of the longitudinal velocity across most of the boundary layer, as indicated by the spacing of dye patches, implies that fluid close to the wall is moving much faster than average.

The processes generating the eruptions and inrushes and their relationship to the shear selected eddies remain open questions. It is often suggested that the eruptions are produced by an instability in the sub-layer region. Certain features of the region resemble markedly features of transition to turbulence in a boundary layer — for example the streaks resemble the development of three-dimensionality described in Section 19.1. However, this interpretation faces the difficulty that essentially identical large-scale motions occur in boundary layers on rough walls, for which the flow structure close to the wall is quite different [68, 121].

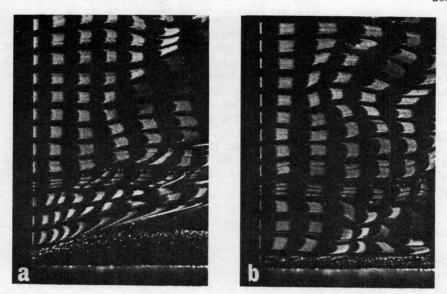

Figure 22.20 Turbulent boundary layer (a) during eruption, (b) during inrush. Flow is from left to right, wall is at bottom; see text for procedure. From Ref. [121].

The eruptions and the inrushes both have structures generating a large Reynolds stress. In fact, between them, they are probably responsible for almost the whole observed Reynolds stress; this implies that they are also the main sources of energy for the turbulence. Orientation of smaller scale motions plays little part in Reynolds stress generation in a boundary layer.

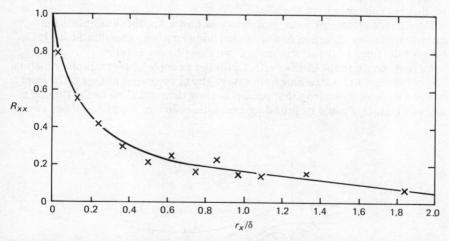

Figure 22.21 Variation of correlation coefficient of longitudinal velocity components with longitudinal separation, r_x, in wall region of turbulent boundary layer, $y/\delta = 0.097$. Note that correlation remains significant at values of r_x of order of boundary layer thickness δ and large compared with distance from wall y. From Ref. [277].

A curious feature of the large-eddy motion close to the wall is that not all quantities associated with it scale in the way implied by the discussion of Section 22.5 [188]. For example it involves a length scale which is large compared with the distance from the wall (illustrated by the correlation function shown in Fig. 22.21). Evidently this scale is being imposed on the wall region by the (less intense) fluctuations further out. At first sight, this invalidates the argument leading to equation (22.18). To provide a reconciliation, it has been suggested [68, 269] that the large eddies near the wall involve a 'universal' or 'active' motion — with a length scale proportional to the distance from the wall — and an 'irrelevant' or 'inactive' motion — with a much larger length scale. The idea requires some modification to fit in with current models of the large eddies, but some such separation of the roles of different length scales must apply; the occurrence of the logarithmic velocity profile is well established.

22.7 The Coanda effect

Suppose a two-dimensional jet emits into a region bounded by a side wall, as shown in Fig. 22.22. It is found that the jet is pulled down on to the wall giving the type of flow shown in the figure. This behaviour is known as wall attachment and is an example of what is called the Coanda effect.

The reason for it can be understood as follows. In the case of an unconfined jet, entrainment (Section 22.3) produces an inflow of fluid from the sides. In the presence of a wall, the jet cannot draw fluid into itself in this way. Instead it is drawn down on to the wall.

Because of the higher entrainment rate, the Coanda effect occurs much more strongly when the flow is turbulent; for example, a turbulent jet will attach to a more distant wall than a laminar jet. Similarly, two-dimensional flows exhibit the Coanda effect more strongly than three-dimensional; in the latter case fluid for entrainment can enter from the sides.

The Coanda effect can occur in a variety of flows. Another example is the reattachment after transition of a separated boundary layer (Section 11.4). It can also take the form of the attachment of two flows to one another.

We may illustrate the Coanda effect with the example of two turbulent thermal plumes (Section 14.6) attaching in this way. The photographs in Fig. 22.23 were obtained by having two long thin parallel heating elements close to the floor in a tank of water. Dye could be introduced into the inflow to the plumes from two

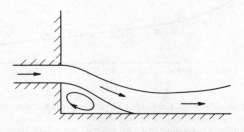

Figure 22.22   Schematic diagram of wall-attaching jet.

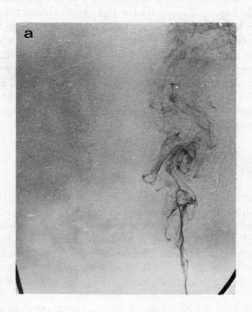

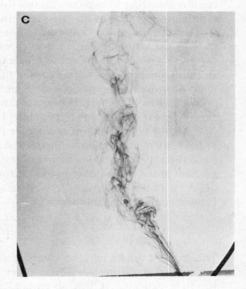

Figure 22.23 (a) Single plume; (b) plumes showing Coanda effect; (c) the same flow as in (b) but with dye on only one side.

sources, also close to the floor, a little way to the side of each element remote from the other element. In Fig. 22.23(a) only the right-hand element is switched on and the single plume can be seen. In the other two pictures both elements are being heated. Each plume would normally entrain fluid from the space between them. However, since there is no way in which this fluid can be replaced, this entrainment is not possible. Instead, the two plumes are drawn together into a single plume rising above the line midway between the two elements. Figure 22.23(b) shows this flow. Figure 22.23(c) shows the same situation, but only the right-hand dye source is present; the change in direction of motion of fluid from the right as it meets fluid from the left can be seen.

22.8 Stratified shear flows

Turbulent flow of stratified fluids is a topic of some importance for its geophysical applications. It has been the subject of some laboratory studies, but not enough for any very full account to be based on these alone. Many of the most important ideas have been developed in a meteorological context, principally the study of the lowest layers of the atmosphere as the wind blows over hot or cold ground [172, 205, 243]. This is too large a subject to be discussed here. Hence, this section just introduces some of the basic ideas without attempting to show their origin in any detail.

We are concerned with the predominantly horizontal mean flow of a fluid whose mean density varies vertically. The mean velocity also varies vertically, and we shall confine attention to two-dimensional flow. Hence, the specification of the situation is primarily in terms of the two gradients, dU/dz and $d\rho_0/dz$.

The velocity gradient can lead to generation of turbulence in the usual way through the action of inertia forces (Section 20.4). The role of the density gradient depends on its sign. If the density increases upwards, then buoyancy forces provide an additional source of energy for the turbulence. If the density decreases upwards, then the turbulence must do work against buoyancy forces, which therefore produce a loss of turbulent energy additional to viscous dissipation; turbulence cannot persist when the density gradient is too large.

From the considerations of Chapter 16, we expect the quantitative formulation of the relative importance of inertia and buoyancy forces to be made in terms of some form of the Froude number (equation (16.7)). The role of the velocity gradient in the dynamics of turbulent flow suggests that U/L should be replaced by dU/dz. Also it is convenient to work in terms of the reciprocal of the square of this Froude number; that is in terms of

$$\text{Ri} = -\frac{g(d\rho_0/dz)}{\rho_0(dU/dz)^2} \tag{22.25}$$

This is called the Richardson number (sometimes the gradient form of the Richardson number to distinguish it from other forms defined somewhat differently). As was to be expected, it depends on the sign of the density gradient but not on that of the velocity gradient.

Negative Richardson number corresponds to a destabilizing density gradient; both shear and buoyancy give rise to turbulence generation. When $-\text{Ri}$ is small, the former is dominant and the motion is essentially of the type we have been considering hitherto. When −Ri is large, the latter is dominant and the turbulence may be more like the free convection turbulence described in Section 4.3.

Positive Richardson number corresponds to a stabilizing density gradient; turbulent motion cannot be sustained when Ri becomes large.

Various experiments have been carried out to discover the more detailed dynamics of these processes. The simplest configuration in principle (although not in practice) is a flow with uniform velocity and density gradients. Such a configuration has been achieved using a special wind-tunnel with graded heated elements and flow resistance grids at its entry [290]. It was used for investigations with positive Richardson number. The numerical details of the results may not be generally applicable, since the flow was still developing in the downstream direction at the observing station (and the Reynolds number may not have been high enough for Ri to be the only parameter); but the results should indicate well the general trends. The damping action of the stratification on the turbulence is illustrated by Fig. 22.24, which shows the variation of the temperature fluctuations relative to the temperature gradient as a function of Richardson number (since the geometry was constant, the fact that the ordinate is not non-dimensional is unimportant). The turbulence is almost completely suppressed when Ri reaches 0.45.

Changes in the structure of the turbulence also occur. Figure 22.25 shows the variations of the correlation functions $-\overline{uw}/(\overline{u^2}\,\overline{w^2})^{1/2}$ and $-\overline{w\theta}/(\overline{w^2}\overline{\theta^2})^{1/2}$ (where θ is the temperature fluctuation); the former is the normalized Reynolds stress, whilst the correlation $-\overline{w\theta}$ plays a role in the transport of heat by the turbulence corresponding to the role of the Reynolds stress in momentum transport. The latter falls off more rapidly, indicating that the turbulence changes in a way that makes it relatively less efficient as a heat transfer mechanism than as a momentum transfer mechanism. This can be understood physically in this way: a fluid particle that is

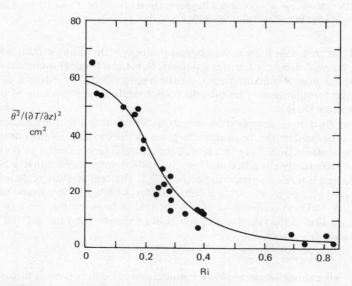

Figure 22.24 Variation of intensity of temperature fluctuations with Richardson number in a stratified shear flow. From Ref. [290].

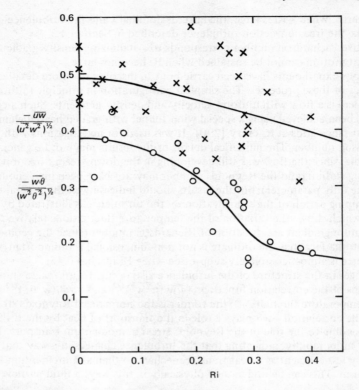

Figure 22.25 Variation of normalized Reynolds stress (x) and heat transfer (o) with Richardson number in a stratified shear flow. From Ref. [290].

displaced but then falls back to its original position without any mixing with its new environment does not transfer any heat, but it can transfer momentum through the action of pressure forces. At the higher values of the Richardson number, the turbulence may be thought of as a random superposition of internal waves (Section 16.4).

In other situations, complexities may arise from variations in the Richardson number, as defined above, from place to place. As an example of the consequences of this we consider flow close to a horizontal upward-facing heated or cooled surface — sufficiently close that the velocity scale is determined entirely by the wall stress and is u_τ as discussed in Section 22.5. The temperature scale is then similarly determined by the vertical heat transfer, which, like the stress, varies little in the region under consideration. If H is the rate of heat transfer per unit area (taken as positive if the transfer is upwards, for example from hot ground to cooler air), this scale is

$$\theta_H = H/\rho C_p u_\tau \tag{22.26}$$

u_τ enters this expression because the temperature variations needed to produce a given heat transfer are smaller when the turbulence is more vigorous. Specification of the problem in terms of u_τ and θ_H is particularly useful in application to the atmospheric boundary layer, as these are often known when the dynamics of the whole system are not.

If stratification is having little effect on the dynamics of the turbulence, we know that the velocity gradient in the region under consideration is given by equation (22.17),[†]

$$\partial U/\partial z = u_\tau/Kz \tag{22.27}$$

Similar considerations applied to the temperature field lead to[‡]

$$\partial T/\partial z = -\theta_H/Kz \tag{22.28}$$

Whether the turbulence is indeed unaffected by the stratification is indicated by the Richardson number

$$\text{Ri} = \frac{g\alpha \, dT/dz}{(dU/dz)^2} = -\frac{g\alpha K\theta_H z}{u_\tau^2} = -\frac{g\alpha KHz}{\rho C_p u_\tau^3} \tag{22.29}$$

The Richardson number and thus the relative importance of the stratification increase with height. It is useful to introduce the height $|L|$ at which $|\text{Ri}| = 1$

$$L = -\rho C_p u_\tau^3/g\alpha KH \tag{22.30}$$

This is the Monin–Obukhov length; like the Richardson number it is defined to be positive when the stratification is stabilizing and negative when it is destabilizing.

For either sign, when $z \ll |L|$, the effect of stratification is slight; for example, provided that z can still be large enough compared with ν/u_τ, the logarithmic profile will be observed. This is therefore known as the forced convection layer. As z is increased, the changes due to stratification become more important and finally dominant.

With destabilizing stratification, this means that when $z \gg -L$ buoyancy is the main source of turbulence generation. This is therefore a free convection layer. A principal feature of the flow as a whole may then be the following [272] : large eddies of the eruption type originate close to the wall as described in Section 22.6; as they move away from the wall they become increasingly influenced by buoyancy, until, at large heights, they resemble the free convection plumes described in Section 4.3.

With stabilizing stratification the primary effect of the temperature variations again appears far from the wall, but, because this is now a damping effect, it can alter the whole structure of the flow. If the outer part of a boundary layer ceases to be turbulent, it loses its Reynolds stress (note that, because $\overline{u^2}$ and $\overline{w^2}$ decrease, the Reynolds stress falls much more rapidly than the correlation function shown in Fig. 22.25). But it is this stress that keeps the fluid closer to the wall moving. Thus if the outer turbulence is damped this fluid is much slowed down by viscous friction at the wall. In terms of the above analysis, u_τ is reduced and the 'forced convection' layer is affected.

[†] Notation: it is conventional to denote the direction normal to the wall by y except when this is explicitly vertical, and then to denote it by z.

[‡] It is a moot point whether the constant here should be the same as that in equation (22.27), but the two are found to be sufficiently close that we need not make any distinction for the present purpose.

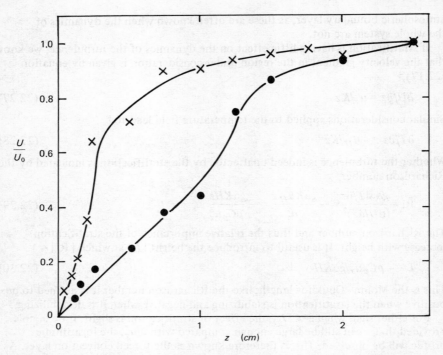

Figure 22.26   Velocity profiles of boundary layer below heated surface at 24 cm (x) and 74 cm (•) downstream from start of heated section. Data from Ref. [189].

Experimental observations of this effect were made in the boundary layer under the top wall of a wind-tunnel, one section of which was heated [189]. Turbulence established before the heated section decayed in the stably stratified region. Figure 22.26 shows velocity profiles at two distances downstream from the start of the heated section. The deceleration of fluid close to the wall is apparent.

It is this effect which is responsible for the common observation of the wind 'dropping' on a clear evening as the ground cools by radiation.

22.9 Reverse transition

In the last section, we saw an example of the reversion of turbulent motion to laminar. This process, known as reverse transition or relaminarization, can occur in a variety of configurations. In addition to a boundary layer entering a region of stable stratification, flows in which it has been observed include boundary layers that enter a region of strongly favourable pressure gradient [53]; pipe and channel flows in which the Reynolds number is reduced by a change of geometry [52, 230]; and pipe flow in which the viscosity is increased and/or the density is decreased by heat transfer [56].

It has recently become apparent that reverse transition involves its own characteristic mechanisms; it is not just a matter of the viscous dissipation becoming

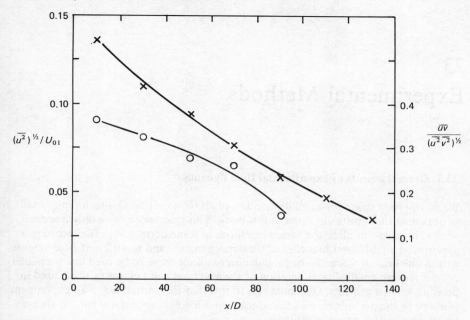

Figure 22.27 Variation of longitudinal intensity (x) and normalized Reynolds stress (o) with distance downstream during reverse transition in channel flow. Both quantities plotted are maxima with respect to position across channel. ($Re_{2a} = 1730$). Data from Ref. [52].

too large for the turbulent energy production to sustain the turbulence. As an example, we may consider observations [52] made in a channel of which the dimensions gradually change with distance downstream from 12.7×76 mm to 12.7×228 mm; the consequent drop in speed reduces the Reynolds number (based on the smaller dimension) from a value at which the flow is turbulent to one at which reverse transition occurs. Figure 22.27 shows maximum values, with respect to position across the channel, of the intensity of longitudinal velocity fluctuations and of the correlation coefficient that provides the Reynolds stress, as functions of the distance downstream from the end of the cross-section change. One sees that, as the turbulence decays, the velocity components become less correlated. The structure of the turbulence is thus changing in a way that produces a faster approach to laminar motion.

Various suggestions have been made about the dynamical causes of reverse transition, of which we may mention two. One, applying to all wall flows, is that the formation of the large eddies erupting from the viscous sub-layer (Section 22.6) is inhibited [222]. The other, applying to boundary layers in favourable pressure gradients, is that the region of intermittent turbulence (Section 22.3) becomes so large that it extends to the wall [104].

23
Experimental Methods

23.1 General aspects of experimental fluid dynamics

We do not have space for a full description of all the experimental techniques used in obtaining the results discussed in this book. This chapter can give only a general survey, intended to place the various methods in some perspective. The techniques appropriate to different branches of fluid mechanics — and to different experiments within one branch — are diverse, and decisions about those to be used in a particular project require detailed consideration of the successes and failures of those used in previous related projects. One must add to this that the limitations to an experiment often lie in the performance of transducers, and the experimentalist should always be on the alert for new possibilities.

The purpose of an experiment in fluid mechanics may range from direct verification of a theory (as in Figs. 11.2, 16.12 and 18.8) to a general exploration of the phenomena that occur in a given situation. Most of the experiments that have contributed to the ideas described in this book fall somewhere between these two extremes — although the proportions contributed by theory and by experiment to the final story are very variable. Most often one is dealing with a situation for which mathematical difficulties preclude a full theory, but in which it is still useful to refer to the equations of motion in deciding what measurements to make and how to interpret the results. Studies of the energy balance in turbulent flow, as in Figs. 22.10 and 22.18, provide a straightforward example of this. Even in topics for which there is a wholly adequate theory, primarily exploratory experiments may have played an equally important role. For example, hydrodynamic stability is now one of the more highly developed theoretical branches of the subject — Chapter 18 — but the need for this type of treatment of the equations of motion would not have been apparent without experimental observations of instabilities.

The design of an experiment involves careful attention to the requirements of dynamical similarity. One must ask what range of phenomena one wishes to study and thus what values the relevant non-dimensional parameters should have. Then one must consider how these can be achieved, or, if they fall outside the practicable range, what departures are least unacceptable.

In this process of design, there are three questions that frequently arise: (i) will the work consist primarily of quantitative measurements or of observations of flow patterns? (ii) will the work be done with an existing installation or with specially built apparatus? (iii) what fluid will be used?

The distinction implied by the first question — transducing versus flow visualization — is not complete. One can, for example, measure velocities by timing the movement of dye. However, it does provide a useful general classification of experiments. The decision depends partly on the previous state of knowledge of the topic under investigation — one is most likely to opt for flow visualization in a preliminary exploration — and partly on the efficacy of available transducers in the particular situation. However, the two approaches are often complementary. No purely qualitative study is likely to answer all questions about a flow. On the other hand, measurements are often difficult to interpret without the assistance of flow visualization. Within this book, rather frequent use of the results of visualization experiments has been made because the photographs provide ready illustrations of the flows under discussion. The reader should not conclude that experimental fluid mechanics is primarily a matter of 'look and see'; one always aims to express results as quantitatively as possible.

There is a third category of experiment, quantitative but not involving detailed probing of the flow. In these experiments, some bulk quantity associated with the flow is measured. Examples are the mass flux in pipe flow (Sections 2.3 and 2.7), the torques acting on the cylinders in rotating Couette flow (Sections 9.3 and 17.5), and the heat transfer in convection experiments (Section 4.2 — particularly Fig. 4.4 — and Sections 13.4 and 14.5). The experimental methods involved depend very much on the particular experiment, so they will not be discussed further in this chapter.

Some fluid mechanics laboratories consist mainly of standard flow systems into which different experiments can be introduced. Others consist mainly of equipment that has been built for particular experiments. This depends primarily on the branch of fluid mechanics being studied. The investigation of the flow past obstacles or of boundary layers requires a uniform flow with minimal velocity fluctuations. To obtain this is of itself a complicated matter. Hence, such experiments are normally carried out in a laboratory permanently equipped with a wind-tunnel (the name for any system providing a working air stream), a water flume or channel (similar systems with water), or a towing tank (a large tank of stationary water through which an obstacle can be moved). A few of the many examples of results obtained with such equipment are Figs. 11.2, 11.7, 19.5 and 22.8. Readers interested in more details of such techniques are referred to Refs. [21, 26]. In contrast, many experiments, for example in convection, are difficult to fit into standard systems, and every experiment involves the construction of a special piece of apparatus. Examples of observations made in such experiments include Figs. 4.5, 14.5, 15.2 and 18.5.

The choice of working fluid, unless dictated by the available standard equipment, is usually influenced by two considerations, the achievement of the desired values of the governing non-dimensional parameters and the performance of flow transducers. Whenever possible, of course, either air or water is used. The choice between these two often depends on the type of experiment; more successful techniques for velocity measurement have been developed for air than for water, whilst flow visualization is generally more successful in water than in air. Other considerations may, however, enter. For example, one might face a situation in which the fact that water more readily gave the desired values of the governing parameters (its lower kinematic viscosity is often advantageous in this respect) had to be set against the practical difficulties of containing it in an arrangement with movable probes. Other fluids are sometimes used because they give better values of the governing parameters or because they have properties particularly appropriate to an experiment. For example, silicone oils are widely used in convection experiments: they can be obtained with different viscosities, but otherwise similar properties, which provides a convenient method of varying the Prandtl number; and the viscosity varies with temperature much less than for many fluids.

23.2 Velocity measurement

Obviously the most important quantity to be measured in most flows is the fluid velocity. Here we shall look at the principles by which various methods of measuring velocity work; the reader interested in the arrangements of a full working system and the procedures for operating it should follow up the references. The general name for any instrument for measuring fluid velocity is 'anemometer'.

Two instruments — the Pitot tube and the hot-wire anemometer — are used widely in many different types of experiment. A third — the laser-Doppler anemometer — seems likely to move into this category in the coming years. The remaining techniques have not given rise to general purpose instruments but have proved useful in particular experiments.

The Pitot tube [214] is illustrated in Fig. 23.1. The inner tube with a hole at the nose, S, of the instrument is entirely sealed from the outer tube. Several holes (typically five), of which two are shown in the figure, round the periphery of the tube all lead into the outer annulus. The theory of the operation of a Pitot tube is contained essentially in equation (10.15), Bernoulli's equation applied to the streamline that ends at the forward stagnation point of an obstacle placed in a stream. If the Pitot tube points into the flow, the pressure p_S will occur at the point S and will be measured by a manometer connected to outlet 1 (the manometer must, of course, block the tube, so that there is no flow through it). Calculation of the speed, u, from the relationship, $p_S = \frac{1}{2}\rho u^2 + p$, requires information about the pressure p. This is provided by the peripheral holes, P. These are some distance downstream from the nose so as to be beyond the region of pressure variation. Since the pressure difference across the boundary layer is negligible, the pressure at these holes is the static pressure p. The average pressure from several holes is observed, as the pressure at a single hole would be more sensitive to misalignment of the tube than the p_S-reading. A manometer connected between outlets 1 and 2 reads the pressure $\frac{1}{2}\rho u^2$, thus providing a direct measurement of u. Provided that the Pitot tube is small compared with the length scale of variations of

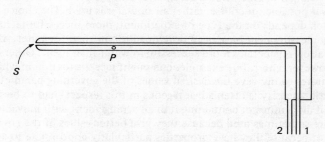

Figure 23.1   A Pitot tube.

the flow, u and p can be interpreted as the speed and pressure that would exist at the position of the Pitot tube in its absence.

Pitot tubes have been most widely used in air, where they can measure speeds from about 1 m s^{-1} upwards. With greater difficulty they can be used in water to measure speeds down to about 3 cm s^{-1} (Ref. [204]). Since one applies inviscid theory to determine the velocity, it is essential for the Reynolds number of a Pitot tube to be high. However, except for specially made tiny instruments, this requirement is fulfilled at all measurable speeds. The main limitations to the use of Pitot tubes are their size and the slowness of their response; they cannot be used in flows of very small length scale, nor to measure rapid velocity fluctuations. In most turbulent flows, for example, only the mean velocity can be measured with a Pitot tube.

The principle of operation of a hot-wire anemometer is virtually indicated by its name. An electrically heated wire is cooled by the flow, the rate of cooling depending on the velocity. In the simplest mode of operation, the current through the wire is maintained constant; its temperature and thus its resistance, measured by the voltage across the wire, depend on the velocity. In an alternative, widely used, mode, a feed-back circuit maintains the wire at a constant resistance and so temperature; the current needed to do this is a measure of the fluid velocity.

Hot-wire anemometers have been most widely and successfully used in gas flows. In general, hot-wires are more sensitive at low speeds than high; except that if the speed is too low, free convection heat transfer takes over from forced convection, making the cooling insensitive to velocity. Hot-wire anemometers can be used in air readily down to about 30 cm s^{-1} ; below this, measurements are more difficult although not impossible.

In recent years the use of these instruments in liquids has been much developed. Here particular use has been made of the hot-film anemometer, a device working on the same principle but geometrically different from the hot-wire. The heated element consists of a thin metallic film on the surface of a wedge-shaped thermally and electrically insulating probe.

Hot-wire (and hot-film) anemometers operate best in just those conditions where Pitot tubes fail. They are small and rapidly responding. They have thus become the principal instruments for studying fluctuating flows, in particular the phenomena of transition and turbulence. They have the additional advantage of giving the information in electrical form, which can be processed electronically to give quantities such as intensities, correlations, and spectra. Nearly all the measurements presented in Chapters 19 to 22 were made with hot-wire anemometers.

Although a hot-wire anemometer is simple in principle, its actual use is a matter of some complexity. A large body of information [29, 38, 197] — and a certain amount of 'folklore' — has grown up around hot-wire anemometry. This covers topics such as: the calibration of hot-wires (this is always necessary — hot-wires are not absolute instruments); the geometrical combinations of hot-wires needed for measuring different components of velocity fluctuations (a particularly important arrangement being two wires in the form of an X, as shown in Fig. 23.2); the particular problems in achieving accuracy that arise when the velocity fluctuations are not small compared with the mean velocity; the problems associated with velocity measurements in the presence of temperature variations, to which a hot-wire probe is also sensitive; and much else.

The laser-Doppler anemometer measures velocity by measuring the Doppler

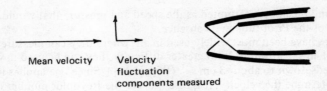

Figure 23.2   An '*X*-wire', which, when arranged so that the mean velocity is in the plane of the *X*, can be used to measure both components of velocity fluctuation in that plane.

shift of light scattered within the moving fluid. With the advent of lasers, sufficiently monochromatic light beams are available for this effect to be measurable. The scattering centres are the tiny particles of dust that are present in any liquid or gas; these are small enough that they are always moving effectively with the instantaneous fluid velocity.

Figure 23.3 shows schematically the principle of operation of a laser-Doppler anemometer. (The full optical systems are, of course, much more complex than this, and take a variety of forms [196].) The incident and scattered beams are inclined to one another so that the point of intersection locates the point at which the velocity is being measured. The scattered beam interferes at the photomultiplier with an attenuated beam direct from the laser to give beats, the frequency of which is a measure of the Doppler shift.

Like hot-wire anemometers, laser-Doppler anemometers have the advantage that they respond to rapid fluctuations in the velocity and thus can be used to study the details of transitional and turbulent flows. They have the additional advantage that there is no probe to disturb the flow. On the other hand, in some situations there are severe practical difficulties in mounting a precision optical system around a flow. (Also, laser-Doppler anemometers are costly.)

Almost every effect of fluid motion must at some time have been tried as a means of measuring velocities. We now look briefly at various devices that have proved useful on occasion. The list does not pretend to be exhaustive.

Mechanical systems have the advantage of simplicity. They are widely used on

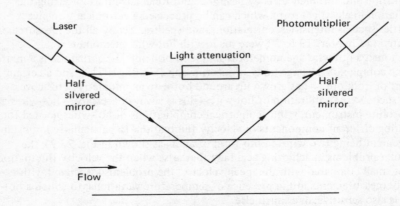

Figure 23.3   Schematic diagram of laser-Doppler anemometer.

the large scale, a familiar example being the cup anemometer used in everyday meteorological applications. They are more difficult to adapt to the small scale of laboratory work. However, two methods that have been used are: observation through a telescope of the deflection of the free end of a cantilevered quartz fibre [148] ; and mounting a vane on the extended arm of a moving coil milliameter [124]. Such arrangements can give high accuracy in low-speed laminar flows. They are much less satisfactory, but still sometimes useful, in turbulent flows [275].

The frequency of the vortex street behind a cylinder (Section 3.3) is a measure of the velocity. This is particularly convenient as a means of calibrating a wind-tunnel or water-channel below the Pitot tube range (once the Reynolds number — Strouhal number relationship has been established). The technique has, however, also been used in a special probe [290].

In liquids, use may be made of the 'electrokinetic' or 'streaming potential' method, although, so far, this has been tried only in water [281]. At the interface between a liquid and a solid, as at the interface between two solids, a double layer is formed, a layer of positive charge on one side and a layer of negative on the other. If the liquid is moving, its charge may be advected introducing measurable potential differences depending on the velocity.

Heat-transfer devices may take other forms than the hot-wire anemometer. For example, the faster a fluid is moving the smaller the temperature rise produced by a given rate of heat input. This fact is used in the arrangement shown in Fig. 23.4 [261]. The middle wire is heated at a fixed rate. The temperature difference between the outer wires is then, over certain ranges, inversely proportional to the velocity component in the direction shown. The wires are made long and set in different directions, so that this remains true in the presence of other velocity components. This device can operate in flows with their own temperature variations.

Finally, it should be emphasized that methods depending on the simple timing of the passage of marked fluid from one point to another are not to be scorned. Many flow visualization experiments can be made quantitative in this way. Heat is sometimes used instead of a visible marker. A good way of determining the speed of a wind-tunnel, when this is low, is to put an alternating current through a fine wire stretched across the tunnel and to measure the wave-length of the resulting temperature variations. A probe — a thermocouple, for instance — is traversed along the tunnel, and the phase variations between the input to the heated wire and the output from the probe are observed. This is tedious, but it does provide an absolute calibration, below the Pitot tube range, on which other devices can be based. Probes for local velocity measurement, based on the timing of the passage of a heat pulse from a source wire to a detector wire, have also been developed [67, 267].

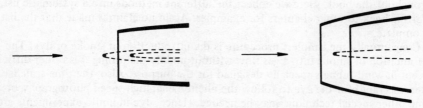

Figure 23.4 Two perpendicular views of the wire arrangement in a temperature rise anemometer.

23.3 Pressure and temperature measurement

We need not consider at any length the methods used for measuring flow parameters
other than the velocity, since these methods do not differ significantly from those
used in other branches of physics.

The pressure at a point on a wall may be measured through a small hole, similar
to the ones in a Pitot tube, linked to a manometer. Alternatively, a small diaphragm
may be set in the wall, its movement changing a capacity or compressing a piezo-
electric crystal. The diaphragm method has the advantage of much more rapid
response, so it can be used to measure the pressure fluctuations at a bounding wall
of a turbulent flow.

The measurement of pressure in the interior of a flow has been considered above
in connection with Pitot tubes. There is at present no satisfactory device for
measuring rapid pressure fluctuations within a flow.

An important aspect of pressure measurements, as well as of velocity measurements with Pitot tubes, is the design of sensitive manometers. The various types are
described in Ref. [26].

It should be added that, whilst pressure measurements are often very useful in
wind-tunnel and similar studies, the pressure variations occurring in many experiments, for example in the field of free convection, are too small to be measured.

In experiments on convection, particularly free convection, measurements of the
temperature field [148] are usually both easier and more accurate than measurements of the velocity field. The former, therefore, often provide the main source
of information about the structure of the flow. However, we can consider the
methods used very briefly, since they are, at least in principle, wholly straightforward. The transducers most widely used are resistance thermometers and thermocouples [63]. A resistance thermometer often conveniently takes the form of a
'hot-wire anemometer' with a very low current through it. Thermistor beads are
also often used as the sensitive elements of resistance thermometers. The junction
of a thermocouple can also be made very small, so all these devices can be made to
respond rapidly.

Optical systems can also sometimes give quantitative information about temperature fields; however, these will be considered under the heading of flow visualization.

23.4 Flow visualization [32, 80, 291]

The variety of methods of flow visualization is illustrated by the photographs
throughout the book. Here we collect the different methods into a systematic list,
referring back to other chapters for examples. Again no claim is made that the list
is complete.

Conceptually the simplest procedure is the introduction of smoke or dye. The
introduction of smoke into a gas flow without unduly disturbing it is rather difficult
except in wind-tunnels specially designed for the purpose. Also, the time scale is
often too rapid for the eye to follow the phenomena; high-speed photography or
some other special technique may be needed. Hence, dye-in-liquid experiments are
often preferred. Nevertheless very good results can be obtained with smoke [26],
as is illustrated by Figs. 14.6, 16.1 and 19.6. A system widely used in smoke

tunnels produces a smoke of fine droplets of paraffin, by evaporating the liquid and allowing it to recondense in the flow. A particularly effective dense white smoke is produced by exposing titanium tetrachloride to the atmosphere, but this is both toxic and corrosive. A convenient way of producing 'instant smoke' for simple exploratory experiments is the reaction between hydrochloric acid and ammonia vapours, but again its extensive use has its dangers.

Many of the photographs in this book illustrate the use of dye; a selection, illustrating different dyes and different ways of using them, consists of Figs. 3.4, 3.5, 3.9, 12.6, 15.4, 17.11, 19.5 and 22.7. Convenient and effective dyes for introducing into water flows include potassium permanganate, gentian violet, and methyl blue. The first has the advantage of producing particularly strong contrast, but at the cost of a sometimes inconveniently large density increase.

As alternatives to introducing dye, there are several ways in which marker can be produced electrically — the hydrogen bubble technique, the tellurium technique, the electrolytic precipitation technique, and the pH technique. The first works best at high speeds, such as those in many water channel experiments; the second and third at intermediate speeds; and the last at the low speeds likely to be encountered in convection and rotating fluid experiments.

In the hydrogen bubble method a wire stretched across the flow is the cathode of an electrolytic system, the anode being, for example, a wall of the channel. Typically 10 volts are needed with tap water, larger voltages with deionized water. Provided the wire is very fine (typically $10-100\ \mu$m), the hydrogen bubbles produced at it are small and numerous enough to move with the flow and give the appearance of a white dye. By insulating portions of the wire and/or pulsing the voltage, patches of dye can be produced, giving most effective pictures like those in Figs. 22.1 and 22.20.

A cathode made of, or coated with, metallic tellurium releases a dense brown dye, which is effective for flow visualization [295]. Care is needed to avoid toxic effects.

In a similar way a white colloidal cloud is produced at an anode made of certain materials [247]. Those containing tin (in water containing sodium carbonate) are particularly effective; solder is thus a convenient material. This method — known as the electrolytic precipitation method — requires rather larger voltages than the others, typically 30–50 V.

The last of these electrical methods [55] makes use of the fact that there is a change in pH (the measure of acidity or alkalinity) in an electrolyte in the vicinity of an electrode. Hence, if the working fluid contains an indicator and is titrated to be close to the end-point of that indicator, the application of a voltage between a fine wire and some other point in the flow can produce a local colour change at the wire. This method has two marked advantages: the production of the dye produces no density change or displacement of the flow; and the dye gradually reverts to its previous state, so the system can be run continuously without becoming filled with dye. It has the disadvantage that it can be used only in closed systems, not in flows where fluid is continuously entering and leaving. The most usual indicator is thymol blue; this changes from amber (neutral) to dark blue (basic) at a cathode and so gives clearly visible marker. Figures 4.14 and 15.2 were obtained in this way. With both this method and the tellurium method, it is important that hydrogen bubbles should *not* be produced. For both methods, voltages in the range 1–10 V are satisfactory, and this gives no trouble in deionized water.

Other flow visualization experiments make use of suspended particles (e.g. Figs. 15.17, 16.8 and 17.5). Of the various particles available, polystyrene beads are particularly useful in water, as their density is only slightly greater than that of water. In silicone oils and other highly viscous fluids, aluminium powder has been very widely used for flow visualization ('silver' paint is a convenient source of sufficiently fine particles). The aluminium particles are small flakes which align with the shear in a flow; when light enters from one direction and is viewed from another, bright and dark patches are seen depending on the local orientation.

In all flow visualization experiments it is necessary to give some thought as to what features of the flow are shown up. Smoke and dye experiments usually show particle paths or streaklines (Section 6.1). The electrical methods allow other possibilities; one can, for example, release dye all along a wire at a given instant and obtain information from its subsequent locus. Similarly, suspended particles may be used in various ways. Photographing them for an interval gives portions of particle paths, which, if short enough, can be used to synthesize a streamline pattern even in unsteady flow (e.g. Fig. 3.7). Other techniques can give overall information about the structure of the flow; this is particularly true of the aluminium powder method (e.g. Figs. 4.5, 14.9 and 15.12) and Fig. 17.4 shows polystyrene beads used in a special way for this purpose.

The last group of flow visualization methods to be considered consists of optical techniques making use of refractive index variations in the fluid [129]. Such variations occur as a result of density variations associated with a temperature or concentration field. They are thus particularly appropriate for studies of convection and stratified flow. However, even in nominally constant density flows it may be possible to introduce density differences which are large enough to allow the use of one of these techniques whilst keeping the internal Froude number high enough for the flow to be unaffected.

In the shadowgraph method, parallel light enters the fluid and is deflected where there are refractive index variations. If the second spatial derivative of the refractive index is non-zero the amount of deflection varies giving a pattern of bright and dark regions related to the flow structure. Figures 4.16, 14.1 and 14.4 are shadowgraphs.

In the schlieren method, parallel light is again used, but is brought to a focus after passing through the fluid. A knife-edge or other stop at this focus blocks off some of the light. If the light has been deflected in the fluid the amount passing this stop will be increased or decreased. Changes in intensity thus relate to the first spatial derivative of the refractive index. By having an optical arrangement in which the stop is at a conjugate point of the source whilst the observing screen is at a conjugate point of the fluid, one can obtain an image of the flow pattern with these intensity variations. There are many variations in the details of the arrangement [129]. Figures 16.11, 16.13, 22.3 and 24.20 are schlieren photographs. (It should be noted that the name 'schlieren' is occasionally used to refer to optical methods in general rather than this specific one, which is then known as the Töpler—schlieren method.)

In an interferometer [251], light that has passed through the fluid interferes with light from the same source that has not passed through the fluid. Whether this interference is constructive or destructive depends on the optical path difference, and so the pattern of bright and dark bands reflects the pattern of isotherms in the fluid. Again there are various optical systems. Figure 18.8 shows two interferograms.

All these techniques work best in two-dimensional configurations, as the observed pattern is the integrated effect of the passage of the light through the fluid.

24 Practical Situations

24.1 Introduction

The main body of this book has been concerned with developing a basic understanding of the phenomena of fluid motion. Applications have been ignored, apart from passing references to illustrate a particular point. One does not capture the full flavour of the subject without some emphasis on the fact that moving fluids occur in a wide variety of practical situations. Some of these applications have had a profound effect on the directions of advance of the basic studies.

It would not be possible in the space — nor perhaps very interesting — to give a systematic survey of applied fluid mechanics. Instead, we look at, and discuss briefly, a selection of particular topics. The selection has been made with two purposes in mind: to illustrate the variety of branches of applied science in which fluid dynamics arises; and to show applications of different topics in the main body of the book. The applications discussed are thus not intended to be those of greatest importance or topicality. They are, however, all topics of current or recent research.

24.2 Cloud patterns

The very varied patterns formed by clouds reflect the variety of dynamical processes that occur in the atmosphere, and are often a useful immediate indication of these processes [201, 227]. Clouds form when moist air is cooled so that the saturation vapour pressure falls below the actual vapour pressure. Although cooling can occur in a variety of ways, the most common is the cooling associated with expansion as air rises; that is cooling associated with the adiabatic temperature gradient (Section 14.3). One may thus observe situations in which cloud is forming in rising air and evaporating in descending air to give a pattern of cloudy and clear patches related to the flow.

Of the many possible illustrations of this, we choose 'cloud streets'. One can fairly frequently observe clouds in long parallel lines, quite evenly spaced. These are usually either convection rolls aligned by the mean flow as considered in Section 16.1 (cf. Fig. 16.1), or billows generated by shear instability in stably stratified air as considered in Section 17.6 (cf. Fig. 17.12). The two processes can be distinguished, even if the stratification is unknown, by the orientation of the cloud lines with respect to the wind direction; convection cells are aligned along the wind, billows across it. Lee waves (Section 16.3) can also cause such patterns if the ridge producing them is sufficiently long and straight.

Figure 24.1 is a satellite photograph of aligned clouds. (It was taken over the south-east USA; the coastline of Georgia can be seen, the clouds being over land.)

The lines are at a height of about 1 km and have a spacing of about 3 km, so the
pattern would not be seen by an observer on the ground. Such large-scale patterns,
the occurrence of which has been appreciated only since satellite observations have
been available, probably involve their own distinctive dynamical processes. It has
been suggested [74] that they arise from instability of the atmospheric Ekman
layer; i.e. they are the counterpart of the laboratory patterns in Fig. 15.10.

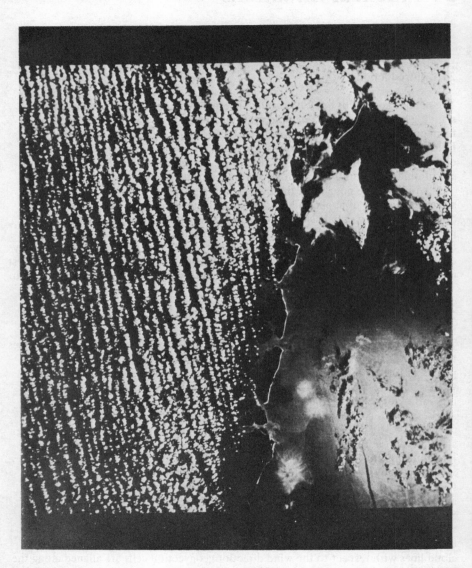

Figure 24.1   Apollo photo of Georgia coast (10 a.m. local time, 4 April 1968) from height of
200 km. From Brown, R. A., 'A Secondary Flow Model for the Planetary Boundary Layer',
J. Atmos. Sci., **27**, 742 (1970). By permission of the American Meteorological Society.

However, convective instability also plays a role [151, 158], so the overall effect may be an interaction between the types of motion represented by Figs. 15.10 and 16.1.

24.3 Waves in the atmospheric circulation

The large-scale circulation of the atmosphere frequently involves wave motions. These are prominent at mid-latitudes in both the northern and southern hemispheres. Figure 24.2 illustrates this. It shows the trajectory of a balloon designed to float in the atmosphere at positions of constant air density; that is effectively at a constant height, of, in this case, about 12 km. The balloon was released in New Zealand, and its position observed through radio signals for 102 days. Wavelike oscillations in latitude as it travels round the earth in the prevailing westerly winds are apparent. Similar features in the northern hemisphere can be seen in the isobar patterns shown in Fig. 20.1, although the development of strong cyclones within the wave pattern makes this situation rather complex.

The longest waves (three or four wavelengths round the Earth) are dynamically similar to Rossby waves [202]. The theory of Rossby waves for a spherical shell is slightly different from that given in Section 15.7, but the fact that they may occur may be understood through the fact that the depth of the atmosphere parallel to the axis of rotation varies with latitude. Sometimes the waves form a fixed pattern arising from disturbance of the general circulation by mountains; i.e. they are a natural counterpart of the flow illustrated by Fig. 15.15. Waves progressing relative to the earth may also be observed; their origin is less apparent.

Shorter waves are probably more often associated with temperature variations between pole and equator — they are baroclinic waves rather than barotropic. These temperature variations are responsible for the general westerly flow on which the waves are superimposed; the Coriolis force turns the meridional circulation that would arise on a non-rotating earth. This process is modelled by the laboratory experiments described in Section 15.8. The generation of the waves can now be understood as an instability. Despite the difference in geometry, the atmospheric waves may be compared [108] quite closely with some of those observed in the laboratory (Fig. 15.17). The non-linear development mentioned in Section 15.8 has its counterpart in the development of the jet-stream, a similar narrow region in which much of the momentum of the atmospheric circulation is concentrated.

24.4 Continental drift and convection in the Earth's mantle

The important role of fluid mechanics in meteorology and oceanography is obvious. Its role in the geophysics of the Earth's interior is somewhat less familar, and we consider here an example of this.

The main divisions of the Earth (discovered through the reflection and refraction of elastic waves originating in earthquakes) are a solid crust (the top few tens of kilometres), a solid mantle (extending from the bottom of the crust to a radius a little over one half the Earth's radius), a liquid core, and, probably, a solid inner core. One would expect fluid dynamical problems to arise in the core; motions

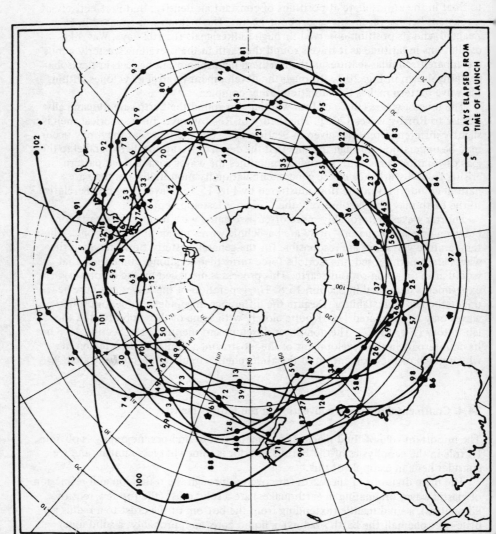

Figure 24.2 Trajectory over 102 days of a balloon released from New Zealand and circulating at height of about 12 km. From Ref [174]

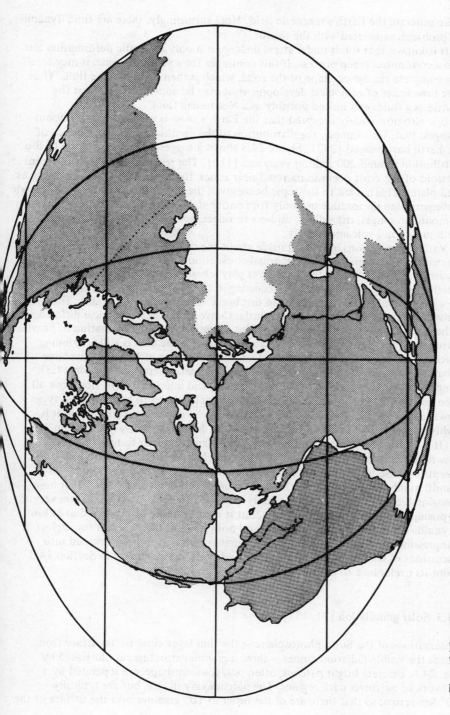

Figure 24.3 Reconstruction of continental distribution around 200 million years ago. (At the bottom Madagascar and India lie between Africa and Antarctica, and a portion of Australia is seen to the right of Antarctica.) After A. G. Smith, from *Understanding the Earth*, Artemis Press Ltd, 1972.

there generate the Earth's magnetic field. More surprisingly, there are fluid dynamical problems associated with the mantle.

It is known that solids under stress undergo not only an elastic deformation but also a continuous creep process. If this continues for a very long time, it may result in a complete change of shape of the solid, which is then behaving as a fluid. Thus, over time scales of geological development, it may be appropriate to treat the mantle as a fluid, and indeed possibly as a Newtonian fluid.

It is also now widely accepted that the Earth's crust is undergoing continuous changes; that, for example, the distribution of the continents over the surface of the Earth has changed [252]. Figure 24.3 shows a suggested reconstruction of this distribution around 200 million years ago [110]. The relative motions of different portions of the crust occur in narrow linear zones, the regions in between moving as rigid plates. This has led to the topic being given the name 'plate tectonics'. The plate movements are responsible not only for continental drift, but also for the formation of mountain ranges, rift valleys, mid-ocean ridges, and ocean trenches and for earthquakes and volcanic activity.

Various suggestions have been made about the cause of the movements; the majority involve some aspect of thermal convection [273, 279]. It is a matter of discussion whether the plates themselves play a basic role in the dynamics or whether they are driven by a flow occurring in the mantle below. It is the latter view that would make concepts from this book more directly applicable. Thermal convection could well occur in the mantle. Convection due to chemical differences, rather than temperature differences, is also a possibility, if the separation of heavier materials to the centre which has led to formation of the core is still continuing. Much of the discussion has been based on our knowledge of Bénard convection (Chapter 4) and on its counterpart with internal heat generation (Section 17.3). Simple cellular flow, boundary layer type flow, and quasi-turbulent flow have all been considered. However, it may be an oversimplification to apply Bénard-type flows to the mantle. The only summary that can be made at present is that it is highly probable that mantle flow occurs but its details remain very uncertain.

(It is worth noting that mantle convection is an exception to two statements elsewhere in this book that certain ideas are rarely relevant to applications. The exceptions arise because one is concerned with an extremely viscous fluid — the Prandtl number is around 10^{24}. Firstly, compressibility effects — and other non-Boussinesq effects — do enter marginally into the problem. This might seem very surprising when the velocities are tiny, but it is an example of the fact that at low Reynolds number relationship (5.61), and not (5.59), is the criterion for neglect of compressibility. Secondly, the Rayleigh number criterion is often invoked into discussions of whether convection occurs — despite the statement in Section 14.3 about its irrelevance to natural situations.)

24.5 Solar granulation [71, 157]

Observations of the Sun's photosphere — the thin layer close to its surface from which the visible radiation comes — show a granular structure, as illustrated by Fig. 24.4. Discrete bright patches, often polygonal in shape, are separated by a network of narrower dark regions. The patches vary in size, but are typically 10^3 km across, so that there are of the order of 10^6 granules over the surface of the

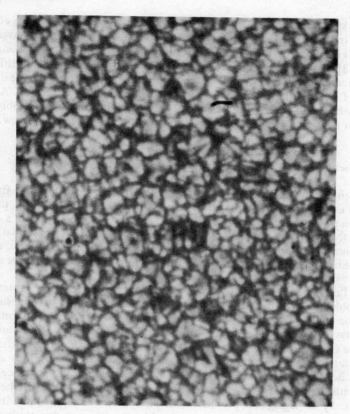

Figure 24.4 Solar granulation. (Photo obtained by Project Stratoscope of Princeton University sponsored by National Science Foundation, National Aeronautics and Space Administration, and Office of Naval Research.) From Bahng, J. and Schwarzschild, M. (1961) *Astrophys. J.* **134**, 312, published by the University of Chicago Press. (Copyright 1961 by the University of Chicago.)

Sun. The pattern is a continuously changing one, the lifetime of an individual granule being typically ten minutes. Doppler shift measurements of velocities indicate that the bright (hot) regions are ascending and the darker (colder) regions are descending.

The pattern is thus almost certainly a convection pattern. Its resemblence to Bénard convection (Chapter 4) in the regime in which a cellular structure is retained although the flow within the cells is turbulent (Figs. 4.11 and 4.12) is noteworthy. It may be that the motion is basically of this type, although there is some difficulty in making the comparison quantitative; the Rayleigh number must be very much larger (by a factor of perhaps 10^5) than ones at which such patterns are observed in the laboratory.

It is plausible that the convection may be little affected by the Sun's rotation and by magnetic fields; for example, the Rossby number based on observed velocities and granule sizes is around 10^2. Of various causes of differences from the laboratory situation, two are certainly important. Firstly, non-Boussinesq effects (appendix to Chapter 14) will be very marked; the length scale of the convection is probably determined by the scale height rather than by the depth of the unstable region [232]. Secondly, the convecting region is overlaid by a stably stratified region and possibly most of the photosphere is in this; the pattern may be a manifestation of a convecting region below rather than in the observed region. A marked periodicity has been observed in the velocity fluctuations; this is presumably due to waves in the stably stratified region, stimulated by the convection below.

24.6 Effluent dispersal

The problems of both air pollution and water pollution evidently involve fluid dynamical considerations amongst their many other aspects. In principle, the type of question posed is usually the same — where is pollutant, emitted from a source, subsequently found and in what concentration? In practice, the flow situations in which pollution may occur are very varied, and different branches of fluid dynamics are involved in answering the question in different cases. We thus consider a particular example.

This is the discharge of sewage or other effluent into the sea or an estuary. The design problem is, evidently, to ensure that the contaminant has become sufficiently dilute to be unobjectionable before reaching places where it could be harmful — an aim that has, of course, not always been fulfilled in the past. Sewage has approximately the same density as fresh water. It is therefore buoyant when discharged into salt water. The problems involved are thus broadly the same as those associated with the discharge of hot water into cold, a matter of practical importance in connection with the return of cooling water from power stations. Excessive heating can be biologically damaging (the problem sometimes known as thermal pollution). Also it is important that the warm water should not return too directly to the power station intake with consequent loss of thermodynamic efficiency.

A major aspect of the investigation of any system or proposed system is the determination of the pre-existing flow patterns, due, for example, to tides or ocean currents. Field observations are usually supplemented by experiments with models of the site; the model may be either a physical one in a laboratory or a numerical one in a computer. To illustrate laboratory modelling, Fig. 24.5 shows a model of the Tees estuary on the north-east coast of England, and Fig. 24.6 shows a simulation of tidal flows in such a model made during an investigation of the best location for a sewage outfall [180].

Despite the fact that each site has its own characteristics, there are many fluid dynamical topics of general relevance. To illustrate this, we consider the example of buoyant effluent being emitted horizontally into stationary ambient water [181]. The principal features of the flow, which may be expected to be turbulent, are shown schematically in Fig. 24.7. The effluent at first travels horizontally as a jet (Section 11.8). The action of buoyancy causes this jet to curve upwards, and in time its motion becomes nearly vertical, its properties then being essentially those of a thermal plume (Section 14.6). How quickly the upward curving takes place depends on the internal Froude number of the initial jet. Throughout this jet/plume flow the processes of turbulent entrainment and mixing (Section 22.3) are taking

Figure 24.5   Model of Tees estuary at the Hydraulics Research Station, Wallingford.

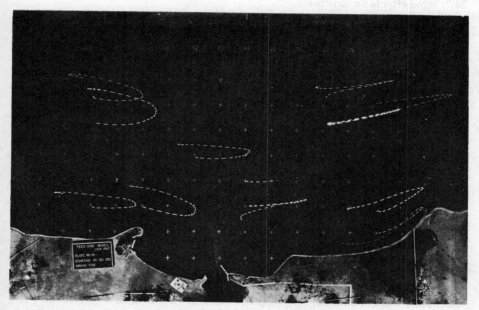

Figure 24.6   Trajectories of candle floats in Tees-side model at Hydraulics Research Station, Wallingford.

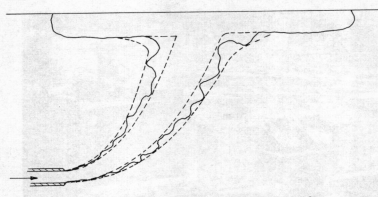

Figure 24.7   Sketch of buoyant jet below free surface.

place, leading to dilution of the effluent. When the plume reaches the surface, the buoyant fluid spreads out in a surface layer. This is stably stratified and so mixing is inhibited (Section 22.8). Further dilution may occur here but is a much less efficient process. Thus the contaminant concentration where the effluent reaches the surface is an important quantity — determined by the characteristics of turbulence in stratified jets and plumes.

24.7 Wind effects on structures

During recent years greatly increased attention has been given to the effect of the wind in the design of buildings and other structures [193, 213]. Both the direct effect of possible wind damage to the structure and the indirect effect of possible undesirable changes to the surrounding wind pattern due to the presence of the structure are matters of importance. In this section we look at two examples of the former. One is an economically trivial example, chosen because the fluid dynamics is straightforward, yet interesting. The other — the collapse of the Ferrybridge cooling towers — was a major incident that illustrates the complexity of a more typical situation. It should be emphasized that, although in both these examples the trouble was not foreseen, the majority of the work in this field is, of course, concerned with prevention not cure; wind-tunnel experiments of the type mentioned below are now frequently performed at the design stage.

Figure 24.8 shows the 'crowning feature' of the Civic Centre at Newcastle-upon-Tyne; three 'castles' are mounted on prongs in a form corresponding to the city coat-of-arms. Sometime after erection the two outer castles developed an oscillation, moving in antiphase in the plane of the 'trident'; their supporting prongs were behaving like a tuning fork. Cine-film of the oscillation shows the distance between the   stles varying by up to 5 per cent, but larger oscillations almost certainly occurred. The wind at the time was roughly perpendicular to the plane of the trident and was not unusually strong (about 15 m s^{-1}). This behaviour resulted from resonance between the frequency of eddy shedding by the cylindrical castles and the natural frequency of the tuning fork mode of oscillation. We saw in Section 3.3 that, because of eddy shedding, the spectrum of the velocity fluctua-

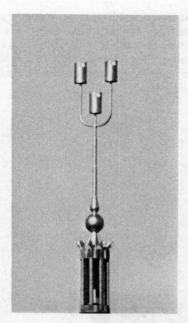

Figure 24.8   The crowning feature of the Civic Centre, Newcastle-upon-Tyne.

tions and consequently that of the force fluctuations on the cylinder, has a sharp peak at a frequency corresponding to a Strouhal number of about 0.2, even at very high Reynolds numbers. In this case, the behaviour was sufficiently simple that it could be diagnosed without any experiments, but it illustrates the point that, when instabilities occur, it is not necessarily the strongest winds that are most dangerous. It was cured by adding a load inside the castles to change the resonant frequency and by filling the support tubes with sand to damp the oscillations.

On 1 November 1965, three cooling towers at Ferrybridge, Yorkshire, collapsed in a gale (Fig. 24.9). The three were members of a group of eight in two rows of four. All three were in the leeward row, indicating that the interaction between the towers had been important. Elucidation of the mode of failure was quite a complicated story, but essentially it was a quasi-static tensile failure, i.e. a tensile failure that would have occurred in a steady wind of the highest speed actually reached temporarily, of the shell under the wind loading [75]. There were two main stages in this elucidation. Firstly, wind-tunnel tests on a model of the complex (Fig. 24.10) determined pressure distributions over the towers; it was not possible to achieve the full-scale Reynolds number as is ideally required (Chapter 7), so it was hoped that the highest possible value would serve. Secondly, the results of these were fed into membrane theory computations of the stresses in the shell produced by the combination of the wind pressures and the shell's own weight. The results were very sensitive to the details of the pressure distribution. Even though the total wind force on the leeward towers was less than that on an isolated tower, the redistribution of the forces by the presence of the other towers could lead to failure. In this case, it was not thought that any dynamic effect (such as that in the example above) played a role; the leeward towers will have experienced larger velocity fluctuations due to the presence of the front row (and these might have contributed to the velocity temporarily reaching the critical value), but the frequencies were not appropriate to any resonance. Clearly the subtlety of a situation like this is such that either very extensive model testing is necessary at the design stage or large safety margins must be allowed.

Figure 24.9   Collapse of third tower at Ferrybridge. From Ref. [75].

Figure 24.10   Wind-tunnel model of Ferrybridge power-station. From Ref. [75].

24.8 Boundary layer control: vortex generators

We have seen in Chapter 11, particularly Sections 11.4 and 11.5, that the effect of boundary layer behaviour often extends beyond the boundary layer itself. Whether a boundary layer is laminar or turbulent, whether and where separation occurs may have a marked or even controlling influence on the performance of a whole flow system. Attempts to change or control the character and development of boundary layers may thus be worthwhile. Such boundary layer control [153] has found application principally in aeronautical engineering. There are, however, other applications; for example, vortex generators, the devices to be described below, have been used to suppress wind-excited oscillation of a bridge [287] (cf. Section 24.7).

In aeronautics, the purpose of boundary layer control varies from one situation to another [153]; aims have been as diverse as attempting to keep the entire boundary layer on a wing laminar (so as to minimize the viscous stress) and promoting transition to turbulence right at the leading edge (to prevent separation). We cannot here mention all the variety of methods used in boundary layer control, so we will look at one example, the use of vortex generators, illustrated by Fig. 24.11.

This photograph shows the wing of a Trident 1 aircraft. (It was taken during

Figure 24.11   Trident wing with vortex generators. Photo provided by Hawker-Siddeley Aviation Ltd.

development flying and one can see the tufts attached to the wing to show the flow pattern over it.) The vortex generators are the line of specially shaped protruberances close to the leading edge.

In general, vortex generators are introduced to prevent or delay separation in a situation in which the fact that the boundary layer is turbulent is insufficient to do so. Each vortex generator produces a longitudinal vortex extending downstream from it — by a process somewhat analogous to the generation of wing-tip vortices (Fig. 12.8). These enhance the mixing across the boundary layer, bringing rapidly moving fluid from outside the boundary layer in close to the wall. This supplements the mixing due to the turbulence. It is apparent from Fig. 11.3 that the change in velocity profile will inhibit separation.

Vortex generators were introduced on the Trident wing (Fig. 24.11) to cope with a particular problem. The suppression of separation is important during take-off and landing when the leading edge droop is down. The purpose is partly to delay stall (Section 12.2) but more particularly to avoid instability of the aircraft when the angle of attack is close to the stalling angle. Flight and wind tunnel tests showed that separation started on one part of the wing and spread progressively in such a way as to produce a nose up pitching moment which tended to further increase the angle of attack. Introduction of the vortex generators at the critical parts of the wing changed this unstable behaviour into a stable one by delaying the outer wing separation until the flow on the inner wing had separated.

24.9 Fluidics

A significant technological development of recent years has been the introduction of 'fluidic' devices [51, 83, 135, 186]. These serve purposes similar to those normally served by electronic devices but operate on certain features of fluid motion. The most successful fluidic elements have been logic elements for use in control systems, which are essentially small-scale computers intended for a specific purpose, such as the control of a machine tool through a programmed sequence of operations. In such elements the signal takes an off/on form, corresponding to the binary digits 0 and 1; in both types of device considered below, the signal is 'on' if a jet of air is issuing through a certain orifice. These devices cannot normally compete in smallness, speed, or cost with electronic devices, but they can operate in certain circumstances where electronic systems are unsatisfactory: in extremes of temperature; in the presence of ionizing radiation; where there is a fire risk; and (surprisingly) in the presence of severe vibration.

We illustrate this with brief descriptions of two types of device, chosen for the interesting fluid dynamical principles on which they operate.

The first type operates through the phenomenon of wall attachment (the Coanda effect — Section 22.7). Consider a system like that in Fig. 22.22, but with the jet situated symmetrically between two walls. Despite the symmetry, the jet always attaches to one wall; which depends on the small disturbances present. It can be located on a particular wall if fluid for entrainment is supplied on the opposite side. Thus in the arrangement shown schematically in Fig. 24.12, if there is a signal at input 1, the power jet is located as shown and there is a signal at output 1 but not at output 2. This signal will remain even when the input signal is removed. The jet will switch to output 2 only when a signal is put on to input 2. Thus the arrangement constitutes a fluidic bistable, a device which, because it has a memory, is the building block of storage and counting systems.

Alternatively, the power jet can be placed asymmetrically between two walls so that it always attaches to a particular wall unless fluid is supplied from that side (Fig. 24.13). In this arrangement the jet returns to its original position as soon as the signal is removed. Thus this provides a logic element. If the output is taken

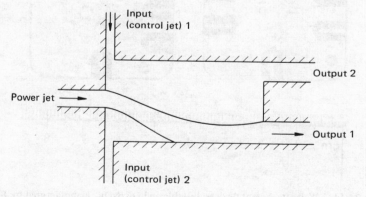

Figure 24.12   Schematic arrangement (cf. Fig. 22.22) of a wall-attachment bistable device.

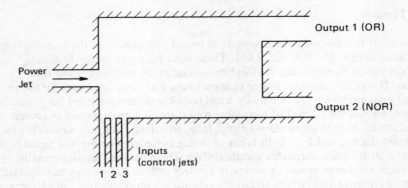

Figure 24.13   Schematic arrangement of a wall-attachment OR/NOR device.

from side 1, it is an OR element, there being an output signal if there is a signal on one or more inputs. If the output is taken from side 2, it is a NOR element.

The diagrams illustrate only the principles involved. The geometrical details of actual devices are, of course, more complicated; for example, the asymmetry in an OR/NOR element may be provided by inlets from the room of different sizes on the two sides. Figure 24.14 is a photograph of a wall-attachment bistable (with two inputs on each side) and an OR/NOR element (with three inputs).

Another type of device is the turbulence NOR element (often known as the 'turbulence amplifier'), shown schematically in Fig. 24.15 and photographed, with cover plate removed, in Fig. 24.16. Its operation is based on the fact that there is a

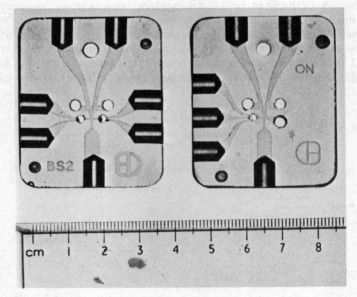

Figure 24.14   Wall-attachment devices, bistable and OR/NOR, manufactured by British Fluidics and Controls Ltd. of Ilford.

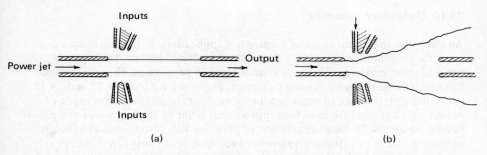

Figure 24.15   Schematic arrangement of NOR unit ('turbulence amplifier'). (a) No input: laminar jet; (b) Input: turbulent jet.

wide Reynolds number range over which a jet will remain laminar if sufficiently undisturbed but will become turbulent in the presence of a large disturbance (cf. Section 19.2). Thus, in the absence of a signal on any of the input jets, the power jet remains laminar; a laminar jet spreads only slowly and so most of the air leaves through the output (Fig. 24.15(a)). If there is a signal on one or more of the inputs, transition is promoted, and the much more rapid spreading of a turbulent jet results in so little of the air leaving through the output that it gives no signal (Fig. 24.15(b)). This is consequently a NOR element, there being a signal at the output only if there is no signal at any input. Other logic components can be built up from combinations of NOR units.

However, this type of device is currently finding its principal applications in interface equipment, providing the primary information for fluid control systems. For example, the presence of a component on a production line can be detected by the interruption of an input. The sensitivity of jets to sound (Section 19.2) is useful in this connection; the input can be an acoustic signal rather than a bulk flow.

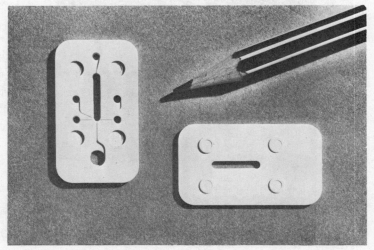

Figure 24.16   Turbulence amplifier (and cover plate) manufactured by CompAir Maxam Ltd. of Camborne.

24.10 Undulatory swimming

An obviously important range of biophysical applications of fluid dynamics concerns the propulsion of animals — the flight of birds and insects, the swimming of fish and other creatures. There are various types of propulsion. Here we consider just one, related to topics in earlier chapters, illustrated by Figs. 24.17 and 24.18. (Both these pictures are of organisms being used for research into this mode of swimming.) Various species of long thin animals swim by sending waves along their bodies. Figure 24.17 shows *amphioxus* (a primitive fish, also known as a lancelet) swimming in this way; it can do so either head-first or tail-first [289]. Other examples are snakes, leeches, eels, and some species of marine worm. In some cases, there may be several wavelengths within the body length. Various micro-organisms propel themselves by sending a wave down a flagellum attached to the body; Fig. 24.18 shows the spore of a water mould [178], and other examples include spermatozoa and some types of bacteria.

The physical principle of such swimming may be understood by considering the force on each portion of the body or flagellum as if it were in isolation. A cylinder moving through a fluid in a direction perpendicular to its axis experiences a larger drag than one moving parallel to its axis. Correspondingly, the drag on a cylinder in oblique motion is not directly opposite to its velocity. Thus it is possible for an animal swimming with every portion of the body moving forward nevertheless to have some portions producing a propulsive force. We may illustrate this by considering an inextensible body in a perfectly sinusoidal wave motion [78, 260]. Figure 24.19 shows two consecutive positions of one wavelength of the body for a case in which the forward swimming speed is one-third the speed at which the wave travels backwards relative to the body. The short lines joining corresponding points of the body indicate approximately the direction in which each portion is

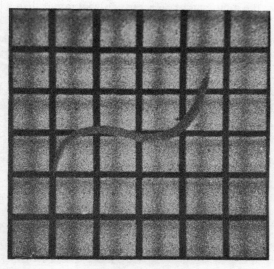

Figure 24.17   *Amphioxus* swimming, head first from left to right. Photo provided by J. E. Webb, Westfield College.

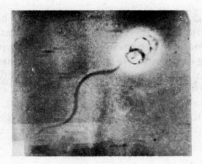

Figure 24.18 Spore of *Blastocladiella emersonii*. From Ref. [178].

instantaneously moving through the water. The resulting forces on the body may then be in the directions indicated by the double-headed arrows. It is seen that enough of these may have a forward component to overcome the drag in the regions where they have a backward component.

An interesting feature of this swimming mode is that it can be effective over all Reynolds number ranges. For the examples in Figs. 24.17 and 24.18, the Reynolds number (based on body diameter and swimming speed) is respectively around 10^3 and around 10^{-4}. It is clear that the difference in drag associated with different directions of motion is essential to the mechanism. At high Reynolds numbers this difference may be large (a cylinder in transverse motion developing a large drag as

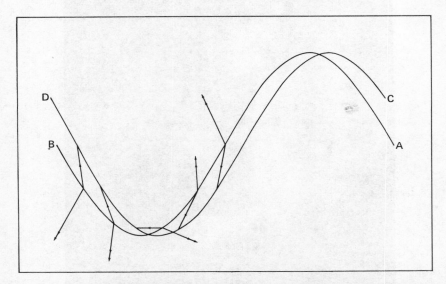

Figure 24.19 Consecutive positions AB and CD of length of body swimming from right to left by sending wave from left to right. Single arrows indicate motion of portions of body; double arrows indicate possible resulting forces on these portions.

discussed in Section 11.5), and so this swimming mode can be quite effective. However, at high Reynolds numbers, there are many other modes available [165], and this one is not usually found in species highly adapted to swimming. At low Reynolds numbers, the drag differences are much smaller (because motion of a body in any direction brings a lot of fluid into motion with it — Section 8.2). They are sufficient for swimming to be possible, but a vigorous wave is necessary to produce only slow forward motion. The swimming is thus inefficient, but since most other swimming modes fail altogether at low Reynolds number, the existence of this mode is important.

24.11 Convection from the human body

Because the ambient air is usually cooler than the human body, convection currents are set up around the body. In the absence of other causes of appreciable motion,

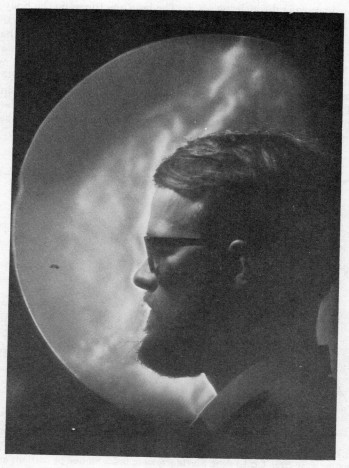

Figure 24.20   Schlieren photograph of free convection from man's head. Photo provided by R. S. Clark, National Institute for Medical Research.

free convection boundary layers, broadly similar to those described in Section 14.5, surround the body.

In recent years it has been realized that this flow may be of considerable medical significance. The concentration of airborne micro-organisms is markedly higher in the boundary layers than in the surrounding air. In particular, the body is constantly losing skin scales (about 10^{10} per day) through the rubbing actions of limbs and clothes, and many of these scales have micro-organisms attached. It has, for example, been suggested [160] that convection may produce the observed connection between skin disease and respiratory disease (e.g. eczema and asthma), by transporting organisms from the skin to the nose; and that it may account for the increase in respiratory infections after a fall in air temperature, which would result in more vigorous convection. An understanding of the role of the boundary layer in transporting skin scales is important for the reduction of infection during orthopaedic operations. It enters into the design of air flow systems in operating theatres, infant incubators, and industrial clean rooms, and into the design of protective clothing such as operating gowns.

As a starting point for investigating these phenomena, detailed studies have been made of the convection from a naked standing man and from a full-scale heated model of a man [87, 160]. The distribution, thickness, and general behaviour of the boundary layers were investigated by the schlieren method (Section 23.4), giving photographs such as that in Fig. 24.20. Hot-wire anemometers (Section 23.2) and thermocouples were used to obtain more information about the velocity and temperature distributions. These are similar to the distributions for a heated vertical plate (Section 14.5), and transition similarly occurs; the flow is laminar on the legs but becomes turbulent further up the body. On a clothed man, the Grashof number may be low enough for the flow to remain laminar over the whole body.

The next stage is, of course, the extension of this work to the more complicated situations related to the applications. An important additional aspect is the development of instruments to detect small airborne particles; a successful method has used a modified hot-wire anemometer system, a pulse being generated by the sudden cooling of the wire on the impact of a particle [79].

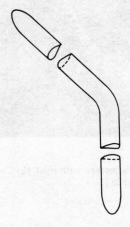

Figure 24.21 Sketch of boomerang with 'breaks' to show cross-sections of arms.

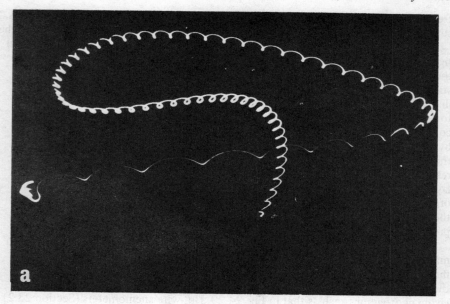

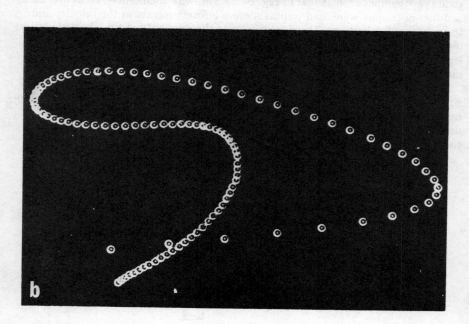

Figure 24.22   (a) Flight of boomerang with light. (b) Computer simulation of view of boomerang flight. From Ref. [125].

24.12 The flight of a boomerang

The inventors of the boomerang somehow chanced on a design that requires aerofoil theory for an understanding of its performance. Whilst the name boomerang is commonly associated with a device that returns to its thrower, there are also boomerangs which fly almost straight. These were used for hunting food and in war, having the advantage over an ordinary projectile of travelling much further and striking harder; the good 'aerodynamic design' gave small viscous energy losses and stability of flight. The differences between returning and non-returning boomerangs are outwardly rather slight; small changes in the detailed shaping have a large effect on the trajectory. The essential features of a boomerang are shown in Fig. 24.21. Each arm has a cross-section of aerofoil shape, with the leading edges on opposite sides of the two arms. There will thus (Section 11.6) be little resistance to rotation of the boomerang in its own plane (anticlockwise in Fig. 24.21). Actual boomerangs are usually rather more complicated than this, often being slightly twisted so that the two arms are not in the same plane. The flight paths can be correspondingly complicated, with changes in the orientation of the boomerang producing different detailed dynamics over different parts of a flight.

However, the basic mechanism by which a boomerang returns can be understood fairly simply in the following way [125]. A returning boomerang has its aerofoil sections shaped or oriented so that a sideways force is generated (as discussed in Sections 12.1 and 12.2). The bend in the middle is not essential to the performance, although it may be important for ease of throwing. Consider a boomerang flying in a vertical plane, so that an observer positioned appropriately sees it travelling from right to left and rotating anticlockwise. Sideways forces act on the two arms, but unequally. The arm instantaneously nearer the top is moving through the air faster than the other, because the linear motion adds to the rotational motion for the upper arm and subtracts from it for the lower. The consequent difference in sideways forces produces a couple on the boomerang. In the absence of rotation, such a couple would twist the boomerang out of the vertical plane. But gyroscopic action associated with the rapid spin of the boomerang leads to it turning about a vertical axis. The boomerang thus travels on a curved path whilst remaining vertically oriented.

Computations based on refinements of this basic idea have provided detailed information about the behaviour of boomerangs of various designs [125]. Figure 24.22 shows a comparison of an actual flight path shown by a boomerang with a light on one tip and the result of such a computation (the programme including a perspective correction so that the pattern corresponds directly to the photograph).

Notation

The following list omits some items which appear in only one section of the book and are defined there.

Where a symbol has more than one meaning (either all listed below or some defined only in the text), the use in any place should be apparent from the context.

Dimensions of quantities below are indicated where this provides a useful reminder of the definitions. Primary dimensions are denoted: M = mass; L = length; T = time; Θ = temperature.†

Subscripts: Symbols with a subscript specific to the symbol are listed below. Other subscripts have general uses. Subscripts corresponding to a co-ordinate indicate the corresponding component of a vector (e.g. u_ϕ = azimuthal component of velocity; k_x = x-component of wave number). The subscript 0 indicates a reference or ambient value; a quantity with this subscript is usually a constant, but is occasionally a basic variable specifying a situation (e.g. $u_0(x)$ = velocity outside boundary layer; $\rho_0(z)$ = basic density stratification). Subscripts 1, 2 indicate values at boundaries. Subscripts $_{av}$ and $_{max}$ indicate average and maximum values.

Superscripts: An overbar, $^{-}$, indicates an average value. A cap, $^{\wedge}$, indicates a unit vector (e.g. $\hat{x}$ = unit vector in x-direction; $\hat{n}$ = unit vector normal to surface).

a	half-width of channel
	radius (pipe, cylinder, sphere, liquid column)
	length specifying geometrical similarity
	speed of sound
b	length specifying geometrical similarity
c	chord of aerofoil
	length specifying geometrical similarity
	concentration
c_g	group velocity
c_p	phase velocity
d	diameter (pipe, cylinder)
	thickness of fluid layer
f	similarity form of stream function (boundary layer, jet)
	isotropic turbulence longitudinal correlation function
$f(\ )$	general function of quantity(ies) in brackets

†When heat is involved its dimensions (ML^2T^{-2}) are written as a separate group. The reason is that, when interactions between mechanical energy and thermal energy are not physically important (as in the Boussinesq approximation), heat can sometimes be treated as a further primary dimension.

g	$|\mathbf{g}|$
	similarity form of velocity profile (boundary layer, jet)
	isotropic turbulence transverse correlation function
$\mathbf{g}$	acceleration due to gravity
h	height (vertical slot, Rossby wave layer)
i	$\sqrt{-1}$
j	isotropic turbulence triple correlation function
k	thermal conductivity $((ML^2 T^{-2})L^{-1}T^{-1}\Theta^{-1})$
	wave number (L^{-1})
	horizontal wave number, $(k_x^2 + k_y^2)^{1/2}$
$\mathbf{k}$	wave number (L^{-1})
l	length (channel, plate)
	co-ordinate along streamline
dl	element of length
m	exponent $(u_{\max} \propto x^m)$
n	co-ordinate normal to boundary
	frequency
	exponent $(\Delta \propto x^n,\ \mathrm{Nu} \propto \mathrm{Gr}^n)$
p	pressure $(ML^{-1}T^{-2})$
	pressure fluctuation in turbulent flow
p_h	hydrostatic pressure
p_s	stagnation pressure
q	$|\mathbf{u}|$
	total velocity fluctuation in turbulent flow
r	polar co-ordinate
	space separation (correlations)
$\mathbf{r}$	general position
	space separation (correlations)
s	period of integration
	time separation (correlations)
t	time
u	x-component of velocity
	x-component of velocity fluctuation in turbulent flow
u_τ	wall flow velocity scale
$\mathbf{u}$	velocity
	velocity fluctuation in turbulent flow
v	y-component of velocity
	y-component of velocity fluctuation in turbulent flow
w	z-component of velocity
	z-component of velocity fluctuation in turbulent flow
x	Cartesian co-ordinate
	distance in main flow direction
x_0	origin of x for self-preserving development
y	Cartesian co-ordinate
	distance perpendicular to main flow direction
z	Cartesian co-ordinate
	co-ordinate perpendicular to planes of two-dimensional motion
	vertical co-ordinate (positive upwards)
	co-ordinate parallel to axis of rotation

A	constant of integration
	non-dimensional quantity in theory of Boussinesq approximation
B	constant of integration
	non-dimensional quantity in theory of Boussinesq approximation
B	general vector quantity
C	numerical constant of proportionality
	non-dimensional quantity in theory of Boussinesq approximation
C_D	drag coefficient (dimensionless)
C_L	lift coefficient (dimensionless)
C_p	specific heat at constant pressure ($(ML^2T^{-2})M^{-1}\Theta^{-1}$)
D	drag (MLT^{-2})
	drag per unit length (MT^{-2})
	non-dimensional quantity in theory of Boussinesq approximation
D/Dt	substantive derivative
E	rate of kinetic energy transport (ML^2T^{-3} in three dimensions, MLT^{-3} in two)
	energy spectrum (with respect to wave number) (L^3T^{-2})
	internal energy
F	spectral transfer function (L^3T^{-3})
F	body force per unit volume ($ML^{-2}T^{-2}$)
G	pressure gradient ($ML^{-2}T^{-2}$)
H	heat transfer per unit area per unit time ($(ML^2T^{-2})L^{-2}T^{-1}$)
H	heat flux ($(ML^2T^{-2})L^{-2}T^{-1}$)
J	rate of internal heat generation per unit volume ($(ML^2T^{-2})L^{-3}T^{-1}$)
K	constant of proportionality
	Kármán constant
L	length scale
	Monin–Obukhov length
	lift (MLT^{-2})
	lift per unit length (MT^{-2})
M	rate of momentum transport (MLT^{-2} in three dimensions, MT^{-2} in two)
N	Brunt–Väisälä angular frequency
P	difference between pressure and hydrostatic pressure
	pressure amplitude (wave or perturbation)
	mean pressure in turbulent flow
	probability distribution function
Q	heat (in thermodynamic considerations)
	density amplitude (wave or perturbation)
R	gas constant
	correlation coefficient
R_{xx}	correlation coefficient between x-components of velocity at two positions
S	general surface
	cross-sectional area of streamtube
	entropy
	$N/2\Omega$ (dimensionless)
$d\mathbf{S}$	element of surface
T	temperature
	mean temperature in turbulent flow

T_a	adiabatic temperature
U	velocity scale
	x-component of velocity amplitude (wave or perturbation)
	x-component of mean velocity in turbulent flow
	bulk velocity superimposed on wave
U_F	velocity of front of turbulent plug
U_R	velocity of rear of turbulent plug
$\mathbf{U}$	velocity of boundary
	velocity amplitude (wave or perturbation)
	mean velocity in turbulent flow
V	transverse velocity scale
	y-component of velocity amplitude (wave or perturbation)
	y-component of mean velocity in turbulent flow
	general volume
	$1/\rho$
dV	element of volume
W	vertical velocity scale
	z-component of velocity amplitude (wave or perturbation)
	work done by heat engine
Ek	Ekman number
Fr	Froude number
	internal Froude number
Gr	Grashof number
Ma	Mach number
Nu	Nusselt number
Pe	Péclet number
Pr	Prandtl number
Ra	Rayleigh number
Re	Reynolds number
Re_a	Reynolds number in which the length scale is a
Ri	Richardson number
Ro	Rossby number
St	Strouhal number
α	coefficient of expansion (Θ^{-1})
	angle of attack
	angle between boundaries
α_c	coefficient of density variation with concentration
β	compressibility $(M^{-1}LT^2)$
γ	ratio of specific heats
	gradient of layer depth
	intermittency factor
δ	transverse length scale
	boundary layer thickness (99 per cent thickness)
δx, etc.	small change in x etc.
δ_{ij}	Kronecker delta
ϵ	small distance
	turbulent energy dissipation per unit mass (L^2T^{-3})
ϵ_{ijk}	alternating tensor
ζ	z-component of vorticity, ω_z, when $\omega_x = \omega_y = 0$

η	similarity form of distance across boundary layer or jet
	y-component of vorticity, ω_y, when $\omega_x = \omega_z = 0$
θ	polar co-ordinate
	angle between wave number and vertical
	potential temperature
	temperature fluctuation in turbulent flow
θ_H	wall layer temperature scale
κ	thermal diffusivity $(L^2 T^{-1})$
κ_c	concentration diffusivity $(L^2 T^{-1})$
λ	molecular mean free path
	length of blocked region, Taylor column
	second viscosity coefficient $(ML^{-1} T^{-1})$
μ	viscosity $(ML^{-1} T^{-1})$
ν	kinematic viscosity $(L^2 T^{-1})$
ξ	non-dimensional wave number
ρ	density (ML^{-3})
ρ_h	hydrostatic density field
σ	force per unit area in main flow direction on surface $(ML^{-1} T^{-2})$
	amplification coefficient in stability theory (T^{-1})
σ_r, σ_i	real and imaginary parts of amplification coefficient
τ	tangential stress in shear flow $(ML^{-1} T^{-2})$
τ_W	value of τ at wall
ϕ	polar co-ordinate
	velocity potential $(L^2 T^{-1})$
	energy spectrum (with respect to angular frequency) $(L^2 T^{-1})$
ψ	stream function $(L^2 T^{-1})$
ω	angular frequency
$\boldsymbol{\omega}$	vorticity (T^{-1})
Γ	circulation $(L^2 T^{-1})$
Δ	length proportional to thickness of boundary layer, jet, etc.
	Ekman layer thickness
Δx etc.	finite difference in x etc.
ΔP	pressure difference scale
Θ	temperature difference scale
	temperature amplitude (wave or perturbation)
Π	longitudinal pressure variation scale
Σ	torque per unit length (MLT^{-2})
	turbulence kinetic energy per unit volume $(ML^{-1} T^{-2})$
Υ	transverse pressure variation scale
Φ	gravitational potential $(L^2 T^{-2})$
	energy dissipation per unit volume $(ML^{-1} T^{-3})$
Ψ	time scale
Ω	angular velocity (local)
	angular velocity of reference frame
$\boldsymbol{\Omega}$	angular velocity of reference frame.

Problems

For the purposes of the following problems, air may be taken as a perfect gas with density 1.2 kg m^{-3}, kinematic viscosity 1.5×10^{-5} m^2 s^{-1}, and specific heat at constant pressure 1.0×10^3 J kg^{-1} K^{-1}; water may be taken to have density 1.0×10^3 kg m^{-3}, kinematic viscosity 1.0×10^{-6} m^2 s^{-1}, and coefficient of expansion (at $20°C$) 2.1×10^{-4} K^{-1}.

1. A layer of fluid (viscosity μ, density ρ) of depth d flows under the influence of gravity down a wide plane inclined at an angle θ to the horizontal. Assuming that d is constant and that all conditions are steady, find the velocity as a function of the normal distance y from the plane. Determine also the ratio of the average velocity to the maximum velocity, and the mass flux per unit width of the plane. (The free surface supports no viscous stress and the pressure above it may be supposed uniform.)

2. A vertical tube of diameter 2 mm has its upper end open to the atmosphere. At the lower end water is maintained at a pressure of 10^4 N m^{-2} above atmospheric. What is the longest length of tube for which this pressure will produce a flow through the tube? (Ignore surface tension.)

   What volume of water will pass through the tube per second if the length is half this? (Assume that the flow is laminar and ignore the entry length.)

3. A two-dimensional channel of constant width d, containing fluid of density ρ and viscosity μ, has one wall at rest and the other moving in its own plane with speed U. The fluid moves under the action of a negative pressure gradient, $-G$, applied parallel to U. In what circumstances will the flow speed exceed U in some region?

   What can you say about the stress on the moving wall when the conditions for this are just not fulfilled?

4. A fluid flows under a pressure gradient G down a channel with parallel walls of effectively infinite extent. The width of the channel is d. The temperature of the fluid varies linearly with the distance y from one wall,

$$T = T_1 + (T_2 - T_1)y/d$$

The viscosity of the fluid varies exponentially with the temperature,

$$\mu = \mu_0 e^{k(T - T_0)}$$

Supposing that the temperature and velocity profiles are the same at all stations downstream, determine the distributions of velocity and vorticity.

Under what circumstances do you think the supposed temperature distribution would be a realistic one?

5. A jet is specified by the diameter of the orifice, the momentum per unit time of of the fluid issuing from the orifice, and the density and viscosity of the fluid. What will be the form of the criterion determining whether the jet is laminar or turbulent?

6. For flow of nitrogen in a pipe of diameter 10 mm at a temperature of 300 K, estimate how low the pressure may be without violation of criteria (5.1) and (5.2) for the applicability of continuum mechanics. (Avogadro's constant $= 6 \times 10^{23}$ mol^{-1}; collision cross-section of nitrogen molecule $= 6 \times 10^{-19}$ m^2.)

7. Show that the continuity equation (5.9) may be rewritten

$$D\rho/Dt + \rho \, \nabla \cdot \mathbf{u} = 0$$

Derive the equation in this form from first principles, starting with the fact that the mass of fluid in a volume V moving with the flow is conserved; that is $D(\rho V)/Dt = 0$.

8. Show that a change of frame of reference as in Fig. 3.1 results in a change of each of $\partial \mathbf{u}/\partial t$ and $\mathbf{u} \cdot \nabla \mathbf{u}$, but leaves $D\mathbf{u}/Dt$ unchanged.

9. Verify relationship (5.61) as the criterion for compressibility effects to be negligible in a low Reynolds number flow.

10. The water supply in the apparatus of Fig. 2.1 is suddenly turned off. Supposing that the instantaneous flow pattern throughout the pipe is that of Poiseuille flow, derive an expression for the time in which the height of the water above the pipe entry falls to one half of its original value.

Formulate criteria for the negligibility of the inertial effects associated with (a) the acceleration of the water into the pipe, and (b) the changing velocity within the pipe.

Evaluate the above time for a pipe of diameter 1 mm and length 10 m leading out of a tank of horizontal cross-section 10^{-2} m^2. Check whether the above criteria are fulfilled if the initial height is 100 mm.

11. Show that the streamlines of the motion

$$u = -\Omega y \quad v = \Omega x \quad w = w_0$$

(where Ω and w_0 are constants) are

$$x^2 + y^2 = a^2 \quad x = a \sin(\Omega z/w_0 + \alpha)$$

(Note: do this by forward integration, not by substitution of the result.)

12. In each of cases (i) and (ii) below, a flow is described in a Lagrangian way by giving, as a function of time t, the co-ordinates (x, y, z) of the fluid particle that is at (x_0, y_0, z_0) at $t = 0$. For each flow, (a) formulate the equations for the path of this particle, (b) derive the Eulerian equations ($u = u(x, y, z, t)$ etc.), (c) consider whether the flow is steady, (d) consider whether the flow satisfies the incompres-

sible continuity equation, and (e) derive a general equation for a streamline. What is the nature of the flows?

(i) $x = x_0 e^{-2t/s}$ $y = y_0 e^{t/s}$ $z = z_0 e^{t/s}$

(ii) $x = x_0 e^{-2t/s}$ $y = y_0(1 + t/s)^2$ $z = z_0 e^{2t/s}(1 + t/s)^{-2}$

$(t > 0; s = \text{constant} > 0)$

13. Derive the general equation for a streamline in the two-dimensional flow (an approximate form of Rossby wave)

$u = u_0$ $v = v_0 \cos(kx - \alpha t)$

where u_0, v_0, k, and α are constants. At $t = 0$, what is the equation for the streamline passing through $x = 0$, $y = 0$?

Derive also the equation for the path of the particle which is at $x = 0$, $y = 0$ at time $t = 0$.

Comment briefly on the comparison of the streamline and the particle path in the two limiting cases, $\alpha = 0$ and $k = 0$.

14. Show geometrically that for cylindrical polar co-ordinates

$$\partial \hat{r}/\partial \phi = \hat{\phi} \quad \text{and} \quad \partial \hat{\phi}/\partial \phi = -\hat{r}$$

Hence, by writing

$$\mathbf{u} = u_r \hat{r} + u_\phi \hat{\phi} + u_z \hat{z} \quad \nabla = \hat{r}\frac{\partial}{\partial r} + \frac{\hat{\phi}}{r}\frac{\partial}{\partial \phi} + \hat{z}\frac{\partial}{\partial z}$$

show (i) that the inertia term takes the form given in equations (5.26), (5.27), and (5.28); and (ii) that, for the case when $u_r = u_z = 0$ and u_ϕ depends on r alone, the viscous term takes the form given in equation (9.3).

Note: the order of operations is indicated by writing $\mathbf{u} \cdot \nabla \mathbf{u} = (\mathbf{u} \cdot \nabla)\mathbf{u}$ and $\nabla^2 \mathbf{u} = (\nabla \cdot \nabla)\mathbf{u}$.

15. (i) Show that, for an unsteady flow in which only the x-component of velocity is non-zero and this varies only in the y-direction, the Navier–Stokes equation reduces to a form analogous to the equation of unsteady one-dimensional heat conduction in a solid.

(ii) An effectively infinite flat plate bounding a semi-infinite expanse of fluid oscillates in its own plane with velocity

$$U = U_0 \sin \omega t$$

Supposing that the induced fluid motion is an oscillation of the same frequency, how do the amplitude and phase vary with distance from the plate?

(iii) For a geometry similar to that in (ii), the plate is suddenly brought into motion at time $t = 0$ and then moves in its own plane with constant velocity U_0. Both the plate and the fluid were at rest for $t < 0$. Show that, for $t > 0$, the fluid velocity is

$$u = U_0 \, \text{erfc}\,[y/2(\nu t)^{1/2}]$$

Find the force per unit area (as a function of time) needed to produce this motion.

Hence, find the total work done after any given time, and determine what proportion of this work has appeared as kinetic energy and what proportion has been dissipated.

$$\left[\text{erfc } x = \frac{2}{\sqrt{\pi}} \int_x^\infty e^{-x^2} \, dx; \quad \text{erfc } 0 = 1; \quad \int_0^\infty (\text{erfc } x)^2 \, dx = \frac{2 - \sqrt{2}}{\sqrt{\pi}} \right]$$

16. Show that for an axisymmetric vorticity distribution $\boldsymbol{\omega} = (0, 0, \zeta(r))$ in cylindrical polar co-ordinates (r, ϕ, z), the vorticity equation reduces to

$$\frac{\partial \zeta}{\partial t} = \frac{\nu}{r} \frac{\partial}{\partial r} \left(r \frac{\partial \zeta}{\partial r} \right)$$

If there is a concentrated line vortex along the z-axis at time $t = 0$ in an otherwise irrotational fluid, show that the vorticity distribution at any subsequent time is

$$\zeta = \frac{\Phi}{4\pi\nu t} \exp(-r^2/4\nu t)$$

What is the corresponding velocity distribution?

17. If, for turbulent flow through a pipe, it is observed that the pressure gradient is proportional to $Q^{7/4}$ (where Q is the volume rate of flow), predict how the pressure gradient would vary with the viscosity and density of the fluid (for fixed Q).

18. The figures below represent observations of the power needed to propel two objects (e.g. toy submarines) through a fluid at various speeds. The objects are geometrically similar, the second being five times as large as the first (linear dimensions). Show that, although the relationship between speed U and power P is different in the two cases, all the figures are consistent and can be combined in an appropriate way. (The other relevant quantities are the density and the viscosity of the fluid.)

Comment on the interpretation of the different relationships between U and P. Small object ($L = 1$ length unit):

U	1	2	3	5	10	speed units
P	1.0	4.5	12	50	400	power units.

Larger object ($L = 5$ length units):

U	1	2	3	5	10	speed units
P	10	80	270	1250	10000	power units.

19. A circular disc is set spinning with angular velocity Ω in an incompressible viscous fluid. Use dimensional analysis to find the general functional form of the expression for the time t in which the angular velocity falls to $\Omega/2$. Assume that this depends only on Ω, the radius of the disc a, the density of the disc σ, the density ρ and the viscosity μ of the fluid.

Could you designate any of the parameters involved as a Reynolds number?

In an experiment of this type using a fluid having $\rho = 1.0 \times 10^3$ kg m^{-3} and $\mu = 1.0 \times 10^{-3}$ kg m^{-1}s^{-1}, t was observed to be 100 s when Ω was 20 rad s^{-1}.

What can you conclude from this about the motion of the same disc (a) in a fluid with $\rho = 1.0 \times 10^3$ kg m^{-3}, $\mu = 2.0 \times 10^{-3}$ kg m^{-1} s^{-1}, and (b) in a fluid with $\rho = 0.75 \times 10^3$ kg m^{-3}, $\mu = 3.0 \times 10^{-3}$ kg m^{-1} s^{-1}?

Suppose now that one argues on physical grounds that t must be directly proportional to σ (because this enters the problem only through the moment of inertia of the disc and not through the resisting fluid motion). How can the general expression for t be simplified?

What can you now conclude in cases (a) and (b) above?

20. A string of density σ, diameter d, length l is held in tension across a channel through which fluid of kinematic viscosity ν flows. The string vibrates when its fundamental natural frequency coincides with the Kármán vortex street frequency. The following observations were made of the tension F at which resonance occurred for various flow speeds U of a fluid with $\nu = 1.0 \times 10^{-5}$ m^2 s^{-1}:

U(m s^{-1})	0.2	0.4	0.6	0.8	1.0	1.2	1.4
F(N)	0.096	0.43	1.03	1.92	3.00	4.3	5.8

Suppose now that the fluid is changed to one with $\nu = 5.0 \times 10^{-5}$ m^2 s^{-1}. At which of the following speeds can the resonance tension be predicted and then what is it?

U(m s^{-1})	0.4	1.0	5.5

(You may assume that the only properties of the string that enter the problem are σ, d, and l, and that changes in the density of the fluid have no effect (except through the kinematic viscosity); and that no harmonics are generated.)

21. A plate bounding a region containing fluid of density ρ and kinematic viscosity ν is subjected to a tangential oscillatory force, F per unit area, of frequency n so that

$$F = F_0 \sin 2\pi n t$$

As a result the plate oscillates with frequency n and with amplitude A_0. Experiments show that, when the resulting motion of the fluid is laminar, A_0 is proportional to F_0 (all other quantities being held constant) and, when it is fully turbulent, $A_0 \propto F_0^{1/2}$. How would you expect A_0 to change (a) for laminar motion, (b) for fully turbulent motion, and (c) in the transition region between the two, for the following cases?

(i) when the frequency is doubled (at constant F_0, ρ, and ν)

(ii) when the frequency is doubled and the fluid is changed to one of half the original viscosity (at constant F_0 and ρ).

You may suppose that the other boundaries of the fluid region are distant (so that no length characteristic of the region enters the problem) and that the inertia of the plate is negligible (so that F_0 is entirely balanced by the fluid resistance to the motion).

Note: it is not necessarily possible to make a prediction in every case.

22. An effectively two-dimensional jet of fresh water is emitted horizontally from a slit of width a with an average speed U close to the top of a tank containing salt water. The density of the salt water exceeds the density, ρ_0, of the fresh water by a

controllable amount, $\Delta \rho$. $\Delta \rho$ is sufficiently small that its only effect on the dynamics of the jet is in changing the gravitational force on fluid particles. In a series of experiments the lowest value of U at which the jet became turbulent was observed for various values of $\Delta \rho$. The results were:

$a = 5.0$ mm; $\rho_0 = 1000$ kg m^{-3}; μ(viscosity) $= 1.0 \times 10^{-3}$ kg m^{-1} s^{-1}

$\Delta \rho$ (kg m^{-3})	0	2	4	8	12	16
U (mm s^{-1})	10	25	33	43	51	58

Similar experiments can be done with changed slit-width and with different fluids and contaminants. Will the flow be laminar or turbulent in each of the following cases?

	(i)	(ii)	(iii)
a (mm)	10	5.0	50
ρ_0 (kg m^{-3})	1000	1.0	2.0
μ (10^{-3} kg m^{-1} s^{-1})	1.0	0.010	0.020
$\Delta \rho$ (kg m^{-3})	2.0	0.020	0.0010
U (mm s^{-1})	25	400	20

(You may assume that the walls of the tank have no effect on the motion; and that the diffusivity of the contaminant may be ignored. g may be taken as 10 m s^{-2}.)

23. Determine the conditions for dynamical similarity of steady incompressible flow of an electrically conducting fluid in a magnetic field, governed by the equations:

$$\nabla \cdot \mathbf{u} = 0$$

$$\nabla \cdot \mathbf{B} = 0$$

$$\mathbf{u} \cdot \nabla \mathbf{u} = -\frac{1}{\rho} \nabla p + \frac{1}{\rho \mu} (\nabla \times \mathbf{B}) \times \mathbf{B} + \nu \nabla^2 \mathbf{u}$$

$$\mathbf{u} \cdot \nabla \mathbf{B} = \mathbf{B} \cdot \nabla \mathbf{u} + \frac{1}{\sigma \mu} \nabla^2 \mathbf{B}$$

Briefly make any comments on the results that you consider to be of interest. (Notation: $\mathbf{u}$ = velocity; $\mathbf{B}$ = magnetic field; p = pressure; ρ = density; ν = kinematic viscosity; μ = magnetic permeability; σ = electrical conductivity.)

24. (i) Determine the vorticity distribution in rotating Couette flow (Section 9.3). Determine the circulation round *any* path containing the inner cylinder when the radius of the outer cylinder becomes infinitely large.

(ii) For fixed Ω_2/Ω_1 and a_2/a_1, compare the magnitudes of the tangential force per unit area acting on either cylinder and the difference between the normal forces per unit area on the two cylinders in terms of the Reynolds number.

25. (i) What is the largest size of water drop (assumed spherical) for which the rate of free fall in air can be calculated using Stokes's formula (9.17) and what is its rate of fall?

(ii) How small must a water drop be for its fall under its own weight to be negligible when it is in a 1 m s^{-1} wind generating turbulence of intensity equal to 10 per cent of the mean velocity?

26. (i) Is the motion incompressible for the flows given by the following velocity potentials? If so, determine the corresponding stream functions.

(a) $\phi = C(x^2 + y^2)$

(b) $\phi = C(x^2 - y^2)$

(ii) Is the motion irrotational for the flows given by the following stream functions? If so, determine the corresponding velocity potentials.

(a) $\psi = C(x^2 + y^2)$

(b) $\psi = C(x^2 - y^2)$

Sketch the streamlines for all cases and the lines of constant ϕ where possible.

27. Show that if the effect of the hydrostatic pressure is significant, Bernoulli's equation becomes

$$p + \tfrac{1}{2}\rho q^2 + \rho gz = \text{constant}$$

where p is the true pressure and z is the vertical co-ordinate (positive upwards).

Hence, show that the velocity of liquid emerging from a small hole in a tank with a free surface is the same as the velocity that would be acquired by free fall from the level of the surface to that of the hole.

28. Find how the constant in Bernoulli's equation varies with radius for each of the two velocity fields, equation (6.17) and equation (6.19).

29. Fluid flows out of a reservoir (so large that the fluid in it can be considered stationary) through a circular tube with a Venturi constriction in it. The radius of the tube is 10 mm, reducing to 5 mm in the constriction. If the pressure (above atmospheric) is 200 N m^{-2} in the reservoir and 190 N m^{-2} in the main part of the tube, what is it in the constriction? Suppose that the flow is incompressible and inviscid (low Mach number, thin boundary layers).

30. (i) Sensitive liquid level manometers can be read with an accuracy of about $\pm 10^{-2}$ mm of water. What is the lowest air velocity that can be measured to within 5 per cent with a Pitot tube?

(ii) It is found empirically that buoyancy effects upset the calibration of a hot-wire anemometer when $Gr^{1/3} > Re/2$. (Why is this of a different form from equation (13.14)?) What is the lowest air velocity that can be measured when the ratio of the absolute temperature of the wire to that of the air is 1.5?

31. Show that all the conditions for inviscid incompressible flow past a fixed circular cylinder of radius a (with uniform velocity at large distances) are satisfied by a velocity potential in cylindrical polar co-ordinates of the form

$$u_0 \left(r + \frac{a^2}{r} \right) \cos \phi$$

Show that the corresponding expression in spherical polar co-ordinates for flow past a sphere is

$$u_0 \left(r + \frac{1}{2} \frac{a^3}{r^2} \right) \cos \theta$$

What are the pressure distributions over the surfaces of the cylinder and sphere?

32. In spherical polar co-ordinates (r, θ, ϕ), the velocity potential

$$\Phi = -kr^2 P_2(\cos \theta) = -\tfrac{1}{2}kr^2 (3 \cos^2 \theta - 1)$$

represents the axisymmetric flow produced by the confluence of two equal and opposite streams. Sketch the streamline pattern in any plane through the axis of symmetry.

If now a solid sphere with surface $r = a$ is placed in this flow, how is the velocity potential modified? Hence, determine the distribution of velocity and pressure over the surface of the sphere.

State briefly the principal ways in which a real flow would be expected to depart from this ideal one.

33. (i) For (a) inviscid flow past a sphere and (b) Stokes flow past a sphere, determine the distance to the side of the sphere (measured in sphere radii) at which the difference from the free-stream velocity falls to 1 per cent.

(ii) For high Reynolds number flow past a cylinder, estimate the distance at which the difference from the free-stream velocity falls to 1 per cent (a) to the side of the cylinder and (b) directly downstream of the cylinder.

Note: refer to the solutions of Question 31 and to Fig. 22.6.

34. Compare the two-dimensional boundary layers on plane and curved surfaces below the same inviscid velocity distribution $u_0(x)$, where x is the curvilinear co-ordinate in the surface. Find the order of magnitude of the pressure variation across the boundary layer for the latter case, by considering the balance between the pressure gradient and the centrifugal force associated with the curved flow. Hence, show that the boundary layer equations are the same for the two cases provided that $\delta/R \ll 1$, where δ is the boundary layer thickness and R is the radius of curvature of the surface.

35. In the two-dimensional flow away from a stagnation point on a flat wall, the inviscid velocity at the wall is

$$u_0 = a x$$

where x is the distance along the wall from the stagnation point (cf. the inviscid flow in Question 26(i)(b)). Show that the boundary layer below this flow, in the region where the Reynolds number ax^2/v is large, has constant thickness. If the stream function in the boundary layer is written

$$\psi = k a x f(y/\delta)$$

show that it is appropriate to put

$$k = \delta = (v/a)^{1/2}$$

and that the governing differential equation is then

$$f''' + ff'' - f'^2 + 1 = 0$$

Formulate the boundary conditions for this.

36. The growth of a boundary layer can be inhibited by sucking some of the fluid through a porous wall. In appropriate circumstances, this can give a boundary layer of which both the thickness and the velocity profile remain constant with distance downstream. Consider this situation for a two-dimensional flat plate boundary layer in zero external pressure gradient. Determine the velocity profile, by considering first the continuity equation and then the momentum equation with boundary conditions:

$u = 0$ and $v = -v_0$ at $y = 0$

$u = u_\infty$ at large y.

Whereabouts on a wall of finite extent would you expect this solution to apply?
How does it relate to the solution when $v_0 = 0$? Mention another situation in which the introduction of an extra parameter gives rise to a simpler solution in a similar way.

37. Show that the velocity profile (11.53) satisfies each of (11.63), (11.64), and (11.65). (Note: by use of the appropriate variable this can be done without detailed integrations.)

38. (i) Use a procedure similar to that in Section 11.9 to show that, in the wake behind a two-dimensional obstacle fixed in a stream of velocity u_0,

$$dM/dx = 0, \qquad \text{where } M = \rho \int_{-\infty}^{\infty} u(u_0 - u)dy$$

Interpret M as the rate of transport of the momentum deficit produced by the drag on the obstacle.

(ii) Correspondingly, the rate of transport of kinetic energy deficit is

$$E = \frac{1}{2} \rho \int_{-\infty}^{\infty} u(u_0^2 - u^2)dy$$

Show that

$$E = u_0 M - \frac{1}{2} \rho \int_{-\infty}^{\infty} u(u_0 - u)^2 dy$$

Hence, for a self-propelled body (i.e. a body holding itself fixed against the flow) for which $M = 0$, show that the wake involves transport of kinetic energy away from the body.

39. (i) The displacement thickness and the momentum thickness of a boundary layer are defined respectively by

$$\delta^* = \int_0^\infty \left(1 - \frac{u}{u_0}\right)dy; \qquad \delta^{**} = \int_0^\infty \frac{u}{u_0}\left(1 - \frac{u}{u_0}\right)dy$$

Show that for Blasius flow each of these is a constant proportion of the 99 per cent thickness.

(ii) Show, also for Blasius flow, that

$$u_0^2 \, d\delta^{**}/dx = \nu(\partial u/\partial y)_{y=0}$$

(Hint: relate each side to an integral in terms of the non-dimensional parameters η and f, and then prove that the two integrals are equal.) Interpret this result in terms of Newton's second law.

40. Show that the velocity field (in two-dimensional polar co-ordinates (r, ϕ))

$$u_r = -u_0 \left(1 - \frac{a^2}{r^2}\right) \cos \phi$$

$$u_\phi = u_0 \left(1 + \frac{a^2}{r^2}\right) \sin \phi + \frac{\Gamma}{2\pi r}$$

represents a solution of the equations of inviscid irrotational motion around a circular cylinder of radius a, tending to a free-stream velocity u_0 far from the cylinder and with circulation Γ round the cylinder. Determine the pressure distribution over the surface of the cylinder, and hence show that the lift per unit length is given by the Kutta–Zhukovskii result, $L = -\rho u_0 \Gamma$.

41. From the information that an aircraft of mass 10^4 kg has wings of average chord 3 m and total span 30 m, estimate the magnitude of the air speeds associated with circulation around the wings during level flight at a speed of 100 m s^{-1}.

42. Consider a smooth ball of diameter 40 mm and density 1.2×10^3 kg m^{-3} travelling (instantaneously) horizontally at a speed of 20 m s^{-1}. Check that the experimental data in Fig. 12.9 are applicable and use them to determine (a) the radius of curvature in a horizontal plane of its trajectory when it is spinning about a vertical axis at an angular velocity of 600 rad s^{-1}, and (b) how rapidly it would need to spin about a horizontal axis in order to counteract 20 per cent of the gravitational force.

43. (i) Consider forced convection in a circular pipe of radius a with the Poiseuille velocity profile, equation (2.17). Suppose that the temperature of the pipe wall increases linearly with distance along the pipe, and that, in consequence, the same constant axial temperature gradient $\partial T/\partial x$ exists everywhere in the pipe. Determine the radial temperature distribution. Determine also the heat transfer from the pipe wall. Express the latter result in the non-dimensional form, equation (13.22) (defining the temperature difference scale as the temperature change in a length of the pipe equal to its diameter, $\Theta = 2a\partial T/\partial x$).

(ii) Show how the above solution can be extended to apply to Poiseuille flow occurring with uniform internal heat generation in a pipe with a thermally insulating wall. Explain why, for this flow to establish a uniform axial temperature gradient, there must be a temperature difference between the fluid at the wall and that at the centre, and derive an expression for this difference.

44. Write the equations of free convection in the approximate form appropriate to a two-dimensional boundary layer. Hence, verify the relationships (14.29) for the variation of boundary layer thickness and maximum velocity in free convection from a vertical plate.

By making the substitutions

$$\psi = [g\alpha(T_1 - T_0)\nu^2 x^3]^{1/4} f(\eta); \qquad (T - T_0) = (T_1 - T_0)\theta(\eta)$$

where

$$\eta = [g\alpha(T_1 - T_0)/\nu^2 x]^{1/4} y$$

show that the differential equations governing this flow are

$$4f''' + 3ff'' - 2f'^2 + 4\theta = 0$$

$$4\theta'' + 3\mathrm{Pr}f\theta' = 0$$

Write down the boundary conditions for these equations.

Show that the heat transfer dependence on $(T_1 - T_0)$ takes the form of relationship (14.36).

45. Convection in a layer between two vertical walls at different uniform temperatures (as described in Section 14.7) of large enough aspect ratio (h/d) can have a region in the middle vertically in which the velocity and the temperature depend only on the horizontal co-ordinate and not on the vertical. Show that, in this region, the temperature profile is unaffected by the flow and determine the velocity profile. Express the latter result in terms of the dependence of the Reynolds number, based on the maximum velocity and the layer width, on the Grashof number.

46. (i) Movements of the Earth's mantle are inferred with speeds around 10^{-9} m s^{-1} (see Section 24.4). Supposing these are produced by free convection in a homogeneous fluid of kinematic viscosity 10^{17} m^2 s^{-1} and coefficient of expansion 10^{-5} K^{-1} and that the length scale of both the velocity and temperature fields is 10^6 m, what are the temperature differences associated with the flow?

(ii) If the thermal diffusivity of the mantle is 10^{-7} m^2 s^{-1}, what is the thickness of the thermal boundary layers associated with the above flow? If the temperature variations are confined to such boundary layers, how is the answer to (i) modified?

47. A tank of fluid rotates in rigid body motion. Superimposed on this is a 'jet-stream' type of motion in which some of the fluid is moving azimuthally with a different angular velocity. Show that an observer at rest in the laboratory regards the modification to the force field by this stream as a change in the centrifugal force; that an observer rotating with the tank regards it as either a Coriolis force or a Coriolis force plus a contribution to $\mathbf{u} \cdot \nabla \mathbf{u}$ (depending on whether the Rossby number is low or not); but that the two are agreed on the radial pressure gradient associated with the motion.

48. A demonstration of the action of the Coriolis force in fluid dynamics can be made by introducing a capillary tube into a uniform flow in a rotating channel. The basic flow, the tube, and the axis of rotation are all mutually perpendicular. Explain

briefly why there is a flow through the tube, and calculate the ratio of the mean speed of this flow to the speed of the basic flow when the angular velocity of rotation is 0.5 rad s^{-1}, the radius of the capillary tube 0.2 mm, and the kinematic viscosity of the fluid 1 mm^2 s^{-1}.

To an order of magnitude, how much higher is the water level on the French coast than on the English coast when there is an eastwards tidal flow through the English Channel at a typical speed of 1 m s^{-1}?

49. Apply the laminar theory of the Ekman spiral to the case of a semi-infinite expanse of fluid with a boundary moving in its own plane at a constant velocity U with respect to a frame of reference rotating with angular velocity Ω about an axis perpendicular to the boundary. The fluid far from the boundary is at rest in this frame. How does the flow vary with distance from the boundary? What is the smallest distance at which the flow direction is exactly opposite to that of the boundary?

This theory may be applied to the motion of the upper layers of the ocean under the action of the wind stress, with the difference that the viscous stress at the surface, not the velocity, is prescribed. Show that the surface moves in a direction at 45° to the direction of the stress, and the net mass flux over the whole flow is at 90° to the direction of the stress. (It may be assumed that only the vertical component of the Earth's angular velocity need be considered.)

50. An Ekman layer becomes unstable at a Reynolds number (based on the geostrophic velocity and the layer thickness) of about 55. Experiments are performed in water in a rotating annulus of inner and outer radii 0.45 and 0.55 m. Ekman layers are observed on boundaries normal to the rotation axis (a) by moving the boundary relative to the annulus at a speed of 30 mm s^{-1}; (b) by producing a transient geostrophic flow by suddenly changing the rotation rate by 10 per cent; and (c) by producing a geostrophic flow by maintaining a pressure difference between the inner and outer walls 10 per cent greater than that needed to balance the centrifugal force. In each case, what is the maximum or minimum rotation rate at which the instability could be observed? Also, at this rotation rate, is the assumption that the Ekman layer is thin compared with other relevant dimensions fulfilled?

51. For Rossby waves of the type analysed in Section 15.7, show that the criterion for non-linear inertial effects to be negligible is that the Rossby number based on the velocity in the direction of the depth gradient and on the wavelength should be small.

52. (i) A cyclone has pressure differences of about 10 mbar (10^3 N m^{-2}) over horizontal distances of about 10^3 km. What is a characteristic wind speed?

(ii) A tornado has pressure differences of about 50 mbar over horizontal distances of about 10^2 m. What is a characteristic wind speed?

(Briefly justify your choice of procedure in each case.)

53. (i) For free convection in a rotating fluid, determine the non-dimensional parameter that indicates the relative importance of Coriolis and inertia forces (ignoring viscous forces).

(ii) For free convection in a fluid rotating about a vertical axis sufficiently rapidly that the Coriolis force is dominant, show that the Taylor–Proudman theorem still applies to the vertical component of the velocity, but is modified for the horizontal components. Illustrate the physical significance of the new form by discussing briefly the vorticity balance associated with the increase in speed with height of westerly winds at mid-latitudes.

54. For a region close to the ocean surface in which the temperature decreases from 25°C to 15°C and the salinity increases from 3.50 to 3.55 per cent by weight over 100 m increase in depth, which of the temperature stratification, the salt stratification, and the Earth's rotation will have the most significant effect on the dynamical behaviour?

55. In Section 16.1, it is shown that when the Reynolds and Péclet numbers are both large, the criterion for stratification to affect a flow strongly is that Fr^2 should be small. Show that the corresponding criteria in the cases of (a) small Reynolds number but large Péclet number and (b) small Reynolds number and small Péclet number are respectively that Fr^2/Re and $Fr^2/RePe$ should be small.

56. It is desired to investigate the lee waves associated with the flow of a wind of 10 m s^{-1} past a hill in an isothermal (and therefore subadiabatic) atmosphere at 300 K, by towing a $1:10^4$ scale model of the hill at 50 mm s^{-1} in a channel in which a uniform vertical salt gradient has been established. If the channel depth is 200 mm and the water at the top is fresh, what should be the salt concentration (expressed as weight of salt per unit weight of water) at the bottom, assuming that the water volume does not change when salt is dissolved in it? (Assume that viscosity and diffusion may be neglected.)

57. A horizontal cylindrical body is oscillated periodically but *non*-sinusoidally in a stratified fluid at a frequency equal to 0.3 times the Brunt–Väisälä frequency. For each of the internal wave modes generated, determine the direction of the group velocity, the direction of the phase velocity, and the ratio of the group velocity to the phase velocity.

58. Derive the principal properties of inertial waves in a rotating fluid (as shown in Fig. 15.12) by the procedure applied to internal waves in a stratified fluid in Section 16.4. (Start with the linearized, inviscid, but time-dependent equations for motion in a rotating fluid and substitute velocity and pressure fields of the form of equations (16.18) and (16.19).) In particular, show that

$$\omega = 2\Omega \mid \cos \theta \mid$$

where θ is the angle between $\mathbf{k}$ and $\mathbf{\Omega}$, and that the group velocity is perpendicular to $\mathbf{k}$ in the plane of $\mathbf{k}$ and $\mathbf{\Omega}$. Consider the significance of the limiting cases $\omega = 0$ and $\omega = 2\Omega$.

59. The capillary instability of a stationary cylindrical column of liquid may be investigated by introducing a disturbance of a controlled wavelength. The table below gives the amplification rate (reciprocal of e-folding time), in units of s^{-1}, as a function of the radius of the column and of the wavelength, for a liquid with

density 1.5×10^3 kg m^{-3}, surface tension 6×10^{-2} N m^{-1} and kinematic viscosity 1.0×10^{-4} m^2 s^{-1}. For a 1 mm radius column of another liquid with density 1.0×10^3 kg m^{-3}, surface tension 2×10^{-2} N m^{-1}, and kinematic viscosity 0.5×10^{-4} m^2 s^{-1}, what would be the amplification rate of a 10 mm wavelength disturbance and what wavelength would give the maximum amplification rate?

		Radius (mm)		
		0.5	1	2
	5	660	0	0
	10	750	310	0
	15	580	340	85
Wavelength (mm)	20	480	300	135
	30	340	230	135
	40	290	180	120
	60	180	140	90

60. Show that the non-dimensional parameter governing the onset of the variable surface tension instability described in Section 17.4 is $\chi \Delta T d/\rho v \kappa$ (the Marangoni number) where χ is the negative rate of change of surface tension with temperature, ΔT is the horizontally averaged temperature difference across the layer, and other symbols are as in the text.

The critical Marangoni number in the absence of buoyancy effects is 80. The critical Rayleigh number (for free upper surface with no horizontal heat transfer) in the absence of surface tension effects is 670. For a layer of oil with $\rho = 1.0 \times 10^3$ kg m^{-3}, $v = 1.0 \times 10^{-4}$ m^2 s^{-1}, $\kappa = 1.1 \times 10^{-7}$ m^2 s^{-1}, $\alpha = 1.0 \times 10^{-3}$ K^{-1}, and $\chi = 6 \times 10^{-5}$ N m^{-1} K^{-1}, estimate the depth at which the predominant destabilizing mechanism changes. What is the minimum temperature difference necessary to produce motion at depths of each of 1/10 and 10 times the above depth?

61. Write down the velocity distribution in rotating Couette flow for the two special cases of (a) two cylinders rotating in the same sense with the same angular velocity, and (b) a single cylinder rotating in an infinite expanse of fluid. Hence, show that according to the inviscid stability criterion (the Rayleigh criterion) the former is stable and the latter is neutrally stable.

Show that the Rayleigh criterion may be reformulated as indicating that the motion is unstable if the vorticity has the opposite sign to the fluid angular velocity.

62. The tendency for buses on a frequent service to form bunches can be understood as follows: if one bus is slightly delayed, more passengers will accumulate at the next stop and the delay will be increased; another bus that gets slightly early will similarly become earlier still. A simple quantitative model of this can be formulated by considering an infinite homogeneous bus route. If the nth bus is a time t_n late, its additional delay at a stop may be taken proportional to the excess time since the last bus; that is to $(t_n - t_{n-1})$. After ΔN stops

$$\Delta t_n = A(t_n - t_{n-1})\Delta N$$

If both the buses and the stops are sufficiently close together, t_n can be treated as a continuous function of n and N. Then one may write

$$\partial t_n/\partial N = A(t_n - t_{n-1})$$

Or; approximating by the first two terms of a Taylor expansion,

$$\partial t_n/\partial N = A \partial t_n/\partial n - \tfrac{1}{2}A \partial^2 t_n/\partial n^2$$

Consider the evolution in time (i.e. with respect to N) of a disturbance that is periodic in space (i.e. with respect to n).

Discuss the extent to which this treatment is analogous to the methods used for studying hydrodynamic instability.

63. Consider whether any significant part of the boundary layers might be laminar in the cases of (a) a ship of length 100 m sailing at a speed of 10 m s^{-1}, (b) a fish of length 0.5 m swimming at 2 m s^{-1}, and (c) the aircraft of Question 41.

64. It is planned to carry out a vibrating ribbon experiment to verify the boundary layer stability curve shown in Fig. 18.7 for Reynolds numbers up to 5000, using a wind-tunnel with speeds ranging from 1 to 50 m s^{-1}. Owing to limitations in the electrical and mechanical system, the ribbon can be vibrated only in the range 15–300 Hz. Also, so that the ribbon does not significantly block the flow, it is desired that the boundary layer thickness should be at least 5 mm. Show that the experiment can be performed within these constraints, but only by varying the distance of the ribbon from the leading edge. Determine the range of variation needed.

65. The flow in a pipe is in the regime described in Section 19.3 in which turbulent plugs are produced periodically. The pressure difference is such that, if the flow were entirely laminar, the Reynolds number would be 9000. A plug is generated close to the pipe entry whenever the Reynolds number rises above 6000. Use the information in Figs. 2.11 and 19.10 to estimate the fraction of the flow that is turbulent (a) when a plug is just being generated, (b) when the rear of a plug is passing out of the pipe, and (c) when the front of a plug is passing out of the pipe. Estimate also the range over which the Reynolds number oscillates during the cycle. (Ignore entry length effects on laminar and turbulent flow properties.)

66. Formulate an equation for the energy of the mean motion in a turbulent flow (by multiplying equation (20.13) by U_i) and rearrange the term representing the interaction with the fluctuations to exhibit (a) a loss term equivalent to the production term in the turbulence energy equation, and (b) a term representing energy transport by the turbulence (integrating to zero over the whole flow).

67. The solar radiation falling on the planet Venus has an intensity of 2.6×10^3 W m^{-2}. About 70 per cent of this is reflected and about 1 per cent reaches the planet's surface. The remainder is absorbed in a cloud layer, 15 to 30 km thick. Cellular convection is observed in the sub-solar region of this cloud layer. Suppose that such convection can occur only if the Rayleigh number of Section 17.3 is in the range 10^3 to 10^6, and that it is brought into this range by small-scale turbulence producing an effective kinematic viscosity and thermal diffusivity (equal to one another). In what range must this eddy viscosity lie? (For order of magnitude purposes, suppose that the atmosphere has the properties of CO_2 at 300 K and 10^5 N m^{-2}, and that g is the same as for the earth.)

68. Show that equation (21.1) for the correlation functions in isotropic turbulence implies that

$$\int_0^\infty gr\, dr = 0$$

provided that $f \to 0$ more rapidly than r^{-2} as $r \to \infty$. Indicate why one would expect this result from continuity considerations.

69. (i) The energy dissipation in isotropic turbulence (denoted by ϵ in Section 21.3) depends only on the r.m.s. velocity fluctuation $(\overline{u^2})^{1/2}$ and a length scale l of the large eddies. Use dimensional analysis to infer the form of this dependence.

(ii) The length scale η of the dissipating eddies (the Kolmogoroff length scale) depends only on the energy dissipation and the kinematic viscosity. Use dimensional analysis to infer the form of this dependence.

(iii) Supposing that one requires $\eta/l < 10^{-3}$ for the inertial sub-range to be observable (so that there is a decade in wave number between $10/l$ and $1/10\eta$), express this as a condition on the Reynolds number based on $(\overline{u^2})^{1/2}$ and l. (Assume that the proportionality constants involved in parts (i) and (ii) are ~ 1.)

(iv) With the observations that $(\overline{u^2})^{1/2} \sim U/30$ and $l \sim M/3$, where U is the mean velocity and M is the grid mesh length, determine the minimum UM/ν for an experiment to observe the inertial sub-range. Show that, with the condition that the flow must be incompressible, the experiment requires a very large wind-tunnel.

70. Determine the pattern of two-dimensional, irrotational, incompressible motion produced when a spatially sinusoidal normal velocity is imposed on the boundary of a semi-infinite region of fluid; that is the boundary conditions are

$$v = v_0 \cos kx \quad \text{at } y = 0$$
$$u, v \to 0 \quad \text{as } y \to \infty$$

This analysis is the starting point for a theory of the irrotational velocity fluctuations in fluid adjacent to a turbulent region. Explain why analysis of the response to a sinusoidal disturbance is relevant to this, and show that the resulting motion does not generate a Reynolds stress.

71. (i) If the velocity and length scales of an axisymmetric jet are of the form

$$u_{\max} \propto x^m; \quad \Delta \propto x^n$$

what are m and n for (a) laminar flow (b) turbulent flow?

(ii) If the velocity, length and temperature difference scales of an axisymmetric plume are of the form

$$u_{\max} \propto x^m; \quad (T_{\max} - T_0) \propto x^p; \quad \Delta \propto x^n$$

what are m, p, and n for (a) laminar flow (b) turbulent flow?

72. The ratio u_τ/U_0 of the wall stress velocity to the free-stream velocity for a turbulent boundary layer on a smooth wall varies with Reynolds number sufficiently slowly that it may be taken as typically $1/30$. Estimate the total skin friction (i.e.

that part of the drag due directly to viscous forces on the surface) acting on the wings of the aircraft in Question 41.

If the engines have a power of 2000 kW, compare the above drag with the total drag on the aircraft.

For the assumption that the wings are smooth to be valid, any roughnesses must be within the viscous sub-layer. How small does this require them to be?

73. In turbulent flow with a boundary that supports no stress (e.g. a free water surface), the stress varies linearly with distance from the boundary,

$$\tau = \rho \sigma y$$

Use arguments analogous to those in Section 22.5 to show that the counterpart of the logarithmic profile (22.18) is

$$U_s - U = A(\sigma y)^{1/2} + B(\sigma \nu)^{1/3}$$

where U_s is the velocity of the surface and A and B are numerical constants.

(Hint: show that the velocity profile given by assuming that $\partial U/\partial y$ depends only on σ and y gives an absurd viscous stress at $y = 0$; hence, infer that the region of applicability may have its velocity origin shifted by an amount that depends on σ and ν.)

74. Evaluate the Monin–Obukhov length L for the atmospheric boundary layer over smooth flat ground for conditions in which the wall stress velocity $u_\tau = 0.3 \text{ m s}^{-1}$ and the vertical heat flux $H = 200 \text{ W m}^{-2}$. What are the gradients of the mean velocity and mean temperature at a height of $L/10$? (Check that the adiabatic gradient may be neglected in these considerations.)

75. (i) Formulate the equation for the mean temperature in a turbulent boundary layer type flow (i.e. apply to equation (13.12) – with $J = 0$ – the procedure leading from the Navier–Stokes equation to equation (20.14)). Show that the turbulence produces a heat transfer across the flow proportional to $\overline{w\theta}$, in the notation of Section 22.8. Consider the physical significance of non-zero $\overline{w\theta}$.

(ii) Rederive equation (20.21) for a flow in which buoyancy forces are significant. Show that for a horizontal mean flow, there is an additional term, proportional to the vertical heat transfer, representing a production or removal of turbulence energy depending on whether the flow is unstably or stably stratified.

(iii) Show that if the Reynolds stress is assumed proportional to the mean velocity gradient and the heat transfer to the mean temperature gradient, then the ratio of the additional term in (ii) to the production term, $-\overline{uw}\partial U/\partial z$, is essentially the Richardson number.

Bibliography and References

I *Introductory reading*

This list includes books which give a good elementary account of fluid dynamical topics in the context of an application.

1   Cottrell, A. H. (1964) *The Mechanical Properties of Matter* (Wiley).
2   Sutton, O. G. (1965) *Mastery of the Air* (Hodder & Stoughton).
3   Hidy, G. M. (1967) *The Winds* (Van Nostrand).
4   Goody, R. M. and Walker, J. C. G. (1972) *Atmospheres* (Prentice-Hall).
5   Little, N. C. (1967) *Magnetohydrodynamics* (Van Nostrand).
6   Shapiro, A. H. (1961) *Shape and Flow* (Heinemann).

II *Classical texts*

References [7] and [8] together still serve as sourcebooks for work done up to the 1930s, the former primarily for theory and the latter primarily for experimental work. The other books, of which Refs. [9] and [11] are also primarily experimental, are less comprehensive but full of useful insights.

7   Lamb, H. (1932 − 6th edn.) *Hydrodynamics* (Cambridge/Dover).
8   Goldstein, S. (ed.) (1938) *Modern Developments in Fluid Dynamics*, 2 vols (Oxford/Dover).
9   Prandtl, L. (1952) *Essentials of Fluid Dynamics* (Blackie).
10   Prandtl, L. and Tietjens, O. G. (1934) *Fundamentals of Hydro- and Aero-mechanics* (McGraw-Hill/Dover).
11   Prandtl, L. and Tietjens, O. G. (1934) *Applied Hydro- and Aeromechanics* (McGraw-Hill/Dover).

III *Theoretical texts*

Of the books on fluid dynamics written for applied mathematicians or theoretical physicists, the following may be the most useful to readers of the present book.

12   Batchelor, G. K. (1970) *An Introduction to Fluid Dynamics* (Cambridge).
13   Curle, N. and Davies, H. J. (1968) *Modern Fluid Dynamics*, Vol. 1: *Incompressible Flow* (Van Nostrand Reinhold).
14   Hunt, J. N. (1964) *Incompressible Fluid Dynamics* (Longmans).
15   Landau, L. D. and Lifshitz, E. M. (1959) *Fluid Mechanics* (Pergamon).

IV *Engineering texts*

Many books on fluid dynamics have been written for engineers; the following are among those giving extensive treatment of basic fluid dynamics.

16 Daily, J. W. and Harleman, D. R. F. (1966) *Fluid Dynamics* (Addison–Wesley).

17 Duncan, W. J., Thom, A. S. and Young, A. D. (1970 – 2nd edn.) *Mechanics of Fluids* (Arnold).

18 Li, W.-H. and Lam, S.-H. (1964) *Principles of Fluid Mechanics* (Addison–Wesley).

19 Massey, B. S. (1975 – 3rd edn.) *Mechanics of Fluids* (Van Nostrand Reinhold).

V *Other general texts*

(References [21] and [22] are broader in their scope than is suggested by their titles.)

20 Richardson, E. G. (1961 – 2nd edn.) *Dynamics of Real Fluids* (Arnold).

21 Rosenhead, L. (ed.) (1963) *Laminar Boundary Layers* (Oxford).

22 Schlichting, H. (1968 – 6th edn.) *Boundary Layer Theory* (McGraw-Hill).

VI *Books on particular branches of fluid dynamics*

The books in this section contain introductory material and could be read alongside the present book. (See also Refs. [21] and [22].)

23 Aris, R. (1962) *Vectors, Tensors, and the Basic Equations of Fluid Mechanics* (Prentice-Hall).

24 Pankhurst, R. C. (1964) *Dimensional Analysis and Scale Factors* (Chapman and Hall).

25 Massey, B. S. (1971) *Units, Dimensional Analysis, and Physical Similarity* (Van Nostrand Reinhold).

26 Bradshaw, P. (1964) *Experimental Fluid Mechanics* (Pergamon).

27 Scorer, R. S. (1958) *Natural Aerodynamics* (Pergamon).

28 Hess, S. L. (1959) *Introduction to Theoretical Meteorology* (Holt/Constable).

29 Bradshaw, P. (1971) *Introduction to Turbulence and its Measurement* (Pergamon).

30 Tennekes, H. and Lumley, J. L. (1972) *A First Course in Turbulence* (M.I.T. Press).

31 Monin, A. S. and Yaglom, A. M. (1971) *Statistical Fluid Mechanics: Mechanics of Turbulence* (M.I.T. Press).

32 Merzkirch, W. (1974) *Flow visualization* (Academic Press).

VII *Further books on particular branches*

The books here are more specialized than those above.

33 Turner, J. S. (1973) *Buoyancy Effects in Fluids* (Cambridge).

34 Yih, C.-S. (1965) *Dynamics of Nonhomogeneous Fluids* (Macmillan).

35 Greenspan, H. P. (1968) *The Theory of Rotating Fluids* (Cambridge).

36 Lin, C. C. (1955) *The Theory of Hydrodynamic Stability* (Cambridge).

37 Chandrasekhar, S. (1961) *Hydrodynamic and Hydromagnetic Stability* (Oxford).

38 Hinze, J. O. (1975 – 2nd edn.) *Turbulence* (McGraw-Hill).

39 Batchelor, G. K. (1953) *The Theory of Homogeneous Turbulence* (Cambridge).

40   Townsend, A. A. (1976 – 2nd edn.) *The Structure of Turbulent Shear Flow* (Cambridge).

VIII *Films*

Many fluid dynamical phenomena are, of course, much better illustrated by cine-films than by still photographs. Of the valuable series of films produced by the National Committee for Fluid Mechanics Films, and distributed by Encyclopaedia Brittanica Educational Corporation, the following are the most relevant to this book. Many extracts from these films are also available as short film loops.

41   Shapiro, A. H. *Vorticity*.
42   Taylor, G. I. *Low Reynolds Number Flows*.
43   Abernathy, F. H. *Fundamentals of Boundary Layers*.
44   Fultz, D. *Rotating Flows*.
45   Long, R. R. *Stratified Flow*.
46   Mollo-Christensen, E. L. *Flow Instabilities*.
47   Stewart, R. W. *Turbulence*.
48   Kline, S. J. *Flow visualization*.

IX *Specific references*

49   Akiyama, M., Hwang, G. J. and Cheng, K. C. (1971) *J. Heat Transfer* **93**, 335.
50   Anderson, A. B. C. (1956) *J. Acoust. Soc. Amer.* **28**, 914.
51   Angrist, S. W. (1964) *Sci. Amer.* **211**, 6, 81.
52   Badri Narayanan, M. A. (1968) *J. Fluid Mech.* **31**, 609.
53   Badri Narayanan, M. A. and Ramjee, V. (1969) *J. Fluid Mech.* **35**, 225.
54   Bahng, J. and Schwarzschild, M. (1961) *Astrophys. J.* **134**, 312.
55   Baker, D. J. (1966) *J. Fluid Mech.* **26**, 573.
56   Bankston, C. A. (1970) *J. Heat Transfer* **92**, 569.
57   Barkla, H. M. and Auchterlonie, L. J. (1971) *J. Fluid Mech.* **47**, 437.
58   Bearman, P. W. (1969) *J. Fluid Mech.* **37**, 577.
59   Becker, H. A. and Massaro, T. A. (1968) *J. Fluid Mech.* **31**, 435.
60   Berger, E. (1964) *Z. Flugwiss.* **12**, 41.
61   Berger, E. (1964) *Jahrbuch 1964 WGLR*, 164.
62   Berger, E. and Wille, R. (1972) *Ann. Rev. Fluid Mech.* **4**, 313.
63   Billing, B. F. (1964) *Thermocouples: Their Instrumentation, Selection, and Use* (Inst. Engng. Inspection).
64   Binnie, A. M. and Fowler, J. S. (1947) *Proc. Roy. Soc. A* **192**, 32.
65   Blackman, R. B. and Tukey, J. W. (1959) *The Measurement of Power Spectra* (Dover).
66   Bloor, M. S. (1964) *J. Fluid Mech.* **19**, 290.
67   Bradbury, L. J. S. and Castro, I. P. (1971) *J. Fluid Mech.* **49**, 657.
68   Bradshaw, P. (1967) *J. Fluid Mech.* **30**, 241.
69   Bradshaw, P. (1969) *Nat. Phys. Lab., Aero. Rep. 1287*.
70   Bradshaw, P., Ferriss, D. H. and Atwell, N. P. (1967) *J. Fluid Mech.* **28**, 593.
71   Bray, R. J. and Loughhead, R. E. (1967) *The Solar Granulation* (Chapman and Hall).
72   Brindley, J. (1967) *J. Inst. Maths. Applics.* **3**, 313.
73   Browand, F. K. and Winant, C. D. (1972) *Geophys. Fluid Dynam.* **4**, 29.
74   Brown, R. A. (1970) *J. Atmos. Sci.* **27**, 742.
75   Central Electricity Generating Board, *Report of the Committee of Inquiry into Collapse of Cooling Towers at Ferrybridge 1 November 1965*.

76 Cheesewright, R. (1968) *J. Heat Transfer* **90**, 1.
77 Chu, T. Y. and Goldstein, R. J. (1973) *J. Fluid Mech.* **60**, 141.
78 Clark, R. B. and Tritton, D. J. (1970) *J. Zool.* **161**, 257.
79 Clark, R. P. (1973) *J. Hyg.* **71**, 577.
80 Clayton, B. R. and Massey, B. S. (1967) *J. Sci., Instrum.* **44**, 2.
81 Colak-Antić, P. (1964) *Sitzungsberichte der Heidelberger Akademie der Wissenschaften, Mathem.-naturw. Klasse, Jahrg. 1962/4, 6. Abhandlung* (Springer), 313.
82 Coles, D. (1965) *J. Fluid Mech.* **21**, 385.
83 Cooper, B. J. (1968) *Sci. J.* **4**, 12, 52.
84 Corrsin, S. (1949) *J. Aero. Sci.* **16**, 757.
85 Corrsin, S. (1959) *J. Geophys. Res.* **64**, 2134.
86 Corrsin, S. (1961) *Amer. Sci.* **49**, 300.
87 Cox, R. N. and Clark, R. P. (1973) *Rev. Gén. Therm.* **12**, 11.
88 Davies, J. M. (1949) *J. Appl. Phys.* **20**, 821.
89 Davies, P. A. (1972) *J. Fluid Mech.* **54**, 691.
90 Davis, R. E. (1969) *J. Fluid Mech.* **36**, 127.
91 Debler, W. R. (1966) *J. Fluid Mech.* **24**, 165.
92 Debler, W. and Fitzgerald, P. (1971) *Univ. Michigan, Dept. Engng. Mech., Tech. Rep. EM-71-3.*
93 De la Cruz Reyna, S. (1970) *Geofis. Int.* **10**, 49.
94 Delany, N. K. and Sorenson, N. E. (1953) *Nat. Adv. Comm. Aero., Tech. note 3038.*
95 Dennis, S. C. R. and Chang, G.-Z. (1970) *J. Fluid Mech.* **42**, 471.
96 Dhawan, S. (1952) *Nat. Adv. Comm. Aero., Tech. note 2567.*
97 Dhawan, S. and Narasimha, R. (1958) *J. Fluid Mech.* **3**, 418.
98 Donnelly, R. J. and Fultz, D. (1960) *Proc. Roy. Soc.* A **258**, 101.
99 Douglas, H. A., Hide, R. and Mason, P. J. (1972) *Quart. J. Roy. Met. Soc.* **98**, 247.
100 Elder, J. W. (1960) *J. Fluid Mech.* **9**, 235.
101 Elder, J. W. (1965) *J. Fluid Mech.* **23**, 77.
102 Elder, J. W. (1965) *J. Fluid Mech.* **23**, 99.
103 Faller, A. J. and Kaylor, R. (1967) *Phys. Fluids* **10**, S 212.
104 Fiedler, H. and Head, M. R. (1966) *J. Fluid Mech.* **25**, 719.
105 Finn, R. K. (1953) *J. Appl. Phys.* **24**, 771.
106 Freund, D. D. and Meyer, R. E. (1972) *J. Fluid Mech.* **54**, 719.
107 Freymuth, P. (1966) *J. Fluid Mech.* **25**, 683.
108 Fultz, D. (1961) *Adv. Geophys.* **7**, 1.
109 Fultz, D. and Nakagawa, Y. (1955) *Proc. Roy. Soc.* A **231**, 211.
110 Gass, I. G., Smith, P. J. and Wilson, R. C. (eds.) (1971) *Understanding the Earth* (Artemis).
111 Gebhart, B. (1969) *J. Heat Transfer* **91**, 293.
112 Gebhart, B. (1973) *Ann. Rev. Fluid Mech.* **5**, 213.
113 Gerrard, J. H. (1965) *J. Fluid Mech.* **22**, 187.
114 Gerrard, J. H. (1966) *J. Fluid Mech.* **25**, 401.
115 Gill, A. E. and Davey, A. (1969) *J. Fluid Mech.* **35**, 775.
116 Goedde, E. F. and Yuen, M. C. (1970) *J. Fluid Mech.* **40**, 495.
117 Graebel, W. P. (1969) *Quart. J. Mech. Appl. Math.* **22**, 39.
118 Grant, H. L. (1958) *J. Fluid Mech.* **4**, 149.
119 Grant, H. L., Stewart, R. W. and Moilliet, A. (1962) *J. Fluid Mech.* **12**, 241.
120 Grant, R. P. and Middleman, S. (1966) *Amer. Inst. Chem. Engrs. J.* **12**, 669.
121 Grass, A. J. (1971) *J. Fluid Mech.* **50**, 233.
122 Gurvich, A. S. and Yaglom, A. M. (1967) *Phys. Fluids* **10**, S 59.
123 Happel, J. and Brenner, H. (1965) *Low Reynolds Number Hydrodynamics* (Prentice-Hall).

124   Head, M. R. and Surrey, N. B. (1965) *J. Sci. Instrum.* **42**, 349.
125   Hess, F. (1968) *Sci. Amer.* **219**, 5, 124.
126   Hide, R. and Ibbetson, A. (1966) *Icarus* **5**, 279.
127   Hide, R., Ibbetson, A. and Lighthill, M. J. (1968) *J. Fluid Mech.* **32**, 251.
128   Hide, R. and Mason, P. J. (1975) *Adv. Phys.* **24**, 47.
129   Holder, D. W. and North, R. J. (1963) *Nat. Phys. Lab., Notes Appl. Sci. 31.*
130   Howard, L. N. (1963) *J. Appl. Mech.* **30**, 481.
131   Humphreys, J. S. (1960) *J. Fluid Mech.* **9**, 603.
132   Ibbetson, A. and Phillips, N. (1967) *Tellus* **19**, 1.
133   Jeffreys, H. (1961) *Cartesian Tensors* (Cambridge).
134   Kim, H. T., Kline, S. J. and Reynolds, W. C. (1971) *J. Fluid Mech.* **50**, 133.
135   Kirschner, J. M. (ed.) (1966) *Fluid Amplifiers* (McGraw-Hill).
136   Klebanoff, P. S. (1955) *Nat. Adv. Comm. Aero., Rep. 1247.*
137   Klebanoff, P. S. and Tidstrom, K. D. (1959) *Nat. Adv. Comm. Aero., Tech. note D-195.*
138   Klebanoff, P. S., Tidstrom, K. D. and Sargent, L. M. (1962) *J. Fluid Mech.* **12**, 1.
139   Kline, S. J. *et al.* (1967) *J. Fluid Mech.* **30**, 741.
140   Kline, S. J. *et al.* (eds.) (1969) *Proc. 1968 AFOSR-IFP-Stanford Conf. Computation of Turbulent Boundary Layers*, Mech. Engng. Dept., Stanford Univ.
141   Kline, S. J. and Shapiro, A. (1965) Film loop FM-48 *Pathlines, Streaklines and Streamlines in Unsteady Flow* (extract from Ref. [48]).
142   Komoda, H. (1967) *Phys. Fluids* **10**, S 87.
143   Koschmieder, E. L. (1966) *Beitr. Phys. Atmos.* **39**, 1.
144   Koschmieder, E. L. (1967) *J. Fluid Mech.* **30**, 9.
145   Koschmieder, E. L. (1974) *Adv. Chem. Phys.* **26**, 177.
146   Kovasznay, L. S. G., Kibens, V. and Blackwelder, R. F. (1970) *J. Fluid Mech.* **41**, 283.
147   Kovasznay, L. S. G., Komoda, H. and Vasudeva, B. R. (1962) *Proc. 1962 Heat Transfer and Fluid Mech. Inst.*, Stanford, 1.
148   Kraus, W. (1955) *Messungen des Temperatur- und Geschwindigkeitsfeldes bei freier Konvektion* (Braun, Karlsruhe).
149   Krishnamurti, R. (1970) *J. Fluid Mech.* **42**, 309.
150   Krishnamurti, R. (1973) *J. Fluid Mech.* **60**, 285.
151   Kuettner, J. P. (1971) *Tellus* **23**, 404.
152   Kurzweg, H. (1933) *Ann. Phys.* (5) **18**, 193.
153   Lachmann, G. V. (ed.) (1961) *Boundary Layer and Flow Control*, 2 vols (Pergam
154   Laufer, J. (1950) *J. Aero. Sci.* **17**, 277.
155   Laws, P. and Stevenson, T. N. (1972) *J. Fluid Mech.* **54**, 745.
156   Leconte, J. (1858) *Phil. Mag.* (4) **15**, 235.
157   Leighton, R. B. (1963) *Ann. Rev. Astron. Astrophys.* **1**, 19.
158   LeMone, M. A. (1973) *J. Atmos. Sci.* **30**, 1077.
159   Leontiev, A. I. and Kirdyashkin, A. G. (1968) *Internat. J. Heat Mass Transfer* **11**, 1461.
160   Lewis, H. E. *et al.* (1969) *Lancet* **1**, 1273.
161   Liebster, H. (1927) *Ann. Phys.* (4) **82**, 541.
162   Liepmann, H. W. (1943) *Nat. Adv. Comm. Aero., Wartime Rep. ACR 3H30.*
163   Lighthill, M. J. (1966) *J. Fluid Mech.* **26**, 411.
164   Lighthill, M. J. (1968) in McDowell, D. M. and Jackson, J. D. (eds.) *Osborne Reynolds and Engineering Science To-day* (Manchester Univ. Press) 83.
165   Lighthill, M. J. (1969) *Ann. Rev. Fluid Mech.* **1**, 413.
166   Lindgren, E. R. (1957) *Ark. Fys.* **12**, 1.
167   Lindgren, E. R. (1959) *Ark. Fys.* **15**, 97.

168 Lindgren, E. R. (1959) *Ark. Fys.* **15**, 503.
169 Lindgren, E. R. (1969) *Phys. Fluids* **12**, 418.
170 Long, R. R. (1955) *Tellus* **7**, 341.
171 Long, R. R. (1972) *Ann. Rev. Fluid Mech.* **4**, 69.
172 Lumley, J. L. and Panofsky, H. A. (1964) *The Structure of Atmospheric Turbulence* (Interscience).
173 Maccoll, J. W. (1928) *J. Roy. Aero. Soc.* **32**, 777.
174 Mason, B. J. (1971) *Nature* **233**, 382.
175 Mattioli, E. (1959) *Atti Acad. Sci. Torino* **94**, 855 (translated as Adv. Group Aero. Res. Dev., Rep. 263).
176 Maxworthy, T. (1970) *J. Fluid Mech.* **40**, 453.
177 Merk, H. J. (1958) *Appl. Sci. Res.* A **8**, 100.
178 Miles, C. A. and Holwill, M. E. J. (1969) *J. Exp. Biol.* **50**, 683.
179 Milne-Thompson, L. M. (1962 – 4th edn.) *Theoretical Hydrodynamics* (Macmillan).
180 Ministry of Technology (1968) *Hydraulics Research 1967, Rep. Hyd. Res. Station* (HMSO) p. 24.
181 Ministry of Technology (1970) *Hydraulics Research 1969, Rep. Hyd. Res. Station* (HMSO) p. 11.
182 Moore, D. W. and Saffman, P. G. (1969) *Phil. Trans. Roy. Soc.* A **264**, 597.
183 Moore, F. K. (ed.) (1964) *High Speed Aerodynamics and Jet Propulsion*, Vol. **IV** *Theory of Laminar Flows* (Oxford).
184 Mori, Y. and Uchida, Y. (1966) *Internat. J. Heat Mass Transfer* **9**, 803.
185 Mowbray, D. E. and Rarity, B. S. H. (1967) *J. Fluid Mech.* **28**, 1.
186 Moylan, M. J. (1971 – 2nd edn.) *Fluid Logic in Simple Terms* (Machinery Publishing Co.).
187 Nachtsheim, P. R. (1963) *Nat. Adv. Comm. Aero., Tech. note D-2089.*
188 Narahari Rao, K., Narasimha, R. and Badri Narayanan, M. A. (1971) *J. Fluid Mech.* **48**, 339.
189 Nicholl, C. I. H. (1970) *J. Fluid Mech.* **40**, 361.
190 Nield, D. A. (1964) *J. Fluid Mech.* **19**, 341.
191 Orszag, Z. A. (1970) *J. Fluid Mech.* **41**, 363.
192 Ostrach, S. (1953) *Nat. Adv. Comm. Aero., Rep. 1111.*
193 Owen, P. R. (1971) *Quart. J. Roy. Met. Soc.* **97**, 396.
194 Pantulu, P. V. (1962) *M.Sc. thesis*, Dept. Aero. Engng., Indian Inst. Sci., Bangalore.
195 Pao, Y.-H. (1967) *Boeing Sci. Res. Labs., Flight Sci. Lab. Rep. 102 (document D1-82-0488).*
196 Penner, S. S. and Jerskey, T. (1973) *Ann. Rev. Fluid Mech.* **5**, 9.
197 Perry, A. E. and Morrison, G. L. (1971) *J. Fluid Mech.* **47**, 577.
198 Pfenninger, W. (1961) in Ref. [153], p. 970.
199 Phillips, O. M. (1955) *Proc. Camb. Phil. Soc.* **51**, 220.
200 Phillips, O. M. (1963) *Phys. Fluids* **6**, 513.
201 Pilsbury, R. K. (1969) *Clouds and Weather* (Batsford).
202 Platzman, G. W. (1968) *Quart. J. Roy. Met. Soc.* **94**, 225.
203 Polymeropoulos, C. E. and Gebhart, B. (1967) *J. Fluid Mech.* **30**, 225.
204 Preston, J. H. (1972) *J. Phys. E, Sci. Instrum.* **5**, 277.
205 Priestley, C. H. B. (1959) *Turbulent Transfer in the Lower Atmosphere* (Univ. Chicago Press).
206 Ramdas, L. A. and Malurkar, S. L. (1932) *Ind. J. Phys.* **7**, 1.
207 Reynolds, O. (1883) *Phil. Trans. Roy. Soc.* **174**, 935.
208 Rosenhead, L. (1954) *Proc. Roy. Soc.* A **226**, 1.
209 Roshko, A. (1961) *J. Fluid Mech.* **10**, 345.
210 Rossby, H. T. (1969) *J. Fluid Mech.* **36**, 309.

211   Rotta, J. (1956) *Ing. Arch.* **24**, 258.
212   Rotta, J. C. (1962) *Prog. Aero. Sci.* **2**, 1.
213   Sachs, P. (1972) *Wind Forces in Engineering* (Pergamon).
214   Salter, C., Warsap, J. H. and Goodman, D. G. (1965) *Aero. Res. Counc., Rep. and Memo. 3365.*
215   Sandborn, V. A. (1959) *J. Fluid Mech.* **6**, 221.
216   Sato, H. (1959) *J. Phys. Soc. Japan* **14**, 1797.
217   Sato, H. (1960) *J. Fluid Mech.* **7**, 53.
218   Sato, H. and Sakao, F. (1964) *J. Fluid Mech.* **20**, 337.
219   Săvulescu, St. N. (1968) *Tranzitia de la Scurgerea Laminară la cea Turbulentă* (Ed. Acad. Rep. Soc. România).
220   Schmidt, E. (1932) *Forsch. Geb. IngWes.* **3**, 181.
221   Schmiedel, J. (1928) *Phys. Z.* **29**, 593.
222   Schraub, F. A. and Kline, S. J. (1965) *Stanford Univ., Dept. Mech. Engng., Thermosciences Div., Rep. MD-12.*
223   Schubauer, G. B. (1954) *J. Appl. Phys.* **23**, 191.
224   Schubauer, G. B. and Klebanoff, P. S. (1955) *Nat. Adv. Comm. Aero., Rep. 1289.*
225   Schubauer, G. B. and Skramstad, H. K. (1947) *J. Res. Nat. Bur. Stand.* **38**, 251.
226   Schultz-Grunow, F. and Hein, H. (1955) *Z. Flugwiss.* **4**, 28.
227   Scorer, R. (1972) *Clouds of the World* (Lothian/David and Charles).
228   Scriven, C. V. and Sternling, L. E. (1964) *J. Fluid Mech.* **19**, 321.
229   Shen, S. F. (1954) *J. Aero. Sci.* **21**, 62.
230   Sibulkin, M. (1962) *Phys. Fluids* **5**, 280.
231   Silveston, P. L. (1958) *Forsch. Geb. IngWes.* **24**, 29 and 59.
232   Simon, G. W. and Weiss, N. O. (1968) *Z. Astrophys.* **69**, 435.
233   Smith, A. M. O. (1960) *J. Fluid Mech.* **7**, 565.
234   Smith, C. V. (1959) *Met. Office, Met. Rep. 21.*
235   Snyder, H. A. (1970) *Internat. J. Non-linear Mech.* **5**, 659.
236   Somerscales, E. F. C. and Dropkin, D. (1966) *Internat. J. Heat Mass Transfer* **9**, 1189.
237   Sparrow, E. M., Husar, R. B. and Goldstein, R. J. (1970) *J. Fluid Mech.* **41**, 793.
238   Stevenson, T. N. (1968) *J. Fluid Mech.* **33**, 715.
239   Stuart, J. T. (1964) *J. Fluid Mech.* **18**, 481.
240   Stuart, J. T. (1965) *Appl. Mech. Rev.* **18**, 523.
241   Stuart, J. T. (1971) *Ann. Rev. Fluid Mech.* **3**, 347.
242   Suhanek, P. C. and Lawrence, R. L. (1972) *Z. angew. Math. Phys.* **23**, 969.
243   Sutton, O. G. (1953) *Micrometeorology* (McGraw-Hill).
244   Szewczyk, A. A. (1962) *Internat. J. Heat Mass Transfer* **5**, 903.
245   Taneda, S. (1956) *J. Phys. Soc. Japan* **11**, 302.
246   Taneda, S. (1965) *J. Phys. Soc. Japan* **20**, 1714.
247   Taneda, S., Honji, H. and Tatsuno, M. (1974) *J. Phys. Soc. Japan* **37**, 784.
248   Tani, I. (1964) *Prog. Aero. Sci.* **5**, 70.
249   Tani, I. (1969) *Ann. Rev. Fluid Mech.* **1**, 169.
250   Tanida, Y., Okajima, A. and Watanabe, Y. (1973) *J. Fluid Mech.* **61**, 796.
251   Tanner, L. H. (1966) *J. Sci. Instrum.* **43**, 878.
252   Tarling, D. H. and Tarling, M. P. (1971) *Continental Drift* (Bell/Pelican).
253   Tatro, P. R. and Mollo-Christensen, E. L. (1967) *J. Fluid Mech.* **28**, 531.
254   Tatsumi, T. (1952) *J. Phys. Soc. Japan* **7**, 489 and 495.

255 Tatsumi, T. and Kakutani, T. (1958) *J. Fluid Mech.* **4**, 261.
256 Taylor, G. I. (1923) *Proc. Roy. Soc.* A **104**, 213.
257 Taylor, G. I. (1923) *Phil. Trans. Roy. Soc.* A **223**, 289.
258 Taylor, G. I. (1937) *J. Aero Sci.* **4**, 311.
259 Taylor, G. I. (1938) *Proc. Roy. Soc.* A **164**, 15.
260 Taylor, G. I. (1952) *Proc. Roy. Soc.* A **214**, 158.
261 Taylor, R. J. (1958) *J. Sci. Instrum.* **35**, 47.
262 Temple, G. (1958) *An Introduction to Fluid Dynamics* (Oxford).
263 Thompson, H. A. and Sogin, H. H. (1966) *J. Fluid Mech.* **24**, 451.
264 Thorpe, S. A. (1969) *J. Fluid Mech.* **39**, 25.
265 Thorpe, S. A. (1971) *J. Fluid Mech.* **46**, 299.
266 Timme, A. (1957) *Ing. Arch.* **25**, 205.
267 Tombach, I. H. (1973) *Rev. Sci. Instrum.* **44**, 141.
268 Townsend, A. A. (1949) *Aust. J. Sci. Res.* A **2**, 451.
269 Townsend, A. A. (1957) in Görtler, H. (ed.) *Boundary Layer Research, Proc. IUTAM Symp., Freiburg* (Springer) p. 1.
270 Townsend, A. A. (1959) *J. Fluid Mech.* **5**, 209.
271 Townsend, A. A. (1970) *J. Fluid Mech.* **41**, 13.
272 Townsend, A. A. (1972) *J. Fluid Mech.* **55**, 209.
273 Tozer, D. C. (1967) in Gaskell, T.F. (ed.) *The Earth's Mantle* (Academic Press), Ch. 11.
274 Tritton, D. J. (1959) *J. Fluid Mech.* **6**, 547.
275 Tritton, D. J. (1963) *J. Fluid Mech.* **16**, 269.
276 Tritton, D. J. (1963) *J. Fluid Mech.* **16**, 417.
277 Tritton, D. J. (1967) *J. Fluid Mech.* **28**, 439.
278 Tritton, D. J. and Zarraga, M. N. (1967) *J. Fluid Mech.* **30**, 21.
279 Turcotte, D. L. and Oxburgh, E. R. (1972) *Ann. Rev. Fluid Mech.* **4**, 33.
280 Turner, J. S. (1969) *Ann. Rev. Fluid Mech.* **1**, 29.
281 Turpin, J. L. (1972) *Phys. Fluids* **15**, 968.
282 Uberoi, M. S. (1963) *Phys. Fluids* **6**, 1048.
283 Van Atta, C. (1966) *J. Fluid Mech.* **25**, 495.
284 Vaziri, A. and Boyer, D. L. (1971) *J. Fluid Mech.* **50**, 79.
285 Veronis, G. (1970) *Ann. Rev. Fluid Mech.* **2**, 37.
286 Vest, C. M. and Arpaci, V. S. (1969) *J. Fluid Mech.* **36**, 1.
287 Walshe, D. E. and Isles, D. C. (1969) *Nat. Phys. Lab., Aero. Special Rep. 023.*
288 Warner, C. Y. and Arpaci, V. S. (1968) *Internat. J. Heat Mass Transfer* **11**, 397.
289 Webb, J. E. (1973) *J. Zool.* **170**, 325.
290 Webster, C. A. G. (1964) *J. Fluid Mech.* **19**, 221.
291 Werlé, H. (1973) *Ann. Rev. Fluid Mech.* **5**, 361.
292 Wieselsberger, C. (1921) *Phys. Z.* **22**, 321.
293 Willis, G. E. and Deardorff, J. W. (1965) *Phys. Fluids* **8**, 2225.
294 Willis, G. E. and Deardorff, J. W. (1970) *J. Fluid Mech.* **44**, 661.
295 Wortmann, F. X. (1953) *Z. angew. Phys.* **5**, 201.
296 Zdravkovich, M. M. (1969) *J. Fluid Mech.* **37**, 491.

Index